ARMORED THUNDERBOLT

ARMORED THUNDERBOLT

THE U.S. ARMY SHERMAN IN WORLD WAR II

Steven Zaloga

STACKPOLE
BOOKS

Published by
STACKPOLE BOOKS
5067 Ritter Road
Mechanicsburg, PA 17055
www.stackpolebooks.com

10 9 8 7 6 5 4 3 2 1

FIRST EDITION

Library of Congress Cataloging-in-Publication Data

Zaloga, Steven.
  Armored thunderbolt : the U.S. Army Sherman in World War II / Steven Zaloga.
      p. cm.
  Includes bibliographical references and index.
  ISBN 978-0-8117-0424-3
  1. World War, 1939–1945—Tank warfare. 2. United States. Army—Armored troops. 3. United States.
Marine Corps—Armored troops. 4. Sherman tank—History. I. Title.
  D793.Z34 2008
  940.54'1273—dc22
                                        2008003234

Contents

Introduction

WHEN I WAS GROWING UP in the 1950s, the Sherman tank was regularly portrayed in the press and on TV as one of the great war-winning weapons of World War II. A half-century later, this image has been completely reversed. A popular book about American tanks in World War II is grimly entitled Death Traps. Television documentaries enthusiastically embellish this gruesome theme. Suicide Missions was the title of one popular TV show about Sherman tank crews. So which is it: death trap or war winner? This book aims to examine how and why the Sherman tank was developed and how it performed in combat during its greatest challenge, the battles in the European theater of operations (ETO) in 1944–45.

This book is the result of more than three decades of research on tank technology and military history. I have been researching and writing about tank development since I was in college in the early 1970s. Starting in the late 1970s, I worked for a defense research firm where I tracked the development of the new generation of U.S. Army armored fighting vehicles, including the M1 Abrams tank and M2 Bradley infantry fighting vehicle. Over the years, I have interviewed the designers of the latest generation of American armored vehicles as well as the Russian and Ukrainian designers of the T-72 and T-80 tanks, the French designers of the Leclerc tank, and the German designers of the Leopard II tank. I have also worked for a government think tank where I was involved in studies of contemporary Russian and Chinese armored vehicle development. In the 1990s, I gave courses on armor and antiarmor technology for Technology Training Corporation.

My long-standing interest in military history has led me to interview many American tank crewmen and commanders from World War II, as well as from later conflicts in Korea, Vietnam, and Operation Desert Storm. As the son and grandson of U.S. Army veterans of World War II, I have naturally gravitated toward the history of that conflict. I have written numerous books on U.S. tanks and armored vehicles in World War II, as well as those of the Soviet Union and other countries, and have also written a number of books on the campaigns of the U.S. Army in the war. This has given me the opportunity to visit many of the battlefields mentioned in this book—Omaha Beach, the bocage country of Normandy, the battlefields of Lorraine, and the Ardennes—and most of the world's major tank museums.

I have detailed my own professional background because it explains the approach I take in this book. This is not a lawn-mower catalog of the Sherman tank and its many production variants. Nor is it a collection of accounts of Sherman units in combat. Rather, it is an attempt to explain how and why the Sherman tank was developed and how its evolution was affected by U.S. combat experiences in World War II.

There are several histories of the Sherman tank in print, most notably Dick Hunnicutt's monumental study. Most of these books look at the Sherman primarily from the technical standpoint and the perspective of the Ordnance Department of the U.S. Army, which was responsible for designing the Sherman. Other studies, such as Charles Baily's groundbreaking Faint Praise, broadened the coverage to examine the interplay between ordnance and other elements of the army bureaucracy, such as the headquarters of the Army Ground Forces and Armored Force. This book attempts to add another critical layer to this story by examining the interplay between the technical and bureaucratic aspects of the development of the Sherman tank, the evolution of the enemy threat and its impact on that development, and finally the role that the combat use of the Sherman by the U.S. Army played on its further evolution.

I have received the generous help of many people in my research over the years. My earliest

inspiration for the study of American tank development was Col. Robert J. Icks, who served in Ordnance during World War II designing armored vehicles such as the M3 75mm GMC tank destroyer. Bob Icks was responsible for the first serious writing about tank development in the United States, starting with his book *The Fighting Tanks* in 1933. He continued to write about tank development until his death in 1985. Bob generously helped younger writers like me, and his enthusiasm for tank history was infectious.

One of Bob's disciples was Col. James Loop, an air defense officer who had a similar passion for tank history. Jim was connected with a number of early publishing ventures on tank history, such as *AFV-G2* magazine, and like Bob, he offered enthusiastic encouragement of other tank buffs. During his tour of duty in Vietnam, Jim's commander was Col. James Leach, who had led Company B, 37th Tank Battalion, 4th Armored Division, during the Battle of the Bulge. During the 1980s, we would meet at the annual Association of the U.S. Army convention in Washington, DC, and Jimmie Leach would impart his considerable knowledge about tank combat in World War II. His dedication to the history of the U.S. Armored Force broadened my interest beyond the technical issues to the tactical issues of Sherman history. Another of my early influences was Bruce Culver, who wrote some of the earliest articles on Sherman history for *IPMS Journal* and other magazines. In the 1970s, Bruce and I squandered a fair amount of our summer vacation time traveling down to Washington to poke through the archives looking for "Sherman stuff."

The circle of tank historians is a fairly small one, and two other people whom I would like to acknowledge are George Bradford and Janusz Magnuski. George founded the premier magazine on tank history, *AFV News,* in which he published my first article back in 1968. Janusz was the leading researcher on Soviet tank history back in the dark days of the 1960s, 1970s, and 1980s when virtually nothing was published on this important subject in the Soviet Union. Janusz was my mentor on Soviet tanks and helped me to gain a broader appreciation for worldwide tank development in World War II. In

Britain, Peter Brown and Ken Jones have tried their best to interest me in British tank history, with mixed results. David Fletcher of the Tank Museum at Bovington, the foremost historian of British tank development in World War II, has always provided his help when my research on U.S. tank subjects has bumped up against British issues. Dick Hunnicutt and Joe DeMarco are the two most knowledgeable specialists on the history of the Sherman tank and have always been helpful when I needed to pester someone about the most arcane details of Sherman history. One of my colleagues and fellow tank nuts while working at DMS Inc. in the 1980s was Lee Ness, who has given me a great deal of help based on his own extensive archival research.

Research on the Sherman tank has taken me to many archives and museums over the years. Charles Lemons and Candace Fuller of the Patton Museum at Fort Knox have always been a big help during my visits there. Likewise, Jack Atwater, Alan Killinger, Pete Kinsvatter, and Ed Heasley have been helpful during my frequent visits to the Ordnance Museum at Aberdeen Proving Ground. Much of my archival research on U.S. Army history has been done at the U.S. Army's Military History Institute at Carlisle Barracks, Pennsylvania, and its superb staff has made my trips there both enjoyable and productive. The National Archives is the main repository of U.S. government records, and I would like to thank its excellent staff since I first began doing research there in 1974. Alan Aimone of the library at the U.S. Military Academy at West Point has been most helpful during my research trips there.

The numerous photos here are all official U.S. Army photos unless otherwise noted. These have come from a variety of archives and museums including the original depository at the Pentagon, the Defense Audio Visual Agency in Anacostia, the current repository at the National Archives and Records Administration at College Park, Maryland, as well as other army facilities and museums such as the Patton Museum at Fort Knox, Kentucky, the U.S. Army Military History Institute at Carlisle Barracks, Pennsylvania, and the U.S. Military Academy at West Point, New York.

CHAPTER 1

War of the Machines

WHEN THE SECOND WORLD WAR broke out in Europe on September 1, 1939, the U.S. Army's tank force was smaller and more backward than Poland's. In the two years between the fall of Poland and Pearl Harbor, the United States had to transform its ill-equipped, second-rate army into that of a great power, able to challenge the world's most powerful. The development of the Sherman tank was a small but significant part of this process.

Tanks had become a vital new means of warfare in the concluding years of World War I. New forms of firepower, especially the machine gun and long-range field gun, had annihilated horse cavalry and made the battlefield too hazardous for infantry. The balance between offensive and defensive combat was upset, and static trench warfare was the grim result. While tactical improvements eventually restored the balance, technological innovations such as tanks and other armored fighting vehicles (AFVs) helped to swing the balance back in favor of the offense. Tanks could assist the infantry in escaping the horrors of trench warfare by providing a means to overcome murderous adversaries like machine-gun nests.

Although the early tanks were a sound tactical innovation, they were a technological mess. Formidable weapons when they were in working order, they broke down too quickly and were difficult to repair in the field. Early German tanks were so mechanically unreliable that fewer than half could be kept in motion for a single day of combat, and afterwards, all surviving tanks had to be sent back to depot for rebuilding. British and French tanks were only slightly more durable.

THE FIRST YANK TANKS

The U.S. Army got its first taste of tank combat in 1918 while using Renault FT light tanks obtained from the French. Curiously enough, their commander was a young officer named George S. Patton, and the officer in charge of tank training back in the United States was Dwight Eisenhower. The United States manufactured the Renault FT under license as the Six-Ton Tank, the first significant mass-produced American tank. It formed the backbone of the U.S. Army's tank companies through the early 1930s. The Renault FT was the most modern tank of World War I, pioneering the classic layout centered around a main gun turret. But it suffered the same mechanical limitations of all early tanks—very slow speed and poor mechanical reliability. Many officers remained skeptical of the future of tank warfare because of the arthritic performance of these primitive early tanks.

Tank development in the United States in the interwar years of 1919 to 1939 was slow and unproductive. So many Renault and Six-Ton Tanks were on hand that there was little reason to build new ones during the 1920s. America's isolationist foreign policy shaped army policy. There was widespread public opposition to any participation in future European wars, and the U.S. Army settled back into much more limited responsibilities in homeland defense and patrolling overseas possessions like the Philippines. Such missions did not require expensive tanks, and so tank development was starved of funds.

The army's Ordnance Department undertook the development and manufacture of tanks in the United States at two of its main facilities, Rock Island Arsenal in Illinois, which built the tanks, and Aberdeen Proving Ground in Maryland, which tested them. By the early 1930s, the Renault Six-Ton Tanks were getting a bit long in the tooth, and Ordnance began the development of a new generation of tanks, patterned on the popular British Vickers six-ton export tank. In fact, Ordnance had to produce two parallel lines of the same tank: a "tank" version for the infantry and a "combat car" version

The first tank in widespread use with the U.S. Army was the French Renault FT, which served under the command of the young Lt. Col. George S. Patton in its initial combat in the Meuse-Argonne campaign in France in September 1918. A total of 514 Renault FT tanks were received from France during World War I.

A shortage of tanks obliged the American Expeditionary Force to call on the support of allied British and French tank units like this British Mk IV tank, shown here training with the 107th Infantry Regiment of the 27th Division in 1918.

In addition to the Renault FT, the AEF also received British Mk V and Mk V* heavy tanks, which equipped the 301st Heavy Tank Battalion, seen here near St. Souplet in northern France on October 17, 1918.

for the cavalry. Congressional legislation in 1920 forbade the cavalry from operating tanks, and this law was skirted by the fig leaf of terminology. Both the infantry light tanks and cavalry combat cars were based on a related chassis, but the infantry favored multiple machine-gun turrets while the cavalry favored a single turret with a more powerful .50-caliber machine gun. Not counting experimental types, the U.S. Army procured only 321 light tanks from 1930 to 1939, and the cavalry an additional 148 combat cars.

With the rise of Nazi Germany and Fascist Italy in the 1930s, the possibility of another war in Europe loomed ominously. The harbinger of the future conflict was the Spanish Civil War, which began in 1936, with Germany and Italy supporting the Nationalist insurgents and the Soviet Union backing the Republicans. This was the first war since 1918 to see the extensive use of modern tanks and so was an experimental proving ground for tank development. The war offered important technical and tactical lessons. In the early 1930s, the Germans

Three types of tanks were manufactured in the United States in 1918–19: the tiny Ford Three-Ton Tank Model 1918, the Six-Ton Tank Model 1917, and the large Mark VIII "International" tank patterned on British designs.

The first American tank design to enter mass production was the Ford Three-Ton Model 1918, of which 15,000 were ordered. This small tankette was armed with a single machine gun, and although a few were delivered to France before the armistice, none saw combat in World War I. The production contract was cancelled after only fifteen were completed.

had switched to the French World War I–era policy of building large numbers of inexpensive tanks, such as their *Panzerkampfwagen* (PzKpfw) I, instead of small numbers of a bigger and more complicated design as they had done in World War I. The PzKpfw I was armed with two machine guns, which were more than adequate to deal with enemy infantry. It was not at all useful against enemy tanks, but tank combat in World War I had been a rarity.

The Soviets on the other hand had been manufacturing a copy of the Vickers six-ton tank as the T-26, armed with a dual-purpose 45mm gun that could fire high-explosive rounds at enemy infantry or artillery or armor-piercing rounds if facing enemy tanks. Tank-versus-tank combat was not especially common in the Spanish Civil War, but it was common enough that most armies now wanted gun-armed tanks. After facing the Soviet T-26 with

The Six-Ton Tank saw some overseas service in the 1920s, such as these serving with the U.S. Marine Corps Light Tank Platoon, East Coast Expeditionary Force, in Tientsin, China, in 1927.

The U.S. Army ordered 4,440 Six-Ton Tank Model 1917s, the American copy of the Renault FT, but only 950 were actually manufactured in 1918–19 before the contracts were cancelled. These tanks formed the bulk of American tank units well into the 1930s and were used as training tanks by the Canadian Army in the early 1940s.

their PzKpfw I tanks, the Germans realized that they needed larger, gun-armed tanks that could engage enemy tanks and infantry in trenches and buildings with high-explosive fire. This would lead to the production of the PzKpfw III tank, the iron backbone of the panzer force during the blitzkrieg years of 1939–41. The other lesson from Spain was that con-temporary tanks were too weakly armored to resist the new generation of infantry antitank guns. By the 1930s, many European armies were adopting compact antitank guns in the 37mm to 45mm range that could pierce an inch of armor at 500 yards. These saw extensive use in Spain and in several cases stopped major tank attacks.

The first new tank developed after World War I was the T1E1 light tank, seen here on trials at Aberdeen Proving Ground in 1928. It was an archaic design that offered little over the Renault FT and never entered series production.

The Christie T3 medium tank was never popular in U.S. Army service because of its technical problems. Two of the seven purchased are seen here serving with the 67th Infantry (Tanks) during summer war games.

The first medium tank acquired after World War I was the Christie M1931, known as the convertible medium tank T3 in U.S. Army service. It had an advanced spring suspension and was designed to run on its wheels for high speed on roads or on its tracks for cross-country travel.

Because of the unreliability of the Christie tank, Rock Island Arsenal proceeded to develop its own design as the M1 convertible medium tank, seen here during Third Army maneuvers at Fort Benning, Georgia, in April 1940. Only eighteen were built, and they were the only significant medium tanks manufactured by the U.S. Army in the 1930s.

After purchasing a British Vickers six-ton tank, Rock Island Arsenal used the lessons from this design to build ten M2A1 light tanks in 1935. It was armed with a .50-caliber heavy machine gun as its principal antitank weapon with a coaxial .30-caliber light machine gun. This tank of the 66th Infantry is seen on exercise without its weapons.

The success of the M2A1 light tank led to a parallel combat car for the cavalry, the M1. It had a more spacious turret and was armed with a .50-caliber heavy machine gun as its principal antitank weapon, plus two more .30-caliber machine guns.

The M1 combat car was the first American tank produced in significant numbers since the 1920s, with some ninety being completed in 1935–37. It is seen here in service with the 1st Cavalry during summer war games.

After the short-lived M2A1 light tank, the infantry switched to twin-turret versions, popularly dubbed "Mae Wests" by the tankers because of their two round turrets. This is an M2A2 light tank of the 1st Armored Division on exercise with the 1st Armored Division at Fort Knox, Kentucky, in 1941.

The last of the cavalry's combat cars was the M2, which entered production in 1940. Its principal armament was the .50-caliber heavy machine gun, a completely inadequate weapon by 1940 standards. Maj. Gen. George S. Patton used this particular M2 when he commanded the 2nd Armored Division in 1942.

THE ARMS RACE BEGINS

The lessons from Spain and the looming threat of war triggered a substantial arms race in Europe in the late 1930s. In 1934, Germany, France, and Britain had produced barely 150 tanks. By 1937, at the height of the Spanish Civil War, this had increased tenfold to more than 1,500 per year, and production continued to increase steadily until the outbreak of war in 1939. In the United States, the pace was slower, but tank development began to overcome the lethargy of the previous decade. Still in the grips of the Great Depression, the budget would not yet permit the design of a tank incorporating the lessons of the Spanish Civil War, since thick armor would require a new design significantly larger and heavier than the existing light tanks. As a temporary solution, the infantry's M2 light tank was improved by replacing its machine-gun turrets with a single 37mm gun turret. Production of the new M2A4 light tank began in the spring of 1940.

The European arms race of the late 1930s left the U.S. Army behind in tank design. Although American light tanks of the mid-1930s were comparable to their European counterparts, by 1940 the M2A4 light tank was not. The U.S. Army had begun to develop a heavier medium tank beginning in the mid-1930s, but by the time it emerged as the M2 medium tank in the summer of 1939, it was already obsolete. The basic concept behind the M2 medium tank was flawed because its armor was too thin to defend against antitank guns and it was armed with a dysfunctional mixture of sponson machines and a single 37mm gun. By way of comparison, new European medium tanks such as the French S-35 and German PzKpfw III had armor that could withstand 37mm antitank fire and centered their armament around a powerful main gun. The most startling design to emerge after the Spanish Civil War was the Soviet T-34 tank, which entered production in 1940. Soviet tank "volunteers" had served in large numbers in Spain, and their experiences convinced Soviet tank designers that a future tank had to withstand infantry antitank guns while at the same time being capable of defeating enemy tanks. The Soviet designers based the T-34 design on the critical paradigm that a new tank had to be designed not merely to defeat the contemporary threat, but also to defeat a more advanced future threat. So instead of being designed to defend against the 37mm guns of the 1930s, the T-34 was designed to defend against more powerful guns in the 50mm to 75mm range. To defeat tanks as well protected as itself, the T-34 was equipped with a powerful dual-purpose 76mm gun. The T-34 represented a revolutionary leap in the "holy trinity" of tank design: firepower, armored protection, and mobility. It

The Soviet T-26 light tank was a license copy of the British Vickers six-ton tank, but fitted with a larger turret and armed with an excellent dual-purpose 45mm gun derived from the German Rheinmetall 37mm antitank gun. The T-26 was so successful that Franco's forces paid a bounty for the capture of these tanks from the Republican tank units. This trophy served with the Spanish Foreign Legion tank battalion alongside German PzKpfw I tanks.

The Spanish Civil War of 1936–39 was the crucible of European tank technology prior to World War II. Germany provided its machine gun–armed PzKpfw I to Franco's Nationalist forces, where it proved to be too weakly armed to deal with the Soviet T-26 light tank seen behind it.

Lessons from the Spanish Civil War led the Soviet Union to develop a radically more powerful tank design that emerged in 1940 as the T-34. Its blend of high mobility, thick armor, and a potent dual-purpose 76mm gun made it the benchmark for world tank design in the first years of World War II.

entered series production about the same time as the U.S. Army's M2 medium tank but was a generation ahead in all respects. The T-34 would set the pace for world tank development in the early years of World War II from 1941 to 1943.

The T-34 had a curious American heritage. In the early 1930s when the Soviet Union began to manufacture tanks, their designers scoured the world for suitable designs to copy. They eventually settled on the British Vickers six-ton, which later emerged in modified form as the T-26 infantry tank. They also bought a small number of light tanks designed by the eccentric American Walter Christie. The Christie tanks were well known for their speed, capable of more than forty miles per hour on the road. Part of this resulted from the use of a powerful Liberty aircraft engine, but Christie had also come up with a novel suspension system using large road wheels and substantial internal springs to provide a smooth ride in rough terrain. The Soviet Union eventually began to manufacture a modified copy of the Christie tank as the BT (the Russian acronym for fast tank) cavalry tank. The U.S. Army bought a handful of Christie tanks, calling them the T3 medium tank. They proved to be "hangar queens," too badly engineered for sustained use and not well enough armed to be worth

The Christie tank was license-manufactured in the Soviet Union but with locally designed turrets. The BT-5 cruiser tank was fitted with the same 45mm gun turret as the T-26. These two Spanish Republican BTs were knocked out during the fighting along the Ebro River in 1937.

The T-34 was secret until the German invasion of June 1941, when its appearance shocked the Wehrmacht and led to the development of the Panther, which entered combat two years later in the summer of 1943. Many, like this one, were found abandoned or broken because of the poor training of the Red Army in 1941.

the trouble. The BT tank saw combat in Spain—curiously enough, with some of the crews being American volunteers. When Soviet designers developed its replacement, they kept the Christie suspension with the new wider tracks but completely redesigned the armor, powerplant, and weapons. The result was the legendary T-34. While some tank buffs suggest that the U.S. Army's refusal to adopt the Christie tank cut off this promising avenue of tank development, the Christie tank by no means guaranteed success. It is often ignored that the other army to widely adopt the Christie suspension, Britain's, had a far poorer track record than the Soviets. The British used the Christie on a succession of cruiser tanks, including the A.13 cruiser tank, Covenanter, Crusader, and Cromwell. None of these matched the T-34, which suggests that features other than the Christie suspension determined the T-34's success.

THE FRENCH EARTHQUAKE

The U.S. Army was finally shocked into action by the German defeat of France in June 1940. The U.S. Army had strong ties with the French Army beginning with World War I when the French trained and equipped the American Expeditionary Force. Many ambitious young officers like George S. Patton had received advanced training at French staff schools in the 1920s. The French Army was widely regarded in Washington as the best and most modern in Europe. What was especially shocking was the rapidity of France's defeat—barely six weeks. The villain in this debacle was the German panzer force and its new "blitzkrieg" tactics.

The French Army in 1940 had more tanks than the Germans, and in many cases, they were technologically more advanced, with better armor and better guns. German tanks were technically sound but not exceptional. What distinguished the Wehrmacht from the French Army was the way that tanks were employed, concentrated in massed panzer divisions and panzer corps. In contrast, the French had scattered their tank strength in various directions—with some tank battalions directly supporting the infantry, others being assigned to the cavalry's light divisions, and yet others forming tank divisions with their own separate mission.

The fall of France ended the American debate about the future of its own tank force. The infantry had continued to insist that tanks were no more than another supporting weapon like machine guns and so should remain subordinate to the infantry. The cavalry remained wedded to the horse and saw the combat car as an ancillary form of horse cavalry. With neither of the traditional branches taking a progressive position on tank power, senior army leaders took matters into their own hands and created a new organization, the Armored Force, headquartered at Fort Knox, to form and train the new tank units. The Armored Force absorbed both the infantry's tanks and the cavalry's combat cars. In practice, the formation of the Armored Force in July 1940 circumvented the traditional horse cavalry generals and recreated the cavalry in a new mechanized form. The first Armored Force commander,

German tanks of 1940, like the PzKpfw IV seen here, had few technological advantages over their French adversaries, but the Wehrmacht's tactical doctrine was more advanced. The PzKpfw IV was armed with a short 75mm gun and was the benchmark for American tank design in 1940–41 when the Sherman tank was first conceived.

The fall of France led to the establishment of the U.S. Army's Armored Force in July 1940. The 7th Cavalry Brigade (Mechanized) at Fort Knox was used to form the core of the 1st Armored Division, and Gen. Adna Chaffee, the first head of the Armored Force, is seen here to the left in front of most of the army's extant M2A4 light tanks.

The French Army in 1940 was well equipped with modern tanks like the Char B1 bis seen here, but their organization and doctrine were not as successful as the Wehrmacht's. As a result of French attempts to license the manufacture of tanks in the U.S. in 1939–40, the U.S. had good information on the Char B1 bis, which inspired the M3 medium tank.

Adna Chaffee, was a cavalry general. Most ambitious cavalry officers knew that the days of the horse cavalry were over and so switched to the Armored Force. Among them was George S. Patton, who would lead the new 2nd Armored Division. In contrast, the infantry was greatly expanding in size, so there was little incentive for infantry officers to shift to the Armored Force. As a result, the Armored Force would have a distinctly cavalry flavor in its training and tactics in the early years of the war.

The defeat of France and Britain's stubborn resistance to German aggression increased the likelihood that America would eventually be dragged into another European war. Franklin Roosevelt began to take steps to prepare the nation for war, and modernization of the army was a key ingredient. The new Armored Force could not be expanded without tanks, and two decades of inattention had limited American resources in this area. The only facility manufacturing tanks was Rock Island Arsenal, which

When the Armored Force was formed in July 1940, its most numerous modern tank was the M2A4 light tank, which had entered production only in 1940. It was based on the lessons of the Spanish Civil War and armed with a 37mm gun instead of the machine guns found on previous infantry light tanks and cavalry combat cars.

was strictly a small-scale affair with the capacity for a few hundred tanks per year at most. Clearly, new factories had to be brought on line. The obvious solution was to contract private industry to manufacture tanks, but this would take time, since none had built tanks before. Two industrial approaches were taken. First, the army issued contracts to large industrial firms to convert existing facilities to tank production or to add new production lines. Railroad firms were especially prominent on this list since they had the capacity to deal with large machines. Second, new factories were created from scratch. The president of Chrysler, K. T. Keller, suggested that the army build an arsenal specifically for tank production, so in August 1940, Chrysler was contracted to erect and manage the enormous new Detroit Tank Arsenal. The original plan was to manufacture 100 tanks per month, but the facility was designed for expansion, and by September 1941, the monthly production goal had been increased to 750 tanks. The work force there grew from 230 at the time of Pearl Harbor in December 1941 to 5,000 a year later. The Detroit Tank Arsenal would eventually manufacture more

than 25,000 tanks during the war—as many as all the German tank plants combined.

Beyond the mobilization of industry, the other issue was the type of tank needed by the army for the new divisions. At the time, nearly all of the U.S. Army inventory consisted of light tanks, and the only type of tank in mass production was the M2A4 light tank. The Spanish Civil War had raised questions about the viability of these poorly armored and weakly armed tanks. The Germans had made extensive use of light tanks in their blitzkrieg campaign in Poland and France, and the U.S. Army decided that it would have to make do with light tanks as the basis of the new armored divisions for the time being, even if they should be replaced with medium tanks as soon as possible. As an expedient, more armor was added to the M2A4 light tank, resulting in the M3 light tank, which entered production in March 1941 at the American Car & Foundry Plant in Pennsylvania, the first of the newly converted industrial tank factories. The M3 light tank, later nicknamed the Stuart by the British Army, would form the core of new American tank units in 1941–42.

AMERICAN BLITZKRIEG

The U.S. Army's future tank needs were heavily shaped by the emerging tactical doctrine, the American equivalent of Germany's blitzkrieg. Until 1940, the army's tanks had been primarily viewed as infantry-support weapons. As in World War I, they were intended for use in small units to support the advance of infantry by helping to eliminate machine-gun nests and other enemy defenses. Infantry-support tanks needed armor protection against likely enemy weapons, and they needed tank weapons suitable for destroying typical enemy defenses such as machine-gun nests, antitank guns, and pillboxes. The M3 light tank was not especially suitable for the modern infantry role since its armor was too thin to resist the German 37mm antitank gun, and its 37mm "squirrel shooter" was not especially useful against entrenched enemy infantry or antitank guns.

Although infantry support was the traditional role assigned to tanks, visionary thinkers in the 1920s and 1930s had begun to consider the use of the tank as a mechanized equivalent of the cavalry with an independent role on the battlefield. Instead of being tied to the infantry, large tank units could use their mobility to punch through enemy lines and charge deep into enemy territory, encircling and annihilating enemy defenses. The culmination of these debates was evident in the Wehrmacht's new panzer divisions. In contrast to some tank enthusiasts who saw the armored division primarily as a tank formation, the Wehrmacht saw it as a combined-arms team. The panzer was the centerpiece of the panzer division, but the panzer regiments were supported by panzer-grenadier (armored infantry) regiments, as well as by a motorized artillery regiment. Panzers alone were vulnerable to enemy infantry and antitank guns, but a careful blend of tanks, infantry, and artillery made a much more versatile formation. The Wehrmacht hoarded nearly all of its armored vehicles into the new panzer divisions and rejected the French practice of allotting a large fraction of its tank force to the infantry support mission. In the long run, this doctrine would prove to be a mistake. But in 1940, after the fall of France, it certainly seemed wise to follow the German example.

As a result, the new U.S. Armored Force focused on the armored division. The existing tank battalions were consolidated into the division's armored regiments, to which were added the other necessary ingredients such as mechanized infantry in half-tracks, self-propelled field artillery, and supporting arms. Gen. Adna Chaffee, the first head of the Armored Force and a prominent proponent of cavalry mechanization in the 1930s, saw the armored division's role as that of a modern-day offensive cavalry force: "The role of the armored division is the conduct of highly mobile ground warfare,

The M3 medium tank finally became available in the autumn of 1941. The M3 medium tank was a novelty at the time, and public demonstrations of its power were popular during press junkets at Fort Hood, Texas, like this display by the 753rd Tank Battalion.

A shortage of medium tanks forced the U.S. Army to use light tanks in their place. This 5th Armored Division exercise at the Desert Training Center in the Mojave Desert in September 1942 shows Company E of the 34th Armored Regiment with M3 light tanks—with the letter "M" for medium painted on the turret sides.

The M2 was quickly superseded by the marginally improved M2A1 medium tank, which used an enlarged turret and thicker 30mm armor on its vertical surfaces. It suffered from an archaic armament layout—a paltry 37mm gun in the turret—while the hull was festooned with four .30-caliber light machine-gun barbettes. Production did not start until December 1940, by which time it was clearly obsolete by European standards, and was halted after only ninety-four had been built.

particularly offensive in character, by a self-sustained unit of great power and mobility . . . on missions either strategical or tactical, whose accomplishments will effect to the maximum the total destruction of the enemy."

Since the main focus of the Armored Force was armored divisions rather than infantry tank battalions, the U.S. Army's new medium tank design was shaped by the technical requirements of the armored divisions and not by infantry-support requirements. Infantry-support tanks of the time, such as the British Matilda and Churchill or Soviet KV, placed the accent on armored protection over mobility since the tank would be needed to directly confront enemy defenses. In contrast, the doctrine for the new armored divisions was patterned on traditional cavalry tactics. The infantry would accomplish the breakthrough of enemy positions, and only

The main technical flaws of the M2 medium tank—pictured here during 1st Armored Division war games at Fort Knox in 1941—were its inadequate armor and its cramped turret. Nevertheless, it remained in service through 1942.

then would the armored division be committed to exploit the penetration and race deep into the enemy's rear. Such tactics did not require especially heavy armor, but they did require excellent mobility. Tank engineering, like all engineering, is a matter of compromise. Too much armor, and the tank loses mobility. Too big a gun means a much larger and more expensive tank, leading to a vicious cycle of added armor weight, more horsepower to propel more armor, and so on. When the new U.S. Army medium tank was developed, the compromise occurred mainly in the area of armor since the tactics dictated mobility rather than defensive strength.

In terms of firepower, the U.S. Army sought a good dual-purpose gun able to fire a potent high-explosive round to deal with most targets as well as an antitank round to tackle the occasional enemy tank. Tank-versus-tank fighting was not regarded as a primary mission of the American armored division since it did not seem to be a particularly common occurrence on the modern battlefield. The U.S. Army knew of few large confrontations of German and French tanks in the 1940 campaign and saw this as a model of future warfare. In this respect, the army was mistaken, but intelligence on the 1940 French campaign was poor.

These tactical developments formed the basis for the design of the U.S. Army's first significant medium tank, the M3. Confusingly, the army used the model (M) designations across a wide range of weapons: for example, the M1 rifle, M1 105mm howitzer, M1 155mm howitzer, and so on. In the case of tanks, there was the M3 light tank and the M3 medium tank. When the British Army began receiving U.S.

The backward state of the U.S. Army's equipment is nowhere more evident than in this view of 1st Armored Division exercises at Fort Knox in 1941. In the lead is an M2A1 medium tank followed by an even more weakly armed "Mae West" light tank.

Production of the new M2 medium tank began at Rock Island Arsenal in the summer of 1939, shortly before the outbreak of the war in Europe. The design was so fundamentally flawed in concept that it was cancelled after only eighteen were built. This one is on summer exercises with the 67th Infantry (Tanks) at Fort Benning in 1940.

tanks under the Lend–Lease program in 1941, they avoided this confusion by naming the tanks after American Civil War generals. So the M3 light tank was named the Stuart after the Confederate cavalry general J. E. B. Stuart, while the M3 medium tank was named the Lee in its basic American version and the Grant in a modified version that used a British-designed turret. The U.S. Army did not use these names during World War II, though they did become popular after the war. Hence, the M4 medium tank is far better known by its British name, the Sherman, than by its American designation. (This book makes use of the British names for convenience and because of their popular use since 1945.)

Besides the M designation, Ordnance also used the temporary T designation for pilot models of weapons. For example, the Sherman pilot was called the T6 before it was type-classified standard as the M4. Once a weapon had a standardized M number, experimental variants within the series received an E suffix. So for example, the pilot of the M4 with the T23 turret and 76mm gun was the M4E6.

KINDERGARTEN TANK

Design of the new M3 medium tank began in July 1940 in the wake of the French defeat. An air of crisis existed in the U.S. Army over the lack of modern equipment, and design of the new medium tank was rushed. The army wanted a modern medium tank—*now*. There were two clear demands to the Ordnance engineers at Aberdeen and Rock Island: the tank had to have at least two inches of frontal armor to protect against the German 37mm antitank gun, and it needed a 75mm gun capable of firing a worthwhile high-explosive round. Ideally, most American tankers wanted a design comparable to the most powerful German tank of the day, the PzKpfw IV. This tank was armed with a short 75mm gun in a turret, along with a single machine gun mounted in the hull for self-defense and a second machine gun in the turret, coaxial with the main gun, which was used against targets too small to attack with the main 75mm gun.

Ordnance had no experience building turrets capable of housing a 75mm gun. They were not certain how large the turret ring would need to be to withstand the recoil forces and had not developed a recoil system compact enough to fit inside a tank turret. In addition, they were leaning toward the use of a cast-steel turret to speed up tank production, but industry had yet to prove the ability to manufacture such a large armor casting. These issues could have been solved with time, but in the crisis atmosphere of the summer of 1940, there was no time to experiment. An old engineering adage sums up this design dilemma: "The engineer's triangle is inescapable: good, fast, cheap. Pick any two." The U.S. Army wanted a tank fast and cheap; it wasn't as good as many wished.

British officials began arriving in Washington with order books in hand, wishing to buy tanks to make up for those lost in France in 1940. So there

Although the M3 medium tank was a major improvement over the M2A1, some Ordnance design features were remarkably shortsighted. The M3 tank turret was surmounted by yet another turret housing a .30-caliber light machine gun that was difficult and awkward to operate.

This wooden mock-up of the M3 was built out of wood at Aberdeen Proving Ground and shows its basic features compared to the obsolete M2A1 medium tank. A 75mm M2 gun is mounted in the right sponson in place of the extravagant machine-gun barbettes of the M2A1, and a cast turret has been used in place of the angular plate-steel turret of the M2A1 to speed production.

The evolutionary link between the M3 medium tank and the earlier M2 series was the experimental T5E2 medium tank. Built in the summer of 1940, the T5E2 attempted to give the M2 more firepower by adding a 75mm howitzer in a side sponson, patterned after the French Char B1 bis tank. That gun was too weak for tank fighting, however, and the sponson mount did not provide enough traverse to defend the tank adequately.

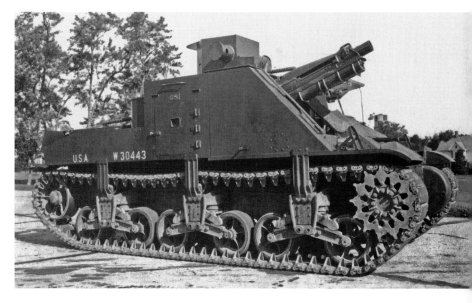

was pressure not only from the U.S. Army for tanks, but also from Britain. The British had an immediate requirement for 3,650 medium tanks, about six times what the U.S. had manufactured in the entire previous decade.

As a result of these demands, Ordnance proposed a hybrid design patterned after the French Char B1 battle tank, which placed the main 75mm gun in a sponson on the right side of the hull to fire high-explosive, while a small turret armed with a 37mm gun provided antitank firepower. The original design was a land battleship festooned with numerous machine guns, a throwback to the infantry tanks that Ordnance had been designing for the past two decades. The Armored Force immediately insisted that the excessive machine guns be dumped, though a few remained, including a cumbersome machine-gun cupola for the tank commander on top of the

This is the first M3 medium tank completed at Rock Island Arsenal in March 1941. Series production was undertaken at five industrial plants starting in June 1941.

37mm gun turret and a pair of fixed hull machine guns in front of the driver. The hull and powertrain were based on the earlier M2A1 medium tank, which was by now a dependable design from an automotive standpoint. The M3 medium tank was far from an optimal design, having a clumsy armament solution and other slapdash design features. But it could be designed and manufactured quickly. Detail design was completed in January 1941, and the first prototype was assembled at Rock Island Arsenal in March 1941, barely nine months after the program was started. Serial production began in June 1941, and eventually, five plants were involved in its manufacture.

Another problem beset the early tank program: the need to ramp up production from a few hundred medium tanks per year to more than 10,000. At the outset of the war, the army planned to raise 216 divisions, including 61 armored divisions. At nearly 400 tanks per division, this entailed the manufacture of 25,000 tanks, plus additional tanks for training and attrition—not to mention that Britain was buying large numbers of tanks and the U.S. had further Lend-Lease commitments. When President Roosevelt prepared his "arsenal of democracy" speech to lay out America's enormous wartime goals, he asked Ordnance for their recommendations. The plans were for an astonishing 45,000 tanks in 1942 and 75,000 in 1943. On top of this, the army was planning to field 200 tank destroyer battalions, requiring substantial production of these armored vehicles as well.

In August 1941, Maj. Gen. Jacob Devers replaced the ailing Gen. Adna Chaffee as head of the Armored Force. Devers was not happy with the claptrap and hasty M3 design and insisted that production be limited to 750 tanks before switching over to a more acceptable single-turret design. Devers preferred the new M7 tank being developed at Rock Island Arsenal. This started off as a light tank to replace the inadequate M3 light tank and was armed with the British 6-pounder, known as the

This is a good example of the initial configuration of the M3 medium tank with the early M2 75mm gun.

Gen. Jacob Devers favored adopting the new M7 tank over an M3 replacement since he felt it could serve as a universal tank replacing both the M3 light and M3 medium tanks. It took another year to develop the M7, which grew into an overweight medium tank inferior to the Sherman and was cancelled before production began.

The M3 continued to evolve during production. This M3 on exercise on Perham Downs in England in December 1942 shows the later-production configuration with the lengthened M3 75mm gun, deleted side doors, and the counterbalance under the 37mm gun indicating that the tank has been fitted with gun stabilization.

57mm in its U.S.-manufactured version. Devers thought the M7 could become a universal tank, replacing both the light and medium tanks. While an intriguing idea, M7 development was not far enough along for this to occur in 1942.

Senior army leaders, under pressure from Roosevelt's ambitious tank program, overruled Devers. The army wanted an adequate tank now, not a perfect tank sometime in the indefinite future. As a result, the M3 medium tank was produced in far larger numbers than originally planned and remained in production even after the start of M4 Sherman production simply to fill out the outrageously high demand for medium tanks.

The British were in the same predicament as the U.S. Armored Force. They did not like the M3 medium tank since it didn't fit comfortably into their usual scheme of infantry and cruiser (cavalry) tanks. But the British Army in the North African desert was desperate for tanks and took what it could get. A British tank specialist in 1942 commented that "the battle of Waterloo may have been won on the playing fields of Eton, but this war will be won on the drawing boards of Detroit."

The British Army insisted on one major change, a modified turret with a bustle to house the tank radio near the commander and without the preposterous machine-gun cupola on the roof of the turret. The version with the British-designed turret was called the Grant while the M3 in its original American configuration was called the Lee. This program started an important interplay between American and British tank experts, with the British trying to impart their hard-won battlefield experience to the Americans in the hope of getting better tanks. The American response was as varied as the many individuals involved in the process. Many U.S. tank engineers, who were familiar with the dismal quality of British tank design, were wary of accepting British advice. American Ordnance officers with the advantage of overseas tours in North Africa to learn the lessons from seasoned British tankers were far more

solicitous of British advice. One way or the other, British influence began to creep into U.S. tank design. The bustle-mounted radio in the Grant led to the U.S. Army's decision to mount the radio in the next U.S. medium tank, the M4 Sherman, in the bustle. One of the most important innovations in U.S. tank gunnery, the switch from periscopic sights to telescopic sights in the autumn of 1942, was largely forced on the U.S. Army by the British.

As the Pearl Harbor panic gradually subsided in 1942, the manic American military programs gave way to more sober plans. In May 1942, the army trimmed back its plans to 187 divisions with 47 armored divisions. As 1942 wore on, the armored divisions were cut to 26, then to 20 by the end of the year; the size of the tank contingent in each division was also reduced. The U.S. Army would form 16 armored divisions during the course of the war instead of the original plan for 61, although some 70 separate tank battalions that had not been included in the original plans eventually were organized. Industrial realities also affected the army's plans, and in September 1942, the enormous demand for steel by the U.S. Navy's shipbuilding program led to reductions in the 1942 and 1943 tank programs. Instead of the 120,000 tanks announced by President Roosevelt, the actual programs resulted in the production of about 24,000 light, medium, and heavy tanks in 1942 and 29,500 in 1943. While this production was only about half of Roosevelt's original scheme, it represented a hundredfold increase in U.S. tank production since 1940, an astonishing industrial accomplishment.

The M3 medium tank came as quite a shock when first issued to the new U.S. armored divisions because of its sheer size compared to the more familiar light tanks. It was soon dubbed "the Iron Cathedral" for its ungainly height. It was widely used for training by the army but would see very little combat in American hands. The most important role that the M3 medium tank played in U.S. tank development was that it helped create a U.S. tank industry.

THE SCHOOL OF TANK TECHNOLOGY

The M3 medium tank was the kindergarten for the tank industry as well as for the army. All of the plants manufacturing it were new to the tank business and needed time to become acquainted with the unique demands of handling armor steel, tank guns, and many other new components. Besides training the factories in tank production, the M3 medium tank established the first widespread collaboration between the design engineers in U.S. government arsenals and the engineers in private industry. American tank engineering experience up to 1941 rested on a handful of teams at Rock Island Arsenal and Aberdeen Proving Ground who could not possibly cope with the scale of tank development and manufacture now being undertaken. The obvious solution was to cooperate with the vast pool of trained automotive and railroad engineers available in the industry, but it took months, if not years, to bring them up to speed on tank technologies like armor plate

and guns. Soon engineers from Chrysler, Pullman Car, American Locomotive, and many other firms were designing key components of American tanks and in some cases entire tanks. Much of this process evolved during the production of the M3 medium tank in 1942–43.

The enormous requirements of both the U.S. and British armies for medium tanks quickly caused bottlenecks, especially regarding powerplants. The M3 medium tank was powered by a Continental radial gasoline engine derived from the Pratt & Whitney aircraft radial engine widely used in U.S. training aircraft. The U.S. War Production Board allotted various levels of priority to scarce industrial resources, and tank production usually came out below the aircraft industry in priority. As a result, new sources of tank engines had to be developed swiftly. William Knudsen, the chief of war production, turned to the "big three" automobile firms,

Ordnance contact with French engineers in 1939–40 opened American eyes to the possibility of using large armor castings as a method to expedite production. After proving casting techniques on the M3 medium tank turret, Ordnance next turned to designing an entire hull casting for the M3A1 medium tank. At the time, this was the world's largest steel armor casting.

The M3A1 used a large, single-piece casting for its hull. This did not completely replace riveted or welded hulls since industrial casting capacity did not exist in 1942–43.

Ford, General Motors, and Chrysler, and asked them to design a 500-horsepower tank engine from available resources as fast as possible. No obvious commercial sources existed since tank engines had to be significantly more powerful than truck engines and at the same time much smaller than ship and locomotive engines. As a result, the auto plants came up with some ingenious solutions. The M3A3 and M3A5 medium tanks used a pair of two General Motors diesel bus engines mated by a common drivetrain. The M3A4 had the even more unusual Chrysler A57 "multi-bank" engine that consisted of five small gasoline bus engines mated together in a star pattern with a common drivetrain. Ford offered their GAA, a new lightweight aircraft engine that had been rejected by the U.S. Army Air Force because of its technical immaturity. It was so plagued with problems that it did not go into series production for the M3 medium tank family. But once it reached maturity in 1944, it became the U.S.

Army's preferred tank engine, eventually powering the M4A3 Sherman and M26 Pershing tanks.

Besides the propulsion innovations, American industry was new to the fabrication of tank armor. Until 1941, all U.S. tanks were constructed from riveted armor plate. Riveting was a well-established industrial practice offering excellent strength. It had some significant military drawbacks, however, since the holes in the armor plate were potential weak points, especially as armor became thicker. Rivets posed a combat hazard because when hit, the portion inside the tank could sheer away and propel around inside the tank like a projectile. While some expedient solutions were developed to minimize the hazards of rivets in combat, other technologies were sought to deal with the thicker armor plate now demanded. Two technologies came to the fore, casting and welding. Casting had been widely used in U.S. industry for many decades, but the casting of armor steel was relatively new. The M3 medium

Another of the innovations pioneered by the M3 medium tank was the use of welding to replace riveting on tank armor. The M3A3 used a welded hull and was powered by a GM 6046 diesel engine instead of the gasoline engines used in the M3 and M3A1 versions.

tank was the first mass-produced American tank to use a cast turret, and many other components were cast as well. It took far less time to cast a complex structure than to fabricate it out of multiple plates of steel, making casting attractive under the time pressures imposed by the war. On the other hand, American industry had limited casting capacity, so casting represented only a partial solution to the tank manufacturing process. The most ambitious casting effort on the M3 medium tank project was the M3A1 version of the tank, whose entire upper hull was made out of a single large armor casting.

The other innovation in tank construction was the introduction of welding, which was used on the hulls of the M3A2 and M3A3. Although industry widely used welding at the time, welding of armor plate presented a significant challenge. Very hard armor steel with a high carbon content posed a real problem because the welds did not withstand shock very well and would crack when hit by an enemy projectile. Designers gradually developed solutions using various alloy combinations—for example, by adding the alloy molybdenum to the steel armor, which resulted in a good balance between hardness, the ability to handle shock, and the ease of welding. Luckily for the United States, molybdenum was abundant; unluckily for Germany, its nearest supplies were in Finland and Norway.

STRANGER IN A STRANGE LAND

Ultimately, the M3 medium tank saw far more combat in foreign hands than with the U.S. Army. Of the 6,258 tanks built, almost 70 percent were diverted to other armies under the Lend-Lease program. The first shipments of M3 medium tanks to Britain and the Soviet Union began in late 1941.

The Grant tank first arrived in North Africa at the end of 1941 to rebuild the British Army after its heavy losses to Rommel's Afrika Korps in the Operation Crusader battles in November 1941. Unlike the U.S. Army with its light and medium tanks, the British Army categorized tanks by their two principal missions: the cruiser tanks in the armored divisions and brigades oriented toward defeating panzers, and infantry tanks oriented toward close support of the infantry. The British Army categorized the Grants as cruiser tanks even though they did not fit either category comfortably, lacking the armor of infantry tanks and the speed of cruiser tanks. However, British losses in Africa and lingering problems with British tank designs made the Grants a welcome addition to the British arsenal. In spite of its awkward armament configuration, the Grant represented a major increase in firepower for the beleaguered British tank regiments. British cruiser tanks at the time were armed initially with the 2-pounder and later the 6-pounder guns, which provided excellent antiarmor performance but no high-explosive

punch. This became a serious drawback in the desert war because Rommel's tactics skillfully combined antitank guns with the small panzer force. The German antitank guns, such as the PaK 38 50mm, were small targets and nearly impossible to knock out by tank guns firing armor-piercing shot. The Germans often used the 88mm Flak gun in an improvised antitank role in the desert because of its long-range accuracy and tremendous power. The 88mm Flak gun could stand off at a great distance—2,000 yards or more—and still wreak havoc with the British tank forces. The Grant offered an antidote to the antitank gun threat since it could fire an effective high-explosive projectile that had a much greater chance of disabling an antitank gun.

As important as its firepower advantages, the Grant also proved more durable than existing British designs. The British tanks of the period were notoriously unreliable and suffered unacceptably high breakdown rates. British industry was stretched too thin, and tanks had a lower priority than aircraft and warships. The haste of British tank design did not leave enough time for testing and correcting flaws, resulting in a lack of durability. Some taste of this problem is evident from the title of the best history of British tank design, *The Great Tank Scandal*. In contrast, the Grant was based on components that had been in development for more than five years.

The British Army favored the version of the M3 medium tank with their own turret design but ended up with some that had the American turret, which they called the General Lee. This is one at a training center in Egypt in 1942. MHI

The Lee tank was accompanied by a U.S. Army Ordnance team to assist with any technical problems. The American officer second from the right is Col. G. B. Jarrett, who played an important role in technical intelligence during the war and later founded the Ordnance Museum at Aberdeen Proving Ground. MHI

The chassis and powertrain were improved versions of the design used on the failed M2 and M2A1 medium tanks, but the real problem with these older designs lay in the armor layout and armament, not the chassis. As a result, by the time the M3 medium tank entered production, vigorous testing had wrung most of the bugs out of the automotive components.

The British first committed the Grants to action in May 1942 during the Gazala battles. In May 1942, British units had 167 Grants with the Eighth Army's 1st and 7th Armoured Divisions and more in Egypt equipping other units or being used for training or reserve. This made it the second most common tank in the armored divisions, compared to 257 British-built Crusaders and 149 American-built Stuart light tanks. At the time, the Grant represented one of the best tanks in the desert, offering better antitank punch than the 50mm gun on the German PzKpfw III and better armor protection. In spite of the new

Grant tanks, the May–June Gazala battles went badly for the Eighth Army. The problems were not technical, but tactical. The Afrika Korps continued to display greater combat effectiveness in spite of technical and numerical shortcomings because of better tactics. The Grant performed well during the battle, and its 75mm gun proved an unpleasant surprise for the Germans in numerous encounters. The August fighting at Alam Halfa again saw the Grant as one of the mainstays of the British armored force, with 164 Grants among the 713 tanks in the forward-deployed units. On the German side, the Alam Halfa battle represented the arrival of the long-barreled 75mm gun on the PzKpfw IV Ausf. F2 tank, an echo of the arms race taking place on the Russian front since 1941 and a better tank than the Grant. This was the last time the Grant would be the principal British cruiser tank. In the autumn of 1942, a dynamic new leader, Lt. Gen. Bernard Montgomery,

The Grant tank was the M3 medium with the British-designed turret, which had a rear bustle to place the radio near the tank commander, as was standard British practice. This particular Grant belongs to the Royal Scots Greys, who in September 1942 were reequipping in Egypt after fighting against the Vichy French in Syria. AUSTRALIAN WAR MEMORIAL PHOTO 025033

"A Grave for Seven Brothers" was allegedly the Russian nickname for the M3 medium tank in Red Army service. While not up to the standard of the T-34, the M3 medium tank was still a worthwhile combat vehicle compared to some of the wretched Soviet tanks of the time.

arrived, along with the first shipments of the new American M4A1 Sherman tank. The Sherman had all of the advantages of the Grant, including its 75mm gun and its automotive dependability, but none of its vices, such as the awkward gun configuration or excessive silhouette. When the second battle of El Alamein started on October 23, 1943, the British armored forces included 270 Shermans and 210 Grants. The Grant remained in service as a battle tank through the end of the Tunisian campaign in May 1943, but in dwindling numbers.

In all, Britain received 2,855 Grants and Lees through Lend-Lease, which amounted to 45 percent of total M3 medium tank production. With the arrival of the more modern Sherman, the British deployed most of their Grants to secondary theaters or dumped them on Commonwealth units. Nearly 800 were delivered to units in Australia and about 900 to India. They remained in combat use in the Pacific theater, performing admirably in the fighting in Burma in 1944–45.

Another British offshoot of the Grant/Lee family was the Canadian Ram tank. In 1941, plans were underway to extend M3 medium tank production to the Montreal Locomotive Works owned by the American Locomotive Company in Schenectady, New York, which was already producing tanks for the U.S. Army. Before this began, the British convinced their Canadian colleagues that the M3 medium tank design was unacceptable and should be redesigned with a single turret to better conform to British cruiser tanks. Designated as the Ram cruiser tank, it used the lower hull and automotive components of the M3 medium tank, with a new cast upper hull and turret. Unfortunately, the Canadians followed British advice on the armament and kept the narrow sixty-inch turret ring of the M3 medium tank since it was compatible with the British 2-pounder. More far-sighted Canadian officers had recommended an enlarged turret ring to accommodate a bigger gun, but as in the United States, the delirium for maximum production overrode the desire for a better design. By the time the Ram was ready for production in December 1941, it was obvious that the 2-pounder was inadequate. Only fifty Ram Is were built with this weapon before production switched to the Ram II with the more powerful 6-pounder (57mm) gun then being adopted on British cruiser tanks like the Crusader. Although the 6-pounder offered antiarmor performance as good as the American dual-purpose 75mm gun, it offered poor high-explosive performance, and a high-explosive round was not yet available. So once the Ram II was ready for service, the Grant had already demonstrated the advantages of the dual-purpose 75mm gun. As a result, none of the Rams saw combat in World War II as battle tanks, though some were used in other roles, such as turretless Ram Kangaroo

infantry carriers, Badger flamethrowers, and Ram artillery observation posts. The sad outcome of the Ram program was a reminder that the success of the Sherman was not preordained. The British had also tried to convince the Americans to shift to the 6-pounder on the Grant follow-on tank—advice that was fortunately ignored.

The Soviet Union received nearly a quarter of M3 medium tank production, totaling 1,368 tanks. Some of its earliest battles occurred on the Russian front, starting with the 114th Tank Brigade on the southern front in May 1942. The M3 medium tanks were most commonly used in separate tank battalions and brigades to provide close support to the infantry and were generally not deployed with the Red Army's tank and mechanized corps (the Soviet equivalent of U.S. armored divisions). The M3 medium tank was called M3S in Soviet service, the S standing for *sredniy,* or medium; the M3 light tank correspondingly was called the M3L, for *legkiy,* or light.

Russian accounts from the Soviet era derided the M3 as a "grave for seven brothers." This was typical Cold War rhetoric; the Soviets would have complained about capitalist perfidy if they had been given atomic bombs and laser-beam weapons. The M3 medium certainly performed better than many of the Soviet tanks used in the infantry-support role, like the T-60 and T-70 light tanks. While not as effective as the T-34 in the tank-fighting role, the M3 was still a useful weapon for infantry support. The Soviets lost many of the M3 medium tanks in the costly battles in the summer and fall of 1942, as much because of the inexperience and poor training of Soviet tankers as because of the faults of the M3 medium tank. Some survived into 1943, and at the time of the titanic Kursk battles in the summer of 1943, the Soviet 48th Army on the central front had eighty-five M3 medium tanks in two of its separate tank regiments. Russian records indicate that at least one M3 medium tank was still in service on the Baikal front at the time of the war with Japan in August 1945.

CHAPTER 2

Birth of the Sherman

IN VIEW OF THE OBVIOUS SHORTCOMINGS of the M3 medium tank, design of a more modern tank began before the final design of the M3 was even completed. Given the pilot designation T6, the new design began development in February 1941, with a wooden mock-up being finished at Aberdeen Proving Ground in August. To speed along development, the T6 was based on the same chassis as the M3 medium tank. The most critical difference between the M3 and the T6 was the turret and armament. The T6 placed the 75mm gun in a fully traversable turret, not a hull sponson. The initial pilot used a cast hull and cast turret, but plans were underway to build welded-hull tanks in parallel to maximize industrial capacity. The first T6 pilot was completed at Aberdeen Proving Ground in September 1941, only six months after the M3 medium tank pilot. Tests of the pilot and inspection by the Armored Force led to some immediate changes. The infatuation of the Ordnance engineers with extraneous machine-gun positions annoyed the tankers. The T6 pilot had the same dubious machine-gun cupola on the turret roof as the M3 medium tank, and the hull had a ball-mounted machine gun plus two more fixed machine guns that could be aimed by the driver while steering the tank. All these were eventually dumped as worthless diversions. The hull had doors in the sponson sides for crew escape, but these compromised the side armor protection and also reduced the capacity for hull ammunition stowage. So these features were also deleted. Notwithstanding these modest changes, the T6 was deemed fully acceptable by both the U.S. Army and its other sponsor, the British Army, which wanted to purchase a more modern design than the M3 medium tank. Indeed, the British government funded the first

A curious evolutionary offshoot of the M3 medium tank, the Canadian Ram combined the chassis of the M3 with a new cast upper hull and turret. It is a useful reminder that the success of the Sherman was not preordained. The Canadians followed British doctrine, arming the Ram first with the 2-pounder and then, on the Ram Mk II, with the 6-pounder, ending up with an inferior cruiser tank that proved unsuitable for combat.

production line for the new tank at the Lima Locomotive Works in Ohio. When accepted for U.S. Army service in December 1941, the new tank became the M4 in its welded-hull version and the M4A1 in the cast-hull version; the British Army named it the Sherman after Gen. William T. Sherman, the famous Union Civil War commander.

Manufacture of the M4A1 Sherman began at the Lima plant in February 1942, followed by production of both the welded M4 and cast-hull M4A1 at Pressed Steel Car Company. As in the case of the M3 medium tank, production gradually shifted to more plants, including the Pacific Car and Foundry Company, the Baldwin Locomotive Plant, and the American Locomotive (ALCO) Company. The Sherman faced the same industrial bottlenecks as the M3 medium tank, and the builders relied on the same process to alleviate the shortage of engines. To power the new M4A2, they adopted the General Motors bus diesels that had been used to power the M3A3 and M3A5. The unusual Chrysler A57 multi-bank engine, used to power the M3A4, was now used to power the M4A4 version of the Sherman. A fourth alternative was eventually added, the Ford GAA gasoline engine, which powered the M4A3 version. This was the most delayed of the options as the new design had numerous teething problems, especially connecting rod failures.

The T6 pilot suffered from Ordnance's obsession with excessive machine guns, having not only a swivel-mounted .30-caliber machine gun but two fixed machine guns as well. These were deleted shortly after the Sherman entered production.

The T6 pilot shows the clear legacy of the M3 medium tank in its chassis, but the upper hull and turret are completely new designs. The side access hatch was deleted before the T6 entered production as the Sherman tank.

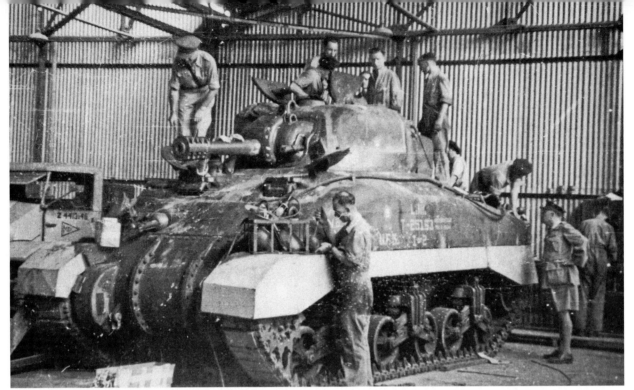

A handful of the first M4A1 Sherman tanks retained some features of the T6 pilot, such as the short M2 75mm gun with counter-weight and the more elaborate early gunner's sight. This British Sherman II is in a workshop in Egypt being fitted with sand shields and other British modifications prior to the second battle of El Alamein.

The M4A1 Sherman was the first production version of the Sherman tank. It differed from the T6 pilot in numerous small details, but most notably in the substitution of the more powerful M3 75mm gun in place of the shorter M2 75mm gun.

The M4 went through constant evolutionary improvement during its production run in 1942. This M4 shows the "heavy duty" bogie suspension adopted in autumn 1942. It had heavier springs and can be distinguished by the trailing return roller. The officer in the center of the group is Maj. Gen. Leven Campbell, Chief of Ordnance, seen here visiting Aberdeen Proving Ground in 1942 to inspect the new tank.

The M4A1 was soon followed into production by the M4, which used a welded hull instead of a cast hull. The first production line at Pressed Steel Car Company shows the very early production features, including the initial style of bogie suspension and the direct vision blocks for the driver in the front of the hull. The second incomplete chassis also has an experimental appliqué over the transmission housing that was soon deleted from production.

INSIDE THE SHERMAN

Aside from the obvious change to a single-turret configuration, the Sherman also introduced important improvements in the crew layout. The M3 medium tank had an oversize crew of seven, largely to man the numerous gun positions. The Sherman tank reduced this to a more efficient five, essentially the same as in contemporary German tanks like the PzKpfw IV. As in the M3 medium tank, the three-man turret crew consisted of the tank commander, gunner, and cannoneer (more commonly called the loader).

Generally a young lieutenant in the platoon's command tank and sergeants in the platoon's remaining four tanks, the tank commander held the senior position in the tank. The commander was responsible for directing the tank in combat and operating the radio in the rear turret bustle to communicate with other tanks in the platoon. In the initial versions of the Sherman tank, his primary means of observation was through a rotating periscope located in the hatch of the cupola over his head. In practice, this did not offer a very good view, and tank commanders were encouraged to fight "unbuttoned"—that is, with their heads outside the tank. In late 1944, an all-vision cupola was introduced with multiple view ports around the cupola to provide much better vision.

The gunner ranked next in seniority in the turret and sat in front of the tank commander in the right side of the turret. As the title implies, the gunner was responsible for aiming the main gun and the coaxial .30-caliber machine gun. On the initial versions of the Sherman in 1942, the gunner's primary sight was an M4 periscope that incorporated an M38 telescopic sight. This was not ideal since the periscope tended to move in its mounting, disrupting the boresight between sight and gun. The British encouraged the U.S. to switch to a more stable and powerful direct telescopic sight, which was introduced at the end of 1942 as the M55 telescope in the M34A1 gun mount. The gunner required considerable training to attain a high level of accuracy

A Sherman commander spent much of his time with his head outside the tank observing the terrain and communicating with his crew via a hand-held microphone or a throat mike. In front of him is the periscopic sight, his only means of seeing when the hatch was closed. The wartime tanker's helmet was developed from a Rawlings football helmet and had earphones for the intercommunication set. Seen here during the Lorraine fighting on October 2, 1944, Capt. J. F. Brady was the commander of Company A, 35th Tank Battalion, 4th Armored Division.

SHERMAN TANK CREW

Sherman tank crew illustration. AUTHOR'S COLLECTION

with the gun. Although the commander was supposed to assess the range to the target and the gunner simply use this figure to aim the weapon, in practice gunners had to have a good ability to estimate range and introduce an appropriate addition to the gun elevation to compensate for the range. The telescopic sights did include stadia markings to assist in this process, but it was still a far cry from the laser range finders and ballistic computers of modern tanks. The gunner traversed the turret using a power traverse for coarse movement and a handwheel for fine adjustments; gun elevation was by a handwheel. One of the Sherman's innovations was the gun stabilizer, a gyroscopic device that kept the gun trained in elevation even when the tank was on the move. This feature was controversial as it required careful maintenance to function properly. Since U.S. tank gunnery practice was to fire after halting, the gyroscope was most useful in keeping the gun roughly aligned to the target while moving. Well-trained crews found it handy, but as combat casualties cut into the ranks of trained gunners in the autumn of 1944, its use tapered off in many units.

The final member of the turret crew was the cannoneer, who stood by himself in the left side of the turret. His principal duty was to load the main

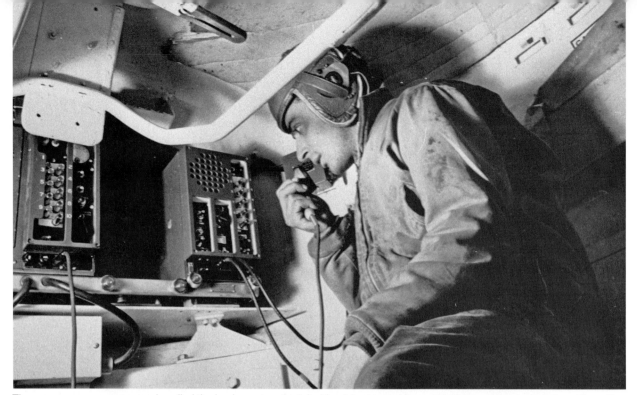

The cannoneer, more commonly called the loader, sat on the left side of the turret. His responsibilities often included working with the tank radio that was located in a bustle at the rear of the turret.

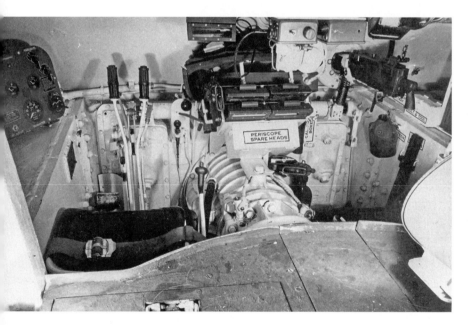

This is a view from the turret looking into the driver's compartment of a M4A1 (76mm) with the driver's station to the left and the bow gunner's station to the right. In the first-generation Shermans, a turret basket wall separated the turret crew from the driver's compartment; it was removed on the second-generation Shermans, as seen here.

gun based on the instructions of the tank commander, and so this position is more commonly called the loader. This position required the least skill of the three turret positions and so usually fell on the most junior member of the crew. In some units, the loaders were also trained in the operation of the radio to assist the commander.

In the front of the hull sat the driver and assistant driver. The driver sat on the left side of the transmission and operated the tank using a set of brake handles, as on a tractor, which slowed or stopped the track on one side, causing the tank to turn. The driver usually ranked third in seniority in the crew after the gunner since the position required good tactical

Inside the Sherman, the gunner sat immediately in front of the commander on the right side of the tank turret.

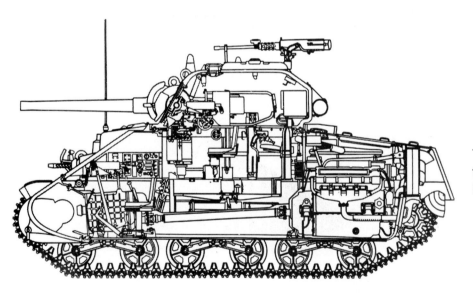

This cross-section view shows the first-generation M4A3 with Ford GAA gasoline engine.

judgment regarding the use of terrain to reduce the vulnerability of the tank to enemy observation and fire. The assistant driver was more often called the bow gunner, or BOG, since he actually had no driving responsibility. In 1942, before the U.S. Army finally settled on locating the radio in the turret, the radio was sometimes mounted in the sponson to the right of the BOG, so this was his responsibility. Once the radio was moved up to the turret, the BOG's sole tactical assignment was the operation of the ball-mounted .30-cal light machine gun. This was used primarily to defend the tank against enemy infantry, though it could also supplement the turret machine gun. The BOG did not have a dedicated sight but had to observe the fall of the machine-gun fire by means of its tracer rounds via his periscopic sight.

The driver sat in the left front corner of the hull. He steered the tank using tractor-style hand-brakes and observed the terrain through a periscope.

This is a view of the gunner's station in an M4A3E8 (76mm) looking down from the commander's seat. The mass of plumbing in front of the gunner's seat is primarily involved in the hydraulic turret traverse system.

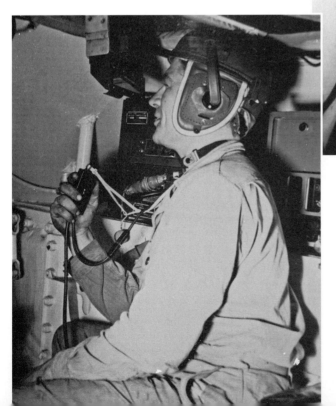

The assistant driver, more commonly called the bow gunner or BOG, sat in the right front corner of the hull. Some early Shermans had the radio in the sponson to his right, but after the army standardized the British style of locating the radio near the commander, the BOG's main responsibility was operating the bow-mounted .30-caliber light machine gun.

THE DYNAMICS OF U.S. TANK DEVELOPMENT

Tank development was a complex interplay between a variety of organizations, each with its own agenda and viewpoint. In theory, the requirements of the Armored Forces, as approved by Army Ground Forces headquarters and designed by the Ordnance Department, initiated tank development, and then tank production was managed by the Army Service Forces. In reality, the relative balance between these various bureaucracies shifted over time because of the personalities and policies of the day.

The Ordnance Department—in particular Gen. Gladeon M. Barnes, chief of its Technical Division—dominated American tank development during the war. That development effort was a very small-scale affair in 1940–41, but it grew enormously during the war with the sudden influx of large numbers of reserve officers with engineering backgrounds. Ordnance was the conduit for contracts to private industry, so it could also bring political pressure to bear when needed. Barnes and the Ordnance Department developed a tendency to go their own way in tank development, often against the wishes of the user and army headquarters.

The Ordnance Technical Committee, later simply the Ordnance Committee, coordinated the interests of the Armored Force, Army Ground Forces, infantry, engineers, and other army organizations in weapons development. This group met weekly to discuss current weapons programs, and its members included representatives of the various offices such as the Armored Force, AGF, ASF, engineers, and so on. Barnes chaired the committee and outranked the colonels and lieutenant colonels from the other organizations. His voice had unusual sway on the Ordnance Committee. In theory, the decisions of the committee were translated into Ordnance Committee Meeting (OCM) recommendations that had to be approved by the army's adjutant general to take effect. In practice, this was a rubber stamp, and it was rare for OCM recommendations to be rejected unless one of the branches was in adamant opposition. The OCM recommendations ranged from technical trivia, such as the formulation for new machine oil, to authorizations for new weapons, such as new tanks.

The Ordnance Committee represented Barnes's main avenue for circumventing the Armored Force and AGF in starting new tank programs. Ordnance would propose some new development at the weekly meeting, the colonels around the table would meekly agree, and a multimillion-dollar tank program would start with little input from either Armored Force or AGF. British tank experts stationed in the U.S. to handle the extensive British Lend-Lease tank purchases were aghast at Barnes's aura of infallibility and the way that Ordnance ran roughshod over the services. One of these specialists, G. MacLeod Ross, later commented that "Ordnance objectives seemed far removed from Armored Force requirements. . . . The Armored Force did not have the strong lobby that Ordnance enjoyed, and so the latter continued in a paternal fashion to dispense to the user what they considered good for them." One of Britain's chief weapons designers, Gen. E. M. Campbell Clarke, wrote after the war that "Ordnance necessarily lacks military background to exercise the powers over [Army] Ground Forces equipment that has been given it. On the other hand, the Ground Forces lack staff with sufficient technical training and background to be entrusted with weapon policy direction, over the purely technical execution of it by Ordnance. The lack of common military background must tend to make joint collaboration between the two partisans difficult and, at the best, reluctant."

One of the primary institutional weaknesses of Ordnance in World War II was its lack of experience in designing and building tanks. The dynamics of tank design fundamentally differ from that of more traditional weapons. Until World War II, U.S. Army Ordnance mainly had designed antipersonnel weapons such as rifles, grenades, machine guns, and field artillery, all of which are primarily designed to kill enemy soldiers. Technological change in antipersonnel weapons tended to be slow. Although a Springfield rifle from World War I might not kill as effectively as the World War II M1 Garand rifle, it was still a lethal weapon and was used in combat in World War II. Many American infantry weapons of World War II were designed during or shortly

Maj. Gen. Gladeon M. Barnes, head of the Technical Division of the Ordnance Department, was the single most influential U.S. Army officer in the development of wartime tank designs.

after World War I, including the BAR squad automatic weapon, the .30-cal light machine gun, and the .50-cal heavy machine gun. The U.S. Army used artillery weapons such as the French 75mm field gun and French Schneider 155mm howitzer through 1943. Antipersonnel weapons did not become obsolete overnight. The U.S. Army had even developed a special category, "limited standard," for these old weapons that were still viable even if not ideal. The tanks designed by Ordnance in the 1930s were heavily influenced by foreign designs and were at best mediocre. Ordnance had a good track record in weapons development during the 1930s and 1940s, and its field artillery weapons ranked among the best in the world.

Unfortunately, the same did not hold true for Ordnance tank design. Ordnance had little experience in designing tanks, and up to 1940, most of its

efforts had taken place on only a single family of light tanks and cavalry cars that resulted in the M3 light tank of 1941. Not only did Ordnance lack a strong history of tank design, but tanks represented a fundamentally different type of weapon intended for machine-versus-machine combat, fighting against enemy tanks and defending itself against a growing variety of antitank weapons. The development of tank and antitank technology proceeded much more rapidly than antipersonnel technology and included significant interplay between enemy offensive and defensive weapons and the tank design. The most successful paradigm for dealing with the challenge of machine-versus-machine weapons was that a new tank must be designed to deal with the future threat, not the present threat. If the tank designers waited until the future threat had appeared, it was already too late since it would take months, if not years, to come up with a suitable antidote. Ordnance showed little appreciation for this paradigm during the war, and U.S. tank development suffered as a result.

This paradigm was already self-evident to other U.S. services, such as the navy and army air force. Warships have always been designed with the likely configuration of enemy warships in mind; likewise, fighter aircraft have always been designed with an eye toward the threat that will exist when the new fighter enters service. Ordnance was institutionally unaccustomed to this paradigm.

Ordnance's institutional weakness was further exacerbated by related difficulties in handling technical intelligence about enemy weapons. Ordnance was traditionally responsible for evaluating technical intelligence on foreign weapons, even if it was collected by other army organizations like the U.S. Army's Military Intelligence Division (MID). In past decades, technical intelligence focused on exploiting novel technology in new foreign weapons that could be useful for American weapons. This approach sufficed for small arms and artillery since new developments in these fields seldom had any immediate and dramatic influence on the battlefield. However, in the new realm of machine-versus-machine warfare, technical intelligence took on an important new dimension since a clear understanding of enemy tanks and antitank weapons necessarily underpinned the formulation of plans for American weapons.

This intelligence was needed in an extremely timely fashion because of the much faster dynamics of tank and antitank weapons development in World War II. In addition, this information had to be adequately conveyed to other combat branches, such as the Armored Force and Army Ground Forces, so that they appreciated the need for a new weapon and would therefore support an expensive and time-consuming new weapons program. As will be mentioned repeatedly in this book, antitank weapons went through multiple generations during World War II, starting with the prewar generation of 25–37mm antitank guns and evolving into 50–57mm guns in 1941–42, 75–76mm guns in 1944, and 88–90mm guns in 1945. Tank armor likewise went through several changes during the war in response to the evolving threat.

During World War II, Ordnance largely failed to develop an organizational structure to translate the gathered technical intelligence into useful information for weapons designers and field commanders. As will be evident in the chapters that follow, Ordnance did a good job collecting data about current German weapons but failed to develop and disseminate an analysis of what this data meant to key army decision-makers.

Contrary to the widely held view that soldiers are addicted to new weapons, the opposite is often the case. Most field commanders of the World War II era were not especially keen on receiving new weapons since it took a great deal of time and effort to train troops to use and maintain them, especially complex weapons such as tanks, which required daily maintenance. Combat officers showed little enthusiasm for new weapons unless they saw a clear need for them and were averse to new designs simply for their technical novelty.

Aside from these institutional problems in the Ordnance Department, the U.S. Army's failures to use technical intelligence in World War II can be traced to a lack of experience. British, German, and Soviet officers had firsthand experience with the evolution of tank and antitank technology from the Spanish Civil War, through the early blitzkrieg years, to the midwar years. The U.S. Army's involvement in large-scale tank development and production really started only in 1940, several years behind most of the European armies. Until 1943, American experience was all secondhand and lacked the urgency seen in European tank programs in 1942–43. This problem became most acute in the summer and autumn of 1943 when the U.S. Army had to decide whether the Sherman would be adequate to face the threat in 1944.

ARCHITECT OF THE ARMY

Although Ordnance designed the tanks, the ultimate decision to build a new tank rested in the hands of the headquarters of the Army Ground Forces, headed in 1942–44 by Lt. Gen. Lesley McNair. During World War II, the U.S. Army included three major headquarters: the Army Ground Forces (AGF), the Army Air Force (AAF), and its industrial arm, the Army Service Forces (ASF). The least known of the major U.S. Army leaders of World War II, McNair was nevertheless one of the most important. Aptly dubbed "the architect of the U.S. Army of World War II," he was not a great combat commander but rather an administrative genius. His office oversaw the raising and equipping of the army's new divisions, the establishment of their training programs, and the setting of their tactical doctrine. In the case of the tank force, McNair played a major role in creating the new armored divisions, determining their size and composition, and selecting their equipment.

As an old artilleryman, he developed a reputation as a scourge of the Armored Force because of his frequent clashes with their leaders. It was more a case of "tough love" than antipathy to the new branch. In the summer of 1940, after the Armored Force was first formed, many of its young commanders strutted around with their new insignia, boasting that the Armored Force would soon be the predominant power on the modern battlefield. McNair decided that the cocky new tankers needed to prove themselves, and during the course of the 1941 war games, he put them to the test. As an artilleryman who had written the book on artillery antitank tactics, McNair loaded the rules in favor of the antitank artillery. Flour-bag "antitank" grenades used in the war games were deemed powerful enough to stop a tank, leading the tankers to complain bitterly. Even if the rules were unfair, young tankers like George S. Patton tried harder to overcome the odds. The games ended with no great tank victories, but they did uncover problems in armored division organization and tactics that were addressed in early 1942 before the Armored Force entered battle in earnest.

McNair established the criteria for army weapons acquisition, based in large measure on the memories of the poor showing of U.S. weapons in World War I. During World War I, American industry responded only slowly to the needs of the U.S. Army, and most of its key weapons, including artillery, tanks, and aircraft, came from the French or British. The American products that did reach the U.S. Army, such as trucks, often proved vulnerable on the battlefield. Memory of these misfortunes shaped the attitudes of McNair and other senior American commanders in World War II.

The two principal AGF criteria for army weapons were battleworthiness and battle need. Battleworthiness meant that the weapons had to be both combat effective and durable. Since troops would be fighting 3,000 miles or more from the arms factories, the weapons had to be well tested in advance so that they did not need frequent repair or replacement. There was no sense shipping a tank 3,000 miles only to have it break down after a few hundred miles of travel as trucks and tanks did too often in World War I. Ordnance developed a bad reputation during World War II for trying to foist half-baked designs on the Armored Force, but McNair's AGF would not let them transition from design to production unless they were durable enough. U.S. tank designs went through more rigorous testing than in any army of the war. The automotive test tracks at Aberdeen Proving Ground were the main center for this effort, but other test tracks were established in the Midwest near the tank plants and also in areas like the Yuma desert to test performance in desert terrain. McNair's insistence on battleworthiness would play a major role in the automotive excellence and durability of American tanks in World War II.

McNair's other demands proved more controversial and lay at the heart of some of the Sherman's problems later in the war. "Battle need" seems to be a very sensible requirement, insisting that weapons be accepted for production only if they are really needed. McNair wanted to avoid Ordnance's "mad scientist" disease that was rampant in 1941–42, with every engineer and design team coming up with hare-brained schemes for war-winning wonder

As head of the U.S. Army Ground Forces, Lt. Gen. Lesley McNair played a pivotal role in all major decisions regarding the production of army tanks, their tactical doctrine, and the training of tank troops.

Maj. Gen. Levin Campbell Jr. (left) was Chief of Ordnance in 1942–46 and is seen here conferring with McNair.

weapons. Some of the ideas were good, but many were amateur junk. From the perspective of the AGF, the process was clear: using branches such as the Armored Force or infantry would inform Ordnance of their requirement, and Ordnance would try to develop a weapon to satisfy their need. The final decision whether the weapon would be accepted for incorporation into the army usually rested with McNair's AGF headquarters, although in rare cases, McNair's decision could be appealed to the final arbiter, Gen. George C. Marshall and the War Department. McNair's office sponsored a program of sending observers overseas to the combat theaters to solicit information from troops to see how weapons were performing and to talk with field commanders about what improvements of existing weapons were needed.

The problem with battle need was the tyranny of time. Modern weapons take months, if not years, to develop, so there could be no fast response to a sudden technological crisis in the theater of battle, such as the appearance of a new antitank weapon or a new enemy tank. Battle need was a reactive philosophy; it presumed that action would not be taken

Left: Maj. Gen. Jacob Devers, the youngest major general in the U.S. Army at the time, was the second head of the Armored Force from August 1941 until May 1943, replacing the ailing Gen. Adna Chaffee.

Right: Maj. Gen. Alvin Gillem replaced Devers as the third head of the Armored Force. Although he played an important role in reinvigorating army attention to the need of tank support for the infantry divisions, by this time the influence of Fort Knox was waning.

until the enemy acted first. This was not much of a problem with antipersonnel weapons, which became obsolete much more slowly and gradually. But in the case of tanks, a new enemy tank impervious to the American tank's gun could unexpectedly appear. The development of a new tank gun to deal with the new enemy tank could not be designed overnight, and even if a bigger gun was already available, it would take months to modify tanks to accommodate it, months to ramp up ammunition production, and months more to ship the gun and ammunition overseas from the United States. The AGF's reactive battle need doctrine, combined with Ordnance's weakness in the use of technical intelligence to predict likely German developments, lay at the root of the Sherman's shortcomings in 1944–45.

BAPTISM OF FIRE

On June 21, 1942, while in the Oval Office of the White House at a strategy meeting with President Roosevelt, Winston Churchill was informed that the garrison at Tobruk had finally fallen to the onslaught of Rommel's Afrika Korps. "What can we do to help?" Roosevelt asked. "Give us as many Sherman tanks as you can spare and ship them to the Middle East as quickly as possible!" Churchill answered. As a result, the Sherman tank would first go into combat in British hands. When U-boats sank one of the transport ships full of Sherman tanks off Bermuda in July, Roosevelt intervened and diverted M4A1 tanks intended for the U.S. 1st Armored Division to make up the loss. This explained why the 1st Armored Division still employed M3 medium tanks in Tunisia in November–December 1942.

British troops warmly received the Sherman, which had all the advantages of the M3 Grant but none of the disadvantages. Its 75mm gun was powerful and versatile, able to defeat the German panzers of the time with armor-piercing ammunition and deal with the antitank threat with a high-explosive round. The turret design was a major improvement over the awkward M3 Grant layout, and the crew

was reduced from an excessive seven to a more practical five men. The Continental radial engine offered good power and mobility, and the armor protection, while not impervious to German fire, was substantial. The Sherman's baptism of fire was during the second battle of El Alamein in October 1942, the turning point of the war in the desert. Under the command of Gen. Bernard Montgomery and with substantial advantages in tanks and artillery over the Germans and Italians, the British Eighth Army finally sent the Afrika Korps into headlong retreat.

A group of observers from Army Ground Forces returned from Britain in February 1943 and reported that

> At practically every British armored force installation visited, considerable voluntary praise was heard on the American M4 tank, both of its mechanical efficiency, and its armament and armor. Four different general officers of the Royal Armoured Corps voiced an "off the record" recommendation that this tank be adopted throughout all British armored units as a single universal tank type

The Sherman saw its baptism of fire in British hands during the second battle of El Alamein in October 1942. This is a Sherman II (M4A1) of the 9th Lancers, 1st Armoured Division, during training prior to the battle.

The U.S. Army stationed liaison teams with the British Army in North Africa to study the tactical and technical lessons of the fighting. Here a British and American team inspect a Sherman II knocked out during the El Alamein battles by an 88mm gun south of Rahman.

and the further production of British tanks be diverted to other war equipment or possibly the manufacture of such component parts of the M4 as local facilities permit. . . . The M4 tank appears to be unquestionably far superior to the newly developed "Cromwell" which had not yet reached a pilot model test.

The Sherman tank proved so successful in North Africa that it would become the backbone of the British tank force in Italy in 1943 and France in 1944.

The combat debut of the Sherman in American hands was not so fortuitous, though the problems resulted from the inexperience of U.S. tankers, not tank design. During the June 1942 meetings in Washington, Roosevelt had agreed to a British plan to end the campaign in North Africa by landing a substantial American force in the French colonies of Morocco and Algeria, putting the Axis forces in a vise with the Americans approaching from the west and the British Eighth Army from the east. Operation Torch began in November 1942 and included

the U.S. 1st and 2nd Armored Divisions. With Morocco and Algeria in Allied hands following the French capitulation, elements of the 1st Armored Division took part in initial operations to take control of neighboring Tunisia. Because of the vast distances involved and the limited logistics, the scale of American operations in the first months of fighting was limited.

The first U.S. medium tank battalion deployed in combat was the 2nd Battalion, 13th Armored Regiment (2/13th Armored) of the 1st Armored Division, which took part in the failed race to Tunis in December 1942. Still equipped with the older M3 medium tank, the inexperienced battalion took a beating in the December fighting. American tank training was unrealistic, and many tank units used bold and dangerous tactics, charging forward with little regard for reconnaissance or terrain. The popular imagination conceived tank combat as a noble clash between two armored knights, with tanks facing each other on the field of battle on equal terms. The veteran tankers of the Afrika Korps had long ago dismissed this romantic nonsense and adopted

The turretless, charred hulks of a platoon of M4A1 tanks are a grim reminder of the sacrifice of Lt. Col. Louis I. Hightower's 3rd Battalion, 1st Armored Regiment, in its ill-fated attempt to repulse the German offensive through Faid Pass toward Sidi Bou Zid on February 14, 1943. These Shermans were knocked out at long range by a combination of 88mm guns and the new Tiger I heavy tank.

The M4A1 first saw combat with the U.S. during Operation Torch, the landings in French North Africa in November 1942. Some M4A1 tanks took part in the landings and subsequent actions against Vichy French forces, but the Shermans saw little, if any, combat.

the tactics of a wary hunter, waiting in ambush for the prey to wander into their gun sights. In offensive operations, German tanks advanced slowly and cautiously, trying not to kick up dust clouds that would give away their positions. They expertly used terrain to avoid silhouetting their tanks against the horizon, and they sent small reconnaissance detachments of armored cars forward in the vanguard to discover the location of enemy formations. It took the American tankers time to learn these lessons, and eventually, the 2/13th Armored would become the best U.S. tank unit in the Tunisian theater.

But it was not the experienced 2/13th Armored that was the first American Sherman battalion to see extensive combat, but their newly arrived and inexperienced compatriots from other battalions of the

An M4A1 medium tank of Company G, 1st Armored Regiment, pulls an M3 half-track out of a wadi near Sidi Bou Zid during the fighting there on February 14, 1943. Most of this unit was knocked out the next day during fighting with the German 21st Panzer Division.

The olive-drab camouflage color of American tanks was ill-suited to the desert, and many 1st Armored Division tanks were roughly camouflaged using local mud. This is *Major Jim*, the M4A1 tank of Maj. James Simmerman, executive officer of the 2nd Battalion, 13th Armored Regiment. This particular tank was lost covering the withdrawal from Kasserine Pass in late February.

1st Armored Division. Rommel viewed the arrival of the Americans in Tunisia as an opportunity to redeem his fortunes after his defeat at El Alamein. He planned to strike the thinly held American defensive positions around the Faid Pass, expecting that the green American formations would be easy pickings despite the weakened state of his own forces. But Rommel was discredited after El Alamein, soon to be recalled to Germany to recuperate from combat exhaustion; Operation *Früh-*

lingswind would be conducted by the newly arrived 5th Panzer Army of Gen. Hans von Arnim.

The attack began on February 14, 1943, through the Faid Pass toward Sidi Bou Zid with two panzer divisions in the lead. Two U.S. infantry battalions were soon in peril, and Sherman tank companies of Lt. Col. Louis Hightower's 3/1st Armored, 1st Armored Division, sallied forth in a hopeless attempt to rescue them. Vastly outnumbered and outgunned, the Shermans were blasted at long range

This is a Sherman II of the 10th Hussars, 1st Armoured Division, knocked out during the El Alamein fighting by an armor-piercing round that struck the turret side. While the Sherman was a significant improvement over the Grant, it was by no means invulnerable to German antitank weapons of the period.

In a latter-day Custer's Last Stand, Lt. Col. J. D. Alger's 2nd Battalion, 1st Armored Regiment, was wiped out on February 15, 1943, during a hopeless counterattack against the 21st Panzer Division southwest of Sidi Salem. These M4s of F Company, 1st Armored Regiment, 1st Armored Division, were destroyed in the final skirmish in the Oued Rouana wadi. The tank in the foreground, #19, was knocked out by a 75mm round, and the tank in the background, #3, by a 50mm round.

by 88mm flak guns set up for antitank defense, and a company of the new Tiger heavy tanks soon joined the slaughter. Of Hightower's original forty-four tanks, only seven tanks survived the day.

The 1st Armored Division commander seriously underestimated the scale of the German attack and,

the next day, ordered a counterattack by a task force with Lieutenant Colonel Alger's 2/1st Armored in the vanguard, followed by infantry in half-tracks from the 3/6th Armored Infantry and antitank support from the 701st Tank Destroyer Battalion. The counterattack was a grim reminder of the inexperi-

An M4A1 medium tank of Alger's battalion knocked out in the Oued Rouana wadi on February 15. The tank has suffered from a catastrophic ammunition fire that has blown off the turret and collapsed the sponson floor.

ence of the American tank force, and Alger's battalion charged forward without reconnaissance against a force more than five times its size.

Shortly after noon on February 15, the Sherman tanks advanced across the desert in a broad V formation, and a German reconnaissance aircraft soon spotted their plumes of dust. Warned well in advance, the two German panzer divisions stationed around Sidi Bou Zid carefully prepared their defenses and awaited the inevitable. Alger's battalion fell into the trap, and German antitank guns and tanks pounded the Americans from multiple directions. About forty Shermans made it as far as the Oued Rouana wadi, where they were gradually shot to bits during the course of the afternoon as the panzers closed in for the kill, a latter-day Custer's Last Stand. Only four tanks that had been at the rear of the column with the infantry survived the massacre. The decimation of these two Sherman tank battalions around Sidi Bou Zid was the opening disaster of what would later be called the battle of Kasserine Pass.

Lt. Col. Henry Gardiner's experienced 2/13th Armored, by now reequipped with Sherman tanks, would take part in the defense of Sbeitla and the counterattacks in Kasserine Pass in the following days. The superb performance of Gardiner's understrength battalion in this difficult fighting was a clear reminder of the value of combat experience in tank warfare.

The U.S. Army learned hard lessons from the Kasserine Pass debacle. The problem in the tank battalions was not the new Sherman tank but the inexperience of the tank crews, unrealistic training, and serious problems in armored division organization. These would be addressed during the rest of 1943. The desert war also compelled the U.S. to change the Sherman's sight. German tanks had telescopic sights for their guns, giving them better accuracy at long range—a vital asset in desert fighting, since the flat terrain permitted long-range tank engagements. The original versions of the Sherman used a periscopic sight with no magnification. The British

One of the few experienced U.S. tank units at the time of Kasserine was Lt. Col. Henry Gardiner's 2nd Battalion, 13th Armored Regiment, which had been serving in Tunisia since the race for Tunis in December 1942. Gardiner is seen here in front of his new M4A1 tank, named *Henry III*, which replaced *Henry II*, lost in the defense of Sbeitla. HENRY GARDINER

had been pressing for a new sight since 1942, and the desert fighting increased the pressure for this improvement. A new telescopic sight was developed in 1942 and reached production in the spring of 1943.

Furthermore, the Sherman had shown an alarming tendency to catch fire. One of the more popular myths attributes this to the Sherman's use of gasoline rather than diesel engines. German tanks were also gasoline powered, however, and did not exhibit a similar problem. The Sherman's problem lay with the ammunition, which was stowed in ammo racks in the sponsons above the track. Hits on the upper superstructure of the Sherman penetrated its thin side armor and almost invariably struck some of the ammunition, igniting the highly inflammable ammunition propellant. Once ignited, the fire could not be put out since the propellant contained its own oxidant. Once one round of ammunition began to burn, it usually set off neighboring rounds, resulting

in a catastrophic fire that turned the tank interior into a blast furnace, incinerating any crewmen who had been unlucky enough not to escape.

Some engine fires could be handled by the Sherman's existing fire-extinguishing system. In the spring of 1943, a string of reports and letters between Washington and the various field commands reviewed complaints about the vulnerability of the Sherman to fires. Discussions with American tank commanders—including Maj. Gen. Ernest Harmon of the 1st Armored Division and Brig. Gen. Paul Robinett, who commanded CCB, the division's most seasoned combat unit—all concluded that ammunition was the primary culprit. British officers believed that 90 percent of the tank fires resulted from ammunition fires and that in their experience, fires in gasoline- and diesel-powered tanks were comparable in number.

As a short-term solution, the ammo bins were reinforced by welding additional appliqué steel armor

This M4A1, one of the handful of survivors from Alger's battalion, is seen here days after the Oued Rouana wadi massacre at the time of the fighting for Kasserine Pass.

The M4A1 medium tank of Capt. G. W. Meade, commander of Company I, 1st Armored Regiment, 1st Armored Division, on the approaches to Kasserine Pass on February 24, 1943, shortly after the Allies had finally stopped the German and Italian advance.

to the outside of the hull, and ammunition was removed from the inside of the turret basket. In the long term, a new stowage configuration was planned. Called "wet" stowage, it went into production in early 1944. The appliqué armor improvements for the Sherman were incorporated into a "blitz" program for new-production tanks. In addition, tanks that had already been manufactured were sent through field depots where these enhancements were added using kits shipped from American factories. All the Sherman tanks in England awaiting the landings in Normandy incorporated these quick-fix changes.

THE BRITISH SHERMAN

In addition to its central role in the U.S. Army, the Sherman tank eventually formed the backbone of British and Commonwealth tank units in 1943–45. Total Sherman production in World War II was 49,234 tanks, which included 33,671 75mm tanks, 10,883 76mm tanks, and 4,680 105mm assault guns. Of these, the United States delivered 22,098—about 45 percent of production—to other armies via Lend-Lease. By far the largest recipient, Britain received 17,184 Shermans of different varieties—

about 35 percent of total Sherman production. The Soviet Union was shipped 4,102 Shermans, about 8 percent of total production.

Although the U.S. began by shipping Britain the M4A1 "Sherman II," two other types became predominant, first the diesel powered M4A2 "Sherman III" and later the M4A4 with its unusual A57 engine, better known in Britain as the "Sherman V." The British Army initially favored the diesel-powered M4A2 and had received shipments in time

By 1943, the British Army was leaning in favor of the M4A4 (Sherman V) because of its reliable Chrysler engine. With the end of M4A4 production in sight, the U.S. Army transferred about 1,400 M4A4 tanks it had been using for training purposes, like this example with the 12th Armored Division in 1943.

By the time of Operation Husky in July 1943, the British Army had started to receive large numbers of the diesel-powered M4A2, known as the Sherman III in British service. This Sherman III, named *Churchill*, of the 3rd County of London Yeomanry, 4th Armoured Brigade, lands from an LST on Sicily on July 10, 1943.

for the second battle of El Alamein in October 1942. However, the Soviets insisted on diesel-powered Shermans since their own T-34 and KV tanks used diesel engines. As a result, in November 1942, the U.S. Army decided to earmark the M4A4 for the British. In May 1943, because of the decision to simplify Sherman production by ending M4A4 manufacture, British supplies were extended by transferring the 1,400 M4A4 tanks then in stateside

American training units to Britain after they had been rebuilt to current standards.

By the time of the Sicily landings in July 1943, most British tank regiments had left behind their Grants and converted to the Sherman. Grant use after Tunisia was confined to secondary theaters such as Burma or to specialized applications such as CDL tanks, recovery vehicles, and other special-purpose vehicles. The large numbers of Sherman tanks

By the time of the 1944 campaign in northwest Europe, the British Army as well as associated Canadian and Polish units made heavy use of the Sherman V (M4A4), although other Sherman types were in use as well. This M4A4, converted to the Sherman Vc (17-pounder), is being recovered by a U.S. Army ordnance team near the Meuse River in March 1945.

available to the British Army led to its adoption as the standard cruiser tank in 1943, with the larger and heavier Churchill becoming the standard British infantry tank. Therefore, Commonwealth units serving alongside the British Army were equipped on the same pattern, so for example, New Zealand tank units in Italy switched to the Sherman, and the Canadian Army in northwest Europe relied on the Sherman as its principal tank. This also affected other units serving under British command such as the Polish Army, which included tank units of the Polish II Corps in Italy and the Polish 1st Armored Division in northwest Europe.

In addition to the use of Shermans with different engines from the typical U.S. Army types, the British Sherman tanks had numerous small-detail differences. After arrival from the United States, most Shermans were delivered to British depots prior to being issued to British or Commonwealth units. The changes mainly involved preferences in stowage and tools, as well as the fitting of British radios, typically the No. 19 radio transceiver. Otherwise, the British Shermans were identical to American Shermans, but they were seldom exchanged on the battlefield because of the different engine types and radios.

CHAPTER 3

The Panzer Nemesis

WHEN SHERMAN TANKS LANDED at Omaha Beach in Normandy in June 1944, they did not differ much from the Shermans used at El Alamein two years earlier. In the meantime, the Wehrmacht had introduced a whole new generation of tanks, including the formidable Panther, and antitank weapons. Why had Sherman design stagnated for two years? The problems that befell the Sherman program in 1943 and early 1944 can be traced to three main causes, two involving U.S. Army organization and doctrine and one involving intelligence.

THE TANK DESTROYER FUMBLE

The fall of France in 1940 had forced the U.S. Army to reorganize its tank forces under the new Armored Force. This aimed to give the army an offensive capability similar to the German blitzkrieg. At the same time, the U.S. Army attempted to address the defensive problems created by blitzkrieg. The standard method of dealing with the tank threat was the antitank gun.

Throughout most of the 1930s, the standard army antitank weapon was the Browning .50-caliber heavy machine gun, which was capable of penetrating the armor of most tanks of the period. This was used both by the infantry and by light tanks and cavalry cars as their primary antitank weapons.

By the mid-1930s, heavier tank armor was beginning to appear in Europe, prompting armies to adopt more powerful antitank weapons. One approach was the antitank rifle, but this proved to be a dead end since, short of becoming unwieldy and

morphing into a towed gun, it could not be easily adapted to thicker armor. The most practical solution was the antitank gun, a weapon usually in the 25–47mm range during this period. Some armies attempted to adopt a multipurpose infantry gun that could fire both antitank and high-explosive projectiles to deal with other threats such as entrenchments and machine-gun nests. This included types such as the Italian 47mm and Soviet 45mm guns. The more common approach in Western Europe was to adopt a dedicated antitank gun, like France's 25mm and later 47mm, Germany's 37mm, and Britain's 2-pounder (40mm) guns.

The U.S. Army purchased a Swiss Solothurn 20mm antitank rifle, a French 25mm gun, and a German 37mm gun for tests and decided to develop a 37mm antitank gun patterned on the German version. Because of the usual shortage of funding, production did not start until the winter of 1940, at

The U.S. Army began receiving the 37mm antitank gun in 1940, by which time is was already growing obsolete. The infantry was reluctant to switch to a larger gun, preferring instead a weapon light enough to be moved by its crew, as seen here during training at Fort Benning in August 1942.

The American infantry antitank arsenal in 1941–42 was so poor as to be grimly comical. Here infantrymen practice an assault on a plywood mock-up of a Japanese tank using improvised hand grenades. By 1942, Ordnance had fielded an antitank rifle grenade and, later, a rocket-propelled antitank grenade, the bazooka.

The T24 evolved into the T40, which mounted the 3-inch gun lower in the chassis. Although type-classified as the M9 3-inch gun motor carriage, production was cancelled when it was realized that there were insufficient 3-inch gun mounts on hand.

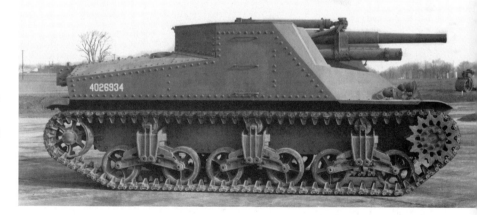

which point the 37mm gun was approaching obsolescence. European armies were already moving on to the next generation of antitank guns, such as the German 50mm, Soviet 57mm, and British 6-pounder (57mm).

The tactical issue that arose in the wake of the defeat of France in 1940 was not primarily technical, but rather tactical—how best to stop a massed panzer attack? The French actually had very good antitank weapons with an ample supply of the 25mm gun and the powerful and compact 47mm gun, the best antitank gun of the period. Why had they failed? The answer was obviously tactical rather than technical as the French guns obviously had the technical performance to defeat the thinly armored German panzers of 1940. In most armies, antitank

Based on mistaken lessons from the French campaign, the first American tank destroyers consisted of antitank guns mounted on trucks or half-tracks. The M6 37mm gun motor carriage was the standard three-quarter-ton weapons carrier with a 37mm gun mounted on a pedestal at the rear. The .50-caliber antiaircraft mount seen here was a local improvisation, not standard equipment.

The first heavy tank destroyer to enter production in 1941 was the M3 75mm gun motor carriage, which combined the venerable French World War I-era 75mm gun with the M3 half-track. Aside from having very modest armor, the gun offered only partial traverse to the front of the vehicle.

guns were distributed to the infantry divisions so that each infantry regiment would have an antitank company with a dozen guns and each of its infantry battalions would typically have an antitank platoon with another three or four guns each. As a result, each infantry regiment could create a thin antitank cordon stretched along a defensive perimeter of a mile or more. This style of cordon defense proved useless in 1940 against panzer tactics. The Wehrmacht concentrated its panzers, so a small number of antitank guns could be quickly overwhelmed by a much larger number of tanks. Traditional cordon antitank defense did not work.

The debate over the best methods to deal with the panzer threat began in the U.S. in the summer of 1940 shortly after the fall of France. The first salvo

The head of the Tank Destroyer Center at Fort Hood, Texas, was Gen. Andrew Bruce, seen here on an M3 75mm gun motor carriage, one of the earliest tank destroyers.

was fired by the chief of infantry, Maj. Gen. George Lynch, who laid out his branch's view of "Antitank Doctrine and Development" in a five-page letter sent to the G-3 (operations) office of the chief of staff. The report argued that the artillery-based solutions then under consideration for enhancing antitank defense were not sound because towed antitank battalions were not mobile enough to respond to panzer attack, were very vulnerable to enemy infantry and tank forces, and had no counterattack potential. Lynch suggested that antitank guns embedded in the infantry and reinforced by corps-level reserves were a starting point. He concluded that "the best anti-tank defense lies in the defeat of hostile armored forces by our own armored units" since

tanks offered the mobility needed to rapidly respond to panzer penetrations, had good defensive capabilities against both enemy infantry and panzers, and offered greater counterattack potential than towed antitank guns. Lynch concluded that the army ought to consider more tank units than were contemplated—not only the new armored divisions, but more general headquarters separate tank battalions for support of the infantry divisions.

Although Lynch's viewpoint was widely shared throughout the army, it was rebutted by one of the most influential officers of the period, Gen. Lesley McNair, who went from commanding the Command and General Staff School to heading the U.S. Army General Headquarters (GHQ), later the

Early Ordnance tank destroyer designs were notoriously bad. General McNair dismissed the M5 3-inch gun motor carriage as the "Cleek-Track," wordplay on its Cletrac chassis and its abysmal technical performance. Although accepted for service use, it never reached mass production.

The first serious attempt at a fully tracked tank destroyer was the T24, which mounted a 3-inch gun in an M3 medium tank with the turret and hull roof removed. It was a crude improvisation and was quickly redesigned.

The Tunisian campaign found the little M6 37mm gun motor carriage to be completely useless on the modern battlefield because of its impotent gun and poor layout. They were quickly withdrawn from service as a danger to their crews.

Gen. Andrew Bruce and the Tank Destroyer Center wanted a fast tank destroyer, and some ingenious, if impractical, solutions were proposed—such as this T55 "Cook Interceptor," seen here at Aberdeen Proving Ground in September 1942. It was rejected because it offered poorer cross-country performance than tracked tank destroyers and the gun had very limited traverse.

wartime Army Ground Forces (AGF). McNair was an artilleryman and had studied the problem of anti-tank defense in the late 1930s, writing the artillery's main study on the subject. His solution relied not on cordon defense thinly spread among the infantry, but on a concentrated, mobile reserve antitank artillery formation that would be kept in the rear until the focus of the panzer attack was evident. Then this formation would rush to the scene of the attack and defeat it with concentrated firepower.

This all sounded theoretically attractive, but how would it work in practice?

To find out, the U.S. Army established a Tank Destroyer Center at Fort Hood in Texas to manage the new program, which was officially created on November 29, 1941. The Tank Destroyer Center was a defensive counterpart to the army's new offensive Armored Force. While Armored Force thinking was dominated by cavalry officers, the Tank Destroyer Center was strongly influenced by the artillery

In Tunisia, the M3 75mm gun motor carriage demonstrated that it could perform adequately when used from prepared positions such as at El Guettar in March 1943, but not under the hyperactive tactics proposed by the Tank Destroyer Center. It was clearly obsolete, however, and was withdrawn from service in favor of the M10 tank destroyer.

branch, especially McNair. The first head of the branch was Col. Andrew Bruce, an infantryman who had earlier headed the general staff's planning branch for tank destroyers. The tank destroyer concept was controversial from the outset. McNair opposed using expensive tracked vehicles as tank destroyers as part of his general preference for keeping army units as light as possible to make them easier to transport overseas and more easily supported once in combat. Bruce saw the critical ingredient of the tank destroyer to be its speed since its principal tactical requirement was the ability to move quickly from the reserve to the point where the panzers were attacking. The tank destroyers' motto was "Seek, Strike, Destroy," and Bruce became fixated

on mobility. He described the ideal tank destroyer as being akin in role to a navy cruiser while the larger, heavier, and slower tank was akin to a battleship. To provide more backing for his position, Bruce pointed to reports from the French campaign that the French Army had success mounting antitank guns on trucks in a portée configuration to provide the speed and mobility needed to move to the scene of the panzer attack more quickly and efficiently. This was largely a myth—symptomatic of the poor intelligence under which the U.S. Army labored in the early years of the war. Even McNair admitted as much in his rebuttal to Lynch's proposal: "The European war to date has supplied no conclusive lessons as to anti-tank defense, other than it has been

The M3 75mm did not do well in Tunisia, though the problems were more closely tied to poor tactical doctrine and training. Here, Rommel inspects an M3 tank destroyer knocked out at Kasserine Pass. Although American combat performance at Kasserine did not impress Rommel, he was disturbed by the high degree of standardization in American military equipment, which foreshadowed the type of industrial warfare the Wehrmacht would soon face.

inadequate." McNair temporarily acceded to Bruce's viewpoint and supported an effort to develop a mechanized tank destroyer.

In the haste to equip the tank destroyer battalions, the first tank destroyers developed by Ordnance were crude expedients. The existing 37mm antitank gun was mounted on a pedestal on the back of a three-quarter-ton truck as the M6 37mm gun motor carriage (GMC). The World War I–vintage French 75mm field gun was mounted on an M3 half-track as the M3 75mm GMC. Bruce was unhappy with both designs as they had limited fields of fire and poor protection for the gun crews. Nevertheless, when the tank destroyer battalions first saw combat in Tunisia in early 1943, they were equipped with these slapdash weapons. The adoption of these weapons soured Bruce on Ordnance's judgment, and relations between the Tank Destroyer Center and Ordnance deteriorated even further in 1942.

No one was happy with the expedient designs, but there wasn't the time to develop a high-speed, tracked chassis that satisfied Bruce's requirements. After Ordnance offered some truly horrible designs, like the M5 and M9 3-inch gun motor carriages, the army finally settled on the idea of mounting the 3-inch gun on a lightly armored version of the M4A2 Sherman tank, resulting in the M10 3-inch GMC. Bruce was very unhappy with the M10, arguing that it didn't have the speed required since it was not appreciably faster than the normal Sherman. It had marginally better firepower than the Sherman, but its armor was much weaker and lacked even a turret roof. McNair overruled Bruce's objections as the army needed an adequate tank destroyer now, not a perfect tank destroyer in 1944. The M10 entered production in 1942, arrived on the battlefield in the later phases of the Tunisian campaign, and became the backbone of the tank destroyer battalions for the

After rejecting the T35, Ordnance modified the design with a simpler and more spacious turret and a lighter hull, resulting in the M10 3-inch gun motor carriage. This would become the standard U.S. Army tank destroyer of World War II, even though the Tank Destroyer Center opposed it as insufficiently mobile. This overhead view shows the turret traversed to the rear of the vehicle in travel mode.

The first effort to mount the 3-inch gun on the Sherman chassis resulted in the T35, which was basically an M4A2 with a new, open-top turret.

The M10 first saw combat in North Africa in early 1943 with the 776th and 899th Tank Destroyer Battalions. It proved to be the best of the tank destroyers in service, though there were still profound doubts about tank destroyer doctrine.

The 37mm gun proved to be completely inadequate for antitank defense when put to the defense at Faid Pass in February 1943 and later at Kasserine Pass. This is a gun of the 136th Infantry, 34th Division, at Sidi Bou Zid on February 14, 1943, at the start of the German offensive that culminated in the battle at Kasserine Pass.

entire war. Bruce continued his quest for the ideal tank destroyer, finally settling on the M18 76mm GMC developed by General Motors. It was the fastest tracked armored vehicle in the U.S. Army in World War II, able to reach speeds of fifty-five miles per hour on roads. It was armed with a lightened version of the 3-inch gun, called the 76mm gun since it used a different propellant casing and the army wanted to avoid confusion between the two incompatible ammunition types.

The Tunisian campaign raised serious questions about the viability of the tank destroyer concept. Part of the problem resulted from the usual litany of woes plaguing the inexperienced U.S. Army in Tunisia: lack of trained crewmen, unrealistic tactical doctrine, and misuse of the tank destroyer battalions by army field commanders who tended to employ them, against doctrine, as tanks or infantry-support weapons. In general, army commanders were thoroughly unimpressed with the performance of the tank destroyers. By the end of the campaign, there were as many tank destroyer battalions in Tunisia as there were tank battalions, yet they had far less to show for their actions. Although touted by AGF and the Tank Destroyer Center as the solution to the blitzkrieg problem, they had failed to have any impact at all during the grim days of February 1943 in stopping the panzer attacks at Sidi Bou Zid, Sbeitla, or Kasserine Pass and had suffered grievous losses. On the one occasion when tank destroyers succeeded in blunting a panzer attack, at El Guettar

on March 23, 1943, the tank destroyers endured horribly high losses. El Guettar also demonstrated that Tank Destroyer Command's aggressive, hyperactive doctrine was dangerous nonsense and the successful use of tank destroyers there had resulted from the use of more passive and prudent tactics. After Kasserine Pass, the tank destroyers were held in such low esteem that during the planning for the Sicily landings, no tank destroyer battalions were included in the initial force despite the known presence of a considerable amount of Axis armor on the island.

The tank destroyer debate continued in the months after the end of the Tunisian campaign. Gen. Jacob Devers, head of the Armored Force, visited Tunisia to study "lessons learned" and came back proclaiming that the "best enemy of the tank is another tank," the same point made by General Lynch in July 1940. His report on the tank destroyer force in Tunisia was scathing:

The separate tank destroyer arm is not a practical concept on the battlefield. Defensive antitank weapons are essentially artillery. Offensively, the weapon to beat a tank is a better tank. Sooner or later the issue between ground forces is settled in an armored battle—tank against tank. The concept of tank destroyer groups and brigades attempting to overcome equal numbers of hostile tanks is faulty unless the tank destroyers are actually better tanks than those of the enemy.

MCNAIR'S FOLLY

Both artillerymen and old friends, Devers and McNair vigorously debated doctrine. McNair had never been very keen on mechanized tank destroyers and still favored the low-cost option of a battalion of towed antitank guns. Little evidence supported this as being a better alternative, but McNair fastened onto British reports of the success of their new 6-pounder antitank gun batteries during the fighting at Medenine in Tunisia on March 6, 1943, as proof of the superiority of towed antitank guns. McNair's argument overlooked the critical detail that the British guns were not part of a dedicated antitank reserve comparable to the U.S. Army tank destroyers, but rather were the usual sort of infantry antitank guns dismissed since 1940 as an inadequate solution. The critical technical feature of the British 6-pounder was that it was powerful enough to deal with the panzers. The U.S. Army in Tunisia was still equipped with the inadequate 37mm antitank gun as the infantry had resisted adopting a heavier and more cumbersome weapon until the Kasserine Pass debacle.

The first AGF team to report back after Kasserine Pass on March 5, 1943, passed on scathing remarks about the 37mm antitank gun:

> Two general officers condemned this gun as useless as an antitank gun and strongly recommended that it be discarded. They stated that it would not penetrate the turret or front of the German medium tank, that the projectiles bounced off like marbles, and the German tanks overrun the gun positions. The G-3 [operations officer] of the Allied Forces informed me that the above recommendation had been approved and they do not want the 37mm gun.

When the U.S. Army decided to adopt the British 6-pounder (57mm) as a replacement for the 37mm gun in the spring of 1943, it had already been in production in the United States for British Lend-Lease requirements for more than year. By the time it saw widespread combat service in the summer of 1944, it was obsolete.

In 1941, Ordnance hastily developed a more powerful antitank gun by mounting the 3-inch gun from the M10 tank destroyer on the carriage and cradle of the 105mm howitzer. While it offered better performance than either the 37mm gun or British 6-pounder, it was not especially powerful for a weapon so large and clumsy. It is seen here next to an infantry 37mm antitank gun as a size comparison.

While the U.S. Army still depended on the 37mm gun for infantry antitank defense in Tunisia, the Wehrmacht had already jumped two generations ahead. This 75mm PaK 40 was one of the first captured by the U.S. Army at Sidi Bou Zid in February 1943, shortly before the German offensive.

Ironically, the 6-pounder antitank gun now touted by McNair had been in production in the United States since March 1942 as the 57mm M1 antitank gun exclusively for Lend-Lease supply, and some of the British guns in Tunisia were in fact American made. The poor performance of the 37mm antitank gun in Tunisia prompted the U.S. infantry to change its mind and switch to the 57mm in March 1943, but by then it was already two years old and growing obsolete. The British were already adopting a 17-pounder (76mm) antitank gun, and the German 75mm PaK 40 antitank gun had also seen combat in Tunisia and would become ubiquitous by 1944. The American debate should have focused on whether its

The German 50mm PaK 38 was introduced in 1941 after the experiences with thickly armored French tanks in the 1940 campaign. It quickly became obsolete with the appearance of the Soviet T-34 tank in 1941 but was used with considerable success by the Afrika Korps in 1942 against thinly armored British tanks. This particular gun is in Washington, DC, for a 1944 demonstration of American and German weapons; the German troops are actually GIs recruited for the performance.

antitank weapons were adequate to counter the existing and future panzer threat. Instead, it got mixed up in the interminable debate over the best tactical organization for antitank defense.

In spite of this muddled analysis of antitank needs, the tide was moving back in favor of towed antitank guns for the tank destroyer battalions. The performance of self-propelled tank destroyers in Tunisia had been so underwhelming that Gen. Omar Bradley, then commander of the U.S. II Corps, began to advocate a return to towed guns that could be easily concealed instead of the very visible self-propelled tank destroyers. Maj. Gen. John Lucas, sent as an observer to Sicily, came back and argued that

> the tank destroyer has, in my opinion, failed to prove its usefulness. I make this statement not only because of the results of this campaign but after a study of the campaign in Tunisia. I believe that the doctrine of an offensive weapon to "slug it out" with the tank is unsound. I think the only successful antitank weapon is one that has a purely

defensive role, has high penetrating power and such a low silhouette that it can be concealed, dug in, and hidden by camouflage. . . . I am of the opinion that the antitank weapon should be a towed gun of great power and low silhouette.

The Lucas report exhibited the extreme satisfaction within the senior ranks of the army over the tank destroyer concept. It disingenuously ignored the fact that no tank destroyer battalions had been deployed in combat on Sicily. The Lucas report provided McNair the final ammunition he needed to reverse course on tank destroyer policy and to revert to towed antitank guns. It would prove to be a mistake for several reasons.

McNair, Lucas, and Bradley had all failed to appreciate that the main reason that British, German, and Soviet towed antitank guns had enjoyed frequent tactical success in 1942 and 1943 was not their tactical disposition but their technical virtues. Unlike the U.S., they had stayed ahead in the armor/antiarmor race by prudently adopting more powerful guns in anticipation of enemy armor

COMPARATIVE ANTITANK GUN PERFORMANCE			
	75mm PaK 40	**3-inch**	**17-pounder**
Combat weight (lbs)	3,306	4,875	4,624
Barrel length (calibers)	L/48	L/50	L/55
Ammunition type	PzGr 39 APCBC	M62 APC	APCBC
Initial muzzle velocity (fps)	2,460	2,600	2,900
Penetration* (mm)	123	115	163

*at 500m, 0 degrees

advances. In 1943 in Tunisia, the U.S. Army was still using the 37mm antitank gun based on a German example from 1936. In contrast, the Wehrmacht had already switched to the 50mm PaK 38 antitank gun in 1941 and the 75mm PaK in 1943. The British had gone from a 2-pounder (40mm) in 1940–41 to a 6-pounder (57mm) in 1941–42 and were moving to a 17-pounder (76mm) in 1943. A significant problem in U.S. antitank defense in 1943 was the recalcitrance of American infantry to adopt a weapon powerful enough to do the job properly. The decision to switch to the 57mm gun in 1943 was too little, too late.

The poor performance of Ordnance in developing a new antitank gun posed a secondary problem. To provide more power than the British 6-pounder/U.S. 57mm gun, Ordnance proposed a towed 3-inch gun for the tank destroyer battalions, simply a towed version of the gun already in use on the M10 tank destroyer. Instead of developing a wholly new gun compact and powerful enough for infantry use—as had been the case with the excellent German PaK 40—Ordnance took the slapdash expedient approach. They simply mated the bulky and heavy 3-inch gun, originally developed in World War I as a coastal and antiaircraft gun, to the existing carriage of the 105mm howitzer. The resulting 3-inch antitank gun was incredibly durable, but unsurprisingly, the infantry was aghast at the idea of equipping its antitank units with this monstrosity. The gun weighed one-and-a-half times as much as its German counterpart (2.4 tons compared to 1.6 tons) and had inferior armor penetration and a much higher silhouette.

The army also failed to appreciate that it was not simply a matter of a towed antitank gun versus a self-propelled gun. Both weapons had their place, and all the other major armies of World War II procured both types. The Wehrmacht adopted the towed PaK 40 for its infantry divisions alongside self-propelled versions of the same gun as *panzerjäger* (antitank) and *sturmgeschütz* (assault guns); the same weapon was used as the KwK 42 tank gun on the PzKfw IV tank. The British adopted a towed 17-pounder but also mounted it on the U.S.-supplied M10 tank destroyer and on a tank destroyer version of the Valentine tank. The Wehrmacht and British Army avoided the failed route of the U.S. Army as they had no overarching ideological preoccupation comparable to the Americans' exaggerated tank destroyer scheme.

Over Bruce's strenuous objections, McNair ordered that a portion of the tank destroyer battalions be converted to towed antitank gun battalions using the towed 3-inch gun. McNair's parochialism further reduced the combat value of a large fraction of the tank destroyer battalions, which would become bloodily apparent in their main test on the battlefields of France and Belgium in 1944. In March 1944, there were sixteen self-propelled and three towed tank destroyers battalions in Britain; by D-Day, those figures had increased, but the balance changed, with nineteen self-propelled and eleven towed tank destroyer battalions.

McNair had ignored one of the key points in both Bradley's and Lucas's arguments—that the antitank gun should be powerful enough to destroy enemy tanks. The 3-inch gun adopted in 1943 was

This display at Aberdeen Proving Ground provides a thumbnail history of German antitank gun development in World War II: the 37mm PaK 36 in the background from 1936, the 50mm PaK 38 in the center from 1941, and the 75mm PaK 40 from early 1943.

The U.S. Army was well aware of the technical performance of the 75mm PaK 40 as this example was sent back from Tunisia to Aberdeen Proving Ground for trials. However, the future implications of this weapon's widespread use in 1944 was not appreciated in time to affect American tank design in 1943.

not capable of defeating tanks already encountered in Tunisia, namely the Tiger I, and there was no promise it would defeat future threats. Indeed, what is so surprising about this debate is the utter failure of the main participants to consider whether the new towed antitank gun could perform its sole function on the battlefield, defeating enemy tanks in a frontal engagement. Planners gave little thought to the likely configuration of the panzer threat in 1944, and instead the debate focused on the tangential issue of the means of propulsion for the gun and its organizational disposition. Had AGF and Ordnance made a more astute assessment of the future threat, the U.S. Army might have had a better towed antitank gun deployed in the infantry divisions rather than one that crippled the tank destroyer battalions.

The other technical misjudgment made by both AGF and Ordnance was their failure to recognize that towed antitank guns were reaching the outer edge of portability on the battlefield and were becoming too cumbersome to use. This first became evident to the Wehrmacht in late 1943 with the advent of the new generation of towed antitank guns. Besides adopting the new 75mm PaK 40 for the infantry divisions, the Wehrmacht was also adopting the towed 88mm PaK 43/41 for special *panzerjäger* battalions deployed at corps and army level, much like the U.S. tank destroyer battalions. The PaK 40, though much lighter than the American 3-inch antitank gun, was still a real burden on the battlefield in infantry units as it was too large to be comfortably handled by its crew. Furthermore, it was not prudent to leave its prime mover near the gun when deployed since this undermined its camouflage, not to mention that the prime mover was unarmored and vulnerable to small-arms fire. In typical battlefield conditions, an antitank gun could be left in position for only a few shots before enemy forces discovered its location and pounded it with small-arms and artillery fire. So antitank guns had to move frequently. This was not a problem with previous antitank guns like the PaK 38 50mm, which was still light enough that it could be moved into a secondary position by its own crew. The Germans kept the 75mm PaK 40 as the primary infantry division antitank gun through the 1944 campaign in spite of this problem because it was a powerful and effective defensive weapon. But Wehrmacht commanders increasingly demanded that it be mounted on a tracked chassis for mobility. This program began in late 1943 and resulted in the Marder series of *panzerjägers,* which placed the PaK 40 on a variety of obsolete light tank chassis and the PaK 43/41 88mm on the tracked Nashorn/Hornisse chassis. As a result, the German infantry divisions in 1944 were equipped with a mixed element of towed and self-propelled 75mm guns, while the corps- and army-level *panzerjäger* units shifted primarily to self-propelled tank destroyers.

The Tank Destroyer Center, which should have been the prime advocate for developing panzer killers, was also too preoccupied with its mobility fetish. Bruce continued to press for his pet project, the nimble M18 76mm GMC, as a better alternative to McNair's towed 3-inch gun. Neither weapon could defeat the new German Tiger I heavy tank that had appeared in Tunisia, but both Bruce and McNair ignored the Tiger, seeing it as a technical curiosity, not as a major threat. They did not understand that the Germans built the Tiger in response to the arms race on the Russian front and that the Wehrmacht was moving in the direction of much thicker tank armor for its medium tanks as well.

The tank destroyer debate distracted the army from addressing the future panzer threat. The Armored Force presumed that the tank destroyers could deal with the panzers, so tankers exerted little institutional pressure for a more powerful tank gun. Devers came back from Tunisia with the British compliments about the Sherman ringing in his ears. "The best tank on the battlefield today" had been the phrase so often heard from British tankers in Tunisia about the Sherman. Tank-versus-tank fighting was not a major focus of armored division tactics even after Tunisia. The Armored Force's cornerstone field manual, *Tactics and Techniques* (FM 17-10), released in March 1942, lumped tank-versus-tank fighting under "special operations" and gave it less than a page of the 400-page manual. Subsequent editions paid slightly more attention, but the focus of armored division doctrine remained exploitation of the breakthrough, and tank-versus-tank fighting continued to be regarded as a defensive mission best left to the tank destroyers.

Regardless of the technical issues, Tunisia decreased confidence in the tank destroyer concept, and the tank destroyer force shrunk accordingly. The initial 1941 plans for 220 battalions had already been reduced to 144 by 1942 and further trimmed to 106 by the end of 1943. Of the 106 battalions formed, 61 were eventually shipped to Europe and 10 to the Pacific theater, leaving 35 in the United States with little demand for their services. The AGF decided that these were surplus and in October 1943 began to disband them or convert them to other roles such as field artillery, tank, or amphibious tractor battalions. The first five were converted in December 1943 and most of the remainder in March–May 1944. The towed tank destroyer battalions would soon prove to be a failure on the battlefield because of these technical and tactical issues.

THE POOR BLOODY INFANTRY

The July 1940 decision to emulate the 1940 panzer force proved to be a mistake that took too long to correct. Nearly all of the new tank battalions formed in 1940 were devoted to the new armored divisions, and the task of developing tank units to support the infantry was neglected. A single "separate" tank battalion, the 70th Tank Battalion (Light) was created when the 1/67th Armored was reorganized in the summer of 1940. In late 1940 and early 1941, a variety of National Guard tank companies scattered around the United States were amalgamated into separate battalions—the 191st to 194th Tank Battalions. Two of these, the 192nd and 194th Tank Battalions (Light), were the first American tank units to see combat after being shipped to the Philippines shortly before the outbreak of the war in the Pacific

in December 1941. These separate tank battalions could be used in support of the infantry, which had been the traditional mission of tanks in the U.S. Army. The small number of these units prompted the infantry branch to complain that the new Armored Force was ignoring its needs, so in June 1941, ten more separate tank battalions were formed, six with M3 medium tanks and the remainder with M3 light tanks. By the end of 1941, five armored divisions had been organized, including thirty tank battalions, while the separate tank battalions numbered fifteen. The plans at the time were to raise more than sixty armored divisions, with no intention to greatly expand the number of separate tank battalions because of the Armored Force's conviction that tanks should not be dispersed in "penny packets."

The principal armored support for German infantry divisions after 1941 was the Sturmgeschütz (StuG) III, which combined the obsolete PzKpfw III chassis with a heavier 75mm gun. By 1944, many German infantry divisions had an organic company of these assault guns, and additional assault gun battalions were deployed at corps and army level for major operations. This StuG III Ausf. G was knocked out on December 26, 1944, during the Battle of the Bulge in Luxembourg.

The British Army had a more balanced approach to tanks than the U.S. Army in the early years of the war, favoring the needs of both the armored divisions and the infantry tank units. The Churchill tank became the standard British infantry tank in 1942–45 and differed from cruiser tanks in its thicker armor.

By 1941, the Wehrmacht realized that its concentration of AFVs in the panzer divisions was a mistake and launched more efforts to support the infantry, deploying Tiger heavy tank battalions at the end of 1942 at corps and army level to aid the infantry during breakthrough operations. Attached to the Hermann Goering Panzer Division, this Tiger I was knocked out in Sicily in July 1943 during an attempt to attack the American beachhead near Gela.

The Armored Force continued to regard the separate battalions as a waste of resources, feeling that the combat lessons of the 1939–40 campaigns held that tank forces should be concentrated to have the greatest impact on the battlefield. While acquiescing to infantry pressure, the Armored Force at the same time created new tank group headquarters that would function as miniature armored divisions, con-trolling multiple separate tank battalions and preventing them from being permanently attached to infantry divisions. This trend was reinforced by McNair's preference for extremely light modular divisions. The AGF commander knew that American units were likely to fight in varied conditions thousands of miles from the United States, so McNair favored a standard modular infantry division that

The T1E2 tank eventually entered production as the M6 heavy tank in December 1942. However, the Armored Force had no interest in a heavy tank at the time, and the program treaded water for most of the war, with little interest shown for such an archaic design.

could be modified in the combat theater by adding necessary supporting components such as tank, anti-aircraft, and engineer battalions.

The organizational disdain for infantry tank battalions in 1940–41 had significant impact on the eventual equipment of the U.S. tank force in France in 1944 and played an indirect role in some of the problems that would eventually plague the Sherman tank. Some European armies did not suffer the wild swings in organizational structure endured by the U.S. Army in 1941–43 and kept a more balanced approach. Both the British and Soviet armies forcefully advocated armored divisions but at the same time recognized a need for a portion of the tank force to be devoted to the infantry-support mission. They generally followed the same doctrinal route as the Wehrmacht and the U.S. Army regarding the

primary role of the armored division in exploiting the breakthrough, but they also strongly felt that some of their tanks should support the infantry in gaining the breakthrough in the first place. Both the British and Soviets saw the need for a distinctly different type of tank for the infantry mission compared to the armored division mission. In particular, both armies wanted heavier armor on the infantry tanks since it was presumed that these tanks would be expected to directly confront enemy defenses including enemy antitank guns and would have to be able to survive antitank-gun fire to conduct their mission. In the British case, this led to the Matilda tanks of 1940–41 and later the larger Churchill tanks of 1942–45. In the Soviet case, this resulted in the KV tank of 1940–43 and later the IS Stalin tanks of 1944–45.

Ordnance actually designed a thickly armored assault tank, the T14, to satisfy British Lend-Lease requirements. By the time it was ready, Britain decided to adopt the Sherman as its cruiser tank and the Churchill as its infantry tank, so the T14 slid into obscurity with little interest from the U.S. Army.

The Wehrmacht gradually realized the mistake of concentrating all their armor in the panzer divisions, especially after the 1941 invasion of Russia. The infantry divisions repeatedly needed armored support, and it was organizationally awkward to break off bits of the panzer divisions to support the infantry. The Wehrmacht began building up its infantry-support force in two ways. To assist the infantry in the breakthrough, it developed a new heavy tank, the Tiger I, which appeared on the battlefield in late 1942. These were assigned to special battalions deployed at corps or army level to reserve them for vital missions. Since German tank production was barely adequate to equip the panzer divisions, the Wehrmacht used the cut-rate approach of supporting the infantry with assault guns *(sturmgeschütz)* instead of tanks. These were based on the ubiquitous PzKpfw III medium tank chassis and armed with a 75mm gun in a fixed casemate instead of a turret. This was a cheaper solution than a turreted tank and could accommodate a larger and more powerful gun than the turreted tank version.

These *sturmgeschütz* could be deployed in battalion-size formations at corps level or in smaller company-size formations as part of infantry divisions. In 1940, German AFV production focused on tanks, which constituted 90 percent of the total. By 1944, tanks represented only 45 percent of German AFV production, assault guns 35 percent, and *panzerjäger* 15 percent. The last two categories were largely used for infantry support, the assault guns being the equivalent of infantry tanks and the *panzerjäger* the direct equivalents of American tank destroyers (minus the doctrinal baggage).

The U.S. Army recognized this shift in German perspective only slowly because, until early 1943, it had no direct firsthand contact with the Wehrmacht. While intelligence reports on German combat tactics in Russia and North Africa abounded, the reports from Russia lacked significant detail about German force composition and were not widely disseminated outside of intelligence circles. British sources provided thorough and detailed information about the Afrika Korps, but the composition of the

The U.S. infantry branch recommended the development of a heavy tank in 1940, which emerged in September 1941 at the Baldwin Locomotive Works as the T1E2 heavy tank. It shows the usual Ordnance profusion of machine guns as well as a 3-inch main gun.

Afrika Korps was extremely unusual compared to the rest of the Wehrmacht for a variety of reasons.

The lack of attention the U.S. Army paid to the infantry support role led to little interest in the development of a tank better suited to this mission. Ordnance actually designed a heavy tank specifically for this mission based on a British requirement, the T14 assault tank, but in the event, the U.S. Army showed no interest in the design, and the British decided to acquire the Sherman for the traditional cavalry/armored division role and their own Churchill for the infantry tank role.

McNair's desire for an austere force structure limited American interest in infantry tanks. Under his direction, AGF did not favor the development of another category of tanks beyond the existing light, medium, and heavy tanks already in development because once overseas in the combat theater, such a tank would simply be one more drain on logistics and maintenance resources. Ordnance's heavy tank

design failed to emerge as a viable candidate for this mission because of its extremely poor design. The M6 heavy tank had been developed in 1940–41 with a poor understanding of any tactical requirements for its features. So instead of being a heavily armored tank able to survive enemy antitank guns, it was simply a clumsy tank with a larger gun and slightly heavier armor than the Sherman, but not enough extra firepower or armor to cover the Sherman's shortfalls in either regard. Although the M6 heavy tank eventually went into small-scale production, its poor conception meant that no army commanders wanted these misbegotten behemoths, and none were ever sent into combat. On the other extreme, the light tank quickly fell out of favor after Tunisia. The U.S. Army had recognized that the M3 Stuart light tank was barely adequate in terms of firepower and armor even before it entered production in 1941. By 1943, in Tunisia, it was obsolete and could not perform most tank missions. In the reorganization of the Armored Force in 1943, nearly all of the light tank battalions disappeared in favor of a new standard battalion based around three companies of M4 Sherman tanks. Against the objections of many tankers, a single company of M5A1 Stuart light tanks remained in each battalion alongside the Sherman companies, but the revised tactical doctrine stressed that they were to be used in secondary missions such as reconnaissance and flank security.

As a result of the decline of the light tanks, heavy tanks, and assault tanks, the Sherman tank would gradually become the universal tank of the U.S. Army in World War II. It would fulfill both the fast cavalry tank role in the armored divisions and the infantry tank role in the separate tank battalions. Preoccupied with armored divisions at the time, the U.S. Army conceived the Sherman in 1941 primarily for that role—in which, it can certainly be argued, it was the finest tank in the world in 1943. It would serve as an infantry support tank by default since there was no custom-designed infantry tank available. Had the army wanted a tank better suited to the infantry mission, it could have either put the T14 assault tank into production or adapted the Sherman. As we shall see a bit later, the Sherman was later modified for the infantry role as the M4A3E2 assault tank, but this version was a classic case of "too little, too late." Compared to the basic Sherman, the main feature needed by an infantry-support tank was more armor. The Sherman was barely able to resist the prevalent German antitank gun of the 1942 period, the 50mm PaK 38. With the appearance of the 75mm PaK 40 in Tunisia in early 1943, the Sherman had become vulnerable to penetration by the standard German infantry antitank weapon at any combat range. This was not immediately apparent to the U.S. Army at the time because of its lack of focus on the infantry-support mission.

The U.S. Army finally began to pay more attention to the infantry-support requirement in the summer of 1943 after Tunisia, as the lessons of that campaign became apparent. As the Germans had learned in 1941, infantry divisions needed armored support, and accomplishing this by splitting off bits of armored divisions, as the U.S. tried to do with the 1st Armored Division in Tunisia, did not work well. Fortunately, the Americans had a small number of separate tank battalions in North Africa, most of which remained in reserve in French Morocco, but the 751st Tank Battalion (Medium) was rushed into Tunisia in 1943 to support the hard-pressed 34th Infantry Division. Combined, the value of the 751st Tank Battalion in the campaign and the difficulties of diverting the 1st Armored Division sparked a revival of tank-infantry cooperation in the U.S. Army. After he returned from Tunisia on a fact-finding mission, Gen. Jacob Devers specifically noted that more attention had to be paid to the "orphans" in the separate tank battalion, in both establishing practical doctrine and beginning to develop specific training for these units to better reflect a reorientation back to the infantry-support role.

This revival of interest in infantry-tank cooperation fortuitously occurred at the same time that the army was reorganizing its armored divisions based on the lessons of Tunisia. The American armored division structure had evolved since 1940 from a very tank-heavy formation with weak armored infantry and armored artillery support to a slightly better balance under the 1942 tables of organization with a mix of six tank battalions, three armored infantry battalions, and three armored field artillery battalions. Tunisia showed that the division still had too many tanks and too little infantry, so McNair authorized a reorganization into a 3-3-3 configuration with three battalions each of tanks, armored infantry, and armored field artillery. This reorganization was the standard configuration for armored divisions fighting in France in 1944. The reconfiguration of thirteen of the sixteen armored divisions in existence in 1943 meant that suddenly there were more than forty tank battalions available. Rather than organize more armored divisions around these, the AGF decided that they would be renamed as separate tank battalions and set aside for the new mission of infantry support.

This marked the final reversal of the 1940 decision to concentrate the army's tanks in the armored divisions. The AGF had gradually come to realize that the original mission of tanks from 1917, infantry support, was still as relevant as the independent missions of the armored divisions. Having made this decision, the army faced, in the summer of 1943, the problem of how to change training, doctrine, and equipment to put it into effect. In August

The fighting for Tunisia quickly clarified the need for tanks to support American infantry divisions. The 751st Tank Battalion, still equipped with the older M3 medium tank, was attached to the 34th Infantry Division to provide tank support in Bizerte at the conclusion of the campaign.

1942, prior to the Tunisia operation, McNair first came up with plans to attach separate tank battalions to armies and corps for combined training, but little was done. In March 1943, the AGF operations officer, Brig. Gen. John Lentz, argued that the separate tank battalions were a bad idea and that the tank units should be made organic to the infantry divisions. McNair opposed this idea, as he still favored his modular infantry division concept and felt that separate battalions could provide a vital mass of firepower and maneuver in the upcoming campaign in France. Instead, McNair issued a directive in April 1943 stressing the need for more combined training by tank and infantry units. In spite of this order, tank battalions were still too few in number to permit each infantry division to train with a tank battalion; moreover, tank battalions and infantry divisions were seldom located at the same base. In June 1943, Maj. Gen. Walton Walker returned from Tunisia and

suggested a more practical solution: after receiving basic training, separate tank battalions should be stationed with a corresponding infantry division for further training and remain with that division during entry into combat. When the new head of the Armored Command, Lt. Gen. Alvan Gillem, returned from his fact-finding mission to Sicily in July 1943, he also tried to reinvigorate the tank-infantry issue. Despite McNair's opposition, momentum was gathering to shift the mission from the massed use of separate tank battalions to support the corps or army to the dispersed use of the battalions to directly support infantry divisions.

The pendulum had swung back again to the traditional role of these units. But with the army in the process of preparing its units for dispatch to Europe for the summer 1944 campaign, little joint training was actually accomplished. Many tank battalions received little or no significant training with infantry units stateside prior to that summer. There were also problems in conducting joint exercises in Britain in the spring of 1944 because of the congestion of American units being funneled into Britain for the invasion. What training that did occur was often unrealistic. The U.S. Army in 1943–44 did not have a great deal of practical experience in combat of the type that would be encountered in Europe in 1944–45. Lessons from the Italian campaign made their way through the system only slowly and were not entirely applicable to the situations that would arise in France. The revived focus on tank-infantry cooperation was not only a problem in the tank units; senior infantry commanders were unprepared to properly employ tank units in conjunction with infantry divisions.

The army's field manuals standardized its tactical doctrine and reflected current army thinking on the best tactics for typical combat situations. The basic tactical manual for junior tank battalion leaders was FM 17-32, *The Tank Company,* which was first approved on August 2, 1942; the corresponding manual for senior battalion leaders was FM 17-33, *The Armored Battalion, Light and Medium,* approved on September 18, 1942. These manuals predated the Tunisian campaign and did not reflect recent thinking on many issues, including tank-infantry cooperation. The army did not revise and reissue FM 17-33 until November 1944. A tentative edition of the new FM 17-36, *Employment of Tanks with Infantry,* was released in March 1944 shortly before the start of the campaign in Normandy; a supple-

ment was published on July 7, 1944, providing more detailed solutions to common tactical problems. These manuals were released too late to have much effect on preparing tank or infantry units for the coming campaign.

From the perspective of the Sherman, these doctrinal changes meant that little preparation was undertaken to adapt the M4 to the infantry-support role. This partly resulted from the widespread conviction in the army that nothing needed to be done. Shermans were being used in the infantry-support role in the Italian theater, and there had not been a major clamor for technical changes. Based on the British and Soviet tank-infantry experience, the most important issue was the need for heavier armor on infantry-support tanks since they seldom had the luxury of maneuvering to accomplish their mission and often had to confront German antitank defenses directly. Yet observer teams sent to Italy in 1943–44 did not hear widespread demands for better armor on the Sherman, and indeed, the consensus seemed to be that added weight would decrease mobility—a decided disadvantage in Italy's mountainous countryside.

What was not apparent at the time was that both the terrain and the threat would be different several months later in France. Only then would the weaknesses of the Sherman appear—painfully. The army perceived no battle need justifying modifications to the Sherman, and Ordnance failed to extrapolate from existing technical intelligence to make the case that future threats would warrant modifications.

ITALIAN LESSONS

The lessons from the Mediterranean theater of operations (MTO) in the summer and autumn of 1943 further validated the need for tanks to support the infantry, and they also demonstrated that American armored division doctrine, when properly applied, was basically sound. Operation Husky, the Allied invasion of Sicily in July 1943, involved the deployment of one armored division and two separate tank battalions. In contrast to the tactical misuse of the 1st Armored Division in Tunisia, the 2nd Armored Division was employed in textbook fashion on Sicily—not surprisingly, since the Seventh Army commander was George S. Patton, who once had led the 2nd Armored Division. Instead of scattering the division, Patton held it in reserve to take advantage of opportunities, eventually launching it on a 100-mile dash through Sicily's rough mountains with the 3rd Infantry Division along a parallel route to seize Palermo. The concentrated use of the 2nd Armored Division was a case study in the intended doctrine for armored divisions.

Two separate tank battalions took part in combat on Sicily, the 70th (Light) and 753rd (Medium). The 70th landed at Gela and helped fight back against the Hermann Goering Panzer Division in support of the 1st Infantry Division, and it later supported the 45th Infantry Division in the advance to the Salso River. Since the 70th was still equipped solely with M5 light tanks, the corps commander assigned a company of M4 medium tanks from the 753rd to provide heavier fire support. The 753rd was used to support both the 1st and 45th Infantry Divisions at various points in the campaign, but the mountainous terrain and narrow mountain roads made it difficult to employ medium tanks, so the 70th saw more extensive use on Sicily. The campaign highlighted the difficulties in the use of armor in mountainous terrain, a lesson that would become all too

An M4A1 of the 3rd Battalion headquarters, 67th Armored Regiment, 2nd Armored Division, comes ashore on Sicily. It is fitted with the new deep-wading trunks locally manufactured in North Africa by the 5th Army Invasion Training Center, an important innovation to get tanks ashore during amphibious operations. Note also the waterproofing over the gun mantlet and other openings.

A Tiger I from Heavy Tank Battalion 504 abandoned in the streets of Biccari, Sicily, toward the end of the campaign. The indifferent performance of the Tiger against the U.S. Army in Tunisia and Sicily bred unfounded complacency in American leaders, who came to believe that the trend toward heavier armor on German tanks was not a serious battlefield threat.

An M4 medium tank of the 751st Tank Battalion climbs one of the hills along the Anzio beachhead on the morning of January 22, 1944. The three platoons of Company A were landed in the predawn hours to support the U.S. 3rd Infantry Division at Anzio.

evident in the subsequent year of fighting on the Italian mainland.

From the standpoint of the panzer threat, Sicily only reinforced the U.S. Army's complacency over the adequacy of the Sherman tank. The Italian tank units on Sicily were equipped mostly with obsolete equipment; for example, the battalion that counterattacked the Gela beachhead fielded French Renault R–35 infantry tanks handed over to Italy as war booty after 1940. As in Tunisia, the Wehrmacht panzer units had the PzKpfw III and PzKpfw IV, though the Hermann Goering Panzer Division had a battalion of Tiger I tanks attached. They were not effectively used, and American infantry and tanks, supported by heavy naval gunfire, beat back violent panzer counterattacks against the beachhead. The

An M4 passes by a PzKpfw IV knocked out during the fighting along the Salerno beachhead. The German LXXVI Panzer Corps, including the 16th Panzer Division and 29th Panzer Grenadier Division, launched a major attack against the beachhead on September 13, causing a crisis in the Allied defense.

U.S. Army came out of Sicily with no particular fear of confronting the vaunted Tiger.

The Allied landings at Salerno on September 9, 1943, reemphasized the need to land armored units as quickly as practical to help defend the beachhead against predictable German counterattacks. The U.S. amphibious landings included two infantry divisions supported by two tank and two tank destroyer battalions. The 191st Tank and 645th Tank Destroyer Battalions were attached to the 36th Infantry Division and the 751st Tank and 601st Tank Destroyer Battalions to the 45th Infantry Division. Both units were configured as medium tank battalions and were equipped with Shermans. These formations saw a considerable amount of combat when the Germans staged a series of violent counterattacks using panzer and panzergrenadier divisions. At the height of the battle, the Germans almost drove a wedge between the two American infantry divisions down the Sele River but were stopped at the last moment by two field artillery battalions, the 27th Armored Field Artillery Battalion with the new M7 105mm self-propelled howitzer, and elements of the newly arrived 636th Tank Destroyer Battalion.

Determined resistance by the infantry divisions and heavy naval gunfire finally turned back the German attacks, but the Salerno operation came close to disaster. The use of armor at Salerno followed the pattern developing in the MTO: attaching a separate tank and tank destroyer battalion directly to each infantry division for support. As on Sicily, the types and quality of German panzers were essentially similar to those encountered in Tunisia and on Sicily, and the army expressed little concern about the performance of the Sherman tank.

The fighting in Italy in the autumn of 1943 held few lessons beyond those already learned in Tunisia and Sicily. The fighting along the Volturno River was largely an infantry struggle because the mountainous terrain prevented the use of any large armored units in the American sector. The fighting on the approaches to Cassino highlighted tactical issues such as the need for better tank-infantry training. Regarding equipment, there was little tank-versus-tank fighting to point out problems, though the advantage accruing to the Wehrmacht with the more widespread use of the longer 75mm gun was becoming clear. By the late autumn of 1943, the

One of the most curious innovations to foster better tank-infantry cooperation was the "battle sled," an idea of the commander of the 3rd Infantry Division, Gen. J. W. "Iron Mike" O'Daniel, at Anzio in the spring of 1944. Each consisted of two trains with six sleds to permit a tank to tow twelve infantrymen behind the tank. During the Anzio breakout in May 1944, one platoon was moved forward about two miles by tanks of the 751st Tank Battalion near Conca, but the infantry was extremely uncomfortable in the sleds because of the heavy dust and exhaust fumes behind the tanks, the very hard ride on the ground, and the tendency of the sleds to flip during a turn.

long 75mm gun was finally replacing the older 50mm antitank gun in German infantry units in Italy. More *panzerjäger* units with this weapon were also being deployed, and the panzer balance was shifting from the PzKpfw III, with its 50mm gun, to the PzKpfw IV, with its long 75mm gun. Sherman crews increasingly complained that this weapon had better long-range firepower than the 75mm gun on the Sherman. At this stage of the war, however, the Sherman was still more than adequate to defeat existing German tanks, except for the rarely encountered Tiger. German records from the Tenth Army, which was defending the Cassino front in May 1944, indicate that the primary Sherman killer was self-propelled antitank guns, followed by towed

antitank guns. Of the 432 tanks killed, 205 (47 percent) were claimed by 75mm PaK 40 towed antitank guns, 93 (21 percent) by 75mm and 88mm self-propelled *panzerjäger,* and 118 (27 percent) by StuG III and Italian Semovente 75mm assault guns; panzers accounted for only 2 kills.

The Allied landings at Anzio in January 1944 did not change this picture to any great extent. Anzio did mark the first appearance of the Panther tank in the west, but the atrocious mud convinced the corps commander to reserve the Panther battalion, which was seldom used except in some long-range engagements in which there was little fear of losing tanks to the Allies. Other new weapons began to appear for the first time, notably German antitank rockets.

THE ROCKET MENACE

One of the unfortunate consequences of the Italian campaign in 1943–44 was that it produced complacency in the U.S. Army about future German threats. For the Wehrmacht, Italy was strictly a sideshow, and the units there did not have high priority for new weapons. While the Wehrmacht had begun to deploy significant numbers of the new Panther and Tiger tanks to the Russian front in the summer of 1943, they were relatively rare in Italy.

Aside from the future panzer threat, Italy provided a poor gauge of trends in German antitank technology, one of the most important changes in which was the advent of new rocket-propelled weapons for the infantry. Ironically, the U.S. was the source of this innovation. The army had been developing rifle grenades with special antitank shaped-charge warheads in 1941 when an enterprising young ordnance officer suggested sticking a rocket engine on the end and shooting the grenade out a tube. Thus was born the M9 2.36-inch (60mm) antitank rocket launcher, better known as the bazooka. The Germans captured some of these weapons in late 1942 or early 1943, though when and where is disputed. In 1942, the U.S. Army shipped a supply of a secret new weapon to the Red Army, under the codename Whip. Little is known about the use of the Whip in Russian hands, but Ordnance officers later claimed that this was the source of the German trophies. German accounts suggest that the capture of bazookas in Tunisia in February 1943 led to the development of German counterparts.

One of the major innovations in antitank technology in World War II was the U.S. Army's 2.36-inch antitank rocket launcher, better known as the bazooka. Unfortunately, the Wehrmacht also thought it was a great idea and quickly introduced an improved version after capturing some in Tunisia.

The German *panzerschreck* was an enlarged version of the bazooka since the Germans were convinced that a more powerful warhead would be needed to deal with future Soviet tanks. This display was put on in Washington in February 1944, with one of the Tiger I tanks captured in Tunisia in the background.

The original *panzerschreck*, officially designated as *Raketen-panzerbüche 54*, proved a bit heavy and unwieldy, and in late 1944, the Germans introduced the shortened RPzB 54/1, seen in this technical intelligence photo from Aberdeen Proving Ground.

A GI compares the *panzerschreck* on the left with the bazooka on the right. The *panzerschreck* had a much more powerful 88mm warhead compared to the 60mm warhead on the bazooka.

In either event, the Wehrmacht viewed it as very clever idea and began building an enlarged and more lethal version as the 88mm *panzerschreck* ("armor terror"). The *panzerschreck* used a larger shaped-charge warhead than the bazooka since the Germans were concerned about future Soviet tanks and wanted a warhead adequate to deal with them. Unlike conventional antitank guns, which depended on the brute force of kinetic energy to penetrate armor, these new rocket weapons relied on explosive shaped-charge warheads. These warheads consisted of a copper cone with a layer of explosive shaped behind the cone. When the warhead struck the tank, the explosive detonated. Instead of bursting in all directions like standard high-explosive warheads, the shape of the explosive channeled most of the blast forward against the cone, collapsing it into a fine stream of high-speed metal particles that could punch through thick tank armor like a supersonic rapier. The *panzerschreck*

was relatively large and heavy, usually operated by a two-man crew. The Germans went one step better and developed a smaller, one-man antitank rocket launcher called the *panzerfaust* ("armor fist"). This was not as long ranged or as accurate as the *panzerschreck,* but it used a cheap, disposable launch tube so that it could be issued in vast numbers.

These rocket weapons revolutionized the battlefield by increasing the number of deadly antitank weapons available to the average German infantry unit. Prior to their advent in 1943, an infantry regiment had only six antitank guns capable of defeating a Sherman. After the advent of the antitank rockets, the regiment would have the same six antitank guns, supplemented by eighteen of the heavy *panzerschrecks* and hundreds of *panzerfausts.*

The battlefield had suddenly become much deadlier for tanks. This was not immediately apparent to the U.S. or British armies as these new

Shaped-charge warheads from these rocket weapons created a very small hole compared to conventional anti-armor projectiles. Here, the crewmen of an M4A3 (76mm) tank of the 712th Tank Battalion show how a German *panzerschreck* knocked out their tank near Metzervisse in November 1944; the crewman on the right is showing the small penetration hole.

By 1944, an even greater antitank threat appeared in the form of the small *panzerfaust*, which, though not as powerful as the larger *panzerschreck*, was issued in the thousands like grenades. Here a GI demonstrates the firing stance using a captured *panzerfaust*.

weapons were very slow to arrive in Italy. Some showed up in January–February 1944 during the fighting in the Anzio beachhead, but not in the volume they would later be seen in France. The other change not entirely evident in Italy was the continued escalation in German antitank guns. The Wehrmacht had first deployed the new PaK 40 75mm gun in Tunisia in February 1943, but it still had not totally replaced the old 50mm PaK 38 in Italy through 1944. Ubiquitous by the time of Normandy in June 1944, however, it would become one of the main killers of the Sherman tank.

THE PANTHER THREAT

The third problem facing the Sherman was its new German nemesis, the Panther tank. The U.S. Army knew about the Panther tank since its first appearance in battle at Kursk in the summer of 1943 but had seriously misunderstood and underestimated the threat.

The Panther resulted from the great tank panic that befell the Wehrmacht in 1941 following the invasion of Russia. The Wehrmacht had not expected the Red Army to react so quickly to the lessons of the Spanish Civil War and thought that the Soviet tank force, though large, would consist mainly of the same T-26 and BT light tanks it had used in Spain. In secret, the Soviets had developed a revolutionary new generation of tanks, the T-34 cavalry tank and the KV heavy infantry tank. These had frontal armor that was impervious to the German's standard 37mm gun and even to their brand-new 50mm antitank gun. Stunned, the German infantry watched antitank rounds bounce off the advancing Soviet tanks, even when engaged by powerful weapons such as the

division's 105mm field guns. The only weapons capable of dealing with the T-34 and KV were the division's four 88mm Flak guns—hardly enough to stop a major tank attack. Fortunately for the Wehrmacht, the Red Army of 1941 lacked competent leaders after Stalin's brutal purges of the late 1930s had decapitated the senior ranks of the Red Army, and the technological surprise of these impressive new tanks was largely wasted. Nevertheless, the T-34 had suddenly established the new benchmark for world tank design, and it would take the Germans some time to devise adequate countermeasures.

The Wehrmacht responded aggressively by up-arming its stable of PzKpfw III and PzKpfw IV with newer and more powerful guns. Although the PzKpfw III would remain the workhorse of the Wehrmacht through the Stalingrad campaign in the autumn of 1942, its growth potential was severely limited by the size of its turret ring, which could not accommodate a powerful 75mm tank gun. Instead, the PzKpfw IV, which had been intended primarily

The Panther Ausf. D first appeared in combat in the summer of 1943 during the Kursk-Orel campaign. Here a group of Red Army prisoners are seen in the midst of a group of Panthers during the Battle of Kursk.

Although the Tiger first appeared on the Russian front in the winter of 1942–43, the summer fighting of 1943 was its first major campaign. The Tiger proved to be more durable than the Panther, prompting a crash program by the Red Army to develop countermeasures in the form of better tanks, antitank guns, and tank destroyers.

as a support tank with a short 75mm gun, was fitted with a long 75mm gun able to deal with the T-34 on an equal footing. By 1943, the PzKpfw IV had replaced the III as the mainstay of the Wehrmacht and would remain so through most of 1944.

Expedients such as the upgunned panzers sufficed in the short term. But German tank commanders like Heinz Guderian knew quite well that the European tank race was not over but had just begun. They needed a tank that could not only match the T-34 but also deal with its successor, which was likely to appear on the battlefield in a year or two. A new tank was already under development as a breakthrough tank, the Tiger I. A truly impressive counterpart to the Soviet KV, the Tiger was hideously expensive to manufacture and operate, and so it was intended to be issued in relatively modest numbers to supplement the existing panzer force, not to replace it.

The new universal panzer, the Panther, was intended to replace both the PzKpfw III and PzKpfw IV sometime in 1942–43. Daimler-Benz and MAN (*Maschinenfabrik Augsberg-Nurnberg*) created two competing designs. The MAN design was finally selected.

Hitler stuck his finger in the process, insisting on even more armor for the Panther, and its combat weight steadily climbed from around twenty-five tons to more than forty tons. While this would have some beneficial effects and make the Panther virtually invulnerable to frontal attack, at the same time the powertrain had been designed for a lighter tank and the Panther would be plagued with reliability problems throughout its whole career. Indeed, it flopped in its combat debut at Kursk in the summer of 1943. The original Panther Ausf. D broke down at such an alarming rate that at any given time, barely one in four tanks was operational. In response, the Germans instituted a crash program to rebuild the existing tanks and institute improvements in the powertrain. Its operational rate climbed from a ghastly 16 percent in July 1943 to an appalling 37 percent in December 1943. The introduction of the improved Panther Ausf. A helped this situation, and the operational rate increased to 50 percent by February 1944 and 78 percent by May 1944.

The other problem with the Panther was its high cost. German engineers could not overcome their usual penchant for craftsmanship and overengineered the Panther, making the tank too complicated and expensive to build and poorly suited for maintenance in the field. Although the Wehrmacht needed a minimum of 600 Panthers per month to replace the PzKpfw IV, Panther production peaked in 1944 at barely 350 per month; by comparison, Sherman production in 1943 exceeded 2,000 per month. The Wehrmacht lacked a figure like McNair to manage the "mad scientists" in German industry, and the direct involvement of senior German political leaders including Hitler invited disaster. The Nazi leadership was feudal in its understanding of modern industry, and the Wehrmacht leadership was not much better. Warfare in the industrial age required a careful balance between quality and quantity. In the U.S. Army, McNair and AGF headquarters served this function and, for all their faults, did a very good job. The German government and the Wehrmacht failed to establish a proper balance between quality and quantity, trying to obtain both despite limited resources. The Panther was actually one of the better examples of German industrial management. One need only look at the ridiculously clumsy King Tiger heavy tank of 1944 or the preposterous Maus superheavy tank of 1945 to see the confusion in German military industrial planning.

The secrets of the Panther were available to the Allies shortly after it saw its combat debut at Kursk in the summer of 1943. The Red Army recovered a number of intact Panther Ausf. D tanks that had broken down on the Kursk battlefield and displayed one of these at Gorkiy Park in Moscow at an exhibit of captured German weapons. British and American liaison officers photographed the Gorkiy Panther, and the Red Army provided basic statistics, including armor thicknesses and basic performance data. By the autumn of 1943, this was quickly disseminated through the usual technical intelligence channels in the U.S. and British Armies. The first report, undated but widely circulated, was written by a Canadian officer and entitled "German PzKw V (Panther)," which was basically a translation of the data provided by the Red Army combined with notes after inspecting one of the Kursk Panthers on display in Moscow. The first officially disseminated report was issued on September 26, 1943, in *Intelligence Notes* No. 26, a regular technical intelligence digest printed in limited quantities by the Office of

Assistant Chief of Staff, G-2, Allied Forces Headquarters. More detail on the Panther appeared in later issues, including No. 27 (October 3, 1943), No. 35 (November 28, 1943), and No. 41 (January 11, 1944). An even more widely distributed report based on much the same information was printed in the November 4, 1943, issue of *Tactical and Technical Trends,* the periodic journal of the U.S. Army's Military Intelligence Division. Clearly, the problem was not a lack of information on the Panther, but a failure to properly analyze and understand the data.

These reports created little alarm in the U.S. Army because of a serious misunderstanding of the intended role of the Panther. The army had already encountered the Tiger I in Tunisia in 1943, again on Sicily in 1943, and sporadically in Italy. The Tiger was, in most respects, a more formidable tank than the Panther in 1943 as it had thicker side armor and proved to be a good deal more durable and reliable on the battlefield. Yet the Tiger had not caused much alarm since it had little impact on any of the battles with the Americans. The 1st Armored Division was completely unaware of the Tiger's role in decimating Hightower's Sherman battalion at Sidi Bou Zid in February 1943 as the Tigers had managed to obliterate the Shermans at very long ranges. Tigers were encountered sporadically afterwards but had little impact on the Tunisia fighting. On Sicily, the Luftwaffe's inexperienced Hermann Goering Panzer Division controlled the Tigers, which were blasted by intense naval gunfire when they had attempted to counterattack the amphibious landings near the Gela beachhead. In one case, Shermans of the 2nd Armored Division ambushed a column of six Tigers, with a single Sherman knocking out three in quick succession with shots against their thinner side armor. No tank, even one as powerful as the Tiger, was invulnerable if its flanks were exposed. The U.S. Army understood that the Tiger battalions were relatively few in number and were unlikely to be encountered in significant numbers. The combat experiences in Tunisia and Sicily suggested that the Tigers were formidable weapons but not particularly menacing in small numbers.

This assessment of the Tiger spilled over to the Panther. When the Germans first deployed the Panther at Kursk, they organized it into special brigades for its combat debut. The U.S. Army knew

The U.S. Army learned about the Panther by the late summer of 1943, when the Red Army displayed captured examples in Gorkiy Park in Moscow. One of these captured Panthers was shipped to Britain in the spring of 1944.

this from intelligence reports and so assumed that in the future the Germans would employ the Panther in relatively small numbers like the Tiger in special battalions or brigades at corps or army level, as they had done at Kursk. The U.S. did not anticipate that the Germans intended the Panther to form the backbone of its panzer divisions in 1944. As a result, there was very little pressure from within the U.S. Army to develop new antitank guns or a new gun for the Sherman tank to deal with the Panther in 1944. The tank commanders in the field were not pressing for a new tank gun since the 75mm gun on the Sherman seemed perfectly adequate against the panzer during combat in Tunisia, Sicily, and Salerno in 1943 and at Anzio and elsewhere in Italy in 1944. There was no perceived battle need according to McNair's definition, and Ordnance did not initiate the development of an antidote to the Panther. Recognition that the Panther was intended for a fundamentally different level of distribution did not begin to percolate through Allied intelligence channels until February 22, 1944, with the publication of *Intelligence Notes* No. 47, which finally recognized the change in panzer division structure. It took some time before senior Allied commanders appreciated the implications of this report, and indeed there is

little evidence that any senior army commanders, such as McNair, Bradley, or Eisenhower, were aware of this issue prior to D-Day.

It is worth noting that the both the Red Army and the British Army had the same information and reacted in a fundamentally different way. They saw the Panther and immediately began steps to modernize both their antitank guns and tank main guns. The Soviets began a crash program to rearm the T-34 from the 76mm to the 85mm gun and to redesign the KV heavy tank from a 76mm to a 122mm gun as the IS-2. These both appeared in early 1944 before the start of the summer campaign season.

The British made much the same assessment as the U.S. Army regarding the likely role for the Panther, but they did not share the American complacency. The British Army, for all of its shortcomings in tank design, was a very battle-experienced force by 1943. British tanks had started the war with machine gun–armed tanks, which gave way to the 2-pounder (40mm) on some tanks by the battle of France in 1940, then the 6-pounder (57mm) in 1942, and the American 75mm in 1942–43. The German panzer force had continuously upgraded its armor and firepower throughout the war, and there

The Panther first faced British and American forces at the Anzio beachhead in February 1944, but the muddy conditions led the local German commanders to reserve the Panther battalion. As a result, none were captured until the May 1944 offensive toward Rome—too late to have any impact on the U.S. Army's 1944 tank program.

was no reason to expect they would stop in 1944. To deal with the Panther as well as other thickly armored German AFVs, the British Army had begun to develop a 17-pounder (76mm) antitank gun in 1942 that was beginning to reach maturity toward the end of 1943.

The power of tank guns in World War II depended on their armor-piercing ammunition. They could not use the new shaped-charge warheads employed on infantry antitank rockets because the existing mechanical fuzes were too slow for high-speed tank projectiles. It wasn't until after the war, with the development of piezo-electric fuzes, that shaped charge tank projectiles became practical. As a result, it came down to brute force—smashing through enemy tank armor with a projectile. A very rough formula for the penetrating power of wartime tank guns was

$$\frac{1/2 \times velocity^2 \times projectile\ weight}{projectile\ resistance}$$

While the finer details of ballistics can be avoided here, the point to emphasize was that an increase in projectile velocity was far more important than an increase in projectile mass. This was accomplished in several ways. The brute force approach simply packed more propellant behind the projectile, preferably one of the newer and more powerful propellants. Another way was to lengthen the gun tube; a longer gun tube meant that the propellant had more time to accelerate the projectile, which then emerged from the barrel faster, even if the propellant load was the same.

The third method involved tinkering with the projectile. The Germans and Americans pioneered hypervelocity armor-piercing (HVAP) shot, a smaller projectile that could travel faster using a very dense core of tungsten carbide. This worked very well, but production of "hyper-shot" was constrained by limited wartime supplies of tungsten carbide, which was reserved in most countries for the manufacture of vital machine tools. A British innovation was the use of a small "sub-caliber" projectile made of ordinary steel instead of precious tungsten carbide. The sub-caliber round consisted of a "sabot" (French for shoe) that was the same caliber as the gun barrel, but within the sabot was the sub-caliber projectile. When the round—known as armor-piercing discarding-sabot (APDS)—left the barrel, the sabot peeled away, and the smaller core projectile traveled all the way to the target with less wind resistance because of its small size. The problem with this type of ammunition in 1944 is that the dynamics of sabot separation were only vaguely understood, and slight perturbations in the peeling away of the sabots could affect accuracy. As a result, APDS ammunition in 1944 tended to have great penetration capabilities but wildly erratic accuracy. So the 17-pounder initially used a more conventional projectile until technical problems with the APDS round were gradually overcome.

In the event, the new British 17-pounder combined all three approaches. The new ammunition

The British solution to the Panther threat was to mount the more powerful 17-pounder antitank gun on the Sherman turret. One 17-pounder turret was shipped to the U.S. Army for trials and was mounted on an early-production M4A2 hull, as seen here at Aberdeen Proving Ground.

packed a fearsome wallop of nine pounds of propellant, compared to only two pounds in the 75mm Sherman gun. The barrel was especially long at L/55 calibers, compared to the Sherman 75mm at about L/32 calibers. (When measuring barrel length, caliber is the length of the barrel in millimeters divided by the bore diameter. In the case of the Sherman's 75mm gun: 2,443mm ÷ 75mm = L/32.5). Finally, the 17-pouder was designed to fire either conventional armor-piercing ammunition or the erratic but dangerous APDS ammunition. It's worth noting that the Germans took a similar approach with the new 75mm gun on the Panther. It used 8.2 pounds of propellant but an exceptionally long barrel with an L/70 length.

The new high-velocity guns tended to kick up an enormous amount of dust in front of the tank because of the large amount of propellant, and this had a detrimental impact during fighting, making it difficult for the tank crew to adjust its fire if it missed on the first shot. The British (and German) solution to this problem was to fit the gun with a muzzle brake that would divert the gun blast sideways to avoid the worst of the dust. The second problem with these high-velocity guns was that they could not fire thin-walled projectiles with heavy loads of

high explosive and had to rely on thicker projectile casings to withstand the velocity and lower high-explosive fills. This was a significant issue because the vast majority of ammunition fired by tanks is high explosive since most targets are not enemy tanks but trucks, pillboxes, machine-gun nests, and so on. The British had found that the 75mm Sherman high-explosive round was one of its best attributes and were reluctant to lose this capability.

The Germans fielded a special high-explosive round for the Panther that used a reduced propellant load. The British solution to the shortcomings of high-velocity tank guns was to adopt a mixed tank formation. Instead of all the tanks in a tank troop (platoon, in the U.S. Army) having 75mm or 17-pounder guns, the troop would all have 75mm tanks, except for one or two 17-pounder tanks to deal with the occasional encounters with thickly armored German panzers. The British Army began trials of the 17-pounder mounted in Sherman turrets in December 1943, and by D-Day, conversion of normal Shermans into 17-pounder Fireflies was well underway, with the type already in service. British antitank regiments employed a towed antitank version by the end of the Tunisian campaign in 1943.

CHAPTER 4

The Future Sherman: Improve or Replace?

THE U.S. ARMY WAS NOT COMPLETELY oblivious to the future panzer threat but lacked the urgency seen in the Red Army and British Army to field improved antitank weapons in time for the 1944 summer campaigns. This resulted from a stew of interlocking problems discussed earlier, including the distraction of the tank destroyer force, the AGF's reactive battle need procurement doctrine, and the overall inexperience of the American armored force in anticipating the technological dynamics of arms races. As a result, U.S. tank units landing in Normandy were equipped with tanks little different from the Sherman that had debuted at El Alamein two years earlier.

SHERMAN GENERATION 1.5

In the haste to put the Sherman into production, the U.S. Army introduced a continual stream of improvements to correct obvious technical flaws. Eventually, the army established a "blitz" program to coordinate the integration of these many improvements into Shermans being produced at several plants. As mentioned earlier, the lessons from Tunisia led to a package of improvements that were deemed so essential that a special kit was developed to upgrade all Shermans stationed with U.S. tank units already in England that were earmarked for the Normandy campaign. In addition to this upgrade kit, all new production Shermans incorporated these features. On the firepower side, the "quick fix"

included the introduction of the improved M34A1 gun mount with the new M55 telescopic sight. The British had been pushing for this since 1942, and it had been accepted for production in October 1942. However, it took until February 1943 before new production tanks received the feature since it necessitated the redesign of the gun mount with a wider mantlet to cover the new telescope. In terms of defensive features, the quick-fix upgrade kit included appliqué armor to be welded over the side of the sponson ammunition bins in the hopes of reducing the Sherman's vulnerability to penetration and subsequent ammo fires. Besides adding more armor over the ammunition, the quick-fix program

The "blitz" improvement program can be seen on these M4 tanks of the 6th Armored Division on exercise on Salisbury Plain in England on June 23, 1944, prior to being shipped to Normandy with Patton's Third Army. The M4 in the foreground has the factory-applied improvements, including the appliqué armor on the hull side and glacis plate, integral cast-armor additions on the turret, and the improved M34A1 gun mount with telescopic sight.

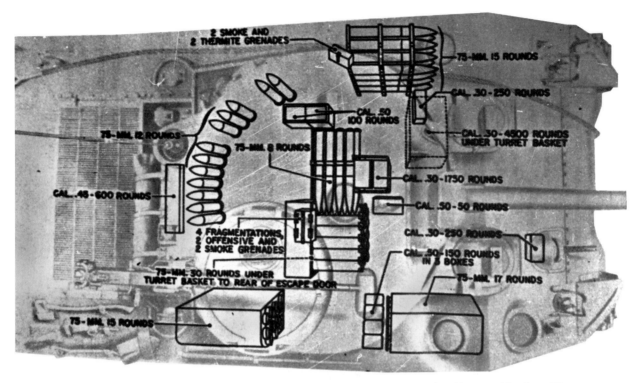

This illustration from the wartime manual shows the ammunition layout in the first-generation Sherman. The three 75mm ammo bins in the sponsons above the track proved to be an Achilles heel of the early Shermans since they were especially prone to being hit, leading to catastrophic ammo fires.

One of the problems uncovered during the fighting in Tunisia was the vulnerability of the ready ammunition stowed around the turret basket in the Sherman turret. A fire in this ammunition had disastrous consequences for the crew, so this ammunition was deleted in the "blitz" program.

also removed the ready rounds stored around the base of the turret since it was found that these posed an especially serious hazard to the crew if ignited.

Appliqué armor was also added over the driver and assistant driver bulges on the glacis plate because the joint was especially vulnerable to penetration. Finally, a curved plate of appliqué armor was added in front of the gunner since during the course of the turret design, it was found that the turret casting was thinner in front of the gunner than elsewhere on the

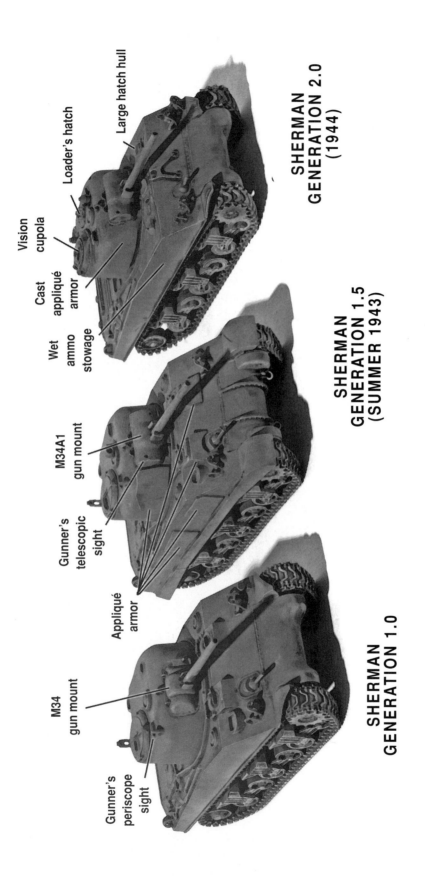

Vision cupola

Loader's hatch

Large hatch hull

Cast appliqué armor

Wet ammo stowage

SHERMAN GENERATION 2.0 (1944)

M34A1 gun mount

Gunner's telescopic sight

Appliqué armor

SHERMAN GENERATION 1.5 (SUMMER 1943)

M34 gun mount

Gunner's periscope sight

SHERMAN GENERATION 1.0

Sherman evolution illustration. AUTHOR'S COLLECTION

Another example of the "blitz" improvement program is this M4A2 at the Armored Board test facility at Fort Knox. On the left hull side, there was only one panel of appliqué armor. This has the other typical upgrades of the program, including the wider gun mantlet to accommodate the new telescopic sight on the right side of the gun.

turret front. Starting in June 1943, Sherman turrets were cast with the additional armor already in place, removing the necessity for the appliqué armor.

Even after the quick-fix kits had been dispatched in England in the summer of 1943, additional improvements continued to be made to the Sherman. For example, the British encouraged the addition to the turret of a 2-inch smoke mortar, primarily a defensive weapon that allowed the crew to quickly fire a round of smoke when attacked to help hide the tank and enable it to maneuver against the enemy. This was added to the upper left corner of the Sherman turret starting in October 1943.

The Sherman tanks that landed in Normandy in June 1944 were in most respects similar to the first-generation Shermans that had fought at El Alamein and in Tunisia. But they did incorporate a host of modest technical changes.

THE 76MM GUN CONTROVERSY

Ordnance had sidestepped AGF regulations about battle need and had been tinkering with gun improvements for the Sherman since 1942. This program was compromised by the lack of a strong demand from either the Armored Force or AGF for a powerful tank-killing weapon, so the Ordnance program meandered for two years with little sense of urgency or direction. The first serious effort to up-arm the Sherman took place in early 1942, shortly after the Sherman entered production. The best American antitank weapon of the time was the 3-inch gun, which had been derived from World War I antiaircraft and coastal defense guns. Of the three methods of increasing antitank performance mentioned earlier, the 3-inch gun used only one, an increased barrel length of L/57, which exceeded the L/32 of the Sherman's existing 75mm gun. The propellant charge was only 3.6 pounds, less than half

that of either the German Panther's 75mm gun or the British 17-pounder. Without permission from AGF or pressure from the Armored Force or Tank Destroyer Center, it proved difficult for Ordnance to justify the development of a whole new antitank gun as was underway in Britain, Germany, and the Soviet Union. Ordnance tried to develop a better gun on the cheap, and U.S. tankers would pay for this short-sightedness on the battlefield in 1944–45.

The existing M7 3-inch tank gun was already in use on the M10 tank destroyer and M6 heavy tank. However, it had a big and clumsy breech and recoil system. Ordnance redesigned the weapon in a more compact fashion specifically for use in smaller tanks and tank destroyers, calling it the 76mm M1 tank gun. The designation 76mm was used for this gun instead of 3-inch since it required a different propellant casing and hence different ammunition than the

The original test-bed for the 76mm gun was this M4A1. A white band has been painted on the gun tube to show the difference in length between the original 75mm gun and the new 76mm gun.

These two crewmen from the 2nd Armored Division show the difference between the 75mm round on the left and the 76mm round on the right. Although the 76mm round is obviously larger because of its bigger propellant case, the size of the actual projectiles was similar.

A dozen of these M4A1 (76M1) tanks were built for operational trials. Careful examination of the turret bustle will show the integral counterweight fitted at the rear to counterbalance the gun. Trials of these tanks, including the tests here at Camp Young, California, with the Desert Warfare Board, suggested that the normal 75mm turret was too small for this gun.

other 3-inch gun, even though the 3-inch M7 gun and 76mm M1 gun both shared the same projectiles. Builders mounted a test example of the new gun in an M4A1 tank and put it through firing trials in the summer of 1942. The gun proved to be well designed, even if a bit much for the Sherman turret. Engineer branch representatives at Aberdeen Proving Ground complained that it violated doctrine since the barrel projected so far in front of the tank that it would be difficult to transport and could get jammed into the ground when a tank descended a hill. As a result, with no special study of the consequences, Ordnance lopped fifteen inches off the front of the barrel, decreasing its length to L/52 and degrading its antitank performance for no especially good reason. This casual change to the gun is a vivid reminder of the low priority afforded to this program by using branches. The shorter gun was designated as the M1A1 76mm gun and would eventually become the standard production type in 1942.

In late 1942, Ordnance proposed building 1,000 Shermans with the 76mm gun in 1943, but AGF did not support this because of the lack of battle need. In November 1942, Gen. Jacob Devers categorically ruled out production of "this untried weapon." This situation changed completely in early 1943 when Devers visited the battlefront in Tunisia and stopped off in Britain on his return to examine British developments, including early work on the new 17-pounder gun. He came back convinced that a more powerful tank gun would be needed by 1944. As a compromise, a dozen M4A1 (76M1) tanks were built at Pressed Steel Car in early 1943 using a slightly improved turret with an integral counter-weight for the gun, which offered better balance. Trials on these vehicles showed once again that the existing turret was not a comfortable fit for the new gun. A better solution would be to use a larger turret, such as that being tested on the new T23 medium tank.

SHERMAN REPLACEMENT: THE M4X

The sad story of medium tank replacements for the Sherman indicated the soundness of the Sherman design, preoccupation with maximizing American tank production at the expense of quality, and the lack of any strong demand for a better tank. As a result, Ordnance work on the Sherman replacement wandered along aimlessly for more than a year, tinkering with intriguing technical improvements. There were two medium tank programs under-way in 1943, though one can be dismissed almost immediately.

The M7 medium tank program had begun in fact as the M7 light tank, intended to replace the anti-quated M3/M5 Stuart family. The main problem with the Stuart light tanks was that their armor was too thin and their gun too small, stemming from their origins in the 1930s as machine gun–armed combat cars and light tanks. For a time in 1942, Devers pro-moted the M7 as the army's future universal tank, able to replace both the M3 Stuart light tank and the flawed M3 Lee medium tank. As the armor and fire-power of the M7 increased to meet this requirement, it grew so heavy that it became a medium tank com-parable in weight to the Sherman. An entire new tank plant was built at Bettendorf, Illinois, where Interna-tional Harvester was slated to undertake M7 tank production. But by the time it was ready for produc-tion in 1943, the Armored Force took a close look at this bloated light tank and refused to accept it for service, recognizing that it offered nothing over the existing Sherman tank. As a result, Ordnance can-celled the M7 program on March 11, 1943, after millions of dollars had been spent on its development and industrialization—one of the lesser-known Ordnance scandals of World War II.

A more ambitious program deliberately aimed at replacing the Sherman, the T23 began in the spring of 1942 after the return of an Ordnance team from North Africa, where it studied the lessons of recent British and German tank combat in the desert cam-paign. The main requirement was to redesign the hull to make the tank more compact. American tank

The first attempt to replace the M3/M4 medium tank series started as the M7 light tank, seen here in its original configuration with a 57mm gun.

By the time the M7 was ready for production in December 1942, it had been rearmed with a 75mm gun and had thicker armor. In most respects, it was inferior to the existing M4 Sherman tank, so production was cancelled after only seven were completed.

The T22 pilots used the same powertrain as the M4A3 medium tank but with a new hull and turret. The armament is the same 75mm gun used on the Sherman series, but it is fitted with an automatic loader fed by a thirty-two-round magazine.

design in the 1930s had focused on the use of radial aircraft engines as a source of compact powerplants. The problem with this selection was that the power-drive from the engine ran through the fighting compartment to the front-mounted transmission and was relatively high since the most economical design simply took power off the main drive shaft rather than running it through an intermediate transmission. This meant that the driveshaft sat fairly high in the fighting compartment. Tanks like the M3 Grant and M4 Sherman had a turret basket for the turret crew, and since this had to ride above the powerdrive, inevitably the hull had to be high to accommodate both features. There were several

This is the pilot of the T20 medium tank at General Motors' Fisher Body Division after completion in May 1943. It is armed with a 76mm gun and fitted with an experimental horizontal volute spring system developed for the Sherman.

The T20E3 pilot was completed by General Motors in July 1943 and introduced the more advanced torsion bar suspension that would later emerge with the final M26 Pershing tank.

alternatives to this configuration, notably the use of a rear-mounted transmission so that the fighting compartment remained clear of the powerdrive.

Design of the T20 began in May 1942 and avoided the narrow and high hull forced on the Sherman by its evolution from the M2 and M3 medium tanks, devising a low and sleek hull topped with a new and larger turret. Ordnance was interested in mounting its new M1 76mm gun in the new design, but lacking any firm battle need from the armored force for such a weapon, it also worked on versions with the existing 75mm gun, including one fed from an automatic loader. There was no particular pressure to push a new design into production,

The T23 pilot incorporated an electric transmission by General Electric. The first two pilot vehicles used the same turret as on the T20 pilot. The T23 used the same vertical volute spring suspension found on the Sherman series.

The third T23 pilot introduced a new, enlarged turret and became the production configuration when manufacture began at the Detroit Tank Arsenal in November 1943. Although ultimately unsuccessful as a tank, the new T23 turret was easily adapted to the Sherman, permitting a more acceptable 76mm version.

so development of the T20 was leisurely by World War II standards, with the pilots delivered in the spring of 1943. Because of the lack of urgency, a variety of spin-offs appeared, such as the T22, which took the powertrain from the M4A3 Sherman instead of the new rear-mounted torquematic transmission used in the T20. The T23, an even more ambitious alternative, used a General Electric electric transmission. Tank designers had dreamed of electric transmissions since World War I since they offered the hope of a

The sixth-production T23 was sent to the Armored Board at Fort Knox for trials in early 1944, but the board rejected it because of its lack of advantage over the 76mm Sherman and the maintenance burden imposed by its sophisticated electric transmission.

The T23 was modified with a torquematic transmission and an enlarged turret with a 90mm gun, becoming the T25 heavy tank. The first pilot version, seen here, was sent to Aberdeen Proving Ground for trials in late January 1944 and was fitted with the horizontal volute suspension found on late-production Shermans. The more heavily armored version of the T25, the T26, would eventually emerge as the M26 Pershing in 1945.

more efficient transmission of power from the engine to the drivetrain than conventional mechanical transmissions. In these designs, the engine powers electrical generators which then use the electricity to run the electric final drives. The French first used such a system on their St. Chamond tank in 1917, a technical flop that was derided as "an elephant on the legs of a gazelle" for its weak suspension and powertrain. The Germans attempted the same sort of advanced electrical drive on the Porsche competitor to the Tiger tank, which later emerged as the flawed Elefant and Ferdinand tank destroyers.

In 1943 and 1944, the T23 became the pet project of Ordnance engineers who were enamored of the technical novelty of the drive system and the more satisfactory armament and armor compared to the Sherman. Trials of the T23 at Fort Knox were not so kind, as the new electrical transmission proved to be troublesome to maintain under field conditions. Ordnance continued to make a hard-sell of their new designs, touting the marvels of the T23.

The most efficient method to add the 76mm gun to the Sherman was to adapt the T23 turret to the Sherman hull. This is the M4E6 pilot, which combined an M4 composite hull with a T23 turret. This proved a simple and practical alternative to the 75mm turret and entered production in January 1944 using the M4A1 hull.

The M4E6 also examined the use of "wet" stowage for the tank ammunition, which placed the rounds in armored bins in the floor where they were less likely to be hit by enemy fire.

SHERMAN GENERATION 2.0

Even if the entire design was too much for production, the T23's new 76mm turret offered a quick solution to uparming the Sherman. The T23 had been designed from the outset with a turret ring the same diameter as the Sherman tank, so the T23 turret was a simple fit on the Sherman hull. A pilot was built in the summer of 1943; called the M4E6, it proved that such a configuration was technically sound and straightforward to produce. Although the technical issue was quickly settled, the procurement issue became contentious. The Armored Force commander, Jacob Devers, had supported the production of a 76mm Sherman since returning from Tunisia earlier in 1943. However, he had been at

loggerheads with McNair at AGF over a variety of issues including the tank destroyer controversy, the reorganization of the armored divisions, and the balance of infantry tank battalions versus the armored divisions. He was booted upstairs in May 1943, becoming head of American forces in the European theater of operations until Roosevelt made his final pick of the commander for Normandy and the European campaign. Alvin Gillem became the new head of the Armored Force but spent the early part of the summer in Sicily to study the lessons of the fighting there. With the departure of Devers, McNair downgraded the Armored Force at Fort Knox, first renaming it Armored Command and

The culmination of the Sherman upgrade program was a completely redesigned hull that had a simplified front glacis plate without the usual bulges over the driver's and codriver's position. More importantly, the new hull incorporated the improved "wet" ammo stowage. Another innovation in the second-generation Shermans was the introduction of the M4 (105mm) assault gun, like this Chrysler-built example, which was used in the assault gun platoons of tank battalions to provide added high-explosive firepower.

later demoting it to Armored Training Center in February 1944. By this stage, Fort Knox's role in determining future tank requirements had been usurped by McNair's command under AGF's requirements section, with Fort Knox having a largely advisory role through its testing arm, the Fort Knox Armored Board.

Pending Gillem's return from Sicily, the Armored Command headquarters recommended in August that 1,000 of the 76mm Shermans be manufactured and that "as soon as the tank has been proven on the battlefield . . . we go to one hundred percent replacement of the M4 with the 76mm gun." This caused a bit of a firestorm at AGF, since it implied that tank production would be in turmoil in the early months of 1944, just as U.S. troops were preparing their biggest operation to date, the amphibious landings in France. On his return, Gillem threw water on the controversy by making clear that the Armored Force was not in fact recommending the abandonment of the 75mm gun, but merely the addition of 76mm tanks as a hedge against German tank developments. Gillem's letter to McNair of September 1, 1943, is a concise summary of the arguments for and against the new 76mm gun:

The 76mm Gun, M1 as a tank weapon has only one superior characteristic to the 75mm Gun, M3. This superior characteristic is in armor penetrating power. The 76mm gun will penetrate on average one inch more armor that the 75mm Gun, M3 at the same range. The high-explosive pitching power of the 76mm gun is inferior to that of the 75mm gun. The 76mm shell weighs 12.7 lbs and has a charge of .86 lbs of explosive. The 75mm shell weighs 14.6 lbs and has a charge of 1.47 lbs of explosive. The exterior ballistics generally of the 76mm gun are less satisfactory for a general purpose Medium Tank than the 75mm gun. The 76mm gun has an extremely heavy muzzle blast such that the rate of fire when the ground is dry is controlled by the muzzle blast dust cloud. Under many conditions this dust cloud does not clear for some eight to thirty seconds. The presence of this heavy muzzle blast makes the sensing of the round extremely difficult for the tank commander and gunner. . . . The characteristics of the complete round of the 76mm gun makes it possible to stow only approximately 70% as many rounds in the Medium Tank, M4 as can be stowed for the 75mm gun. The great length of the 76mm round slows the loader and somewhat slows the rate of fire. . . . In view of these facts, it is considered unwise to equip an armored division or separate tank battalion entirely with 76mm guns to the exclusion of the 75mm gun. It must be remembered in making these comparisons that the 75mm Gun M3 is not entirely helpless against enemy armor. It is believed that a fairly good percentage of 76mm guns should be included in a medium tank unit for the purpose of giving it a sufficient share of additional penetrating power obtainable with the 76mm gun. . . . It appears that 33 percent of medium tank production equipped with the 76mm guns would be a more satisfactory figure from the current viewpoint.

Gillem's support of the 76mm gun provided sufficient battle need to convince McNair to support production of the 76mm Sherman. Production planning for 1944 was still in progress, and Ordnance intended to introduce a new second-generation Sherman design at this time. The second-generation Sherman consisted of a series of small but significant improvements derived from the study of the lessons from Tunisia. Some of these had already been incorporated into the quick-fix Sherman upgrades in the summer of 1943, but the new program better integrated them into the Sherman. At the core of the second-generation Sherman was an improved hull design. The front glacis plate of the Sherman was needlessly complex to manufacture, with a pair of protrusions where the driver and bow gunner sat, which had required the appliqué armor panels in the quick-fix program. The new design eliminated these in favor of a single glacis plate, which at the same time offered better ballistic integrity. The existing Shermans had relatively small hatches for the driver and bow gunner, but crews found that it was difficult to rapidly exit these hatches in combat, and the new

From a combat standpoint, the introduction of the "wet" ammo stowage on the Sherman considerably enhanced crew survivability in combat. The combination of armored stowage bins and the repositioning of the ammo in the floor made it less likely that ammunition would be set on fire if the tank was hit. This view looks down into the loader's hatch of an M4A3 (76mm) as the loader stows ammunition in the new racks.

hull glacis plate permitted the addition of larger and more satisfactory hatches. The most important change, however, was the introduction of "wet" stowage for the ammunition.

The Sherman tank through 1943 had most of its ammunition in unprotected bins located in the sponsons on the side of the tank over the tracks. This made them very vulnerable to enemy fire since a hit on the front or side of the tank had a very high probability of hitting them. When struck by enemy rounds, a catastrophic fire usually ensued because once the propellant in one round was ignited, it usually set fire to neighboring rounds in quick succession. Fire extinguishers could do no good against such a blaze since the propellant, like solid rocket fuel, contained its own oxidant. Although gasoline was often blamed for catastrophic tank fires in combat, American and British researchers had quickly appreciated that ammunition fires were a far more serious threat. Many gasoline fires could be stopped by a fire extinguisher, and the Sherman already had an automated fire extinguisher system.

As mentioned earlier, the short-term solution to the ammunition problem was to weld extra appliqué armor over the ammunition bins, which was done starting in the summer of 1943. The better way around this problem was to make it less likely that the ammunition would be hit and less likely to catch fire if the tank was penetrated by enemy guns. To make it less likely to be hit, the ammunition was

This cross-sectional drawing shows the final-production configuration of the M4A1 (76mm) with HVSS suspension. The dark-colored boxes on the floor below the turret basket contain the tank's repositioned ammo bins.

shifted from high in the sponsons to low in the hull under the turret basket. Not only did this reduce the likelihood of the ammunition being hit, but it also gave the ammunition some passive protection from tank components. An enemy projectile hitting the tank low in the front would not only have to go through the tank's outer armor to hit the ammunition, but it would also have to pass through the very substantial transmission in the lower front of the tank, most likely stopping it before it hit the ammunition. From the sides, the enemy projectile would be likely to hit the large cast bogies of the suspension before even reaching the tank's side armor, once again drastically reducing the probability of reaching the ammunition. In addition, the ammunition was now placed in lightly armored bins surrounded by water or antifreeze. This was not enough to stop a complete projectile, but a frequent source of tank fires was the spray of sizzling metal fragments that careened around inside the tank like supersonic ping-pong balls when a projectile broke up after penetrating the tank's armor; the new bins were enough to stop many of these small fragments.

An army study in 1945 concluded that only 10–15 percent of the wet-stowage Shermans burned when penetrated, compared to 60–80 percent of the older dry-stowage Shermans.

In view of the Armored Command's continuing displeasure over the T23 and the lack of a firm battle need from the theater commanders, the army planned to build a mix of second-generation Shermans in 1944, some with the large 76mm turret, some with the 75mm turret, and some with the 105mm assault gun turret. The 105mm turret was another innovation that appeared in late 1943. Tank battalions wanted even more high-explosive punch than the 75mm gun, and so an assault gun platoon was added to the headquarters company in each tank battalion. At first, the plan was to issue these units the M7 105mm howitzer motor carriage. This was a type of open-top field artillery vehicle based on the Sherman chassis, better known to the British as the Priest because of its machine-gun "pulpit." However, this offered no armored protection for the crew, so instead, the 105mm howitzer was mounted in a modified Sherman tank turret. These "assault gun" Shermans were used to provide indirect artillery fire support for the tank battalions and were not intended for close combat.

By 1944, the U.S. Army was attempting to simplify the variety of Shermans in service. As mentioned earlier, there were basically four families of Shermans that varied by engine type: the M4/M4A1, M4A2, M4A3, and M4A4. Until 1944, U.S. Army units exclusively used the M4 and M4A1, which shared a common Continental radial engine and differed only in hull construction. Other types, like the M4A2 diesel, were used by the U.S. Marine Corps in combat and by the U.S. Army in training, but they were not deployed to the European or Mediterranean theaters of operations for combat use by the army. However, in 1943, the U.S. Army decided to shift to the M4A3, with a new Ford GAA inline engine, which was a better engine than the Continental radial, as soon as practical. This occurred during the transition to the second-generation Sherman.

For 1944, the army planned to begin production of the second-generation 76mm Sherman with the M4A1 (76mm) since this type was the first to be ready for manufacture. This would be quickly followed by 75mm and 76mm versions of the M4A3, with the new second-generation "wet" stowage hull, which would become the preferred type. The M4 remained in production with a new composite hull with the front portion using a large casting derived from the M4A1 hull, while the rear was constructed of welded plate as before. The M4 also was built with the new second-generation welded hull, primarily in the 105mm assault gun version.

THE DEBATE INTENSIFIES

By the end of 1943, AGF and the Armored Force had reached consensus on future tank needs for 1944 with the second-generation Shermans and the new 76mm gun. However, the British were skeptical that the 76mm gun was adequate for the job, and their influence with Devers at ETO headquarters in London led to second-guessing about the program. One of the innovations established in the European headquarters was an armored fighting vehicles and weapons section (AFV&W) patterned after similar British organizations. The duty of the AFV&W section was to examine current and future needs for tanks and other AFVs for the U.S. Army in Europe. This small office was far better informed than most theater headquarters on tank development and the panzer threat.

The AFV&W section began its own crusade to get better weapons for future battles, influenced by their British colleagues, who were not very impressed with the new American 76mm gun, favoring their own 17-pounder, which had much better armor-penetrating power, albeit with some design and accuracy problems. The AFV&W section was well aware that the U.S. Army was not likely to approve a British 76mm gun on top of the M1A1 (76mm) recently approved for production, so they examined other Ordnance initiatives.

The first program to mount the 90mm antiaircraft gun on the Sherman chassis was the ungainly T53E1 90mm gun motor carriage. It proved too unstable as an antiaircraft platform, and when offered to the Tank Destroyer Center, it was also rejected because of its half-baked design.

COMPARISON OF HEAVY TANK GUNS

Type	Length	Projectile	Projectile weight (kg)	Propellant weight (kg)	Initial muzzle velocity (m/s)	Penetration* (mm)
90mm gun M3	L/50	M82	10.9	3.3	810	120
88mm gun KwK 36	L/56	PzGr 39/43	10.1	6.8	930	156
88mm gun KwK 43	L/71	PzGr 39/43	10.1	6.8	1,130	210

*at 500 meters, armor at 30 degrees

The many stories of the Wehrmacht using 88mm flak guns as improvised antitank guns in France in 1940 and in Russia and the North African desert in 1941–42 intrigued Ordnance. The U.S. Army had a very effective 90mm antiaircraft gun, though it was encumbered with sighting devices and autoloading features that made it difficult to convert into an antitank gun. However, these studies did prompt Ordnance to begin to experiment with 90mm antitank vehicles. A 90mm gun was mated to the M4 Sherman chassis as the experimental T53 90mm GMC in the summer of 1942, and remarkably, AGF and Ordnance agreed to manufacture 500 in August 1942. When General Bruce of Tank Destroyer Command found out about this, he went nuts and demanded that the program be stopped. The T53 was extremely clumsy and slapdash, even if it did have a powerful gun. Bruce was still fixated on the need for speed in future tank destroyer designs and had no interest in a weapon no faster than the existing M1 3-inch GMC, even if it did have a bigger gun. So the T53 died before reaching production.

Ordnance still thought that the 90mm gun was the wave of the future and proceeded to design a lightweight, compact 90mm gun that could more easily fit in a turret. Like the 76mm gun, it was based around an existing antiaircraft gun and ammunition and so was not as powerful as a custom-designed tank-killing gun. Technically, it was closest to the 88mm KwK 36 fitted to the Tiger I heavy tank, which likewise had been developed from the German 88mm flak gun. As in the case of the 76mm gun, the selection of an existing gun meant that it had less than optimal characteristics for an antitank weapon, notably a modest propellant charge—only about half that of the comparable German weapon. As a result, its armor penetration capabilities were markedly inferior to the KwK 36 and the later KwK 43 on the King Tiger.

The experimental T7 90mm gun was the most powerful gun suitable for tanks in development in the U.S. in 1943. Ordnance first mounted it in a modified M10 tank destroyer turret but, because of the heavy weight of the barrel, decided that a new turret with a more satisfactory turret bustle was desirable for better turret balance. This emerged in September 1943 as the T71, later known as the M36 90mm GMC when production started. Although this vehicle offered superior firepower to the existing M10 tank destroyer, Bruce was still adamant that he did not want a vehicle that had no more speed than the existing M10, and he continued to push for his pet project, the high-speed M18 76mm GMC. In the event, Ordnance proposals to shift the M36 into the 1944 production plan in lieu of the M10 came to a screeching halt when it ran into another controversy, the 90mm tank.

When Jacob Devers visited Tunisia in early 1943, he heard the first reports about the German Tiger. This led to his belief that the U.S. Army should have an equivalent heavy tank to deal with the Tiger in the 1944 campaigns. While still heading the Armored Force in early 1943, he pushed Ordnance to reorient its T23 medium tank program to incorporate a bigger gun. The Sherman would eventually mount the 76mm gun originally fitted to the T23, so he wanted a 90mm gun on a modified T23. Ordnance developed two versions, the T25 with three inches of frontal armor and the T26 with four inches, both armed with the same 90mm gun as

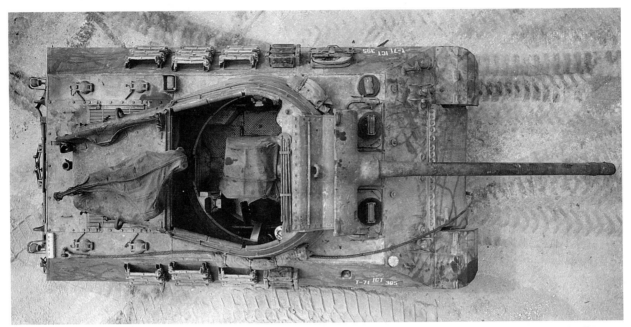

After attempting to mount the lightweight T7 90mm gun in an M10 turret, Ordnance instead developed a new turret for the T71 90mm gun motor carriage pilot seen here. This emerged in 1943 as the M36 90mm gun motor carriage, which became caught up in the 90mm gun controversy in the autumn of 1943.

planned for the M36 tank destroyer. By the time that work had begun, Devers was at his new European headquarters and carried on his crusade from there.

When visited by AGF representatives in London in September 1943 to discuss future weapons needs, Devers requested that development of the T26E1 be accelerated and that 250 of these be manufactured as quickly as possible. Devers wanted the T26 deployed on the scale of one for every five M4 medium tanks—much as the British planned to do with their 17-pounder Firefly tanks. Ordnance concurred, but saddled the proposal with its pet project, advocating production of 1,000 of the advanced but flawed T23 as well. The G-4 section of the war department attempted to reconcile these various proposals by soliciting the advice of field commanders as well as McNair's AGF headquarters in Washington.

On October 14, 1943, the theater headquarters were asked for their advice about the types of tanks desired for the 1944 tank program; brief technical details were provided about the T20, T22, and T23 medium tanks as well as the T25 and T26 heavy tanks. The War Department cable went to Devers in Europe, Eisenhower in North Africa, and the army's South Pacific and Southwest Pacific commands.

Devers's headquarters showed some enthusiasm for the T20, T22, and T23, but with the important caveat that the new types would be desirable only "if the Armored Command accepts it after performance and gunnery tests." Devers continued to push for the development of the T25 and T26 heavy tanks. Eisenhower's headquarters favored the T23 but expressed confidence in existing mechanical transmissions and some concern that the T23's novel electrical transmission must be equally reliable and easily maintained. There was little interest in heavy tanks, with Eisenhower's staff noting that "the T26 tank is not favored because it is not believed that the proposed increased armor protection over that of the present M4 series of medium tanks is justified by the corresponding increase in weight and decrease in maneuverability."

The two armored divisions that had combat experience did not agree on future designs. General Harmon of the 1st Armored Division favored the T23 and recognized the merit of the T25 and T26, just not in armored divisions. His tank regiment commanders had divided opinions. Col. Hamilton Howze argued that the T25 and T26 "were not worth the trouble to build." General Gaffey of the

Gen. Andrew Bruce continued to push the M18 76mm gun motor carriage as the preferred choice of the tank destroyer force, even though its gun was incapable of dealing with the new Tiger and Panther tanks.

2nd Armored Division wanted a T23 with a 75mm gun and mechanical transmission. One battalion commander favored the T25, two others the T23. The lack of consensus gave the War Department little firm guidance. Furthermore, the theater commands, which were not especially well informed about technical and performance issues, based their judgments on the skimpy data provided in the cables. For example, not knowing the limitations of the 76mm gun when facing German types such as the Tiger and Panther, Harmon favored the 76mm on the T23 over the 90mm on the T25 and T26 "if the 76mm can do the job." The tank commanders were largely unaware of armored command's unease with the T23, especially its electric transmission. Ordnance continued to labor away at the T23, but AGF didn't want to interrupt Sherman production for a tank lacking a firm battle need, and the armored force hesitated to foist a new tank on its battalions in Europe on the eve of the upcoming 1944 campaign. As a result, the T23 remained an unwanted orphan.

With opinion from the theater commanders so divided, McNair waded into the debate. The T23 was not a serious contender because of the contin-

ued resistance of the Armored Command over reliability and maintenance issues with the electric transmission. McNair had already agreed to the 76mm version of the Sherman, so he turned his attention to the 90mm issue raised by Devers's advocacy of the T25 and T26 heavy tanks and the M36 90mm tank destroyer. McNair's letter provides the best evidence of the dangerous complacency that permeated senior army leadership, even in the autumn of 1943:

> The M4 tank, particularly the M4A3, has been widely hailed as the best tank on the battlefield today. There are indications that the enemy concurs in this view. Apparently, the M4 is an ideal combination of mobility, dependability, speed, protection, and firepower. Other than this particular request—which represents the British view—there has been no call from any theater for a 90mm tank gun. There appears to be no fear on the part of our forces of the German Mark VI (Tiger) tank. . . . There can be no basis for the T26 tank other than the conception of a tank versus tank duel—which is believed unsound

The more heavily armored T26 eventually emerged as the preferred choice between the T25 and T26 pilots. This is the T26E1 pilot with its turret traversed over the rear. It has numerous small production differences over the eventual T26E3 production version, such as the lack of a muzzle brake on the 90mm gun.

and unnecessary. Both British and American battle experience has demonstrated that the antitank gun in suitable numbers and disposed properly is the master of the tank. Any attempt to armor and gun tanks so as to outmatch antitank guns is foredoomed to failure. . . . There is no indication that the 76mm antitank gun is inadequate against the German Mark VI (Tiger) tank.

McNair's arguments were technically inaccurate and reflected an alarming degree of smugness. His dig at the "British viewpoint" was both a slap at Devers for his openness to British views as well as a reflection of American disdain for the shoddy quality of British tank design. His suggestion that there was "no fear of the Tiger" was preposterous. Few American tankers had encountered the Tiger in combat, and the few that did, such as Hightower's battalion at Sidi Bou Zid, had seen their unit virtu-

ally annihilated. McNair continued to dispute the need for tanks to fight other tanks, a fossilized view appropriate to World War I tank combat but now completely out of date.

From a technical standpoint, McNair's viewpoint was dangerous: the new 76mm gun was not as powerful as many army leaders thought. The M1A1 76mm tank gun firing the M62 APC (armor-piercing, capped) projectile had a nominal penetration of 109 millimeters at 500 yards with the armor angled at 20 degrees. The Tiger's gun mantlet was 120 millimeters thick and the hull front 100 millimeters. In practice, the 76mm gun could penetrate the Tiger mantlet only at ranges of 100 meters or less and the hull at 400 meters, while the Tiger could penetrate the M4 Sherman at ranges more than double these figures. In practice, it was almost impossible for a 76mm gun to penetrate the Tiger frontally. More importantly, the 76mm gun had an even harder time against the Panther. American officers believed that

THE DEBATE INTENSIFIES **125**

the 100-millimeter-thick Panther gun mantlet was vulnerable to the 76mm gun since on paper it was 100 millimeters thick and the 76mm gun could penetrate 109 millimeters. However, the Panther mantlet was rounded, so its effective thickness, unless a lucky hit struck it dead-on, was more than 100 millimeters, and the mantlet was backed by a thick steel gun mount offering additional protection. The Panther's glacis plate was only 80 millimeters thick, which on casual inspection suggested it was vulnerable to the 76mm gun. What many U.S. Army officers overlooked was that the Panther glacis was angled at 55 degrees, meaning that it had an effective thickness against frontal attack of 145 millimeters, far beyond the capabilities of the 76mm gun. The Panther was essentially invulnerable to frontal attack by the 76mm gun, a fact not widely understood by senior American commanders because of Ordnance's inadequate explanation of the threat. Many U.S. Army officers in 1943 were not well trained in the intricacies of tank technology and gun ballistics, and their judgments on these subjects were poor. As data on the Panther continued to spread through the army in Europe, there was a growing recognition that the 1944 tank program might not be adequate.

The program to field a successor to the Sherman proceeded in fits, pushed on mainly by Devers and the AFV&W section of his European headquarters. There had been complaints that the T26 exceeded army regulations regarding weight and width, posing a problem in shipping. When pressed on the issue again on December 10, 1943, Devers responded emphatically that he saw a need for "at least 250 T26 to be produced now." This settled the matter, and on December 16, 1943, Gen. George Marshall finally overruled McNair and authorized the production of 250 T26E1 heavy tanks by April 1945. While this put the army on the right track, the development cycle of the T26 moved too slowly to have any effect on the 1944 campaign in France. In late December, Devers was transferred to the Mediterranean as deputy commander of the North Africa theater; he was slated to lead the invasion of southern France, Operation Dragoon, in the summer of 1944. On December 6, 1943, Eisenhower was finally tapped as commander of the European theater under the new SHAEF (Supreme Headquarters Allied Expeditionary Force) headquarters. This led Army Service Forces to again attempt to derail the program, complaining now about the difficulties of establishing production of the new transmission line. In frustration over the continued bickering, Marshall personally sent a cable to Eisenhower in January 1944 asking whether the original Devers request should be allowed to stand. Eisenhower stated that it should, and the matter was finally settled in favor of manufacturing the Pershing tank. However, the T26 was not yet complete, and production would not begin until the autumn of 1944 no matter how much support came from the European theater.

LAST-MINUTE INNOVATIONS

Fortunately for American armored units in 1944, the AFV&W section made two other proposals that had important short-term effects. Approval of the M36 90mm tank destroyer had been denied when first promoted in September 1943, in no small measure because it had gotten mixed up in the controversy over the 90mm tank. When resubmitted later in the autumn, the request, couched in different language, argued that the M36 was not needed as a tank destroyer, but rather that its firepower would be needed to deal with the bunkers along the Siegfried Line. Even though General Bruce of the Tank Destroyer Center didn't want them, McNair saw the battle need for the M36 and approved the creation of ten battalions. They would prove to be a valuable addition to the army arsenal in the autumn of 1944, the only American AFV capable of dealing with the new generation of thickly armored German panzers.

In a similar vein, the AFV&W section pushed for a long overdue program, a version of the Sherman better suited to infantry-support needs. There was general recognition in Europe that improved German antitank guns were a growing threat to the Sherman's armor and that more armor was needed. In January 1944, the section submitted an urgent requirement to Washington for 250 heavy tanks for the upcoming campaign in France, using the same approach as in the M36 proposal—that they were needed to deal with the Siegfried Line defense. In February 1944, the Development Division of the U.S. Army Ground Forces concurred, but since the new T26E2 heavy tank was not expected to be ready until 1945, the Armored Force recommended an expedient design based around an uparmored M4A3 medium tank. As an alternative, Ordnance proposed that the clumsy and antiquated M6 heavy

Pressure from the ETO headquarters prompted Ordnance to develop a more heavily armored version of the Sherman, the M4A3E2 assault tank, which had a new turret and transmission cover with thicker armor as well as extra armor plate on the glacis plate and hull sides.

Another innovation by the ETO headquarters was a request for the orphaned M12 155mm gun motor carriage. The artillery branch did not want these, but the ETO headquarters rightly believed that they might come in handy for bunker busting along the Siegfried Line on the German frontier.

tank be modified for the role, but AGF strongly opposed this because of the many problems of the M6 that were revealed during testing. These issues were settled in early March 1944, in favor of the M4 assault tank, called the M4A3E2. This differed from the normal M4A3 medium tank in several respects. The M4A3E2 used a new turret with six-inch armor in place of the normal turret that had three-inch armor. The hull armor was substantially thickened with 1.5-inch-thick steel welded to the front glacis and sides. The War Department approved a production run of 250 assault tanks to be available by August 1944, and they were manufactured on a rush basis from May to July 1944. Although the M4A3E2 assault tanks would not arrive in France

until the autumn of 1944, they were evidence that AGF would push through programs if a clear battle need existed.

McNair and AGF made a diligent effort to keep abreast of combat developments in Europe, but the suggestions from the field often contradicted one another and usually came too late. In February 1944, the army sent a New Weapons Board, headed by Col. G. G. Eddy, to Italy and Britain to solicit advice about future weapons requirements. Their report was published in late April 1944. The board found a nearly universal interest in the new 76mm gun for the Sherman, with tankers in the Italian theater complaining that the German PaK 40 antitank gun and its equivalents on the PzKpfw IV tank and StuG

III assault gun were better weapons than the American 75mm gun and represented the main threat to tanks. One of the report's primary conclusions was that "there should be a progressive increase in firepower, such as the 90mm guns in the T20-series tanks. . . . German armament is not static." It is a shame this argument was not made a year earlier; by April 1944, it was too late.

Surprisingly, tankers in Italy saw little need for more armor or protected ammunition racks, arguing that much more armor would not make the Sherman invulnerable but would degrade its automotive performance in the hills of Italy. A handful of Bruce's prized M18 tank destroyers had been shipped to the Anzio beachhead for combat trials, but they were thoroughly disliked for their thin armor and cramped interiors. Unlike Bruce, the tank destroyer crews wanted the more powerful gun of the M36 90mm tank destroyer, not the fast M18. The New Weapons Board also had a chance to examine the new British 17-pounder antitank gun, and while they were impressed with its armor-piercing ability, they remained skeptical because it lacked a useful high-explosive round. The New Weapons Board generally validated the consensus that had gradually emerged in late 1943 about future tank needs, reinforcing the decision to shift to the 76mm gun on the Sherman and offering further backing for the development of the T25 and T26 heavy tanks.

Yet within a few weeks, the first combat engagements in France in the aftermath of the D-Day landings undermined the results of the New Weapons Board. What was not immediately apparent in Washington was that Italy was a peripheral theater for the Wehrmacht and received neither the quality nor quantity of new weapons allotted to the Russian front or to France. The Germans had only a single Panther battalion in Italy, and it did not see widespread use until May 1944 after the New Weapons Board had departed. German infantry units in Italy still made widespread use of the old 50mm PaK 38 antitank gun though it had been widely replaced by many divisions deployed in France with the much more potent 75mm PaK 40. The new rocket antitank weapons had appeared in the Anzio fighting in February 1944, but not in sufficient numbers to have much of an impact.

Hints of these mistakes continued to percolate to the surface in the weeks prior to D-Day, but by then it was too late. On April 30, 1944, Allied intelligence released a new assessment of the organization of the new 1944 pattern German panzer division. It noted that the Panther was not being relegated to the rare heavy tank regiments but was an integral component of the new panzer divisions and would make up half their tank strength. While not known at the time, Panther strength in France had climbed from 25 percent in December 1943 to 46 percent in May 1944, and more were arriving in France every week. The U.S. Armored Command at Fort Knox had begun to recognize that the Panther would present a greater threat than had previously been recognized by American tactical doctrine or technical intelligence. A report on the tank situation from April 17, 1944, grimly noted:

> While it is conceded that the primary objective of our armor is to engage the enemy infantry, artillery, and rear installations, experience has shown that the enemy will always counter an armored penetration with his own armor. Therefore, in order to operate successfully against remunerative and desirable enemy installations, we shall first have to defeat the enemy armor. To do this, we must have a fighter tank which is superior to the fighter tank of the enemy. Available information on characteristics of German tanks compared to those of our nation show that no American tank can equal the German Panther in all-around performance.

A conference at Fort Knox in early April 1944 concluded that the best option to rapidly deploy a tank capable of meeting the Panther would be to mount a 90mm gun on the M4A3 hull since it was felt that the new T26E3 tank would not be available for nearly a year. Chrysler quickly assembled a single test example mounting a T26 turret on Sherman since they shared a common turret ring. But in reality, it would take months to test this tank, shift it into production, and transport it to the combat theater. Ordnance quickly halted work on the hybrid

Fort Knox proposed mounting the T26 turret on the Sherman hull as a fast way to get 90mm guns to the tankers in Europe. A single pilot was assembled by Chrysler in the summer of 1944, but this approach was rejected when it was realized that such tanks would arrive in Europe no sooner than the T26E3 heavy tanks.

T26/Sherman, deeming it a distraction from the main T26E3 effort.

The U.S. Army in Europe would have to make do with what was available. When the army landed on Omaha Beach in June 1944, its Sherman tanks were only modestly improved from those that first went into combat two years before at El Alamein. Because of the time it took industry to change the production lines, the new second-generation Shermans, such as the M4A3 with wet stowage, would not appear on the battlefields until September 1944, and even then only in small numbers.

Even more surprisingly, the M4A1(76mm), which had been in production since February 1944, would not appear on the battlefields in France until late July 1944, even though an initial batch of 130 had arrived in England on April 10, 1944. The fate of these tanks clearly indicates the complacency of the U.S. Army to the future German panzer threat. A

conference was held at Bradley's First Army head-quarters in Britain on April 20, 1944, to discuss how to distribute the newly arrived 76mm tanks. Since none of the officers present had seen the new type, an officer from the AFV&W section of the First Army presented a comparison of the 76mm gun tank to the more familiar 75mm gun tank. He stressed that the tank offered greater accuracy, improved armor, and concrete penetration, but at the same time the tank suffered from blast obscuration, which hindered direct fire control. It also had an inferior HE projectile, lacked suitable smoke ammunition, and had decreased ammunition stowage. It was also pointed out that the higher muzzle velocity of the 76mm gun adversely affected the performance of the gun when firing high-explosive ammunition against typical targets such as enemy antitank guns. More alarmingly, the AFV&W section suggested that the blast obscuration problem of the

Ordnance also proposed sticking the T26 turret on the orphaned M6 heavy tanks, but this proved no more attractive to the Armored Center than the M6 itself as a result of the obvious automotive and operational problems of the archaic M6 tank.

76mm gun could be solved by training the tank commander to observe fire "from the ground laterally displaced from the tank." In other words, when firing the gun, the tank commander would have to dismount and position himself some distance from the tank, where he could observe the target without it being obscured by the gun blast and dust. No suggestions were offered about how the commander could communicate with his crew from this exposed position.

The senior officer present, Maj. Gen. Hugh Gaffey, had commanded the 2nd Armored Division on Sicily but was now assigned to Patton's embryonic Third Army in England. Aghast at the details of the new tank, he complained that it obviously had many bugs. Since there were so few of these tanks available at the moment, he recommended that they not be issued to troops and be allowed to accumulate until Ordnance back in the United States ironed out the problems. He argued that it was too late to introduce the type in view of the training burden it would impose, and he was concerned about the logistics problem its new ammunition type would pose. One of the younger officers, Capt. I. D. Brent from Eisenhower's AFV&W section, stepped into the fray and pointed out that tankers in the Italian

theater had requested that the 76mm tank completely replace the 75mm tanks and that although the 76mm gun failed to provide the desired level of penetration against the German Panther and Tiger tanks, it was still far better than the 75mm gun. A chart shown at the conference indicated that the 76mm gun could penetrate the Panther gun mantlet at 400 yards and the Tiger at 200 yards, while the 75mm gun could not penetrate it at any range. A compromise was suggested by Gen. W. B. Palmer that the 76mm tanks be allotted to separate tank battalions newly arriving in the United Kingdom and that the entire battalions be equipped with the new type rather than mixing the 75mm and 76mm guns in a single battalion as had been General Gillem's plan. In the interim, the new tanks were to be orphaned to depots in Britain until specific battalions were assigned to the task of converting to the new tanks.

After the U.S. First Army was committed to combat in Normandy in June 1944, the AFV&W section officers at Eisenhower's headquarters attempted to interest Patton's Third Army in the mothballed tanks prior to their deployment to France in late July. On June 12, 1944, a firing demonstration of the M4 tank with 76mm gun was conducted for Patton, the commanders of 2nd, 5th, and 6th Armored Divisions, and several other senior commanders. "All the commanders were reluctant to see it take the place of the 75mm tank gun in any quantity." Patton was willing to accept some so long as they were confined to separate tank battalions, but none were allotted to the Third Army prior to its transfer to France. "Patton knew as little about tanks as anybody I knew," commented one of the U.S. Army's best tank commanders in World War II, Gen. Bruce Clarke, striking to the heart of the matter. Clarke was not highlighting Patton's tactical genius, but rather his technical ignorance. Patton knew how to use tanks in combat, but he did not know much about tank design. While McNair's insistence on battle need made intuitive sense, it was based on the false premise that field commanders had the time and technical expertise to make difficult decisions on weapons. Ordnance had forfeited this responsibility by its continued promotion of pet projects, such as the T23, which were not battleworthy because of over-ambitious and flawed technology. So the War Department naturally turned to the field commanders but unfortunately received uninformed and short-sighted advice. Attitudes would soon change when U.S. tanks began to encounter the Panther.

THE BRITISH APPROACH

The British did not share the Americans' confusion over future tank gun needs and had been working on a more powerful 17-pounder (76mm) tank gun since 1941 as a hedge against future threats. A small number of the new weapons made a hasty combat debut as towed antitank guns in Tunisia in the spring of 1943, fitted on 25-pounder field gun carriages as a temporary expedient. The appearance of the Tiger I in Tunisia validated the British approach, and on March 9, 1943, the British General Staff established a new "Policy on Tanks," which noted that "fulfillment of their normal role necessitates that the main armament on the greater proportion of tanks of the medium class should be an effective HE weapon and at the same time as effective a weapon as possible against enemy armour of the type so far encountered in this war. The smaller proportion of tanks of the medium-class require a first-class anti-tank weapon for the engagement, if necessary, of armour heavier than that against which the dual-purpose weapon referred to above is effective."

Since the Sherman was likely to be the principal cruiser tank in the forthcoming campaign in northwest Europe, this inevitably meant that the Sherman would be rearmed with the new weapon once its design had matured. The British Sherman force

The British approach to the Sherman's firepower problem was to mount the 17-pounder antitank gun in the Sherman turret. The first pilots were built in December 1943. The Sherman Vc (17-pounder) shown here belonged to the Polish 1st Armored Division, which was training in England in early summer 1944 before departing for the Falaise Gap battles. PILSUDSKI INSTITUTE

Besides rearming the Sherman, the British also substituted the 17-pounder for the 3-inch gun in their M10 tank destroyers, like this example in France in 1944. PATTON MUSEUM

slated for operations in France would consist primarily of tanks with the existing dual-purpose 75mm gun, while two tanks per troop would be fitted with the new 17-pounder antitank gun. In contrast to the American 76mm gun program, which was pushed along by the development agencies with little enthusiasm from either the Armored Force or AGF, the British 17-pounder program was started earlier and enjoyed broad and official support from the development agencies, the tank force, and the general staff. Optimized for tank fighting, its poor high-explosive performance was simply ignored as irrelevant to its mission. The 17-pounder development was rushed, and its performance was not perfect. The early weapons displayed an alarming amount of flash, even with the muzzle brake, and, more alarmingly, a fair amount of flash at the breech end, even through the breech block. This earned it

the nickname Firefly, which was not an officially sanctioned name in 1944.

The British first proof-tested the 17-pounder in a Sherman turret on December 26, 1943. The fit in the turret was not ideal, but was adequate. However, the large ammunition invariably meant that ammunition stowage was less than in the 75mm tanks. To raise this to a more acceptable level, the bow gunner positions was deemed surplus and the cavity filled with extra ammunition stowage. The principal version of the Sherman converted with 17-pounder guns was the Sherman V (M4A4), which was redesignated as Sherman Vc to mark the difference. Other variants such as the Sherman I (M4) were also converted. The 17-pounder Sherman first saw combat in France starting on D-Day.

Plans to convert their Shermans to carry the more potent 17-pounder prompted the British

Because of the suspension of M4A4 production, the British Army was obliged to accept M4A1 (76mm) tanks as substitutes. These were generally fobbed off to secondary theaters, especially Italy. This is a Sherman IIA of the Pretoria Regiment of the 6th South African Armoured Division in Poiana, Italy, on April 29, 1945.

Army to reject acquisition of the new American versions of the Sherman with the 76mm gun. Nevertheless, Britain ended up with 1,330 M4A1 (76mm) because of the cancellation of further production of the preferred M4A4 (75mm) and most other 75mm types—except the M4A3 (75mm), which was sequestered for the U.S. Army, and the M4A2 (75mm), which was earmarked for the Russians. The M4A1 (76mm) was designated as Sherman IIA in British service. On receiving the M4A1 (76mm) in 1944, the British Army was at a loss about its potential distribution and role. The 17-pounder conversion program was well underway, but a cursory study in the summer of 1944 concluded that "for a variety of technical considerations connected with the positioning of the trunnions, the telescope and the elevating gear, it would be necessary to carry out a major redesign and extensive modification of the turret" to convert the M4A1

(76mm) into a 17-pounder tank. Furthermore, the first conversions would not be ready until April 1945. As a result, the conversion of the 76mm tanks into Fireflies was not pursued. The British Army was not very happy with the 76mm gun for most of the same reasons as U.S. tankers prior to Normandy.

To simplify logistics, the Sherman IIA was mostly earmarked for the Italian theater, where anti-tank performance was not as vital as it was in north-west Europe. As a result, by the end of 1944, four units in Italy were supplied with the Sherman IIA, three British and one South African, and there were 418 Sherman IIA tanks there at the end of 1944, which increased to 484 in 1945. There was no intention to widely distribute the Sherman IIA to units in northwest Europe, but the growing shortage of 75mm tanks to convert into 17-pounder Fireflies changed this policy. The Polish 1st Armored Division had been badly battered during the fighting in

The only element of Montgomery's 21st Army Group to use the Sherman IIA with 76mm gun was the Polish 1st Armored Division, which received them from British stocks after suffering heavy losses while closing off the Falaise Gap in August 1944. Festooned with spare tracks for added protection, this Polish Sherman IIA crosses a Bailey bridge in the Netherlands in 1945. PILSUDSKI INSTITUTE

the Falaise Gap in August 1944, and so it was earmarked to begin receiving the Sherman IIA as replacements. The first batch of Sherman IIAs was received by the Poles on November 20, 1944, and by end of the war, more than 180 Sherman IIA tanks were delivered to the Poles. The Polish 1st Armored Division was the only unit of Montgomery's 21st Army Group to see combat with this type in northwest Europe.

A similar reaction to the panzer threat occurred in the Soviet Union. After confronting the Panther and Tiger during the Kursk campaign in July 1943, the Red Army lifted a long-standing ban on T-34 upgrades that had been in place since 1942 in order to maximize production. The Soviets initiated a crash program to field a T-34 capable of defeating the Panther and Tiger. To speed the program along, the Soviet tank designers developed a new 85mm tank gun based on existing 85mm antiaircraft gun ammunition. This version of the T-34, named the T-34-85, entered production in March 1944, in time to take part in the spring 1944 battles. Likewise, the KV heavy tank was completely redesigned, rearmed with a massive 122mm tank gun, and rushed into production as the IS-2 heavy tank in early 1944.

CHAPTER 5

Bocage Buster

THE U.S. ARMY BEGAN THE CAMPAIGN in France with amphibious landings in Normandy on D-Day; the first American troops ashore from the landing craft rode Sherman tanks. Unlike earlier landings in 1943 in the Mediterranean, the Wehrmacht vigorously defended the Normandy beaches, making Omaha Beach an unexpected bloodbath. More difficulties awaited the U.S. Army as it advanced into the Norman countryside. None of the Allied planners had anticipated the tactical consequences of the Norman landscape, especially the thick hedgerows known as bocage. In such terrain, armored divisions had little use, and the long-neglected infantry tank battalions would have to carry the burden of the tank fighting for the first six weeks of the summer campaign. Through ingenuity and perseverance, the tank and tank destroyer battalions played a significant role in the Normandy campaign.

BLOODY OMAHA

The plans for Operation Overlord anticipated the use of tanks in the initial amphibious landings to reinforce the infantry as had been done in North Africa in November 1942, Sicily in July 1943, Salerno in September 1943, and Anzio in February 1944. The original British planners were heavily influenced by the lessons of the ill-fated 1942 Dieppe raid, during which the Canadian Churchill tanks had faced substantial mobility problems because of the terrain and the Royal Navy's tank landing craft had taken serious losses to German artillery. The technical solution to the landing craft problem was the development of duplex drive (DD) tanks, which converted normal Shermans into amphibious tanks using a canvas skirt for buoyancy and a set of propellers for propulsion in the water. Although the U.S. Army initially went along with this idea and converted 350 M4A1 tanks into the "Donald Duck" configuration, apprehension about this idea grew after exercises on the English coast near Slapton Sands, where a number of tanks and their crews drowned. Lt. Gen. Leonard Gerow, the commander of V Corps, which landed on Omaha Beach, questioned why this unproven and obviously fragile technology was being used, when a proven technology, deep-wading tanks, was available. Deep-wading tanks—waterproofed Sherman tanks fitted with a pair of snorkels to provide air to the engine—were first used on Sicily in July 1943 and again at Salerno and Anzio. This configuration allowed them to be dropped in water up to the top of their turrets, and they could simply crawl to shore under their own power. While it placed the landing craft, tank (LCT) at greater risk to enemy shore batteries, this had not proven to be much of a problem in the previous landings in the Mediterranean.

A pair of M4 medium tanks from V Corps practice amphibious landings on the English coast in November 1943. Both tanks are fitted with deep-wading trunks that permitted them to land in water up to the height of their turret.

An LCT loads at a port in Devonshire on the southern English coast on June 4, 1944, prior to the Normandy landings. It is carrying M4 tanks of the 70th Tank Battalion while one of the unit's T2 tank recovery vehicles backs up the access ramp. These vehicles have the deep-wading trunks and would land at Utah Beach on D-Day.

As a compromise, the tank battalions assigned to the Normandy landings were reconfigured, and instead of each having three companies with sixteen DD tanks each, they would have two companies of DD tanks and one of deep-wading tanks. The plan called for a single tank battalion to support each of the infantry's regimental combat teams, meaning two tank battalions at Omaha Beach and one at Utah Beach. The DD tanks would lead the way, scheduled to arrive at H-Hour minus 5, five minutes before the first wave of infantry.

The relatively modest tank support planned for the Overlord landings was based on the presumption that the landings would be confronted by the same tactics the Wehrmacht had used in the Mediterranean theater. German doctrine argued that it was pointless to try to defend every inch of beach and more prudent to keep a mobile reserve of panzer divisions and motorized infantry some distance from the beach. Once the landing zone was identified, the beachhead could be vigorously attacked by this mobile reserve. Unfortunately, Hitler had other ideas and in 1943 had ordered the creation of the Atlantic Wall along the French coast, studded with bunkers and concrete gun casemates. In fact, the wall was as much a propaganda ploy as a serious fortification and presented a serious barrier only on the Pas de Calais, where the Germans

The Dog White section of Omaha Beach is littered with shattered vehicles and craft at low tide on the evening of D-Day, June 6, 1944. The M4 tank, *C-13 Ceaseless*, is from Company C, 743rd Tank Battalion, and was disabled on the beach after losing a track.

Arriving late on D-Day, LCT(A)-2273 struggles toward the St. Laurent draw, where in the early afternoon, it deposited its two wading tanks and one dozer, which belonged to Company A, 743rd Tank Battalion. Damaged by weather and German fire, the LCT sank later in the day.

expected the Allies to land. In Normandy, the Germans built few fortifications until early 1944, when Field Marshal Erwin Rommel arrived. Hitler personally assigned Rommel the task of defeating any Allied landing in France. Rommel had commanded German forces in northern Italy in the autumn of 1943, when the German counterattack failed to push the Allied landing at Salerno back into the sea. The failure of Salerno and the subsequent failure of the panzer counterattack at Anzio in February 1944 convinced Rommel that German tactical doctrine was fundamentally flawed. He wanted the defense to stop the invasion dead on the beach, instead of waiting for a counterattack. This led to bitter—and

This M4A1 (named *Adeline II*) of Company A, 741st Tank Battalion, was damaged on Omaha Beach on D-Day after its rear bogie assembly was hit by a 50mm antitank gun during a duel with a German bunker in the E-1 St. Laurent draw. The tank could still move in spite of the damage but could not surmount the sea wall to exit the beach. It was later recovered by the battalion's T2 tank recovery vehicle and is seen being towed through Colleville after D-Day for repair.

never fully resolved—arguments between Rommel and the other German commanders in France.

But Rommel's appearance on the scene reinvigorated the Atlantic Wall program, especially in Normandy, where extensive construction began in March and April 1944, long after the Allies had completed planning for Overlord. In February 1944, Rommel visited the Grandcamps sector of lower Normandy and stood on the bluffs near the villages of Colleville and Vierville. He sensed the similarity of the geography to Salerno and told the assembled officers that "the fate of Europe would be decided on this beach." Instead of being held by a single battalion from a third-rate static division, this sector of the beach was reinforced by a fresh, full-strength infantry division newly raised and trained and led by combat-experienced veterans of the Russian front. The stretch from Vierville to Colleville was reinforced by an infantry regiment, parts of the division's artillery regiment, a multiple rocket launcher battalion, *panzerjäger* and assault gun companies, and a hefty increase in concrete for new bunkers and pillboxes. This section of the Grandcamps sector was codenamed Omaha Beach by the Allies, who did

Cannonball, an M4 of Company C, 70th Tank Battalion, drowned in a deep shell crater at Utah Beach and recovered after D-Day. It was one of the tanks fitted for the T40 Whiz-Bang demolition rocket launcher for attacking the Germans' fortified sea walls; this feature was removed prior to the landings because of the hazard it posed to the crew.

The first tank off Utah Beach was this M4A1 duplex drive tank of Company A, 70th Tank Battalion, which was disabled on one of the causeways leading away from the beach. It was pushed over the side of the causeway to permit other tanks and troops to pass.

not discover that the Wehrmacht had moved the 352nd Infantry Division onto the beach in this area until D-Day.

The tank landings on Omaha Beach on the morning of June 6, 1944, had very mixed results. On the western side of Omaha, the 741st Tank Battalion launched its two companies of DD tanks 5,000 yards from shore in spite of rough seas and warnings from navy officers. Only two DD tanks managed to swim ashore, three more were delivered directly to

A group of M4 tanks of the 3rd Armored Division prepares to load aboard LSTs for transport to Normandy in June 1944. Most tanks delivered to France in June 1944 were fitted with deep-wading trunks to permit the LSTs to land them from a short distance off shore. After D-Day, most were landed directly on shore. The 3rd arrived on June 23, 1944.

Although duplex drive tanks were not especially effective during the Normandy landings, they had fewer problems during the landings in southern France on August 15, 1944, as part of Operation Dragoon. This M4A1 duplex drive amphibious tank from the 753rd Tank Battalion landed near St. Tropez. This shows the canvas flotation collar folded down after the tank has reached shore.

A pair of duplex drive tanks is pictured in front of an LST during the landings on the Mediterranean coast of southern France in August 1944. Twenty-eight duplex drive tanks were landed by three tank battalions during Operation Dragoon.

shore from their LCT, and the remaining twenty-seven sank as they struggled to reach the beach. The two DD tanks were the first U.S. troops on Omaha Beach and attacked the Germans despite furious counterfire. Within a few minutes, LCTs arrived with the deep-wading tanks and Sherman tank dozers, although two LCTs had sunk en route and others were delayed. So the 741st Tank Battalion had only sixteen of its original fifty-six Shermans: five DD tanks, six wading tanks, and five dozers landed around H-Hour, 0630 hours.

On the eastern side of Omaha Beach, immortalized in the film *Saving Private Ryan,* the 743rd Tank Battalion achieved greater success because of more prudent judgments about the fragility of the DD tanks. The navy commander in charge of the LCTs convinced the senior army officer that the seas were too rough, and as a result, the LCTs began setting down on Omaha Beach one minute before H-Hour. The LCTs managed to deliver forty-two of the fifty-

six tanks of the 743rd Tank Battalion: thirty-two DD tanks, seven wading tanks, and three dozers.

The Sherman tanks, like the infantry and engineers they were supporting, faced an intense day of fighting along the beach trying to knock out the numerous pillboxes and defensive positions. Their biggest problem was the terrain on Omaha. Unlike the other D-Day beaches, Omaha was lined with high bluffs that were too steep for the tanks to climb. Exit was limited to four ravines, or draws, that the Germans had reinforced with pillboxes, antitank guns, barriers, and antitank traps. As a result, the tanks spent most of the day trying to fight their way through the kill-sacks the Germans had arrayed across the four ravines while the infantry skirted around them by moving over the weakly defended bluffs. By the end of the day, the draws were cleared, and the surviving tanks began moving inland—only 2 tanks of the 741st Tank Battalion and 39 of the 743rd Tank Battalion of their original 112 Shermans.

In contrast to Omaha Beach, none of the duplex drive tanks launched during Operation Dragoon were sunk, although two were lost to mines on shore.

One of the infantry officers later said that the tanks "had saved the day. They shot the hell out of the Germans and got the hell shot out of them."

Utah Beach stood in complete contrast to Omaha Beach. The flat terrain was much more suitable for landings, German defenses were far less extensive, and the German troops were from a third-rate static division. The waters off Utah were more sheltered than Omaha, and the 70th Tank Battalion managed to swim twenty-seven of its thirty-two DD tanks to shore, and LCTs landed twelve of six-teen wading tanks. The parachute landings by the 82nd and 101st Airborne Divisions in the areas behind Utah Beach had weakened the resolve of the German defenders, and the beach defenses were quickly overcome. The main tactical problem at Utah Beach was that the Germans had flooded the flat farmland behind the beach, making exit difficult except along a handful of causeways. By mid-morning, the Sherman tanks of the 70th Tank Battalion had pushed along one of the causeways, heading for a linkup with the paratroopers later in the day.

HEDGEROW HELL

On D-Day plus 1, Sherman tanks fanned out of the Omaha and Utah beachheads in support of the infantry and paratroopers. They were completely unprepared for the terrain that faced them. The Norman countryside was broken up into small farm fields edged on all sides by high hedgerows called bocage, which had been created over the centuries as a means to protect the fields from the harsh Atlantic winds. The bocage was clearly evident in overhead photographs taken by Allied intelligence before the landings, but the Allies presumed that they were akin to the much smaller hedgerows on the English side of the Channel. The French bocage was typically much higher, with the base of the hedge often four to six feet of earth and rock, covered with a tangle of bushes, black thorn, and beech trees. It was, in fact, a natural fortified area. Unlike a man-made fort, it went on for dozens of miles along the coast until it reached the more open farm lands around Caen in the British sector, and it was over twenty miles deep, reaching beyond the city of St. Lô. It would take the U.S. First Army six weeks to fight its way through this "hedgerow hell" to St. Lô.

The bocage greatly simplified German defenses since it provided natural defenses. The few roads that penetrated the bocage could be easily mined, and key crossroads could be covered by antitank guns and *panzerschreck* antitank rocket launchers. Initial attempts to overcome the bocage using tanks proved costly. Many of the hedges were too tall to be surmounted by a Sherman, even if it raced across the field before impacting against the hedgerow. In the case of smaller hedges, the Sherman would expose its thin belly armor as it tried to crawl over the hedge, making it an easy target for German troops on the other side. Tank casualties rose at an alarming rate as the U.S. Army tried to learn the tricks of fighting in the bocage. American planners had anticipated

GIs of the 4th Infantry Division escort a group of German prisoners as an M4 medium tank of the 70th Tank Battalion passes by during the fighting west of Ste.-Mère-Église on June 10, 1944, as part of the VII Corps' effort to expand the Utah beachhead toward Cherbourg.

A well-camouflaged M4 of the 70th Tank Battalion is passed by a medic's jeep in bocage country while supporting the 4th Infantry Division.

An M4 tank from the 740th Tank Battalion supports a group of GIs during the street fighting in Cherbourg, which began in earnest on June 21 with an assault by the 4th and 79th Infantry Divisions.

combat attrition comparable to that in Italy, about 7 percent of tank strength per month. In Normandy, the tank casualties were more than double that.

Bocage fighting required combined-arms tactics: the coordinated use of tanks, infantry, and artillery to secure a common objective. Unfortunately, the U.S. Army had neglected the infantry-support role of the separate tank battalions until late 1943 and offered little or no tank-infantry training. The basic field manuals for tank-infantry tactics were still being distributed, and the infantry divisions and tank battalions in Normandy had to improvise. Fortunately for

A very clear example of why a Sherman was not a good match for a Panther. This particular M4A1 engaged in an unequal duel with a Panther from the Panzer Lehr Division and is seen here on July 20, after the German panzer offensive had been beaten back. Besides the six hits from the Panther's 75mm gun, there are two smaller holes on the M4A1 from *panzerfaust* or *panzerschreck* rocket launchers.

the U.S. Army, the Wehrmacht had realized that the bocage country was not suitable for tank use and had deployed few AFVs in the June 1944 fighting, and most of those were to the east fighting against the British and Canadian divisions in the open farm country near Caen.

Almost immediately, the army abandoned the concept of keeping the separate tank and tank destroyer battalions under corps or army control and instead attached them to infantry divisions—usually one tank and one tank destroyer battalion per division. The usual deployment practice was to assign each of the three Sherman tank companies to the

three infantry regiments in each division. Some regiments used the entire tank company together for missions, while others further distributed the tanks on the basis of one tank platoon per infantry battalion. The remainder of the tank battalion was used in a variety of fashions. The light tank company presented a problem since most infantry units found that the 37mm gun and light armor of the M5A1 light tank made it less suitable for close infantry support than the M4 medium tank, especially in the bocage country. Some divisions assigned the light tank company to the divisional reconnaissance troop, while others kept it as a division mobile reserve to

The incompatibility of tank and infantry radios posed a significant problem in combined tank-infantry operations in the summer of 1944. This infantry radioman with an SCR-300 walkie-talkie could not communicate with the neighboring M4 medium tank because the radios operated in different frequency bands.

reinforce other tank companies. The M4 (105mm) assault guns in the headquarters company were a popular asset to reinforce divisional artillery or as a form of mobile reinforcing artillery that could be assigned as the need arose. Some battalions withdrew the single assault guns in each of the three Sherman tank companies and consolidated them with the headquarters company's assault guns to form a six-gun platoon.

The success or failure of the separate tank battalions depended on the skill of the infantry commanders in the use of tanks. Many infantry divisions had not trained with a separate tank battalion and had a poor appreciation of proper tank tactics. Tank battalions were frequently misused as a result. Most often, the problem was the overestimation of their capabilities and underestimation of the vulnerability of the tanks, especially when used in small sub-units

of company size or smaller. Tank commanders bitterly complained that the infantry thought tanks were invulnerable and ordered them on missions where they faced entrenched German positions bristling with deadly PaK 40 antitank guns and *panzerfaust* rockets. Inexperienced infantry divisions would simply burn up tank battalions assuming that they would get new attachments when needed. In contrast, infantry divisions with a permanently attached tank battalion learned to value the combat support they offered and to use them carefully, knowing they would get no more tanks.

The problems caused by the lack of training between infantry and tanks prior to D-Day led AGF to print a 1st Infantry Division report as "Operations Memorandum 1" on September 2, 1944, outlining the proper methods to employ infantry and tanks successfully in combat. This report was circu-

One solution to the incompatibility of tank and infantry radios was to supply the infantry with tank radios. This is an SCR-509 tank radio mounted on a packboard by the 41st Armored Infantry Battalion. The main problem with this solution was the shortage of extra tank radios and the heavy weight of the radio and its associated battery.

lated in both Washington and Europe as a means to help commanders stay abreast of important new developments. This eight-page report was based on the lessons of fighting in Normandy and was intended to act as a stopgap until the army published a suitable new field manual on tank-infantry tactics.

A later army study concluded that

the combat team has become the keystone of all successful operations. The complexity of the new weapons and the limitations of each gives a complete interdependence of them on others to attain efficiency. Nothing is more helpless than a lone tank without artillery or infantry support. Its inherent blindness, its

weight and size make it a natural target of all enemy fires. If friendly artillery is not coordinated, a hidden group of anti-tank guns will soon get it. Or if there is no infantry near, as soon as the tank slows down it becomes easy prey to an enemy infantryman with an anti-tank rocket. On the other hand, in operations where the tank-infantry-artillery and engineers are given their proper mission, one for which they have trained together as a team, the strength of each will complement the weakness of the other, thus making the strong concerted effort necessary for success.

Infantry divisions had the most success with tanks when the tank battalion was assigned to the

A useful solution to communication between infantry and accompanying tanks was to fit a field telephone on the tank that was linked to the tank's internal intercom system. This is a test of such a set-up on an M4A1 shortly before Operation Cobra in July 1944.

same division for prolonged periods of time, which enabled joint training and an integration of the tank battalion headquarters within the divisional command. Some corps had the sense to semipermanently attach tank battalions to a specific division and leave them attached for several months. In turn, this allowed the tank battalion to regularly assign specific companies to specific regiments on a long-term basis. Under these circumstances, lessons learned in combat led to more effective tactics, and confidence grew between the tankers and infantrymen. The General Board report on tanks after the war noted that if "the battalion had been an organic unit and trained with the division prior to combat, a better mutual understanding and spirit of cooperation would have always prevailed."

The bocage fighting in June–July 1944 highlighted the lack of attention paid to realistic tank-infantry training. Even a day of joint training before a major operation was a big improvement since officers from both units were able to better understand the capabilities, requirements, and limitations of tanks supporting infantry. At the small-unit level, tank-infantry coordination was best managed by assigning a rifle squad to each tank platoon for direct support. The squad was responsible for protecting the tank from close-in attack by German infantry, and regular attachment of the squad avoided the need to continually retrain new units in tank-infantry cooperation.

One of the most significant technical problems in tank-infantry cooperation was the inability of the

The U.S. Army's first extensive contact with the Panther came on July 11, 1944, when the Panzer Lehr Division attempted to push the U.S. 9th Infantry Division back over the Vire River. The attack was a shambles, and numerous Panthers were lost to the infantry's 57mm antitank guns as well as to a battalion of M10 tank destroyers.

tanks and infantry to communicate because of the incompatibility of their radios. The army had belatedly recognized this problem prior to D-Day but had not yet resolved it. American infantry platoons in Normandy had a single hand-held SCR-586 "handie-talkie" AM radio to communicate with other platoons and company headquarters. At company level, the infantry had the backpack SCR-300 "walkie-talkie" FM radio to communicate with higher commands such as battalion headquarters. The standard tank radios, such as the SCR-508, were FM transceivers operating in different bands than the infantry's SCR-300 and unable to communicate at all with the AM SCR-586 at platoon level. So none of these three radios could talk to one another.

The planned methods for communication prior to Normandy were hopelessly unrealistic. The typical deployment of a tank battalion to an infantry division permitted one tank company to be attached to each infantry regiment. The existing tactical doctrine established that the tank company commander would contact the infantry regiment headquarters, which in turn would pass the information to companies and platoons. While this perhaps made sense on paper, it was totally inadequate in combat. Imagine for a moment that a tank is advancing in support of an infantry company and one of the infantry platoons spots a German antitank gun lurking in the bocage. According to doctrine, he would inform his platoon leader, who would radio company headquarters via the SCR-538; the company headquarters would then radio regimental headquarters via the SCR-300; the regimental headquarters would radio the tank company commander via a separate FM radio link; and finally the tank company commander would radio the tank platoon commander nearest the threatening antitank gun. Of course, this warning would come minutes after the German gun had already blasted the tank platoon. In close terrain like the bocage, immediate communication between the infantry and the tanks was essential to their survival in combat and the joint prosecution of their missions.

Voice communication between the infantry and tanks offered an obvious solution but proved unreliable and dangerous. It assumed that the tank commander was standing with his head exposed outside the turret and not wearing his tanker's helmet, which contained the earphones that the commander used to communicate with his crew; while wearing it, he had difficulty hearing anything except for the tank intercom communications. Even if the infantry shouted to the tank commander, the chances of him hearing the shout were small—even less likely given the din of a moving tank and the usual noises on the battlefield. So some form of radio communication was the only practical solution, though a different configuration than the available network.

Tank and infantry units in Normandy began to improvise. Some infantry units tried to give tank commanders spare SCR-586 radios to use from inside the tank, but this seldom worked because AM radios were vulnerable to interference inside a moving tank. (This is why U.S. tanks used FM radios, not AM radios.) Some tank battalions took spare SCR-509 tank radios and gave them to infantry companies or battalion headquarters, which mounted them on infantry pack-boards that allowed them to be carried into combat. This was hardly ideal since the tank radios were heavy and bulky to start with and needed a separate battery supply. Other units experimented with placing infantry SCR-300 walkie-talkies inside tanks with the antenna sticking out through an open hatch. This was actually the most satisfactory of all the improvised radio solutions, but the SCR-300 was new in the summer of 1944, and the lack of surplus radios in Normandy precluded their wide employment.

Even with this stopgap, communication between tanks and infantry at the small-unit level was still limited to infantry company level, which was too far up the chain of command during small-unit operation. Aside from radios, the army also made extensive use of field telephones, which offered another short-term, though hardly ideal, solution. In this case, a tank commander would receive a field telephone, whose wire would be routed out of the turret to the rear of the tank, where a reel of field telephone wire would be spooled out behind the tank as it advanced forward. Needless to say, this was not especially practical if the tank was traveling long distances, and of course, the field telephone wire could be easily broken.

A more satisfactory approach involved wiring the field telephone into the tank's intercom system. This allowed a field telephone to be mounted in a box on the rear of the tank, and an infantryman could walk up behind the tank and give information to the crew. This proved to be a more complicated technical issue than it first seemed since incorrect installation could jam the tank's intercom system. The U.S. First Army developed a standardized design for wiring the tank with an EE-8 field telephone by a process that ordnance units could complete in the field. A conversion program was undertaken prior to the start of Operation Cobra at the end of July 1944. The field telephone usually was mounted in an empty .30-cal machine-gun ammunition box welded to the back of the tank. An infantryman could walk behind the tank and communicate with the crew, pointing out targets. This solution was not perfect: it exposed the infantryman to enemy fire, and he could not accompany the tank if it was moving at normal speeds. But it was better than nothing and remained in widespread use during the European campaign and, later, the Korean War. (The U.S. Army would relearn this lesson in Iraq in 2004.)

The improvised use of the SCR-300 and pack-mount SCR-508 continued until the autumn of 1944, when a dedicated tank-infantry radio, the AN/VRC-3, began arriving. A modified version of the infantry's SCR-300 better adapted to tank use, the army issued them on a scale of two per tank platoon (the platoon leader's and platoon sergeant's tanks) and one at company level. It took from September to December 1944 before they were in widespread use.

Despite this lesson, McNair and AGF refused to make the tank battalion attachments permanent, arguing that there were not enough tank battalions to go around. This was a specious argument: the number of infantry divisions deployed in the ETO was close to the number of separate tank battalions deployed there. The same issue affected the tank destroyer battalions. Although tank destroyer doctrine involved retaining the battalions in a corps or army reserve and then deploying them to resist a panzer attack, this was a completely useless concept when the army was on the offensive. Massed panzer attacks were a thing of the past, and the Germans had the same difficulties as the Americans in operating tanks en masse in the bocage. The infantry constantly demanded more fire support to blast its way out of the bocage, and no commanders were willing to leave the tank destroyers idle because of a patently mistaken tactical doctrine. As a result, the tank destroyer battalions were attached to the infantry in the same fashion as the tank battalions, with the same sorts of problems. Most infantry divisions on the front line in Normandy in the summer of 1944 had both a tank battalion and a tank destroyer battalion attached.

The tank destroyer battalions had some unique problems. By Normandy, a portion of the battalions had switched from the tank-like M10 tank destroyer to towed 3-inch guns because of McNair's mistaken ideas about towed guns. These towed battalions had an impossible time in Normandy since they were far more vulnerable than the armored M10 battalions when providing close support to attacking infantry, and they were not mobile enough to provide a fast response when German tanks or assault guns suddenly appeared. The 3-inch gun was so heavy that it proved very difficult to move in the Normandy hedgerows. Once it was moved into position by its half-track, the gun crews had difficulty getting it into firing position. Besides being clumsy to deploy, the 3-inch gun was large and difficult to conceal, and crews were more vulnerable to small-arms and mortar fire than the M10 tank destroyer. In addition, infantry commanders appreciated the psychological boost that self-propelled tank destroyers gave their troops compared to the towed guns. During the hedgerow fighting, troops used towed guns in their intended antitank role only infrequently. Most of the fighting for the first two months of the campaign was a close-combat infantry struggle, and the towed antitank guns were too clumsy to provide mobile support. As a result, it became standard policy in most battalions of the First Army to leave only two companies for antitank defense and place one company behind the lines in the field artillery role.

One of the few times that the towed tank destroyers were put to the test occurred during the German Avranches counterattack near Mortain in August 1944. The 30th Infantry Division, which bore the brunt of the attack, was supported by the 823rd Tank Destroyer Battalion—the first battalion converted to towed guns in 1943 and hence the most experienced. During the course of the fighting, the battalion claimed fifteen panzers knocked out, but its own losses were heavy: eleven of its thirty-six guns, two platoons overrun, and 104 troops dead or missing. Once again, the combination of infantry 57mm guns and bazooka teams helped to bolster the infantry defense and stem the attack. The fighting at Mortain made it clear that antitank guns and bazookas, in spite of their technical limitations, were still very effective when embedded in a stout infantry defense; operating independently in the tank destroyer battalions, towed antitank guns were very vulnerable to being outflanked and overrun by the panzers.

The problems with the inadequate penetration of the 3-inch gun against the Panther led to improvisations inspired by German examples. During the Panzer Lehr Division's attack in early July, a small number of 90mm antiaircraft guns had been hastily positioned for antitank defense based on the Germans' use of the 88mm flak gun. Later in the summer, with the Luftwaffe little in evidence, the U.S. First Army formalized this option and assigned a single 90mm antiaircraft battalion to each corps for antitank defense. Nevertheless, the 90mm guns were used against German tank attacks only rarely during the summer and fall. Instead, the 90mm battalions were generally employed as field artillery; a First Army report indicated that "very satisfying results were obtained by using this weapon for long-range harassing and interdiction fires beyond the capabilities of divisional artillery." Later, this policy change would have consequences in the Ardennes, where 90mm antiaircraft guns provided an important source of powerful antitank capability in the first few desperate days of the Battle of the Bulge.

The summer fighting convinced Bradley's 12th Army Group that the towed 3-inch gun tank destroyer battalions had failed completely. In a September 1944 report to Eisenhower, the headquarters firmly disagreed with AGF's plans to deploy half of all tank destroyer battalions in this flawed configuration. Of the fifty-two tank destroyer battalions assigned to the ETO, Bradley wanted only twelve left in the towed configuration, and then only if converted to the new and more powerful T5E1 90mm towed antitank gun. This should have been the end of McNair's folly, but armies take time to react, and the towed battalions would still be in service to face their greatest challenge in the Ardennes in December 1944.

The self-propelled tank destroyers proved much more valuable, although they were seldom used in their intended role. In most cases, they functioned as surrogate tanks, with the battalions being deployed much like the separate tank battalions. A report by the commanding officer of the 5th Tank Destroyer Group in Normandy describes their successful use in the fighting:

> What is not in the field manuals on tank destroyer use is the effective support which they render to a fighting infantry at the time of actual combat. An infantryman has his fortitude well tested, and the mere presence of self-propelled tank destroyers in his immediate vicinity gives a tremendous shot of courage to the committed infantryman. For example, at Chambois [during the closing of the Falaise Gap in August 1944], an infantry battalion moved toward the town with utter fearlessness to enemy artillery, mortar, and small-arms fire when accompanied by some M10s. However, the M10s were delayed in crossing a stream for about thirty-five minutes. During this time, the infantry battalion continued to their objective which dominated a roadway leading to Chambois. They fought infantry, they bazooka-ed some armored vehicles including three tanks on the road, but on realizing that the M10s weren't firing, they started a retirement. Leading the parade to the rear was a short lad known as "Shorty." Shorty in the lead was the first man to see a platoon of M10s who had finally gotten across the stream. Shorty took a good look at the M10s, turned around, and

shouted to the others, "Hell boys, what are we retiring for, here come the TDs!" The entire company in mass immediately reversed their direction and returned to their excellent positions, and to say they fought for the next few hours with unusual bravery is stating it mildly. The point I am trying to make is that the appearance and the knowledge that self-propelled tank-destroyers were at hand was a major reason that the infantry attained success and victory. Often many men die or suffer to retain or exploit IF the inspiration furnished by the presence of self-propelled tank destroyers is known. The towed guns can be just as brave and thoroughly trained, but they never give much 'oomph' to the fighting doughboy when the chips are really down.

The army frequently encountered German armor in the bocage fighting, though seldom in large quantities. The most common types were StuG III and StuG IV assault guns attached to the infantry and panzergrenadier divisions and 75mm *panzerjäger,* such as the Marder III, attached to infantry divisions. For example, U.S. paratroopers saw extensive fighting against StuG IVs of the 17th SS Panzergrenadier Division in the fighting around Carentan in June 1944. The first major clashes with German panzers occurred in early July near the Vire River when the Panzer Lehr Division moved into this sector to prevent an American breakthrough to St. Lô. Here the first extensive employment of the Panther took place on July 11 when the Panzer Lehr launched a local counterattack. Infantry 57mm antitank guns and M10 tank destroyers beat off this attack, and Panzer Lehr lost almost a quarter of its effective combat strength in the attack. As the U.S. Army had already found, it was very difficult to conduct panzer attacks in the bocage against determined infantry. Although neither the 57mm antitank gun nor the 3-inch gun on the M10 tank destroyer could penetrate the frontal armor of the Panther, its side armor was not much greater than that of the Sherman and was very vulnerable.

BOCAGE BUSTING

As the Shermans and infantry gradually learned to conduct coordinated operations in the bocage, they began exploring ways to punch through the hedgerows. One method was to use Sherman dozer tanks to smash through the bocage, but these were too few in number in June 1944, and some of the thicker hedgerows were too sturdy even for dozers. The tank battalions wanted a method that could rapidly breach the bocage and surprise the German defenders.

In keeping with their traditional mission of overcoming obstacles and fortifications, American engineers were the first to develop solutions. The 121st Engineer Combat Battalion came up with the idea of placing two twenty-four-pound explosive charges

at the base of the bocage to blow a gap through the hedge. First tried on June 24, 1944, with Shermans of the 747th Tank Battalion providing covering fire, the explosives barely created a gap. The engineers concluded that at least twice the explosive strength would be needed, and the battalion commander calculated that a tank company penetrating one and a half miles through bocage country would encounter thirty-four separate hedgerows, requiring seventeen tons of explosive per company or about sixty tons per battalion. This was clearly impractical.

The engineers continued to experiment with explosive breaching and devised the idea of attaching a pair of pointed wooden beams, dubbed the "salad fork," to the front of a Sherman. The Sherman would

The "salad fork" developed by the 747th Tank Battalion was one of the first attempts to develop a device to cut through the hedgerows. The two pointed timbers created tunnels in the base of the hedge that could be filled with explosives.

A "salad fork" in operation by the 747th Tank Battalion during the bocage fighting in July 1944. This technique led to later and more successful bocage busters.

The "green dozer" was developed after the "salad fork" to push through hedgerows. It was less successful but was used in small numbers by the 747th Tank Battalion. It is seen here on an M4 of the 747th Tank Battalion.

then drive at high speed into the hedgerow, pushing the salad fork deep into the base. When the Sherman backed off and extracted the salad fork, there would be two deep tunnels at the base at the hedgerow that were ideal for blasting a gap. An accompanying engineer team would stuff the holes with a prepackaged demolition charge consisting of fifteen pounds of explosive in the fiber-board ammunition containers used to transport 105mm artillery ammunition. M29 Weasel tracked utility vehicles would follow the tank-engineer team, bringing along extra explosive. This idea proved attractive enough after tests that the

The best known of the bocage busters was the Culin hedgerow cutter, more commonly called the "rhino."

A "rhino" pushes through a hedgerow during First Army trials prior to Operation Cobra.

The 3rd Armored Division used its own distinctive style of rhino, the T2 Douglas device. It can be distinguished by the triangular plates on either side.

29th Infantry Division decided to give it a try during the next major offensive against St. Lô. The division's commander, Maj. Gen. Charles Gerhardt, created a special training area near Couvains to permit the infantry, tanks, and engineers to practice and perfect the method. They developed their own tactics: "one squad, one tank, one field." The salad fork was first tested in combat on July 11, 1944, while supporting the 116th Infantry of the 29th Division, one of the two regiments that had been in the first wave at Omaha Beach. The salad fork and new engineer tactics were so successful that they were copied by other units, including the 703rd Tank Battalion attached to the neighboring 4th Infantry Division.

In studying the results of the July 11 attack, it became obvious that the salad fork was not an ideal solution since the timbers were often bent or wrenched off the tanks during the violent collision with the hedge. Interestingly enough, the impact of the salad fork alone could breach a hedge in some cases. These experiences prompted Lt. Charles Green to devise a more durable bocage-busting device, variously called a "tank bumper," "brush cutter," or "green dozer," made out of lengths of steel

One of the most versatile versions of the Sherman tank was the tank dozer, first used on D-Day to help clear beach obstacles. This tank dozer, named *Apache*, is from Company A, 746th Tank Battalion, and is seen near Tribehou on July 25, 1944, during Operation Cobra.

railroad tracks. A number of these were welded to the tanks of the 747th Tank Battalion in mid-July for the upcoming Operation Cobra offensive.

While this was taking place, the commander of the neighboring 102nd Cavalry Reconnaissance Squadron (CRS), the V Corps' cavalry unit, asked for suggestions from the M5A1 light tank crews of his F Troop about how to get through the bocage. Sgt. Curtis G. Culin Jr. suggested mounting a knife-blade cutter on the front of the tank that could create a gap in the hedgerow. His idea may have been based on scuttlebutt about the experiments in the neighboring units. The cavalry commander ordered his unit's motor officer, Capt. Stephen M. Litton, to build such a device and fit it to one of the unit's M5A1 light tanks. The "rhinoceros" was made from steel beams salvaged from German beach obstructions, the famous "Rommel asparagus" along the

coast. After a number of trials and improvements, the 102nd CRS demonstrated the device to the V Corps commander, Maj. Gen. Leonard Gerow. He was so impressed that on July 14 he staged a demonstration for the U.S. First Army commander, Gen. Omar Bradley, along with several divisional commanders. Bradley had seen the salad fork in action but was concerned about the large amount of explosive that would be needed to use it in the upcoming offensive. He was much more impressed with the rhinoceros and ordered the First Army's ordnance section to begin construction of as many of these devices as possible on an emergency basis. This device received a variety of names, such as the Culin hedgerow cutter, but it was most widely known as the "rhino." Between July 15 and 25, when Operation Cobra started, more than 500 rhinos were manufactured. This was enough for about

Although the rhino is more famous, the bulldozer blades were in fact more effective in breaking through the hedgerows. Each of the separate tank battalions was provided with five or six tank dozers for the Cobra breakout. This dozer tank (named *Here's Dots Mom*) from the 70th Tank Battalion is seen pushing through a hedgerow.

60 percent of the tanks in the First Army taking part in the initial assault. Almost 75 percent of the tanks in the 2nd Armored Division were fitted with the rhino, which was also fitted to tanks of the separate tank battalions supporting the infantry divisions.

On July 22, a modified M5A1 light tank was demonstrated to Gen. George S. Patton and a team from the 3rd Armored Division. After the demonstration, the division was ordered to build its own rhino devices on a crash basis. A workshop was set up in St. Jean de Daye under the supervision of Warrant Officer Douglas, who had been a professional welder in civilian life. Douglas had no plans for the Culin device and devised a modified version that was distinguished by a pair of triangular plates at either end, which he felt would penetrate the hedge better. A total of fifty-seven of these "Douglas cutters" were attached to tanks of the 3rd Armored Division prior to Cobra.

The various types of rhino devices were all considered top secret, and Bradley ordered that none be used until Operation Cobra began. Other units developed their own versions of the rhino based loosely on the Culin-Litton design. Some neighboring British units also adopted these devices, but most of the British sector closer to Caen was rolling farmland without bocage, so rhinos were not as widely used. Culin's rhinos later became wrapped up in myth and legend as a sterling example of Yankee ingenuity and a major cause of victory in Normandy. This was a wartime exaggeration, but the rhino and other devices were excellent examples of the skill the U.S. Army displayed in Normandy to overcome tactical problems with field improvisations, as well as the willingness and enthusiasm of senior American commanders to support and employ these innovations. This level of adaptability was not seen in all armies.

OPERATION COBRA

Operation Cobra was Gen. Omar Bradley's plan to break out of the "green hell" of the bocage into the open country south of St. Lô. The attack began with the carpet bombing of the German front lines on July 25, 1944. Some of the bombs landed too close to the U.S. infantry, and among the dead was Gen. Lesley McNair, who was on a fact-finding mission to France at the time. The bombing shattered the forward German defenses. The Panzer Lehr Division had the decimated remains of its Panther tank regiment along the forward lines, and it was bombed to oblivion, its tanks thrown into craters.

As the dust cleared, American infantry divisions began moving forward to secure the breakthrough. Ahead of them were the separate tank battalions, fitted with rhinos and dozer blades to crunch through the bocage. The rhinos achieved a considerable success with these units. The 741st Tank Battalion had been rebuilt after its heavy losses on Omaha Beach and at the start of Operation Cobra supported the 2nd Infantry Division. Their combined attack on the bocage was a textbook example and succeeded

in rapidly pushing through the defenses of the crack 3rd *Fallschirmjäger* (Parachute) Division. The divisional artillery would fire on a zone about 500 yards deep with air burst shells, and the tanks would then crunch through the bocage, cross the fields, and set up a defensive perimeter near the next hedgerow. The artillery would lift and move to the next field, while the infantry would advance and meet up with the tanks. This systematic approach was used to beat down the German forward positions and continue until the Germans' main line of resistance was overcome, often a mile or more from the initial perimeter. While slow and methodical, the U.S. Army penetrated deep into the German defenses by the end of the day.

Until Operation Cobra, the U.S. First Army had not made extensive use of its armored divisions. American doctrine argued that armored divisions should not be unleashed until the breakthrough had been won, and until Cobra, there had been no breakthrough on the St. Lô front. Earlier in July, impatient with the slow progress, the 3rd Armored

Although the Panther was the best known of German panzers in Normandy, the PzKpfw IV was still the most numerous. This is a PzKpfw IV of the Panzer Lehr Division, knocked out during Cobra.

Operation Cobra opened with a massive carpet bombing of the front line which decimated the remnants of Panzer Lehr Division's Panther battalion. Here GIs look over one of the Panthers that has been blown into a bomb crater.

Operation Cobra saw the debut of the new M4A1 (76mm) with its longer gun and enlarged turret. This M4A1 (76mm) of the 3rd Armored Division is fitted with a T2 Douglas device and is pictured during operations near Reffeuville on August 7, 1944.

An M4 passes by a Panther knocked out near La Chapelle during Cobra.

An M4 fitted with rhino prongs passes by an M10 3-inch gun motor carriage during the opening phase of Operation Cobra in late July 1944.

This M4A1 (76mm) of the 2nd Armored Division is seen with a Rhino hedge-cutter mounted on front.

The rhino was not widely used by either the 2nd or 3rd Armored Division since both units preferred to remain on the roads whenever possible to travel faster. Here *Duke*, an M4A1 (76mm) of Company D, 66th Armored Regiment, 2nd Armored Division, carries an infantry team into action during Cobra.

Division was ordered to attempt a breakthrough over the Vire River via the Airel bridge on July 7–8. The attack had failed, and the general leading the attack was relieved, even though he had argued that the attack contradicted doctrine. For Gen. Lawton "Lightning Joe" Collins, commanding the VII Corps near St. Lô, the tricky question was whether the first day's attacks had indeed penetrated the German defenses. If not, then a tank charge by the 2nd and 3rd Armored Divisions might bog down in the face of remaining German antitank guns and rocket teams. Collins took the gamble and decided that the Germans were in no position to resist the armored advance. On July 26, the two armored divisions began moving forward. The majority of the rhinos had been welded to the tanks of the 2nd and 3rd Armored Divisions, which nevertheless did not widely use them to cut through hedgerows. By the time these two divisions were turned loose to

exploit the initial breakthroughs, they preferred to use roads whenever possible to speed their advance. Their main problem was traffic jams, not German resistance or the bocage. The French country roads were narrow and easily clogged by the mechanized columns of an armored division, which, on the move, extended more than twenty-five miles from spearhead to rear.

In spite of the first day's traffic jams, momentum began to build. Even though most of the German armored force was still tied down against the British near Caen, there was ample German armor in the American St. Lô sector; it had been reinforced in recent weeks as the Germans clearly understood the objective of the American infantry assault. Opposing the U.S. right flank was the 2nd SS Panzer Division "Das Reich," a hardened veteran of the Russian front, and alongside it, the 17th SS Panzergrenadier Division, which had been fighting the Americans

The 2nd SS Panzer Division was decimated in a pocket near Roncey after being encircled during Cobra. This 150mm Hummel self-propelled gun (named *Clausewitz*) and SdKfz 251 half-track headed a retreating column followed by about ninety other vehicles and 2,500 Waffen-SS troops. It was stopped around midnight on July 28 by a 2nd Armored Division roadblock at the crossroads of Notre-Dame-de-Cenilly. The ensuing traffic jam along the hedgerow-lined road left the remainder of the retreating column exposed to American fire, and a savage nighttime battle began in which the column was largely destroyed.

since D-Day. The U.S. Army's approach to dealing with panzer divisions was not to engage them in swirling tank battles but to pulverize them with fighter-bombers and artillery while the armored divisions outflanked and trapped them. The 2nd Armored Division carried out this maneuver in the final weeks of July, trapping large elements of the 2nd SS Panzer Division and much of its heavy equipment in the Roncey pocket.

Operation Cobra saw the first extensive use of the second-generation Shermans, the long-orphaned M4A1 (76mm) tanks that had been sitting in warehouses in Britain since April 1944. After initial encounters with German armor in Normandy, especially after the first encounters with the Panther tanks of the Panzer Lehr Division in early July 1944, U.S. Army commanders suddenly changed their minds about the need for better tank guns. Of the 130 M4A1 (76mm) available, 2nd and 3rd Armored Divisions each received 52, and the rest were handed out in small numbers to the separate tank battalions.

A column of tanks from 2nd Armored Division moves along a tree line near Champ du Bouet. This tank is one of the new M4A1s (76mm).

A column of M4 medium tanks of the 3rd Platoon, Company B, 8th Tank Battalion, 4th Armored Division, passes through the Avranches area on the way into Brittany in early August.

A ten-ton wrecker lifts the Continental R-975 radial engine from the engine compartment of an M4 medium tank of the 2nd Armored Division in a repair yard near Le Teilleul, France, on August 16, 1944.

RONSON LIGHTERS

The Sherman tank developed a bad reputation in the summer fighting, mostly in British rather than American service. British and Canadian armored divisions in Normandy were based around the Sherman tank, while the British infantry tank brigades usually used the heavier and more thickly armored Churchill. The British armored divisions operated in the open farm fields around Caen, where bocage did not constrain mechanized operations. The British and Canadian divisions staged a series of costly mechanized operations against the Wehrmacht in June and July that led to a massive loss of tanks. The Sherman was soon derided as the "Ronson lighter," after the advertisement of the day that it "lights first every time."

Most of the tank-versus-tank fighting in Normandy in June and July 1944 took place in Montgomery's 21st Army Group sector. Seven of the nine German panzer divisions in Normandy faced the British and Canadian forces; only two were in the American sector. Allied armor showed a corresponding imbalance. At the end of June 1944, the U.S. First Army had only 765 Sherman tanks in Normandy, of which 395 were with the 2nd and 3rd Armored Divisions, which had not yet seen extensive combat. In contrast, Montgomery's 21st Army Group had about 550 Churchill and 2,300 Shermans in the field, including 175 of the new Sherman 17-pounder Fireflies. The disproportion in armor on the Allied side had to do with terrain and Allied planning. The more open country around Caen was better suited to large-scale armor operations than the constricted terrain of the bocage country around St. Lô. Large-scale deployment of U.S. armor did not occur until the addition of Patton's Third Army at the time of Operation Cobra in late July when American Sherman strength finally began to approach 2,000 tanks.

The heavy Sherman casualties in the British sector resulted in no small measure from the much more extensive tank fighting there and from the volume of German panzers and antitank weapons. But British tactics also increased the Sherman's vulnerability. By the summer of 1944, the British Army was very thin on replacement troops, especially infantry, and could not afford the costly infantry assaults like those being staged by the U.S. Army around St. Lô. Montgomery realized this and tailored his tactics accordingly. If the British Army was thin on infantry, they were awash with tanks, especially Lend-Lease Shermans. The U.S. attrition reserve in Normandy was 7 percent per month; the British reserve was 50 percent. The British were willing to lose tanks in abundance to carry out their mission, but this did not necessarily imply heavy tank crew losses. During this phase of the war, on average every tank lost to an enemy tank or antitank gun typically lost one crewman, usually the trooper nearest the point of penetration. Crews quickly learned that as soon as the tank was hit, they had no more than thirty seconds to bail out before the ammunition ignited in catastrophic fury. A British battlefield survey after the fighting found that German tank and antitank gun fire was responsible for about 90 percent of the Sherman kills in the fighting in Normandy and that nearly three-quarters "brewed up" (burned) after being penetrated. The main Sherman killers were the various 75mm guns mounted on the German PzKpfw IV, Panther, StuG III assault gun, and the towed PaK 40 antitank gun, which accounted for 82 percent of the Sherman kills; the vaunted 88mm gun accounted for much of the rest.

British tactics differed from American tactics. After the frustrations of the June battles, Montgomery became willing to use his armored divisions to secure the breakthrough, even though this was against doctrine. This was most evident during Operation Goodwood in mid-July 1944 when the 21st Army Group lost about 400 tanks in a few days of fighting in another failed attempt to push beyond Caen with the armored divisions as the spearhead instead of the infantry. The British accepted tank casualties more so than heavy infantry casualties, losing more than 600 tanks and more than 650 damaged but repairable in June and July, the majority of them Shermans. British tank losses in France in June–August 1944 were about 1,530 tanks compared to about 875 U.S. tanks.

The Normandy campaign was costly to Montgomery's armored units. The intensity of the fighting for the Falaise Gap in August 1944 is suggested by this field near Argentan where there are a pair of knocked-out Sherman Vs to the right, a Loyd Carrier in the left foreground, a German StuG III assault gun to the left, and a knocked-out PzKpfw IV in the center.

In the end, Montgomery's tactics succeeded at a heavy but sustainable cost. The British 21st Army Group slowly but surely ground down the German panzer divisions in the fields around Caen, keeping them out of the bocage country near St. Lô while American infantry and tanks ground their way through the hedgerows. Following Operation Cobra, the British and Canadian armored divisions prepared for their own breakout.

The Wehrmacht had started the summer campaign with 1,550 tanks in all of France, including those in southern France, of which 655 were the new Panthers. German losses in the Normandy fighting were heavy: at least 250 panzers and assault guns in June and more than 360 in July. Actual figures were considerably higher but impossible to determine because of German accounting methods. German records indicate that AFV losses in the west were only 830 tanks and assault guns during the heavy fighting

from June to August but a staggering 1,770 in September 1944. In fact, losses from June to August were substantially higher, but some of the knocked-out tanks remained in German hands and were theoretically repairable and not written off the books until September, distorting the record of actual losses in the early summer fighting. While the German losses in June–July 1944 may have been lower than Allied losses, German tank strength in Normandy was much smaller than Allied armor, and replacements could barely keep pace, with German tank strength falling to 1,300 by July while Allied medium tank strength grew to 3,900. German replacement tanks to France in the summer amounted to about 1,120. Following Operation Cobra and the ensuing encirclement battles at Roncey, Falaise, the Seine, and the Mons pocket, total German losses in the summer campaign amounted to more than 90 percent of the force committed—some 2,585 tanks and assault guns.

CHAPTER 6

To Paris and Beyond!

THE FIGHTING IN AUGUST 1944 WAS THE first time that the U.S. Army was able to employ multiple armored divisions in their intended role as a deep exploitation force. No formation better epitomized the potential of armored warfare than George Patton's Third Army. Patton's units had been secretly moved into the Normandy bridgehead throughout July, with an aim of exploiting the Operation Cobra breakout. But instead of heading east with the First Army, Patton was ordered west toward Brittany to seize port facilities such as Brest and Quiberon Bay. Patton's vanguards were the 4th and 6th Armored Divisions, inexperienced but well trained and well led. They made the fastest tank dash of the war, plunging more than 250 miles into "Indian country" and encountering little German resistance.

Hitler was furious at the catastrophic unraveling of the German defense line in France. Contemptuous of American combat prowess, he repeatedly tried to defeat Allied forces by staging counterattacks against the American forces that he considered less battleworthy than their British counterparts. In August, he decided that Patton's audacious charge into Brittany offered the best opportunity and ordered a panzer counterattack called Operation Lüttich to push to the sea at Avranches, cutting off Patton's Third Army. German forces in France had been decimated by the summer battles around St. Lô and Caen, and the Avranches counterattack was conducted by pulling panzer units away from the British sector near Caen. It was a foolish mistake. The Allies controlled the air, and the "jabos," as the Germans called Allied fighter-bombers, were soon swarming on the German tank columns. The numbers of tanks knocked out by Allied Thunderbolt and Typhoon

171

An M4 105mm assault gun of the 8th Tank Battalion, 4th Armored Division, passes through Avranches on its way into Brittany in early August. The 4th and 6th Armored Divisions were the spearheads of Patton's Third Army in its record-breaking drive into Brittany in mid-August. The tanks of the 8th Tank Battalion, unlike most of the division, were painted in a splinter-camouflage pattern.

The infantry's 57mm antitank gun played a crucial role in the defeat of Operation Lüttich, Hitler's August 1944 attempt to stage a panzer offensive to the sea in response to Cobra. This camouflaged 57mm gun is from the 12th Infantry, 4th Division, which covered the shoulder of the attack on Mortain.

fighter-bombers has often been exaggerated, but the air attacks crippled the panzer divisions by destroying their more vulnerable supply columns and restricting their movement during the daytime. Operation Lüttich's second big mistake was to weaken its presence in the British sector, as in the meantime more Allied forces had arrived in France, including more Canadian armor and the Polish 1st Armored Division, which would soon stage a plunge beyond Caen.

Operation Lüttich soon ground to a halt after running into the U.S. 30th Infantry Division near

An M4 medium tank passes by an abandoned Wehrmacht medical evacuation cart during the operations on the approaches to the Seine River in August 1944.

A camouflaged 3-inch gun of a tank destroyer battalion in its defensive position during the fighting in northern France on August 19, 1944. The inadequate performance of the 3-inch gun against the German Panther, as well as its lack of mobility, led American commanders in Europe to insist that it be replaced by a 90mm gun as soon as possible.

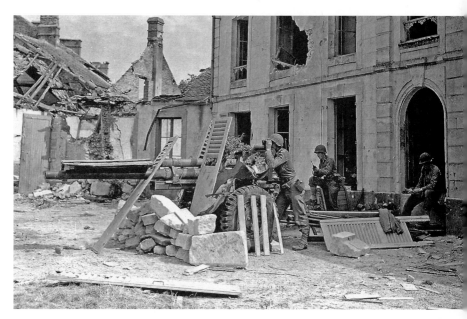

Mortain. If the Allies had a hard time in offensive operations in the bocage, so too did the Wehrmacht. While the panzer divisions were being pummeled by U.S. artillery and fighter-bombers around Mortain, Montgomery's forces had begun their own breakout, heading for Falaise. Operation Lüttich had left the Wehrmacht in Normandy vulnerable to a disastrous encirclement. The first part of the encirclement was a "hammer and anvil" attack with Montgomery's 21st Army Group's hammer swing-

A 57mm gun of the 1st Battalion, 39th Infantry Regiment, 9th Division, is camouflaged behind wooden debris during the fighting around Cherence le Roussel on August 6. The battalion received a Distinguished Unit Citation for its defensive actions against Operation Lüttich.

ing rapidly toward Falaise, while the U.S. First Army created an anvil by taking the town of Avranches. This would create the Falaise pocket.

The second stage of the encirclement began when Patton recognized the futility of the charge into Brittany. The rapidity of the tank advance obscured the simple fact that the Germans would sabotage the port facilities at Brest as they had done in June at Cherbourg. Intact, the port of Brest would have been an invaluable logistical aid for the Allies, but in ruins, it would be nearly worthless.

Patton realized that the Falaise encirclement had created a gigantic vacuum in northeastern France, with the Wehrmacht unable to prevent access to the next defense line along the Seine. Patton won Bradley's and Eisenhower's permission to reorient most of his mobile forces and head east toward Paris. The deep envelopment of the Wehrmacht in August 1944 was one of the most remarkable advances of the summer. The Germans occasionally scraped together enough forces to mount a last-ditch defense in some cities such as Chartres, but

An M4 tank of the 5th Armored Division passes by an abandoned 75mm PaK 40 antitank gun during the fighting in Dreux on August 16, 1944, as part of Patton's Third Army advance on the cathedral cities of Chartres and Orleans.

Patton's main problem was not German resistance but a shortage of fuel.

Patton's race for the Seine in August was made possible by the automotive robustness of the Sherman tank. For all the complaints about its thin armor and weak gun, the Sherman was an ideal cavalry tank. The German Panther tank, for all its defensive power, would have been unsuitable for this type of operation because of its mechanical fragility. The Panther had a life expectancy of only 930 miles, which many Sherman tanks in operation had already exceeded in training and would exceed it again in Normandy. The summer 1944 campaign highlighted the Sherman's other key value to the Allied victory. McNair and AGF had kept a lid on Sherman modifications and more advanced designs like the T23 in order to maximize American tank production. In battle, quantity has a quality all its own. Warfare in the industrial age requires a careful balance between quality and quantity. The Sherman offered a better balance than the Panther, which, because of its cost and complexity, could be built in

An M4A2 tank (named *Franche-Comté*) of the French 3/12 RCA receives an enthusiastic welcome as it advances down Avenue Victor Hugo on August 25.

enough quantities to equip only one of the two panzer battalions in each panzer division. In contrast, there were so many Shermans that they not only filled out the U.S. and British armored divisions, but also were plentiful enough to provide each U.S. infantry division with a tank battalion. In the mid-summer of 1944, Montgomery's 21st Army Group had 2,336 Shermans of various types, including 318 of the new 17-pounder Fireflies; the U.S. First Army had 1,120 Shermans, and Patton's Third Army in August added another 1,035 Shermans—for a grand total of nearly 4,500 Allied Shermans in France, more than three times the size of the panzer force.

TAMING THE PANTHER

The U.S. Army had relatively few encounters with the Panther tank during the summer of 1944, but what they saw of it they didn't like. The first major engagement occurred on July 8, 1944, when the 3rd Armored Division caught a Panther column near St. Jean De Daye in confined terrain, knocked out the lead and trail tanks, and proceeded to destroy the rest. More contact with the Panzer Lehr's Panthers followed on July 11, 1944, when the Germans attempted to push back the 9th Infantry Division's bridgehead over the Vire River near Le Desert. The Panzer Lehr was led by Rommel's aide from the desert campaign, Gen. Fritz Bayerlein, and he found operating panzers in the bocage every bit as frustrating as the Americans had. His Panther regiment took heavy losses to the Americans' 57mm antitank guns, which could easily punch the Panther's weak side armor, even if its frontal armor, was impervious.

Supporting M10s of the 899th Tank Destroyer Battalion claimed a dozen Panthers and a PzKpfw IV. Bayerlein's assessment of the Panther was tart:

While the PzKpfw IV could still be used to advantage, the PzKpfw V [Panther] proved ill adapted to the terrain. The Sherman because of its maneuverability and height was good . . . [the Panther was] poorly suited for hedgerow terrain because of its width. Long gun barrel and width of tank reduce maneuverability in village and forest fighting. It is very front-heavy and therefore quickly wears out the front final drives, made of low-grade steel. High silhouette. Very sensitive powertrain requiring well-trained drivers. Weak side armor; tank top vulnerable to fighter-bombers. Fuel-lines of porous material that

The U.S. Army captured numerous Panthers during the summer campaign, subjecting several to firing tests to learn its secrets. This is a Panther Ausf. A of the 2nd Panzer Division, evident from its trident insignia on the side of the turret.

This is a photo from a technical report by the First Army after three Panthers were subjected to fire from various Allied antitank weapons at Isigny in August 1944. This particular Panther suffered a catastrophic armor failure as a result of the Germans' lack of alloys like molybdenum and use of other alloys that produced hard but brittle armor.

allow gasoline fumes to escape into the tank interior causing a grave fire hazard. Absence of vision slits makes defense against close attack impossible.

But Bayerlein still appreciated the Panther's virtues when used in the right conditions: "An ideal vehicle for tank battles and infantry support. The best tank in existence for its weight."

The first encounters with the Panther and the poor performance of the 3-inch gun led to immediate efforts by Eisenhower's headquarters to find remedies. The SHAEF G-3 (operations) division prepared a detailed report to the G-3 office of the Army Chief of Staff in Washington on July 11, based on the recent combat experiences and hasty tests conducted against a captured Panther on July 10. The report laid out the poor performance of the American 3-inch and 76mm guns, the better performance of the British 17-pounder, and the inferior performance of American 57mm infantry antitank gun ammunition compared to the new British sabot ammunition. The report noted that the confined terrain of Normandy usually afforded U.S. units the ability to maneuver to defeat the Panther as they had at Le Desert, but once the Allies were out in open country, the U.S. Army would be at a disadvantage when facing the improved German AFVs. The report recommended getting 90mm or

17-pounder guns into the hands of American troops as soon as possible and preparing a method to up-armor the Sherman in the field to make up for its clear deficiencies in protection.

The U.S. Army soon learned to fear the Panther and its virtually invulnerable frontal armor. Fortunately, contact with the Panther in Normandy was sporadic, and as Bayerlein commented, the terrain was hardly ideal. The counterattack at Mortain in early August led to the loss of more Panthers against the U.S. infantry's antitank guns.

A number of Panthers were captured more or less intact, so American and British ordnance experts tried to discover its secrets. A captured Panther was set up in a field near Balleroy on July 10 and subjected to fire from a variety of American and British tank guns. A month later, on August 19, a more comprehensive test was conducted using several captured Panthers at an ordnance tank park near Isigny. The Panthers were put in a field and fired on by the whole gamut of Allied antitank weapons, including bazookas, 57mm antitank guns, Sherman 75mm guns, the U.S. 3-inch gun, and the British 17-pounder. The results were extremely discouraging; in most cases, the rounds simply bounced off the front armor of the Panther. It was quite clear that the British 17-pounder was by far the best tank killer in Allied service, but it could penetrate the Panther mantlet and lower bow plate only at close ranges and the glacis plate not at all, even

Although many U.S. Army accounts mention encounters with Tigers in Normandy, in fact there were few or no engagements between American units and German Tiger battalions, which were located in the British-Canadian sector. This Tiger being inspected by French FFI resistance fighters was on a train in the Braine station, which was overrun by the U.S. 3rd Armored Division. As can be seen, it has suffered extensive battle damage and was probably inoperative.

from point-blank range at 200 yards. These results were obtained with standard 17-pounder rounds; the new discarding sabot round had somewhat better penetration but very erratic accuracy. The performance of the U.S. 76mm gun was disheartening, and it had poor all-around performance, unable to penetrate the Panther frontally except for the occasional lucky hit. The Isigny test included a special batch of the new T4 HVAP ammunition for the 76mm gun, which compared in performance to the standard British 17-pounder ammunition. The problem with HVAP was that it would never be available in large quantities, while the British 17-pounder ammunition was made of conventional alloys and therefore was more widely available.

The other alarming news that summer was that newer German AFVs were turning up with much thicker armor. The summer saw the introduction of "Guderian's Duck," the Panzer IV/70, also known initially as the *Jagdpanzer IV.* This was the run-of-the-mill PzKpfw IV chassis armed with the same powerful 75mm L/70 gun as the Panther in a fixed casemate instead of a turret, with armor as thick as the Panther's on the front. The Tiger I had given way to the King Tiger, a monster with an even more powerful 88mm gun. The U.S. captured a few abandoned King Tigers during the race for the Seine and first faced them in battle in the fighting for the Mantes bridgehead north of Paris in mid-August. They were few in number and made little impression after several were ambushed by M10 tank destroyers. Nevertheless, the trend was clearly in the direction of an array of German AFVs that were impervious to U.S. tank guns in frontal attack.

AMERICAN FIREFLY DEFERRED

The Balleroy and Isigny tests and the appearance of these new German AFVs raised the question of whether the U.S. Army ought to take up a British offer to convert some of their tanks with 17-pounder guns as an antidote to the Panther and its menacing new friends. The British had offered some 17-pounder guns as early as December 1943, but the U.S. Army had turned them down after seeing the firing trials and arriving at the mistaken conclusion that the new 76mm gun could deal with the Panther. Early demonstrations of the 17-pounder had shown an alarming amount of flash at the rear gun breech when fired, a hint of poor engineering, and a frightening muzzle flash (the source of its "Firefly" nickname). British offers to provide the 17-pounder to the U.S. Army in the autumn of 1943 led General Devers to insist on a live firepower demonstration to show that it would be worth the effort. Comparative shoots of the American 90mm and British 17-pounder guns were conducted at Aberdeen Proving Ground in the U.S. on March 25, 1944, followed by a similar trial at Shoeburyness in Britain on May 23, 1944. These demonstrations came far too late to have any impact on equipment programs for the summer 1944 campaign since production of both the 76mm Sherman and 90mm M36 tank destroyer were already well underway.

A report on July 26, 1944, suggested that more than 1,000 of the new 90mm M36 tank destroyers would be arriving between August 1944 and March 1945; the 90mm gun performed equal to or better than the 17-pounder. On the positive side, British 17-pounder conversion programs were winding down as British requirements were being completed. On the downside, the supply of the 17-pounder ammunition might reach a bottleneck, certainly complicating an already complex ammunition stream. The program would also tie down 100 to 150 tanks per month while undergoing conversion. While this number might seem trivial in view of the scale of Sherman production, in the late summer of 1944 it was a major issue. The U.S. Army had seriously underestimated the likely rate of tank loss in the summer, basing it on the rate suffered in the Italian theater, which was roughly 7 percent per month. Supplies had been adjusted accordingly. However, the casualties in Normandy in 1944 had been double this level, closer to 15 percent, and as a result, U.S. tank units in France were short of 335 Sherman tanks by September—the equivalent of more than six tank battalions or two armored divisions. Stripping out another 150 tanks per month would adversely affect combat strength, and it would take some months before this situation could be adjusted by requesting more tanks from the United States.

When the British War Office was contacted about the possibility of undertaking 100 17-pounder conversions in August, the AFV&W section was told that no conversions could be undertaken until October 1944 at the earliest. Gen. Omar Bradley's headquarters contacted Eisenhower and asked him to expedite the conversions. When told of the ineffectiveness of the M4A1 (76mm) against the Panther from the Isigny trials, Eisenhower bitterly remarked, "You mean our 76 won't knock these Panthers out? Why, I thought it was going to be the wonder gun of the war. . . . Why is it that I'm the last to hear about this stuff? Ordnance told me this 76 would take care of anything the Germans had. Now I find you can't knock out a damn thing with it." Eisenhower brought up the issue with Montgomery, based on an earlier offer Montgomery had made about transferring 17-pounder Shermans to the U.S. Army.

By early September, the British tank units had been able to replenish their Normandy losses, and the War Office reiterated its offer to convert up to 100 American M4 tanks per month to 17-pounder Sherman Fireflies, taking over about 40 percent of British conversion capacity. The issue had far less urgency in September 1944 after the great summer victories. Brig. Gen. J. A. Holly, the chief of Eisenhower's AFV&W section, wrote to a colleague in early September 1944: "Probably the problem of the Panther will no longer be with U.S. for the remainder of the war. The German, we believe, has lost most of his armor." Holly reported back to AGF in Washington on September 17, 1944, that the 17-pounder effort had "slipped into the background

In the summer of 1944, the British Firefly was the only version of the Sherman that stood a reasonable chance in a frontal engagement with a Panther or Tiger. This particular Sherman Vc (17-pounder) was knocked out near Erf during the fighting in the Netherlands during Operation Market Garden, the failed Allied attempt to seize a Rhine crossing at Arnhem with a combined armored-parachute assault.

because of the scarcity of German armor, the war successes, the shipment of 75mm gun tanks to the Continent instead of the UK and no apparent accumulation of tank reserves . . . battle losses consumed our 75mm gun tank reserves." The tank supply issue was not resolved in 1944 and worsened dramatically in December 1944 because of heavy combat losses in the Battle of the Bulge. By the beginning of January 1945, the deficit was 865 medium tanks, about 30 percent of authorized inventory. As a result of these factors, including the promised arrival of 90mm tank destroyers and T4 HVAP ammunition, the U.S. Army's 17-pounder program was put on indefinite hold through 1944.

The other way to deal with the Panther and its evil friends was to strangle them in their cribs. The U.S. Army Ground Forces began putting pressure on the U.S. Army Air Force (USAAF) for a concerted bombing campaign against German tank plants. There had been few dedicated bombing attacks on the tank plants through the spring of 1944 because of the focus in the spring months on German fighter factories, in the early summer on support missions for D-Day, and in midsummer on a campaign against German oil refineries and synthetic fuel plants. The British night attacks on the tank plants were largely ineffective, and the USAAF daylight raids had so far omitted the tank plants.

As a shortcut, the RAF suggested attacking a key chokepoint in German tank production, selecting the Maybach engine plant since it provided most of the Panther and Tiger engines. This plant was struck by the RAF on the night of April 27–28, 1944, essentially stopping production for five months through September 1944. This would have halted Panther production but for a German decision to disperse production to a second source, the Auto-Union plant at Siegmar, which came online in May 1944; the Germans thus narrowly averted a disaster in the panzer industry. With the panzer menace more evident in the summer, both American and British commanders began renewing their demands for more bombing of the panzer plants.

In August 1944, the RAF and USAAF began a systematic air campaign against the German panzer industry. The main Panther plant, MAN at Nuremberg, was badly smashed up on September 10, 1944, costing the Wehrmacht the equivalent of more than four months of production—about 645 tanks. The Daimler-Benz Panther plant was hit as well, but the second most important Panther plant, the MNH (*Maschinenfabrik Niedersachsen*) in Hanover, was missed until March 1945. The most successful attack was conducted against the Henschel King Tiger plant in Kassel, which shut it down for several months and crippled King Tiger production prior to the Ardennes campaign. However, the bomber commanders were not especially pleased with the results of the attacks, which petered out in October.

The bombing raids had a pernicious, but not immediately apparent effect on German panzers. The head of German war production, Albert Speer, was able to squeeze even more panzers out of the battered industry through the end of the year, but with significant and largely hidden costs. Speer kept panzer production at high levels by shifting plant resources away from other products such as trucks and focusing on tanks. More critically, the panzer plants dramatically cut production of spare parts, which fell from 25 to 30 percent of tank contracts in 1943 to 15 percent by the summer of 1944 and as little as 8 percent by the autumn of 1944. Quality control fell sharply, especially in armor production. When testing Panthers at Isigny, the Allied officers rejected some tests on two of the three Panthers because the armor seemed substandard. What they didn't know at the time was that sloppy quality control at the armor plants was leading to as much as half the thick tank armor being improperly tempered in the quenching process, which degraded its quality 10 to 20 percent. To make matters worse, the German supply of the critical molybdenum alloy had evaporated as Norwegian, Finnish, and Japanese supplies disappeared that summer. Molybdenum gave armor steel its toughness, and substitutes left the armor steel hard but brittle, apt to crack under the shock of attack. The extensive use of slave labor in the panzer plants also undermined the quality of the panzers. Recent museum restorations of Panthers have revealed evidence of deliberate sabotage, such as placing debris in the fuel and oil lines. These issues would come to a head at the end of the year in the Ardennes.

As there were no quick fixes to the Panther problem, the U.S. tankers again used their own initiative to come up with stopgap solutions. A number of tank battalions fighting in the bocage learned that the new 75mm white phosphorus ("Willy Pete") smoke round had some unexpected advantages. When fired against a German tank, it gave the Sherman a temporary advantage since the panzer would be blinded for a minute or more, and then the Sherman could maneuver and engage the enemy from its weaker side or rear. In many cases, the acrid white phosphorous smoke would get sucked into the panzer by its ventilating fan and become so unbearable that the panzer crew would abandon the tank. Sherman crews soon learned to fire a "Willy Pete" smoke round at a well-positioned panzer, wait a few seconds for the smoke to take effect, and then machine-gun the tank in hopes of killing the crew. This tactic didn't work every time, but it offered one approach for dealing with a determined opponent. Army observer teams took note of the tactic, and special "combat lessons learned" were passed around to inform other tank units of the discovery.

The most effective antidote to the Panther was the discovery of its Achilles heel. It had long been known that the Panther had weak side armor, so maneuvering to attack its side was already a well-established tactic, often aided by the Willy Pete smoke trick. However, some tank crews found that a

A British armored column moves over the bridge at Nijmegen on September 21, 1944, during Market Garden. The lead tank is a Sherman Vc (17-pounder).

well-aimed shot at the lower part of the Panther's gun mantlet would ricochet downward through the thin hull roof armor and strike ammo racks directly below. This took a very careful shot, but it offered some hope in cases where a Panther was so well positioned that it could not be overcome by maneuvering.

To deal with the threat of German infantry *panzerfausts,* tank crews began placing layers of sand bags on the fronts of their tanks. Some crews swore that these sandbags deflected the blast of the German rocket grenades, but Ordnance officers scoffed at the idea. In Patton's Third Army, Ordnance officers convinced Patton that it was a bad idea and that it simply added weight to the front of the tank, prematurely wearing out the transmission. As a result, sandbag armor was officially banned in the Third Army. It proliferated elsewhere, gradually becoming an art form in some units, with elaborate structures to support the sandbags.

ON THE FIELDS OF ARRACOURT

American commanders in late August and early September believed that they had licked the panzer problem and that the panzer force had disappeared. In fact, Hitler was preparing a nasty surprise for Patton's hard-charging Third Army, planning once again to cut it off and annihilate it before it reached the German frontier. Instead, the great panzer counterattack was decimated so quickly and so decisively that it is seldom appreciated in many American histories of the war. Yet the tank fighting around Arracourt in September 1944 would be the largest tank-versus-tank battles fought by the U.S. Army in 1944 until the Battle of the Bulge. The Lorraine tank battles were a clear example of the growing proficiency of the U.S. Army in tank warfare and a first sign of the decline in the German panzer force. The Panther tank may have seemed a sure winner against the Sherman on paper, but tank warfare hinges on the skill of the tankers and tank commanders more than on competing technology.

The decimation of the Wehrmacht's Seventh Army and Panzer Group West in the Roncey Pocket, the Falaise Gap, the Mortain counterattack, and the Seine encirclement left the German force routed in fast retreat toward the German border. The second Allied landing in France on the Mediterranean coast of Provence on August 15, 1944, forced Hitler to order the retreat of two more German armies, the First and Nineteenth, in late August, effectively ending German occupation of southern and central France with little resistance. The newly arrived 6th Army Group, commanded by Jacob Devers, headed for Alsace, while Montgomery's 21st Army Group barreled through Belgium and the Netherlands and Bradley's 12th Army Group bolted for the Siegfried Line. Through most of early September, the Wehrmacht was in such chaos that the period later became known as "the void" in German histories of the war.

The juncture of Bradley's 12th Army Group and Dever's 6th Army Group would occur somewhere

The first flop of Hitler's panzer counteroffensive in Lorraine was the failed attack by Panzer Brigade 106 *Feldherrnhalle*, led by the legendary Franz Bäke. On the night of September 7–8, 1944, the brigade attempted to cut off the U.S. 90th Infantry Division near Mairy, France. By the end of the day, the brigade had lost most of its equipment, including 21 tanks and tank destroyers, 60 half-tracks, and more than 100 support vehicles. The Americans left this Panther Ausf. G on the roadside west of Metz for improvised vehicle-recognition training for passing troops.

The second panzer unit to attack in Lorraine was Panzer Brigade 112, which deployed its Panther battalion in Dompaire on the night of September 12. A combat command of the more experienced French 2nd Armored Division beat up the brigade on September 13, 1944, and in two days of fighting, the German brigade had only twenty-one operational tanks out of its original eighty. This Panther was captured intact by the French and for many years was displayed in Paris in front of Les Invalides.

On September 19, Panzer Brigade 113 launched an attack against elements of the 4th Armored Division near Arracourt and first ran into the 704th Tank Destroyer Battalion near Rechicourt-la-Petite. A short-range duel in the early-morning fog led to the loss of several Panther Ausf. Gs (shown here) and M18 Hellcat tank destroyers. PATTON MUSEUM

in Alsace or Lorraine, and the Wehrmacht was determined to slow this consolidation to permit the extraction of as many of its forces from central France as possible. The main threat was Patton's Third Army, which had charged past Paris to the south, aiming for the German border and Frankfurt via the old fortress city of Metz. In German eyes, the rapid pace of Patton's advance, spearheaded by the

4th and 6th Armored Divisions, posed the greatest Allied threat in mid-September.

From Eisenhower's perspective, mid-September should have been the time for pausing and regrouping. The original plan had called for Allied forces to halt in the "Normandy lodgment area" to the west of the Seine River, with Dever's 6th Army Group expected to be no farther north than Lyons in

The crew of Sgt. Timothy Dunn of the 37th Tank Battalion set up a bivouac near Chateau Salins on September 26, 1944, shortly after the tank battles near Arracourt. The vehicle tarp has been erected to create a tent for the crew.

central France. Instead, the stunning summer victories had placed the Allied armies far beyond the plans and at the edge of their logistical lines. The plans had been to secure the ports of Cherbourg and Brest for supply, supplementing supplies coming across the Normandy beaches via the Mulberry harbors at Omaha Beach and Arromanches. The Germans had thoroughly smashed Cherbourg before its capture in June; Brest was still holding out and would be thoroughly smashed as well before its surrender. Nature had been unkind and had ripped apart the Mulberry harbor at Omaha Beach in July. But the real problem was the French railroad network that had been so thoroughly wrecked by Allied airpower during the summer interdiction campaign. In one of the greatest

blunders of the summer campaign, Montogmery's forces had seized the vital port city of Antwerp but failed to clear the Scheldt Estuary, which controlled access to the port. The Germans quickly exploited the oversight, and the Canadian Army would spend most of the autumn fighting bitter battles in the mud trying to wrest control of the estuary. In the south, Marseilles would prove to be an unexpected bonus since the port was intact and the French rail network northward was also largely intact. But it would take weeks to get this issue sorted out. In the meantime, Allied forces were critically short of fuel and ammunition, and tanks need gas.

Montgomery saw the desperate German plight as an opportunity for bold action and proposed an

Lt. Col. Creighton Abrams, commander of the 37th Tank Battalion at Arracourt, used this M4 medium tank, *Thunderbolt V*, as his command tank through the early autumn fighting in Lorraine. The U.S. Army's current M1A1 tank is named after him.

airborne assault to seize a series of bridges to catapult the 21st Army Group over the Rhine and into northern Germany via Arnhem. Given Montgomery's usual caution, Eisenhower had little choice but to accept, paving the way for Operation Market-Garden, the failed airborne/tank assault toward the "bridge too far." Eisenhower's decision to authorize Market Garden inevitably meant that Patton's advance toward Frankfurt would be constrained by a lack of fuel. On several occasions, Patton was reminded to halt and await supplies. He always managed to find an excuse to send forward another "reconnaissance in force to probe German defenses," which looked curiously like a full-fledged advance.

The debates within Allied high command and the growing exhaustion of the Allied fuel supplies were not evident to the Germans. In spite of the summer disasters, Hitler still expected that his panzer forces could win great encirclement battles in the west as they had so often on the Eastern Front, especially against the green and soft American troops. Not surprisingly, he selected veterans from the Eastern Front to conduct his planned panzer offensive in Lorraine. A violent panzer attack against Patton's Third Army was both the most necessary and the most promising option. The Third Army had advanced the farthest east, and its momentum toward the Saar suggested that it would be the first Allied force to enter Germany. Besides blunting this

In 1945, a veteran of the 704th Tank Destroyer Battalion returned to the Arracourt area and photographed several of the Panther tanks that still littered the battlefield. This Panther Ausf. A most likely belonged to one of the panzer divisions taking part in the latter phases of the battle, possibly the 11th Panzer Division. The new panzer brigades were equipped with the newer Panther Ausf. G. PATTON MUSEUM

threatening advance, a panzer counterattack toward Reims would have the added benefit of preventing the linkup between Dever's 6th Army Group, advancing from southern France, and Bradley's 12th Army Group in northern France. On September 3, 1944, Hitler instructed the commander of German forces in the west, Field Marshall Gerd von Rundstedt, to begin planning this attack. Under Hitler's initial plan, the attack would be carried out by the 3rd and 15th Panzergrenadier Divisions and the 17th SS Panzergrenadier Division and the new Panzer Brigades 111, 112, and 113, with later reinforcements from the Panzer Lehr Division, 11th and 21st Panzer Divisions, and the new Panzer Brigades 106, 107, and 108. The skilled Hasso von Manteuffel was flown in straight from the fighting on the Russian front and put in command of the Fifth Panzer Army headquarters that

would control the panzer counteroffensive. The date of the counterattack was set for September 12, 1944.

At the core of the panzer attack were the newly formed panzer brigades, a new type of formation organized in the summer of 1944 to act as "fire brigades" on the Russian front. They were not the usual sort of combined-arms force with a balance of panzers and panzergrenadiers, but rather a tank-heavy force designed to rapidly move against Soviet breakthroughs and smash them with mobility and firepower. In most cases, they were built around a core of experienced Eastern Front veterans. For example, Panzer Brigade 106 had been formed around remnants of Panzergrenadier Division *Feldherrnhalle* and was commanded by one of the most distinguished Wehrmacht tank commanders, Col. Dr. Franz Bäke, who had led a panzer battalion in the climactic tank encounter at Prokhorovka during the 1943 Kursk battles and later led the Tiger tanks of the legendary Heavy Panzer Regiment Bäke on the Eastern Front in 1944.

The first batch of these brigades, numbered from 101 to 110, were in fact closer in strength to a regiment, with only a single tank battalion. Equipment included thirty-six new Panthers, eleven Pz.IV/70 tank destroyers, and four *Flakpanzers* for air defense. The later brigades numbered above 110 had two tank battalions: one of PzKpfw IVs and one of PzKpfw V Panthers. Three of the four brigades in the Lorraine fighting had this heavier configuration. On paper at least, these were formidable units with ninety tanks and ten tank destroyers each—much more armor than most German panzer divisions in the autumn of 1944. But their impressive lineage and talented commanders concealed the fact that they had been raised on the cheap with new panzer crews and completely inadequate training.

In contrast, their eventual foe in the Lorraine battles, the 4th Armored Division, had spent the past six weeks learning valuable combat lessons. Like most American armored divisions in the late summer of 1944, the 4th Armored Division had been in training in the United States for two years before being dispatched to Europe. The summer campaign had provided enough seasoning for the tankers to become experienced without too many casualties to make them battle-weary. The 4th Armored Division had taken part in Patton's advance into Brittany and then the abrupt turnaround and race through the Loire Valley past Paris and into Lorraine. They were equipped entirely with older M4 tanks that had been built in late 1942 and early 1943, but which had undergone the blitz upgrade in the summer of 1943 with the new M34A1 gun mount with telescopic sight and appliqué armor over their ammo racks. They were offered some 76mm tanks and turned them down. Through the August fighting, they had relied on their 75mm guns and preferred to remain with tried and tested weapons rather than experiment with new ones. By September, their Shermans had clocked more than 1,000 miles on their odometers—enough to cripple a Panther—but they were in good automotive shape, with ample spare parts and skilled mechanics.

Hitler's plans for the Lorraine counterattack soon turned into shambles because of the desperate plight of the Wehrmacht. Many of the units scheduled to participate were in a fight for their lives and couldn't easily be extracted to participate. The new panzer brigades arrived slowly because of Allied airpower. In addition, Rundstedt pleaded with Hitler to let him use some of the panzer brigades to deal with the most threatening problems at the front. The carefully hoarded panzer reserve was gradually frittered away to stave off defeat on other fronts. Panzer Brigades 107 and 108 were dispatched to the Aachen front, where Hodges's First Army was threatening to capture the first city in Germany.

The rapid advance of Patton's Third Army over the Moselle River threatened the German defenses before the attack could be staged, and local commanders pleaded with Berlin for permission to use the panzers before it was too late. On September 7, Hitler gave permission to use Panzer Brigade 106 to turn the flank of Gen. Walton "Bulldog" Walker's XX Corps, with the proviso that the brigade be returned to reserve in forty-eight hours. Instead, the brigade stumbled into the U.S. 90th Infantry Division, the "Tough 'Ombres," and was smashed, losing much of its equipment. The French 2nd Armored Division, now part of Patton's forces, threatened to cut off the German LXIV Corps on the west bank of the Moselle River, and the German commander committed Panzer Brigade 112 as a relief force without Hitler's permission. It was trapped by the French Sherman tank battalions at Dompaire and decimated on September 13.

By the time the Lorraine panzer counterattack finally started a week late on September 18, it was a pale shadow of the original plan, with only a fraction of its intended power. Four panzer brigades were absent—two of them shattered and two diverted—and other units were not yet in the area. The initial skirmishing around Luneville on September 18 was so disjointed that Patton had no idea his forces were under attack, and the plans for the next day were for a continuation of operations toward the German border. This led to a rare type of tank-versus-tank encounter, seldom experienced by the U.S. Army in the ETO: a classic meeting engagement in which both sides were offensively oriented and neither side had any defensive advantage.

The main attack picked up steam on the morning of September 19 around the farm town of Arracourt. This was the area of operation of two combat commands of the 4th Armored Division. Combat commands were the combined-arms groupings used by American armored divisions during the war, typically consisting of a mix of one each of tank, armored infantry, and armored field artillery battalions from the division's nine combat battalions. Each division would typically have three combat commands—CCA and CCB deployed on the mission and CCR as the reserve and as a holding formation for units that needed rebuilding, refit, and resupply. That day, CCA and CCB were forward, planning a late-morning advance eastward toward the German frontier.

The Germans planned a two-brigade assault, with Panzer Brigade 113 attacking the eastern spearhead of the CCA forces near Lezey and Panzer Brigade 111 attacking the center near Arracourt. This would have given the Germans more than a four-to-one advantage in armor in this sector. During the predawn approach, Panzer Brigade 111 became lost in the farm fields, allegedly after receiving bad instructions from a French farmer. Even without them, Panzer Brigade 113 still had more than a two-to-one advantage in tanks and equipment.

There had been rumblings of panzers during the night, and the 4th Armored had set up a thin screen of M18 76mm GMC tank destroyers from its 704th Tank Destroyer Battalion. As dawn broke, the rolling farm hills were cloaked in fog as they had been for the past week. One of the tank destroyer officers bumped into the advancing German columns while traveling by jeep, escaped unnoticed, and informed headquarters of the encounter. Shortly thereafter, an outpost of M5A1 light tanks from Company D, 37th Tank Battalion, encountered the same group and withdrew in the thick fog to report.

The spearhead of the German column was a company of Panther tanks leading the eastern column of the Panzer Brigade 113 attack. Moments later, they stumbled into the main U.S. positions, a platoon of M4 medium tanks from Company C, 37th Tank Battalion. The Panther tanks emerged

from the fog about seventy-five yards in front of the Shermans, but the American tankers had been warned and were waiting. Quickly opening fire, three Panthers were knocked out in rapid succession. Stunned and surprised, the German column broke off to the southwest. The U.S. tank company commander raced a platoon of M4 medium tanks to a commanding ridge west of his position to trap the withdrawing panzer column. As the eight surviving Panthers appeared, four were quickly knocked out by close-range shots against their vulnerable side armor. Before the Germans could respond, the M4 tanks masked themselves behind the cover of the reverse slopes. In the dense fog, the Panther crews had no idea where the American tanks were located, and seconds later, the M4 tanks reappeared from behind the ridge and destroyed the remaining four Panthers with a volley against their vulnerable flank.

In the meantime, a platoon of M18 tank destroyers was on the way to reinforce the outposts when it ran into the spearhead of the western column of Panzer Brigade 113. Unnoticed in the thick fog, the M18s took advantage of the terrain and adopted hull-down cover in a shallow depression that protected their thinly armored hulls. Surprised again by a volley of fire from a point-blank range of only 150 yards, the German column quickly lost seven tanks, but three of the four M18 Hellcats were put out of action as well. The German column retreated. As the remainder of Panzer Brigade 113 advanced toward their objective at Rechicourt-la-Petite, a second platoon of M18 Hellcats of the 704th Tank Destroyer Battalion ambushed one of the German tank columns, knocking out eight Panthers and causing the attack to falter. By midafternoon, the tank destroyers had knocked out nineteen tanks but had suffered significant casualties, including the battalion commander, who was killed by mortar fire.

As the tank fighting intensified, the commander of the 37th Tank Battalion, Lt. Col. Creighton Abrams, radioed his scattered tank companies with instructions to rally near Arracourt. In the early afternoon, the Shermans of Companies A and B were formed into Task Force Hunter and sent to counterattack near Rechicourt. The ensuing tank skirmish led to the destruction of nine more Panther tanks, at a cost of three M4 medium tanks. By the

ON THE FIELDS OF ARRACOURT 191

time the lost Panzer Brigade 111 appeared in the afternoon, the fighting was largely over for the day.

Patton visited Arracourt late in the day and talked with the divisional commander, Gen. John Wood, about his plans for the next day. Wood reported that his units had destroyed forty-three enemy tanks during the fighting, mostly factory-fresh Panthers, at a cost of six men killed and three wounded plus three M18 tank destroyers and five M4 tanks knocked out. Patton believed that the German strength in the area had been spent and ordered Wood to continue his advance the next day. He thought that this was simply a local counterattack and not part of a grand panzer offensive.

The following morning, Combat Command A of 4th Armored Division moved out from the area near Lezey on its planned offensive. While it was moving eastward, CCA received frantic radio calls from rear elements of the division near Arracourt reporting that German tanks were attacking again from the Parroy woods toward the town. This was the long-delayed attack by Panzer Brigade 111. Eight German tanks had appeared out of the mist about 1,000 yards from the 191st Field Artillery Battalion as it was preparing to limber up and move out. The 155mm howitzers were quickly swung around and began to take the tanks under fire at point-blank range. A small number of tanks and tank destroyers from other units showed up and beat off the panzer attack under intense fire.

Abrams ordered his 37th Tank Battalion back toward Lezey to clean out what he believed to be a handful of German tanks. In the meantime, a German PzKpfw IV company, supported by antitank guns, took up ambush positions on the approaches to the area where the earlier fighting had taken place. When Company C, 37th Tank Battalion, crested the rise, it was hit with a volley from the tanks and antitank guns below, losing half a dozen M4 tanks in a few seconds. The Americans pulled back over the rise and waited for Company B to reach them. After forming up, the two companies maneuvered to gain a better position and in the ensuing tank fighting knocked out eleven German tanks while losing another six themselves. A further five Panthers were knocked out later in the afternoon when the American task force reached Bures.

There was little fighting on September 21 after Hitler ordered command changes because of the previous three days of failure. After a late start, the German attack struck the northern flank of Combat Command A of the 4th Armored Division, which was screened by elements of the 25th Cavalry Squadron. In the thick morning fog, the German tanks managed to get close to the cavalry outposts, and a series of fierce skirmishes ensued in which seven M5A1 light tanks of Company F were knocked out while desperately trying to fend off attacks by the much more powerful German tanks. The German attack was blunted when it encountered a thin screen of M18 Hellcat tank destroyers of Company C, 704th Tank Destroyer Battalion, which knocked out three tanks. Because of the late start of the attack, the fog was starting to lift. This made the German columns vulnerable to air attack, and for the first time in several days, the P-47 Thunderbolts of the XIX Tactical Air Command came roaring over the battlefield, strafing and bombing the German columns.

While the cavalry screen was delaying the German panzer attack, Abrams reoriented the 37th Tank Battalion northward and occupied a hill looking down into the valley east of Juvelize, where the German reinforcements were moving forward. Company A, 37th Tank Battalion, took the German tanks under fire at ranges of 400 to 2,000 yards and also called in field artillery fire. Among the German casualties was Panzer Brigade 111's commander, Col. Heinrich von Bronsart-Schellendorf. Under air attacks and artillery fire, the attack crumpled, and Panzer Brigade 111 began to withdraw. After the Luftwaffe refused his pleas for air support, Manteuffel committed his last armored reserve, some surviving tanks from Panzer Brigade 113, with no perceptible effect. By the end of the day, Panzer Brigade 111 was down to seven tanks and 80 men from an original strength of more than ninety tanks and 2,500 troops. The following day, the panzer brigade commander, Col. Erich von Seckendorf, was killed when his half-track command vehicle was strafed by a P-47 Thunderbolt. In the three days of fighting from September 19 to 22, the 4th Armored Division's Combat Command A had lost fourteen M4 medium and seven M5A1 light tanks as well as twenty-five men killed and eighty-eight wounded.

Sitting in a jeep, the 4th Armored Division's commander, Maj. Gen. John Wood, talks to the head of Combat Command A, Col. Bruce Clarke, during the fighting in Lorraine in October 1944. Clarke preferred to command CCA while flying in the back seat of a Piper Cub. PATTON MUSEUM

In the process, they had effectively shattered two panzer brigades.

The fighting around Arracourt continued for another week, but under significantly different tactical circumstances. With Operation Market Garden underway since September 17, Bradley informed Patton that he would have to wind down offensive operations and sit tight since he would not be receiving enough fuel to move forward. Two of Patton's four armored divisions were shifted to other formations, and the 4th Armored Division was told to hunker down and take the defensive. The fighting at Arnhem focused Hitler's attention, and most of the fresh German resources were sent to that sector.

Manteuffel's panzer forces were ordered to continue their attacks without fresh resources.

The Lorraine tank battles finally petered out on September 29 after the 11th Panzer Division had taken a beating in futile attacks against the 4th Armored Division's defenses. Of the 262 tanks and assault guns deployed by the German units in the week of fighting near Arracourt, 86 were destroyed, 114 were damaged or broken down, and only 62 were operational at the end of the month. The 4th Armored Division, which had borne the brunt of the Arracourt tank fighting, lost 41 M4 medium tanks and 7 M5A1 light tanks during the whole month of September, and casualties had been 225 killed and 648 wounded. The battle had ended in stalemate, and both sides now faced a frustrating autumn of fighting in the mud as Patton continued his advance toward the Saar. But if the tactical results had been inconclusive, the Arracourt fighting clearly demonstrated the growing problems of the Wehrmacht in waging offensive panzer operations. The Wehrmacht had suffered far higher casualties than Patton's Third Army and had repeatedly squandered tactical and technical advantages.

At the heart of the matter was the declining quality of German panzer crews. The panzer brigades fighting at Arracourt had been hastily raised and trained, even if their senior commanders were Russian front veterans. The 4th Armored Division was well trained, battle-ready, and well led by superb officers like divisional commander John Wood, CCA commander Bruce Clarke, and 37th Tank Battalion commander Creighton Abrams.

Arracourt was not a particularly important battle in terms of its overall impact on the ETO campaign, but it is extremely illuminating regarding the tank balance in the ETO. The technical and quantitative advantage of the panzer brigades in the first few days of the fighting were thrown away by tactical mistakes and poor crew training. The Panther was a superb tank, clearly superior to the Sherman in firepower and armor. This didn't matter when the disparity in crew quality was so different. The U.S. tankers exploited the few technical advantages of the Sherman and benefited from the terrain and weather. The Panther was best suited to long-range tank engagements where its long-range firepower could kill Shermans long before they were within range to respond. The foggy weather and terrain denied the Panthers that advantage. The Panther can best be compared to a sniper; the Sherman to a street fighter. The Sherman's advantages lay in skirmishes at close ranges. The Panther had sluggish turret traverse because its power traverse drew power off the engine and required careful coordination between a skilled driver and gunner; the novice German panzer crews lacked these skills. The Sherman had a faster turret traverse than the Panther and was independently powered. The Sherman gunner had better situational awareness at close range than the Panther gunner since he was provided a periscopic sight for general observation as well as the telescopic sight for aiming; the Panther gunner lacked a periscope, and it took longer for him to acquire a target. This mattered less in long-range engagements than in fast-moving close engagements. The Panther had superb front armor, but this counted for little in a wild tank melee, like much of the fighting in Arracourt, in which its vulnerable side armor was often exposed.

In the wake of Arracourt, the 4th Armored Division was offered the new second-generation M4A3(76mm) as replacements for battle losses. The 37th Tank Battalion didn't want any, preferring to stick to the 75mm gun because of its better high-explosive "pitching power." Even after the tank battles at Arracourt, the experienced 37th Tank Battalion still recognized that in day-to-day tank fighting, it was high-explosive firepower that mattered. Nevertheless, Gen. Bruce Clarke put pressure on Lt. Col. Creighton Abrams to accept a 76mm gun tank to set an example for the rest of the battalion. He knew that if Abrams refused to use the new tanks, so would his troops. Abrams finally relented, and the new tank was nicknamed *Thunderbolt VI*, the sixth tank Abrams had been issued since 1942 and his second Sherman in the ETO. The 4th Armored Division gradually came to appreciate the added firepower and accuracy of the 76mm gun, especially because the new tank offered a more powerful 5-power telescope for aiming instead of the 2.5-power telescope in the older M4 series.

BETTER BULLETS

The inadequacy of the 76mm gun on the Sherman and M18 Hellcat tank destroyer as well as the 3-inch gun on the M10 tank destroyer led to a crash program by Ordnance to develop and field the new HVAP (high-velocity, armor-piercing) ammunition that had been in development since 1943. HVAP rounds used a core made of heavy and dense tungsten carbide surrounded by an aluminum shell. As a result, the shell was relatively light yet had high velocity and very good armor penetration. On impact, the outer shell peeled away, and the smaller tungsten carbide core penetrated the armor. The concept of such rounds had been around for some time and were used in Polish antitank rifles in the 1939 campaign and in later German antitank projectiles. The main problem with these rounds was the scarcity of tungsten, a critical war material that was tightly controlled by the U.S. War Production Board because of its high priority applications in machine tools. A shipment of 2,000 rounds of the experimental T4 76mm HVAP ammunition was airlifted to France in August 1944. Its performance in trials against actual Panthers was poorer than stateside tests against armor plate predicted, but it still was better than the standard M62 APC (armor-piercing-capped) round then in use. It could not penetrate the Panther glacis, but it punched the Panther mantlet at 800 to 1,000 yards, compared to only 100 to 300 yards for the normal M62 APC.

A production order for 20,000 HVAP rounds was issued in the late summer, but production never kept up with demand because of shortages of tungsten carbide. The production requirement for the new HVAP ammunition was set at 43,000 rounds through January 1945 and 10,000 monthly after that. This production was to be equally divided between 76mm and 3-inch, the latter for the M10 3-inch GMC tank destroyer and the towed guns. The HVAP ammunition underwent continual refinement through the autumn. The original T4 had the tungsten carbide core enclosed in a steel jacket within the aluminum body and windshield. The modified T4E17 removed the steel jacket and became the next production standard in the fall of 1944. The third and final version of the ammunition was the T4E20, which used an unground tungsten carbide core that offered about 5 percent better penetration and also introduced an adjustable nose plug. This variant was finally type-classified as the M93 76mm fixed-shot HVAP-T in February 1945 and became standard during 1945.

The first distribution of HVAP ammunition to tank units took place in Belgium on September 11, 1944, based on the first airlifted batch of 2,000

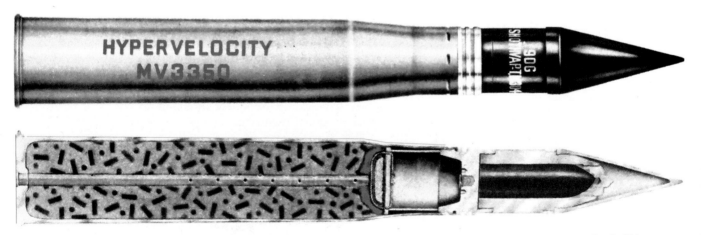

The new high-velocity, armor-piercing (HVAP) ammunition consisted of a sub-caliber tungsten carbide penetrator contained within a lightweight outer shell, as seen in this cross-section of the new 90mm HVAP round.

rounds. Tank and tank destroyer crews were very enthusiastic about the performance of the new ammunition, but it was never available in adequate quantities. The AFV&W section of the 12th Army Group decided to issue it on an equal basis to all units equipped with the M4 (76mm) and the M18 76mm GMC tank destroyer, which used the same ammunition. But this usually meant only one round per vehicle per month. By the end of February 1945, each 76mm tank and tank destroyer had received, on average, only five rounds of HVAP since the autumn of 1944. By early March 1945, a total of about 18,000 rounds of HVAP had been delivered to the ETO, of which about 7,550 were 76mm rounds and the rest was 3-inch ammunition for the M10 tank destroyers. The 6th Army Group, fighting in Alsace in December 1944–January 1945, received little or no 76mm HVAP ammunition. These units faced far fewer German tank units than did 12th Army Group, until the Operation *Nordwind* offensive of January 1945 in Alsace.

AMERICAN BLITZKRIEG

The Sherman succeeded in the 1944 campaign not because of superior technical performance, but because it was an integral element in a better fighting machine than the Wehrmacht. The quality of the Wehrmacht had eroded steadily through the war because of the staggering demands of the Russian front, and German tactical and operational doctrine did not keep pace. While the Wehrmacht was in the forefront of the art of war in 1939–41, it was rapidly falling behind by 1944. The American art of war was fundamentally different from the German or Soviet style, placing a great deal more emphasis on airpower. While American capabilities in tactical combat in World War II have been deprecated as inferior to the Wehrmacht, this is often based on a blinkered approach that artificially compares only the combat effectiveness of the infantry and armored divisions but ignores the broader context of the tactical capabilities provided by artillery and airpower as well as the American emphasis on logistics and industrial warfare. Rommel grimly recognized that "even with the most modern weapons, anyone who has to fight against an enemy in complete control of the air fights like a savage against modern European troops, under the same handicaps and with the same chance of success."

The U.S. Army was one of the few militaries during the war to place so much emphasis on the industrial dimension of modern warfare. The Allied preponderance in weapons was not preordained, as demonstrated by the poor American showing in World War I. Rather, the American lessons of its industrial failures in 1917–18 led to a systematic revolution in American war planning in the 1920s and 1930s to prepare for future wars by focusing more attention on its industrial and logistical dimensions.

There has also been a tendency to criticize American operational art as compared to the Red Army in World War II, contrasting Soviet "deep battle" doctrine with the apparent lack of a similar American doctrine. In fact, the U.S. had a more advanced deep battle doctrine, but unlike the Soviets, U.S. doctrine lacked the ideological pretensions of Soviet war science and emerged by practical example, not by way of field manuals. During World War II, the U.S. developed a form of industrial age warfare that was the most effective combination of the traditional ground combat arms and the revolutionary potential of airpower.

The U.S. Army—i.e., the Army Ground Forces and Army Air Force—devoted a disproportionate share of its resources to airpower not only in terms of industrial production, but also in terms of manpower resources, training costs, and operating expenses. Neither the German nor Soviet armies could compete with the Americans in this regard because of the sheer expense; only the British armed forces made a comparable effort. To put this in some perspective, the U.S. Army spent almost six times as much on aircraft as tanks—$36 billion versus $6 billion in 1941–45. The Wehrmacht—the Heer (army) and Luftwaffe (air force)—did attempt to create a modern three-dimensional art of war and also devoted a disproportionate level of resources to airpower. However, this attempt was largely stifled by the Allied strategic bombing campaigns, which forced the Wehrmacht to strip much of its tactical airpower from the Russian front in 1943–44 and concentrate its attention on strategic air defense of the Reich. The U.S. Army Air Force doctrine was focused on destroying enemy airpower as a prerequisite to further operations. This led to Operation Pointblank in the autumn and winter of 1943–44, which aimed at destroying the Luftwaffe in the air and crippling its related aviation plants. By the spring of 1944, prior to D-Day, this mission had been largely accomplished. The lack of Luftwaffe airpower over the battlefields in France did not result from the Wehrmacht's negligence of this aspect of modern warfighting, but from its defeat in repelling Operation Pointblank.

The American art of war that emerged by 1944 differed considerably from Soviet deep battle, which was primarily a two-dimensional concept involving ground forces. Although Soviet doctrine recognized the desirability of tactical airpower to support the ground forces, its air force during World War II was hamstrung by industrial weaknesses, poor aircrew

The first of the new M4A3 with the Ford GAA engine began appearing in combat in the late summer of 1944. Here, a new M4A3 medium tank of the 737th Tank Battalion fires on buildings near Dombasle, along the left flank of the advance along the Moselle River near Nancy on September 15, 1944, in support of the 320th Infantry Regiment, which was crossing a nearby canal at the time.

training, and doctrinal shortcomings that led to its inability to impose air superiority over the Luftwaffe or engage in counterforce industrial air strikes.

In contrast, the American art of war was three-dimensional, consisting of traditional two-dimensional ground warfare supplemented by the third dimension of airpower. The U.S.'s industrial focus gave rise to a dominant mission of strangling the enemy's economy by means of heavy "strategic" bombers that struck into the depths of the German homeland. A sequential series of strategic air cam-

paigns evolved through 1943 and 1944, with considerable debate and controversy between Eisenhower and his senior air force commanders. In the operational depths, the mission was primarily focused on strangling the Wehrmacht by interdicting its supply of men and materiel from Germany to the battle area through the use of medium bombers. At the tactical level, airpower had the mission of tactical interdiction to deprive the Wehrmacht of its mobility and the Luftwaffe of its tactical ability, to provide firepower beyond the range of traditional artillery.

The Sherman was designed to be repairable under field conditions. Here, the transmission is removed for servicing using a wrecker truck.

The first of the new M4A3 with 76mm gun arrived in France in August 1944. These tanks are being prepared by the 350th Ordnance Battalion prior to being issued to American tank units.

The U.S. Army's penchant for industrial warfare extended to its devotion to field artillery. This was the one ground combat arm in which the U.S. Army had unquestioned tactical and technological superiority over the Wehrmacht. American field artillery was fully motorized and partly mechanized while the German artillery still relied on horse transport for some of its field artillery until the end of the war. The U.S. Army's development of innovative field artillery tactics, such as the use of fire direction centers networked by radio, enhanced its lethality. The quality of its field artillery was further extended by its sheer quantity: more field artillery battalions, more ammunition. Quantity has a quality all its own in field artillery.

The Sherman tank operated within the broader context of this American art of war. The Sherman succeeded on the World War II battlefield not because it was the best tank, but because it was part of the most modern and effective army. German officers complained about the poor quality of American infantry because they would not fight without tanks, would not fight at night, and depended too much on artillery fire support. German war memoirs constantly lament Allied airpower as though it was somehow unchivalrous and unfair to plague the heroic German infantry *landser* and *panzermann* with this impersonal menace. The German commanders did not comprehend that they were facing a more modern military machine that placed greater emphasis on firepower and industrial prowess to dominate the battlefield and therefore depended less on the traditional combat arms. The U.S. Army did not insist on fielding the best tank, but it did insist on fielding enough tanks that were good enough.

CHAPTER 7

Through the Mud and Blood

WHEN THE ALLIED ARMIES OUTRAN THEIR supplies in September 1944, Eisenhower had two principal options. He could halt military operations for the autumn as the Red Army had done on the central front in Poland and wait until logistics caught up, or he could maintain limited military operations along the Siegfried Line to the extent permitted by supplies and continue to grind down the Wehrmacht and prevent it from fully recovering from its summer disasters. Eisenhower decided on the second option, leading to three months of frustrating campaigns along Germany's fortified West Wall. From the standpoint of tank operations, this meant that there were none of the grand maneuvers like Operation Cobra, but rather the relentless attritional warfare closer to the bocage fighting of June and July 1944. The big difference was the weather and the terrain. The autumn of 1944 was the wettest on record in northwest Europe, with twice as much rain as usual. Mud is no friend of the tank, and the farm fields became so sodden that they were often impassable, even to tanks. This led to a condition that commanders called "a front one tank wide." In other words, the lack of mobility caused by the mud forced the tanks to operate on roads, often just narrow country lanes or village streets. As a result, tank units were constrained to the few available roads, which greatly simplified German antitank defense. Every major road intersection could be covered by an antitank gun or a hidden *panzerjäger*. Furthermore, these conditions were ideal for antitank mines, a threat that had not been especially common in France. The second change from the summer was the terrain. The western German frontier near Aachen, the Saar, and Alsace was heavily industrialized and in many areas consisted of sprawling towns. The

On September 13, 1944, Task Force X of the 3rd Armored Division penetrated the Siegfried Line near Roeten, the first American troops into Germany. Here, one of the division's M4 tanks drives through some dragon's teeth along the border on the approaches to Aachen, in the standard olive-drab and black camouflage paint that the division had worn since Operation Cobra.

Two days after Task Force X's penetration of the Siegfried Line, one of its M4 dozer tanks moves through a gap in the dragon's teeth.

autumn campaign saw the first extensive use of the Sherman in urbanized areas.

On the German side, the evaporation of fuel supplies forced the Luftwaffe to disband many squadrons and the navy to dock most of its warships. The personnel from these units were trans- ferred to the army, giving the German infantry a sudden surge of troops for the final defense of the fatherland. Embittered by the savage Allied bombing raids on their cities and towns and now fighting on their native soil, the German soldiers' spirit stiffened after the demoralizing defeats of the summer.

A 3rd Armored Division M4 carrying troops of the 36th Armored Infantry Regiment moves through border defenses near Roeten on September 15, 1944.

The town of Schevenhuette was the site of intense fighting when the German Seventh Army launched a local counterattack on September 17, 1944. Tanks of the 3rd Armored Division move through the town on September 22 after the fighting ended in a bloody stalemate.

The first major German city to come under attack on the Western Front was Aachen, starting on October 11, 1944. Here an M4 provides overwatch as an M10 tank destroyer moves forward on October 20. The German troops finally surrendered the next day when an M12 155mm gun motor carriage was used to reduce the commander's bunker at point-blank range.

GIs of Company M, 26th Infantry Regiment, 1st Infantry Division, advance cautiously along the streets of Aachen on October 15, 1944, as a pair of M4 tanks of the 745th Tank Battalion move down the street. The 745th Tank Battalion supported the Big Red One since Normandy; the tank to the left is still fitted with its rear wading trunk from the Normandy landing.

FORGOTTEN SECRETS: PROJECT CASSOCK

The terrain and weather conditions of the autumn 1944 campaign led to a revival of interest in specialized tanks for dealing with the new threats. At the same time, it led to the ignominious end of the most secret Allied tank program of World War II, Project Cassock.

In the early years of World War II, the British Army began to experiment with various techniques to enable tanks to fight at night. These were conducted under the strictest secrecy, since it was believed that the sudden introduction of a new surprise night-attack tactic would have the most

dramatic effect if reserved only for the most important battles. The most promising technology was also the most obvious—the use of high-power searchlights. Even though the technology was obvious, so too were the shortcomings. High-power searchlights would be clearly visible to the enemy and so could be quickly knocked out. Eventually, British engineers came up with a scheme to mount the searchlights inside an armored tank turret. The searchlight was largely protected by the turret armor, and the light beam was projected through a narrow slit that would be difficult to hit. The engineers came up

The Leaflet tank, also known as the T10 Shop Tractor, was an American version of the British Canal Defense Light. Although six battalions were equipped with these night-fighting tanks prior to D-Day, the extreme secrecy attached to the program doomed it in the end.

A close-up of the turret of a Leaflet tank of the 736th Tank Battalion (Special) in England prior to D-Day. The searchlight beam was emitted through the narrow vertical aperture above the tanker's feet.

with other innovations, such as the use of a shutter to enable the beams to flicker on and off to confuse enemy gunners. Colored filters were also developed to make it more difficult for the enemy to determine the range to the lights. This weapon was named CDL for Canal Defense Light.

The U.S. Army was informed of the program in 1942 and asked to participate. The idea was to create a CDL force in both the U.S. and British armies. At an opportune moment, both armies could launch a coordinated night attack to overcome some particularly stubborn German defense line. In November 1942, the U.S. Army decided to take up the offer, and as a result, a program was begun to manufacture CDL tanks in the U.S., under the code name Project Cassock. There was a clear understanding

between the British and American sides that the U.S. would not use the CDL tanks without coordinating the operation with British officials first.

The American CDL tanks were called T10 Shop Tractors in Ordnance documents and production contracts, but the tank was code-named Leaflet for operational use. In fact, most troops called it by its original British name, the CDL. Production of an American copy of the British CDL began in the spring of 1943, and a total of 500 of these "S Turrets" were manufactured. There was some debate about which was the best tank for the S Turret; both the older M3 and M4 medium tanks were tested in this role. Both Britain and the U.S. finally settled on using the older M3 Grant medium tank since the 75mm gun could be left in place, giving the Leaflet

Because of shortages of minefield-breaching equipment, the U.S. Army obtained small numbers of Crab flails from the British. They were first used by a platoon of the 747th Tank Battalion during Cobra in July 1944. The Americans also received the assistance of the British 79th Armoured Division to provide flail tank support. This Crab is in use near Breinig, Germany, on October 11, 1944.

One of the first units to see combat with the M4A3E2 was the 743rd Tank Battalion, which had fifteen in November 1944 while supporting the 30th Infantry Division. This tank was knocked out near Fronhoven in late November 1944 after being hit by four 88mm rounds from an antitank gun about 800 yards away near Lohn. One bounced off the glacis plate and two off the mantlet before a lucky hit actually entered the telescope opening. Although not immediately apparent, this vehicle was fitted with a flamethrower in the hull machine-gun position.

A T1E3 "Aunt Jemima" mine roller of the 25th Armored Engineer Battalion, 6th Armored Division, near the Moselle River at Liverdun, France, on October 7, 1944.

An M4 tank fitted with a T1E3 "Aunt Jemima" mine roller moves down a road along the German border while supporting the 30th Infantry Division on December 10, 1944. The 739th Tank Battalion was one of two former CDL battalions specifically configured for mine clearing operations and had one company with eighteen T1E1 mine rollers, two companies with twelve T1E3 mine rollers, and six dozer tanks.

tank the capability to fight as well as illuminate targets. By the spring of 1943, the M3 was out of production, so a contract was given to American Locomotive Company in Schenectady, New York, to remanufacture and convert older tanks, bringing them up to the current Sherman standards in terms of many mechanical features. A total of 497 Leaflet tanks were converted starting in June 1943, principally on the M3A1 cast-hull version.

The U.S. Army decided to organize the Leaflet tanks into six separate tank battalions. This was a very substantial commitment of resources, equivalent in tank strength to all of the U.S. Marine tank battalions raised in World War II or two armored divisions. To maintain secrecy, the Leaflet tanks were confined to the 9th and 10th Armored Groups, each with three separate "special" tank battalions: the 701st, 736th, 738th, 739th, 740th, and 748th Tank

During the attempts by Patton's Third Army to overcome the fortifications around Metz, the 735th Tank Battalion made one of the few uses of the demolition snake in combat. This consisted of up to 400 feet of explosive-packed tubing that was pushed in front of the tank and detonated to blow gaps in minefields. This shows the assembly of one of the snakes on October 2 near Gorz.

This is a front view of another M4A3E2 knocked out near Fronhoven. An 88mm hit on the glacis plate obliterated some sandbags on the hull front. Three other hits are evident on the front, including one near the gun tube, one on the upper edge of the mantlet, and one on the upper edge of the glacis plate.

Battalions (Special). Instead of the usual organization, these battalions each had fifty-four "special" tanks and eighteen M4 Sherman "fighter" tanks without the CDL equipment. So each tank company had eighteen Leaflet and five fighter tanks instead of the usual sixteen Sherman tanks. All six battalions were confined to Camp Bouse in the remote Arizona desert to preserve the intense secrecy of the project. The two armored groups began to be transferred to Rosebush camp in southwest Wales in March 1944; they destroyed all records of their training activities before departing for Europe, which is one reason that information about this project is so scarce. Three of the battalions were transferred to Normandy in August 1944, and the rest arrived by September 1944. In anticipation of their arrival, Eisenhower's SHAEF headquarters issued an order on August 10, 1944, that none

The 155mm gun of this M12 155mm gun motor carriage is in full recoil as it fires on a German pillbox near Grossenich, Germany, on November 16, 1944. The field artillery was not especially interested in the M12 for normal fire-support missions, but several battalions were equipped with this self-propelled gun because of the efforts of Eisenhower's AFV&W section, which anticipated the need for them to deal with German pillboxes along the Siegfried Line.

The 6th Armored Division received a number of M4A3E2 assault tanks in November, and this one was hit with six 88mm rounds during fighting near Neid, France, on November 16, 1944. It is seen here being repaired by divisional maintenance crews.

would be committed to action without approval from SHAEF headquarters or moved forward any closer than twenty miles from the front lines. The top-secret status of the Cassock project would prove to be its downfall since few field commanders knew about its role or capabilities. What is so surprising about the project is that the British did not make use of the CDL tanks during their various armored offensives around Caen in the summer of 1944.

By the autumn of 1944, the U.S. Army had institutionalized the practice of attaching a separate tank battalion to each infantry division in combat. However, there was a shortage of tank battalions, yet the six "special" tank battalions were sitting idle behind the lines. Eisenhower's SHAEF headquarters began to discuss converting these back to normal tank battalions and committing them to combat. To avoid the waste of all the time and effort spent raising

A crew from the 70th Tank Battalion tests an E4-5 flamethrower mounted on an M4A3 (76mm) during trials in Belgium. The flame gun was mounted in the ball mount usually used for the .30-caliber machine gun.

The 70th Tank Battalion demonstrated the E4-5 flamethrower to several units in September 1944, as seen here, and two were attached to the 741st Tank Battalion later in September 1944 for attacks against pillboxes along the Siegfried Line.

these units, in October 1944, the commander of the 10th Armored Group began making the rounds of commanders of the U.S. First Army along the German border trying to interest them in the use of the Leaflet tanks for a major offensive operation. Most of the officers were skeptical about the whole idea without an actual demonstration, but the high level of security delayed attempts to stage such a display.

By the end of October, little interest had been forthcoming in staging a major night attack. So on November 4, 1944, SHAEF decided to put the Leaflet tanks in mothballs and begin converting three of the Cassock battalions into normal tank battalions. In the end, three of the battalions would be converted to specialized battalions using other types of "armored funnies."

In anticipation of encounters with bunkers along the Siegfried Line, elements of the First Army were provided with flamethrowers. Four E4-5 flamethrowers were fitted to M4A1 (76) tanks of 70th Tank Battalion on September 11, 1944. Two of these tanks were temporarily attached to the 741st Tank Battalion and were used to attack a German pillbox three days later. This configuration was found seriously inadequate because the tank had to approach to within twenty-five yards of the pillbox, and even after using up its fuel, the pillbox was not knocked out.

An E4-5 flamethrower mounted on an M4 tank of the 709th Tank Battalion is discharged near Zweifall, Germany, on November 24, 1944. Interestingly, the tank is still fitted with one of the rare green dozer hedgerow cutters more commonly associated with the 747th Tank Battalion.

Because of shortages of flamethrower tanks, British tanks were often seconded to American units for support. In this case, a Churchill Crocodile of the 9020 Tank Squadron, 1st Fife and Forfar Yeomanry, was attached to the U.S. 2nd Armored Division during operations in late November along the Siegfried Line. Here a Crocodile attacks a target near Merkstein, Germany, on December 3, 1944.

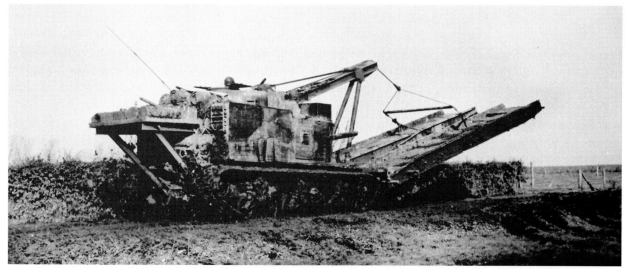

Antitank ditches and other obstructions were a constant hindrance during operations along the Siegfried Line, leading to many improvisations by the armored engineers. One particularly popular innovation was the development of fittings that permitted M31 tank recovery vehicles to carry and deploy treadway bridge sections to breach these gaps. This example is being used by the 17th Armored Engineer Battalion of the 2nd Armored Division near Beggendorf on November 16, 1944, at the start of Operation Queen, the failed offensive to reach the Roer.

PANCAKE MINE ROLLERS

One of the most vexing tactical problems to emerge during the autumn fighting was the growing rate of tank casualties to mines. The muddy ground conditions forced the tanks to use roads, which were vulnerable to mining operations. For example, during the Battle of El Alamein, it took an average of 1,942 mines for every tank knocked out; in the Aachen fighting along the Siegfried Line, it took only 221 mines per tank kill. Mines had been a minor nuisance in Normandy but were becoming a major threat along the Siegfried Line. For example, in the U.S. First Army, tank casualties to mines had only been about five in June 1944 but had risen more than tenfold to fifty-two—almost the equivalent of a tank battalion—by November. Mines eventually became the second most common cause of tank losses after gunfire, accounting for about 20 percent of tank casualties.

The U.S. Army had hoped to acquire British flail mine-clearing tanks for D-Day, but these were slow in materializing because of shortages in the British Army. However, some method to rapidly breach mine fields was needed, so the remaining three Cassock battalions were earmarked for conversion to mine-clearing tanks once the equipment became available. These units were now designated as Tank Battalion MX (mine exploder). The mothballed Leaflet tanks might have been completely forgotten except for an officer in the antiaircraft section at headquarters who thought they might be useful in future operations along the Rhine River, where they could help defend key bridges from night attacks. As a result, they would finally see combat in some very unexpected roles in 1945.

The U.S. Army had some experience with British flail tanks since the Tunisian campaign, when it had acquired some of the early Scorpion flail tanks. These consisted of a frame fitted to a Sherman tank with a small auxiliary motor and a rotating drum at the front of the tank fitted with weighted chains that were used to beat the ground in front of the tank. The weights on the end of the chain, combined with the flailing motion, were enough to detonate most German antitank mines. The Scorpion flail was cumbersome and by 1944 was replaced by the Crab flail, which worked on the same principle. Ordnance was not entirely convinced that a flail system was the best approach. The flail eventually lost so many chains that it became ineffective, and the process was unpredictable; the flail was apparently still intact one moment, then missed a few mines, which exploded under the tank. The American approach was to use heavy steel rollers resistant to mine damage. In addition, it was easier to tell when the mine rollers had been damaged to the point of being ineffective. There were two principal types used in the ETO: the T1E1 Earthworm, which was pushed by an M32 tank recovery vehicle (TRV) based on the Sherman chassis, and the T1E3 Aunt Jemima, pushed by a modified M4 medium tank. The Earthworm consisted of an array of smaller rollers with a set in front of each track and a third set positioned in the center. The Aunt Jemima was nicknamed after the famous pancake batter, and as the name implied, it consisted of a stack of large rollers in two arrays on either side.

A small number of the mine rollers first arrived in the ETO in the summer of 1944, along with an initial shipment of British Crab flails. A total of nine Crabs, twelve T1E1s, and twenty-seven T1E3s were used to equip companies of the 702nd and 744th Tank Battalions in July 1944 for Operation Cobra. The flails and mine rollers were used on a limited scale during Operation Cobra, but the lack of sufficient training undermined the effectiveness of these devices, which were cumbersome even in the best of circumstances. Mines remained a relatively minor risk until the autumn fighting, and so there was little pressure until then to address the threat more vigorously. The one clear lesson from the use of the mine exploders during Operation Cobra was the need for specially trained crews to handle these dangerous devices. This was the genesis of the November 1944 program to convert the three Cassock battalions to mine exploders. In the event, the conversion project took more time than expected because of equipment shortages, and during the Battle of the Bulge, one of the three units, the 740th Tank Battalion, intended for Patton's Third Army was hastily converted into a normal tank battalion and sent into action against Kampfgruppe Peiper in support of the 82nd Airborne Division. In 1945, the remaining two battalions became jack-of-all-trade specialist tanks battalions and were eventually equipped with a strange menagerie of specialized tanks, including mine exploders, some mothballed CDL Leaflet tanks, and even DD Donald Duck tanks for the Rhine River crossing.

BUNKER BLASTERS

Another tactical challenge in the autumn of 1944 was the need to deal with the extensive fortifications along the German frontier, called the Siegfried Line by the Allies and the West Wall by the Wehrmacht. The first specialized tank developed for this role was the M4A3E2 assault tank mentioned earlier, which was basically a normal M4A3 tank with much thicker armor. Although nominally developed for this mission, it was seldom used for this specific antifortification role. By the time M4A3E2s arrived in the ETO in the autumn of 1944, they were quickly assigned to the separate tank battalions, which badly needed a tank with armor sufficient to withstand the ubiquitous German antitank gun of the period, the 75mm PaK 40. With the wet weather frequently restricting tank movement to single roads, the lead tank in a tank column was very vulnerable to destruction. The tactic involved placing the M4A3E2 at the head of attacking columns since it could absorb so much more punishment than a normal Sherman. At first, the armored divisions had resisted the use of these assault tanks, fearing that the added weight would result in a sluggish tank apt to breakdown from the extra stress on its suspension and powertrain. In fact, the M4A3E2 proved to be nearly as mobile as normal Shermans, with only slightly reduced mechanical durability.

The weather-driven tactics led to a change of heart, and soon nearly all U.S. tank units in the ETO were clamoring for their fair share of assault tanks. Only 250 had been shipped to Europe, so they were doled out in small amounts. It is fair to say that the M4A3E2 assault tank was the most popular version of the Sherman in service in the autumn of 1944. Patton's Third Army chief of staff reported, "Everyone wants the M4A3E2," and the commander of the 6th Armored Division recommended that the army's 1945 tank program consist of a mixture of two-thirds M4A3E2 and one-third 105mm howitzer tanks for the remainder of combat operations in Europe. Eisenhower's headquarters telegraphed Washington that the "M4A3E2 assault tank has proved itself in combat and has been most favorably received. The theater has an immediate requirement for the maximum number that can be produced without materially reducing the flow of tanks to the Continent." In the end, the ETO would receive no more assault tanks, forcing American tankers to come up with their own local solutions to improve the Sherman's protection. The shortage of assault tanks was a consequence of the army's belated interest in the infantry-support mission.

Another technical option in attacking fortifications was tank-mounted flamethrowers. The U.S. Army had hoped to obtain the British Crocodile flamethrower for D-Day, but adapted to the Sherman instead of the Churchill tank. In the event, these arrived so late that only four were built before the program was cancelled, and they didn't see combat until February 1945. In the interim, the U.S. Army received flamethrower support from the British Army—for example, the use of a squadron of British Churchill Crocodiles during the siege of Brest in September 1944. In the meantime, the U.S. Army received a smaller U.S.-designed tank flamethrower, the E4-5, which was mounted in the hull of the M4 medium tank in place of the hull machine gun. These arrived in the ETO in September 1944 and were first used in combat on September 18, 1944, by the 70th Tank Battalion. This flamethrower had much shorter range than the Crocodile and was not very popular. The Crocodile had a large reservoir of compressed gas and fuel in a special armored trailer towed behind the tank while the E4-5 had a very modest gas cylinder and fuel cell because of the restricted space inside the Sherman. One tank officer labeled performance of the E4-5 "pathetic," a viewpoint that was widely shared after repeated uses in October 1944 along the West Wall. The flamethrowers were issued on a scale of nine per separate tank battalion. Generally, they were mounted in M4A3E2 assault tanks because of their better armor, but they were also mounted in most other types of M4 medium tanks.

In general, the U.S. Army's flame-tank program in the ETO was a flop, especially compared to their success elsewhere. The Canadian Army in Belgium and the Netherlands became one of the most ardent practitioners of flame-tank operations, finding them to be excellent weapons to pry out the most tenacious German defenders. The actual technical performance of Canadian Wasp flamethrowers was not especially impressive, but mechanized flamethrowers had an enormous psychological impact on the German troops, who feared them more than conventional weapons. Likewise, the U.S. Marine Corps and U.S. Army in the Pacific theater were also enthusiastic proponents of flame-tanks to deal with bunkers.

The most effective bunker buster in the ETO was not a tank at all, but a self-propelled gun. The M12 155mm GMC was another Ordnance orphan. In 1942, Ordnance decided to mount the World War I–era French 155mm gun on the M3 medium tank chassis for the field artillery, building 100 of them even though the field artillery had no interest. The M12 suffered from some of the problems of the old 155mm gun, especially a restricted elevation that limited its effective range. Since the 155mm gun was used in heavy artillery battalions at corps level, it was fired only from secure rear areas, so a self-propelled mechanized version was not necessary. Late in 1943, AFV&W section officers at SHAEF headquarters in England took some interest in the M12 as a potential bunker buster to deal with the Siegfried Line. They put in a request that the mothballed vehicles be taken out of retirement and shipped to Europe. They were dusted off and rebuilt to current Sherman tank standards. Although issued to field artillery battalions, the M12 self-propelled guns were often used in a completely untypical fashion, issued in small firing units of a battery or less and dispatched far and wide along the front to deal with bunkers. Even though the 155mm projectile was not powerful enough to crack open the thicker steel-reinforced concrete bunkers, it was accurate enough that it could be aimed at the bunkers' embrasures or other vulnerable spots.

During the fighting north of Aachen in early October 1944, many were assigned to the XIX Corps. They took part in a concerted campaign to demolish the West Wall bunkers prior to an offensive in this sector. Divisional artillery began the process with barrages to strip away camouflage from the bunkers. The M12 bunker busters were then moved up close to the front under the cover of darkness and set about blasting the bunkers from a few hundred yards away. During the final stages of the siege of Aachen in late October 1944, an M12 was brought into the city to reduce the German commander's hideout, leading to the final surrender. The M12 continued to be used in the bunker-buster role through the remainder of the autumn campaign.

In the event, the U.S. Army never had sufficient specialized tanks to deal with German fortifications and relied on more traditional means, especially combined infantry-engineer teams using satchel charges, flamethrowers, and other tactics. An armored group after-action report described a typical attack on the bunkers: "The assault teams in the main attack were composed of a squad of infantry supported by two tanks, and sufficient engineers to destroyed the pillboxes once they were taken. In six hours, these teams captured eleven pillboxes and took fifty-one prisoners in an area that was strongly defended." Another infantry regiment found that the pillboxes in its area were so tenaciously defended that tank-dozers were used to seal them up. It took about fifteen minutes of work to cover the bunkers, and this also prevented the German troops from infiltrating back and recapturing abandoned bunkers.

Patton's Third Army was particularly handicapped during its attempts to deal with the numerous forts around the border city of Metz in the autumn of 1944. Some of the methods developed by Ordnance simply proved impractical. Fort Driant was a particular menace during the fighting, and an elaborate plan was concocted to assault it. The fort was protected by thick fields of barbed wire which prevented the approach of infantry and hampered the use of tanks. Ordnance had developed a tank version of the Bangalore torpedo, nicknamed the snake, for breaching wire obstructions. The snake was simply a much longer version of the Bangalore torpedo, essentially a long length of pipe filled with high explosive. In early October 1944, four Shermans of the 735th Tank Battalion were modified to push a snake in front of them, with the snakes measuring as long as 400 feet. The snakes proved to be completely impractical under normal field conditions, with three of them breaking apart before reaching the fort and the remaining tank losing its snake moments before pushing it under the first wire barrier.

The U.S. Army had given relatively little thought to specialized armor prior to D-Day, and much of the American use of specialized armor was tied to British equipment. This stands in sharp contrast to the Pacific, where the U.S. Marine Corps fostered the use of specialized vehicles including amphibious tractors (amtraks) for beach landings and flamethrower tanks for assaulting Japanese bunkers. There were a handful of exceptions. As mentioned earlier, the U.S. Army had pioneered the use of dozer tanks, and these proved to be valuable and versatile weapons throughout the campaigns in the ETO. Ordnance also developed the best tank recovery vehicles of the war. The first of these was the T2 TRV, later called the M31, which was based on the obsolete M3 medium tank. This was the workhorse of American tank units in the ETO in 1944. It was gradually replaced by a more refined design based on the Sherman tank, the M32 TRV, which also saw extensive use in 1944–45.

NEW TANK KILLERS

The autumn fighting along the German border saw the introduction of the second generation of Sherman-based tank destroyers, the M36 90mm gun motor carriage. The first forty M36 tank destroyers arrived in France in the first week of September 1944 and were issued to Hodge's U.S. First Army. After preparation and crew training, they first went into action in October 1944 during the fighting along the Siegfried Line. Because of the small numbers originally available, it was not possible to equip entire battalions with the M36. As a result, the initial practice was to issue it to existing M10 battalions, usually on a scale of one company at a time. As more became available, entire battalions were reequipped.

The general conclusion was that the M36 was a definite improvement over the M10 when dealing with the Panther tank, though it was not the complete solution. The existing 90mm ammunition would not reliably penetrate the Panther glacis plate at ranges above 500 yards. Once again, Ordnance had failed to develop a new generation of ammunition specifically configured for tank fighting, and an improved HVAP round was still months away. Using the existing ammunition, crews found that it was better to target the Panther turret, which was more vulnerable. In some circumstances, several 90mm rounds fired in rapid succession at the glacis would penetrate, because of the collapse of the embrittled armor when partial penetrations were hit again by another round. The Panther was very vulnerable when hit from the side. In an engagement with a Panther at 1,500 yards by an M36 of the 776th Tank Destroyer Battalion north of Shalback, "Two hits were scored on the tank: one in the track by AP which blew the track off, and the other round of AP in the turret which blew a hole about six inches in diameter and made cracks in the entire right side of the turret. The seams on the back deck were also ripped. The round went into the turret, blew the breech block off, then blew off about half the turret top." New ammunition, better able to make frontal

The first M36 90mm gun motor carriage began to arrive in France in September 1944, but it did not see combat until October because of the need to train crews. Here, one of the original batches of the new tank destroyers is seen training in France on October 14, 1944.

Shortages of equipment in the autumn of 1944 occasionally led to substitution. The 629th Tank Destroyer Battalion—normally equipped with the M10 3-inch gun motor carriage—uses this M4A3 (76) in Gurzenich, Germany, during fighting on December 14, 1944.

As was the case with all previous tank destroyers, the M36 had an open turret to keep weight down. Here, the loader to the left is loading a round into the 90mm gun breech while the gunner to the right is aiming the gun.

penetrations, was in demand by the crews. The new T30E16 90mm HVAP ammunition for the M36 gun didn't become available until the Ardennes campaign, finally arriving in January 1945. This ammunition finally gave the tank destroyers the ability to penetrate the Panther's thick glacis plate at a range of about 450 yards.

Besides the M36, a growing number of units were being fielded with General Bruce's pet project,

the M18 Hellcat tank destroyer. The first of these had appeared in the ETO in August 1944 with Patton's Third Army, including the 704th Tank Destroyer Battalion of the 4th Armored Division. The M18 proved to be popular for its stunning automotive performance, but it offered little improvement over the M10 in terms of combat effectiveness. An army team interviewed one of the Hellcat commanders who had taken part in the

The M18 76mm gun motor carriage grew in numbers in the ETO as efforts were made to replace the towed 3-inch gun. This is an M18 of the 827th Tank Destroyer Battalion (Colored), one of a number of segregated African-American tank destroyer battalions that served in the ETO in 1944–45.

The M36 was armed with a 90mm gun, and the crew of this tank destroyer of Patton's Third Army loads one of the standard twenty-four-pound M82 armor-piercing-capped rounds near Serrig, Germany, on March 16, 1945.

Arracourt fighting, Sgt. Joseph Tetreault. He had previously served in the North African campaign in one of the original M3 75mm GMCs, so his comments received special attention from the Tank Destroyer Center. Tetreault reported that

> operating under combat conditions and averaging 80 to 100 miles a day during the

Third Army drive from St. Lô to the German border near Strasbourg, my M18 Hellcat was driven 1,870 miles. No repairs were necessary either to the vehicle or engine; only minimum attention was paid to moving parts. . . . M18 engine performance was excellent under the most trying conditions and was highly thought of by all men in my and other

M18 tank destroyer outfits. [The suspension] gave excellent results and was superior to the suspensions of other track systems now being used on all other U.S. vehicles.

Tetrault was pleased with the combat performance of the M18, though it should be noted that the tanks he refers to in his account were in fact Panthers. He continued:

Our most effective vehicle that I've seen to combat the German tank is the M18 Hellcat. Tiger tanks, while heavy armored, are very slow. They must come to a full stop to fire their big 88mm gun effectively. To knock them out, a gunner must remain cool and not fire until they stop. He then must aim directly under the tube. If a gunner is on a Tiger's flank, then he should aim directly at the top of the bogie wheels. If two or more German tanks approach, wait for them. Then fire at the tank that stops first, disregarding if it is the one furthest away. A moving German tank is not dangerous. It must stop to be effective.

The number of M18 Hellcats in the ETO was not especially great, totaling five battalions by October and nine at the time of the Battle of the Bulge in December 1944. The slow growth in M18 battalions resulted from their firepower problems. The 76mm gun on the M18 was no better in antitank performance than the 3-inch gun on the M10, so there was little point in converting the M10 battalions, especially when many units preferred the advantages of the M10, like its larger and more functional fighting compartment. The main advantage of the M18—its greater speed and mobility—was not in high demand in the tank destroyer battalions and did not compensate for its liabilities.

Bruce's quest for the perfect tank destroyer had centered on the need for speed, but this virtue proved to be of marginal value in actual combat. A postwar study by the General Board on tank destroyer employment concluded that "in a very large percent of its employment in this theater, its road speed of sixty miles an hour and its great cross country speed were never needed." Bruce had failed to distinguish between automotive speed and tactical speed. While the M18 was indeed very fast and mobile on a clear road, its speed in reaching the battle area was often limited by the available road net. Once in range of the enemy, the weak armor of the M18 and its open turret prompted experienced crews to move cautiously in order to limit their exposure to enemy fire.

HEAVY TANK—BIG FEET

The sodden soil along the Siegfried Line restricted tank mobility for much of the autumn of 1944. Sherman tanks quickly became bogged down in the mud, and tank crews learned to stay on the roads. Sherman crews became infuriated as they watched heavier German tanks such as the Panther and King Tiger traverse fields that only moments before had frustrated American tanks. Indeed, the Panther, nearly twice the weight of the Sherman, had a significant advantage in soft terrain because of its wider tracks. It had a ground pressure of 12.3 pounds per square inch (psi) while the much smaller and lighter Sherman had a higher 15.1 psi ground pressure. The Panther's wide tracks were a legacy of the Russian front and patterned after the wide tracks of the Soviet T-34. The Sherman's narrow tracks had proven perfectly adequate in Tunisia, Sicily, Italy, and France. But the Sherman was no match for the German mud.

The solution was duck bills, or to use their official name, "extended end connectors." Ordnance was well aware of the Sherman's flotation problem in soft soil and had already developed a solution in the form of a new suspension system. The Sherman had been using a vertical-volute-spring (VVS) sus-pension system, which restricted the width of tracks since it could accommodate only a single road wheel. The new horizontal-volute-spring system (HVSS) could accommodate two road wheels per station, and so mounted a wider twenty-three-inch track that offered a ground pressure of 10.7 psi, better than the Panther's. Production of tanks with the new suspension was authorized in March 1944 and began in August 1944, but the first tanks with this feature would not appear on the front lines until Christmas 1944—a reminder of the problems faced by the U.S. Army when operating so far from home. Germany could get new tanks from the factory to frontline units in about three weeks; for the U.S. Army, it took three months longer.

In the interim, something had to be done quickly. Ordnance had already come up with a simple solution in the form of a modified end connector that extended the existing track by about four inches, reducing the Sherman's ground pressure to 12.4 psi, only a little higher than the Panther's. The problem was that these extended end connectors were in short supply, and it would take months to ship enough to Europe. The solution was to make do with the resources at hand, particularly underutilized

Troops from the 39th Infantry Regiment, 9th Infantry Division, help the crew of an M4 tank of the 746th Tank Battalion attach a section of corduroy matting on the front of the tank on December 10, the day the division started a new attack along the Siegfried Line along with the 3rd Armored Division. The matting consisted of several logs tied together with wire that could be laid down as a carpet in front of the tank when particularly deep mud was encountered. This was a common field expedient in the autumn of 1944.

An M5A1 light tank named *Bric* from the 2nd Armored Division sits in a crater after a mine blew off its front bogie near Loverich, Germany, in late November 1944. The fighting for the Roer area took place in very muddy conditions that made it difficult to employ armor.

The autumn of 1944 was unusually wet in Belgium and along the German border, and the mud created a significant mobility problem for the M4A3 (76mm). This 6th Armored Division tank was knocked out near Hellimer, Germany, on November 25, 1944, after first striking a mine.

An M4 (76) of Company C, 771st Tank Battalion, sets out from Linnich, Germany, while supporting the 84th Division during the Roer offensive. A section of corduroy log matting is strapped to the side of the hull.

A partial solution to the mud problem was the addition of extended end connectors to the Sherman's tracks. More popularly called "duck bills," many of these were manufactured by local factories in Belgium and France as a result of shortages of supplies from the United States. The duck bills on this Sherman of the 6th Armored Division are one of the locally manufactured types.

factories in Belgium and northern France. The extended end connectors were a relatively simple casting that could be managed by many European foundries which were idle because of the chaos of war. Bradley's 12th Army Group simply began having the local firms cast hundreds of thousands of these "duck bills," which were then issued to American and British Sherman units. A shortage of foundries led to local improvisations, such as creating the duck bills by welding an extension to existing end connectors. By November, most Shermans were sporting the duck bills and having an easier time traversing terrain.

But the autumn rains eventually left the ground so sodden that not even the Panther could reliably cross most farm fields without a risk of bogging down. Other expedients were developed, some of which were indirect lessons from the Russian front. The Wehrmacht had inherited a Russian technique of carrying logs the width of the tank. When the tank became bogged in mud, the log would be lashed to the tracks in front, and then the tracks again spun under the tank. The moving log usually helped the tank escape the mire for at least some distance. By November 1944, many American tanks could be seen with logs lashed to the side. One American innovation involved connecting two or three logs with wire to fashion an improvised "corduroy mat," which was even more effective in extracting tanks from deep mud than a single log.

KILLER TANK

There was no consensus about the new 76mm Shermans, even by the late autumn of 1944. Many experienced armored divisions still preferred to have a mix of 75mm and 76mm Shermans because of the better high-explosive firepower of the 75mm gun. In addition, the new white phosphorus "Willy Pete" smoke round, introduced in Normandy and available only for the 75mm gun, proved very useful in combat in 1944. Although originally intended to create smoke screens for concealment, U.S. tankers found that the round had good incendiary effects, so it was often used to start fires in buildings that were under attack.

The attitude toward the Sherman in the autumn of 1944 was summed up in a November 1944 interview by the War Department Observers Board with Maj. Gen. Robert Grow, commander of the 6th Armored Division in Patton's Third Army and one of the best American tank commanders. Grow told the board:

> Our tanks are alright. We have mainly 75mm guns. I'd like to have a platoon of 76mm guns, M4A3 tanks in every company. That would be sufficient. We like the 75HE better than the 76 and we use a lot of WP. I

The main players from the Washington bureaucracy come to see the Pershing at Aberdeen Proving Ground. The civilian to the right is Undersecretary of War Robert P. Patterson, with the chief of the Army Service Forces, Lt. Gen. Brehon Somervell, leaning over the gun barrel with Maj. Gen. Gladeon Barnes and Lt. Gen. Levin Campbell of the Ordnance Department behind him to the left.

The T26 goes through its paces on one of the automotive tracks at Aberdeen Proving Ground alongside a German Tiger I to the right and a Sturmpanzer IV Brummbär assault gun to the left.

A display is held at Aberdeen Proving Ground of the army's tank fleet with a number of officers inspecting the new T26E1.

don't want to lose the smoke, that WP is very effective in village fighting. I've recommended that in the future we have two-thirds of our tanks with 105mm howitzers and one third with 90mm guns. With this set-up I'd give some of each to each company. This recommendation was based on our experiences and I'll admit we haven't had any tank versus tank fights; those that have had will probably have a different attitude.

Units that had been involved in extensive fighting with German AFVs were not entirely happy with the 76mm gun, for many of the same reasons. An Observer Board report prepared in late November with the 3rd Armored Division noted that

those [76mm tanks] that they had were well liked, especially when using HV [high velocity] ammunition. It was the general complaint however that the muzzle blast

One of the options not widely discussed in 1944 was the possibility of issuing tank battalions with a Sherman fitted with the 90mm gun turret from the M36 tank destroyer. When shortages of M10A1 hulls limited the number of M36s produced, this option was pursued as the M36B1, which combined the M4A3 tank hull with the M36 turret. Only tank destroyer battalions used these, like this example from the 899th Tank Destroyer Battalion in Hargarten, Germany, on March 15, 1945.

made it impossible for the gunner to adjust his fire. Some units were employing a system of having one tank observe the fire of another and making adjustments by radio. This of course reduces the fire power of the unit. Even the HV ammunition left much to be desired as it would not penetrate the front plate of either the Mk V [Panther] or Mk VI [King Tiger] tank and various commanders appeared quite disturbed over the fact that their tanks were out-armored and out-gunned by the German tanks.

Even before U.S. troops landed in Normandy, the army was planning for its ideal tank for the 1945 campaign. After the Armor Center at Fort Knox was demoted, future tank requirements were consoli-

dated under AGF's requirements section of the Armored Vehicle Branch, headed in 1944 by Col. G. M. Dean. Following an inquiry from this office in April 1944, the operations division (G-3) of Eisenhower's SHAEF headquarters asked Brig. Gen. Joseph A. Holly and his AFV&W section for their recommendations for tank production for the 1945 campaign. Eisenhower's tank specialists replied that they wanted the obsolete M5A1 light tank replaced entirely with the new M24 light tank and that the future medium tank mixture should be a three-to-one ratio of medium tanks armed with 105mm howitzers and 90mm guns to replace the existing 1944 mix of 75mm and 76mm guns. The recommendations acknowledged the different requirements of the armored divisions and separate tank battalions because of their different combat missions

One of the oddest Ordnance creations of the war was the T28 superheavy tank, armed with a massive 105mm gun. A 1943 Ordnance initiative with little interest from the Armored Force, it weighted ninety-five tons combat loaded and employed two full sets of Sherman tracks and bogies per side. The two pilots were not completed until after the end of the war in Europe.

and also the difficulty of providing two different types of tanks. As a result, the AFV&W section favored a common tank for both types of units, with increased armor on the medium tanks for the separate tank battalions so long as adequate cross-country mobility could be retained. The desired technical characteristics clearly favored a new design such as the T25 or T26 rather than a continuation of the Sherman.

Little confidence in the tank destroyer concept remained, and General Holly derided the tank destroyers as nothing more than a defensive tank as compared to the offensive tanks used by the armored divisions and separate tank battalions. In view of the offensive orientation of the U.S. Army in 1944–45, he saw no need for tank destroyers and recommended that they be re-equipped with medium tanks armed with 90mm guns.

Other organizations were also asked for their recommendations, including the Armored Center at Fort Knox, now under Maj. Gen. C. L. Scott. In contrast to Holly's team, the Armored Center was not yet certain whether a 105mm assault tank was desirable over the existing 75mm gun, and so it passed on this requirement. The Armored Center was principally concerned about Ordnance's failure to date to come up with a "killer tank" comparable to the German Panther. The Fort Knox team was skeptical that any new tanks, such as the T25 and T26, would be available in time to affect the outcome of the war in Europe and suggested that the

M4A3 tank be refitted with the 90mm gun turret that had been planned for the T25 and T26 tanks.

In response to the input from various army organizations and especially Eisenhower's headquarters, in June 1944 the General Staff and Army Service Forces agreed to a plan for the production of 7,800 medium tanks in 1945, consisting of 2,060 T26E1s (90mm), 2,728 T26E1s (105mm howitzer), and 3,000 M4A3s (105mm howitzer). Furthermore, the British wanted 750 T26s (90mm) and 400 T26s (105mm howitzer). The SHAEF request to abandon tank destroyers was accepted, and the M36 90mm GMC production was scheduled for completion in 1944. This plan was far from final, in part because of uncertainties about the duration of the war in Europe, the requirements for the Pacific theater should an invasion of Japan be necessary, and the actual timeframe for introducing the new T26E1 into production. As a result, the General Staff continued to solicit advice from field commanders through 1944, as well as to consult with the procurement branches to balance the ideal tank production plan with actual industrial capabilities. The combat encounters with the Panther and other German AFVs in the summer and autumn of 1944 resulted in a significant shift in planning, and by December 1944, the plans to build a large portion of the T26E1 with 105mm howitzers had been dropped in favor of standardizing the 90mm gun with an objective of 4,716 T26E1s (90mm). The unexpected fighting in the Ardennes in December 1944 would completely change these plans.

THE DYNAMICS OF TANK-VERSUS-TANK FIGHTING

What factors most strongly influence the outcome of tank-versus-tank fighting? Technological superiority? Crew quality? Sound tactical doctrine? These issues were not a major focus of the U.S. Army in the autumn of 1944, but they help to explain the difficulties the Sherman faced in late 1944. During World War II, the new discipline of "operational research" was first being applied to military issues such as this, most notably by the British Army. Operational research by the U.S. Army Ground Forces was not as established as in the U.S. Army Air Force, and a study of tank-versus-tank fighting was not conducted until after the war, somewhat limiting the collection of data. In the spring of 1945, the U.S. Army's Ballistics Research Lab (BRL) conducted the first major American study of tank-versus-tank fighting in an effort to determine which factors led to battlefield success. This was part of a process that underlay efforts to develop future tanks. Comprehensive statistical data was not immediately at hand, so the evaluation team narrowed their attention to the records of the U.S. 3rd and 4th Armored Divisions, which saw as much or more tank-versus-tank fighting than any other American divisions. A total of ninety-eight engagements from August through December 1944 were identified and quantified, including the Arracourt engagements and thirty-three skirmishes in the Battle of the Bulge.

This study immediately noted that the U.S. Army fought very few large tank-versus-tank battles.

During the last two weeks of November, the 2nd Armored Division took part in the offensive to push past Aachen to the Roer River, which was tenaciously defended by panzer units like the 9th Panzer Division. Captured during the fighting, this Panther Ausf. G is being hauled away through Gereonsweiler by an M25 prime mover, the tractor portion of the famous Dragon Wagon tank retriever.
USMA

During mid-November, Patton's Third Army fought a series of engagements with the 11th Panzer Division in Lorraine, east of Chateau-Salins, with the 4th Armored Division engaging in savage tank battles starting on November 14 near Guebling. This is a scene along the road between Guebling and Bougaltrof showing three knocked-out Panther Ausf. Gs and an SdKfz 250 of the 11th Panzer. In the foreground is an M4A3 (76mm) named *All Hell* of Company A, 761st Tank Battalion (Colored).

Most were small-unit engagements, averaging nine tanks on the American side and four on the German side. The study concluded that the single most important factor in tank-versus-tank fighting was which side spotted the enemy first, engaged first, and hit first. This rule meant that the defender had a clear advantage, since the defending tanks were typically stationary in a well-chosen ambush position. The defender was more apt to spot the enemy tanks first because the likely avenues of approach were under surveillance. Furthermore, greater familiarity with the local terrain meant that the defender usually had the ranges to certain objectives plotted in advance, which was an important ingredient in making certain that the first round fired struck its target. In contrast, attacking forces were usually on the move, which often led to a lack of familiarity with the terrain in the battle area, difficulty spotting the defending enemy tanks, and reduced accuracy

because of problems with quickly establishing accurate ranges given the limited technology of the day.

Of the incidents studied by BRL, defenders fired first 84 percent of the time. When defenders fired first, the attackers suffered 4.3 times more casualties than the defender. On the relatively few occasions when the attackers fired first, the defenders suffered 3.6 times more casualties than the attackers. This see-first/hit-first advantage is a statistical correlation, not the cause of the tactical success. The side that saw first and hit first usually had an overwhelming advantage in the first critical minute of the firefight since not only did firing first have such an effect, but neighboring friendly tanks also tended to fire shortly after, overwhelming the enemy force with a sudden volley of fire. Tank-versus-tank engagements tended to be short, violent affairs with the losing side quickly withdrawing rather than face annihilation. Ambush from a concealed position was the

This is a view of the same scene from the opposite direction, showing three of the knocked-out Panthers from the 11th Panzer Division near Guebling.

ideal ingredient in winning a tank-versus-tank fire-fight. A similar British study reached much the same conclusion, finding that in 70 percent of the eighty-three actions studied, the side that engaged first won. The British study also concluded that when one side had numerical superiority and also engaged first, "it was invariably successful." Another grim statistic showed that the side that was ambushed had very little chance of regaining the initiative and that their survivability fell by half every six seconds.

There was very little evidence that technical superiority, such as the imbalance between the Panther and the Sherman, was a major ingredient in the outcome of firefights, partly because of a lack of adequate data from the German perspective. Nonetheless, the popular myths that Panthers enjoyed a five-to-one kill ratio against Shermans or that it took five Shermans to knock out a Panther have no basis at all in the historical records, at least so far as the U.S. Army is concerned. The BRL study concluded that the outcome of tank-versus-tank fight-

ing was more often determined by the tactical situation than the technical situation.

Crew training was an important ingredient in tank engagements since an experienced commander was more likely to spot the enemy first, a well-trained crew was more likely to engage first because of better coordination, and the tank was more likely to hit the enemy first because of the gunner's superior skills. But in the end, a mediocre crew in a mediocre tank sitting in an ambush position had an advantage over an excellent crew in an excellent tank advancing forward. It is worth noting that the U.S. Army conducted another operational research study in the wake of the 1950 tank-versus-tank fighting in Korea. This later study confirmed the see-first/hit-first rule and suggested that it corresponded to a sixfold increase in tank effectiveness. This study also had enough data to assess whether technical advantages had an impact on tank effectiveness and concluded that the new M26 Pershing was about 3.5 times more effective than the

M4A3E8 Sherman. This is an interesting point since the M26 Pershing was in many respects comparable to the Panther in firepower and armor protection.

Even though these studies were intended to provide the scientific groundwork for future tank design, they illuminate the difficulties faced by the Sherman in the 1944 campaigns. The Sherman more often than not was used in offensive operations, often against organized German defenses where the Wehrmacht had the opportunity to position antitank guns and AFVs along likely avenues of approach. Under these circumstances, the Germans had distinct tactical advantages in tank fighting, and the U.S. Army suffered heavy tank casualties as a result. Sherman tank crews constantly complained about having to face Tiger tanks and 88mm guns, but the technological imbalance was not the real problem. Tigers were a rarity in the ETO, as were 88mm guns. The most common enemy was the 75mm PaK 40 and its AFV equivalents, whether mounted on the PzKpfw IV tank, StuG III assault gun, or a wide range of *panzerjäger;* the German 75mm gun could kill the Sherman frontally from standard combat ranges of 1,000 yards or less. It was not the technological imbalance that caused so many Sherman tank losses, it was the tactical circumstances that so often gave the Wehrmacht the see-first/hit-first advantage.

The corollary was true as well. The Wehrmacht suffered disproportionate tank casualties on the occasions when it attempted to conduct offensive operations against the U.S. Army, such as the Panzer Lehr's attack at La Desert in July 1944, the Avranches counterattack near Mortain in August 1944, and the Lorraine panzer offensive in September 1944. The forthcoming fighting in the Ardennes, the heaviest tank fighting of the U.S. Army in World War II, would demonstrate this even more clearly. The BRL study also suggested that a useful tactical option for an offensive-oriented army was to provoke counterattacks. This approach was used by the British at Caen in the summer of 1944 and on numerous occasions by the U.S. Army. The Wehrmacht had a reflexive instinct to respond to attacks with an immediate and violent counterattack. If exploited properly, the Allied side could take up good defensive positions prior to the counterattack, thereby gaining a temporary tactical advantage in the ensuing tank battle. This tactic was not always possible, and the cost of offensive operations on the 1944 battlefield usually was heavy tank losses.

TANK FIGHTING BY THE NUMBERS

Although tank-versus-tank fighting tended to attract the most attention, it was by no means the most common type of tank fighting, nor the most important. The vast majority of tank combat involved actions against non-armored targets including enemy troops, vehicles, emplacements, and others. It is impossible to summarize the actions of thousands of Sherman tanks over several hundred days of combat, but some studies conducted during and after the war at least help to provide some thumbnail sketches of typical tank combat in the ETO.

Fortifications and buildings represented the most common targets for tank guns, accounting for 39 percent of targets. Enemy troops were the next most common target at about 16 percent, while enemy AFVs amounted to about 14 percent. Enemy anti-tank guns and artillery were about 13 percent and wheeled vehicles about 8 percent. This meant that Shermans generally carried and employed far more high-explosive ammunition than armor-piercing ammunition. A typical mix was 60 percent high explosive, 30 percent armor piercing, and 10 percent white phosphorus smoke. Some units such as the 746th Tank Battalion carried as little as 15 percent armor-piercing ammunition since they were mostly involved in infantry support and seldom encountered enemy tanks.

The typical targets also led to the extensive use of machine guns. The Sherman had three machine guns, an independently operated .30-cal machine gun in the bow operated by the assistant driver/bow gunner, another .30-cal machine gun coaxial to the main gun and operated by the gunner, and a .50-cal heavy machine gun on a pintle mount on top of the turret. Crews used the machine guns so extensively that many U.S. tank units modified internal stowage racks to permit the carriage of 10,000 to 12,000 rounds of .30-cal ammunition instead of the 4,750

A classic image of tank support in World War II. An M4 medium tank of the 746th Tank Battalion supports Company I, 60th Infantry Regiment, 9th Infantry Division, during fighting near the Belgian border on September 9, 1944.

An M10 3-inch gun motor carriage of the 893rd Tank Destroyer Battalion moves forward along a firebreak in the Hürtgen Forest west of Germeter on November 4, 1944. During the savage forest fighting, the tank destroyers were used primarily to provide fire support to the beleaguered infantry.

Antitank guns remained one of the primary Sherman killers in the autumn 1944 battles. This 75mm PaK 40 antitank gun was positioned to cover the road outside Kleinhau in the Hürtgen Forest and was captured by the 8th Infantry Division in late November 1944.

The new rocket antitank weapons posed a danger to German as well as American tanks. Here, Pvt. Robert Starkey of the 16th Infantry Regiment, 1st Infantry Division, stands beside the burnt-out hulk of a PzKpfw IV/70 that he knocked out with his bazooka during the fighting near Hamich, Germany, on November 22, 1944. The rocket set off the ammunition inside the fighting compartment, completely blowing it apart.

rounds normally allotted. Besides being used to attack identified targets, machine guns were widely used for "prophylactic fire" to engage a suspicious bush, building, or terrain feature that might harbor an enemy ambush.

The .50-cal heavy machine gun had been included on the Sherman as an antiaircraft weapon, and many tank units found the mounting to be very awkward to use against ground targets. Some units actually left them stowed on the back of the turret. In contrast, other units thought that the .50-cal was the most valuable weapon on the tank in day-to-day combat and used it more often than the main gun. It was very destructive and proved to be very effective in attacking enemy infantry and trucks. It was also powerful enough to penetrate most brick and stucco walls. Gen. Bruce Clarke from the 4th, and later 7th, Armored Division recalled:

I told my men that the greatest thing on the tank was a free .50 cal. in the hands of the tank commander. We were not able to fight from tanks with the tank commander buttoned up—that has never been successfully done. [Buttoned up] he can't hear or see and so pretty soon he unbuttons. Now if he's got a free .50 cal machine gun, all he has to do press his thumb and he can pick out a dangerous spot. It may be a bazooka flash or something. He can throw a burst there without even thinking about giving an order.

Patton was so enamored of tank machine guns in combat that he sent a letter directly to the head of Ordnance, Maj. Gen. Levin Campbell, asking him to look into switching to weapons with a higher rate of fire, such as the aircraft-type .50-cal machine gun

An M4 tank of the 5th Armored Division's Combat Command Reserve (CCR) takes up position on the northeast edge of Hürtgen prior to the renewal of the attack toward the Brandenberg-Bergstein plateau in early December 1944.

as a substitute for the coaxial .30-cal, and a twin .30-cal machine gun in place of the .50-cal mounted on the turret roof. Campbell humored Patton by conducting a quick study and sending him the results in November 1944, but in reality, the logistical problem of altering the machine-gun mix on the Sherman would have been difficult compared to the modest gains in firepower.

The U.S. and British armies collected extensive data on the causes of tank casualties in order to better design future tanks. Enemy gunfire was by far the most common source of Allied tank casualties, amounting to 54 percent of overall tank losses. In

the ETO, the figures were somewhat smaller: 47.7 percent in 1944 and 50.9 percent in 1945. There are no breakdowns of this data to distinguish whether the weapon was on a panzer, *panzerjäger,* or towed antitank gun. Data on the typical caliber of weapons knocking out the tanks is unreliable because Allied crews tended to call virtually any German high-velocity antitank weapon an 88. In the case of one study by researchers of knocked-out Shermans, of seventy-two tanks hit, fifty-two (72 percent) had been hit by 75mm, seventeen (24 percent) by 88mm, and three by antitank rockets. In the ETO, the engagement range of these weapons was

An M4 of the 709th Tank Battalion uses the shelter of a shattered house in the devastated town of Hürtgen on December 5 after the town was taken by the 121st Infantry Regiment. The M4 is still fitted with a rhino hedgerow cutter. In the foreground is a burned-out M4 tank lost in the earlier fighting on November 28.

The 5th Armored Division had significant problems operating in the Hürtgen Forest because of the terrain, the mud, and the mines. Here, an M36 90mm gun motor carriage and a T1E3 Earthworm mine roller vehicle of Combat Command A (CCA) are seen in the muddy field near Grosshau on December 15 during the drive to push to Winden on the Roer River.

typically 800 yards; in Sicily and Italy, it was usually shorter, averaging 350 yards; in Tunisia, the ranges were greater, about 900 yards.

The majority—52 percent—of gunfire hits against tanks were on the hull, with 17 percent on the track and suspension and 31 percent on the turret. In terms of the engagement angle, British records from the fighting in Germany in 1945 indicate that about 37 percent of hits were on the front of the tanks, 60 percent on the side of the hull and turret, and 3 percent against the rear. Another American study of 107 Shermans tanks that had been knocked out found that 21 percent of the gunfire hits were against the front of the hull, 9 percent against the front of the turret, 32 percent against the side of the hull, 18 percent against the side of the turret, and 1 percent against the rear of the hull. Not all tanks penetrated by enemy fire burned, and so some were repairable. It's interesting to note that in Sicily and Italy, 81 percent of U.S. tanks that were penetrated by gunfire burned, while in the ETO only 53 percent burned—an indication of the value of the wet stowage program. Of those knocked out by gunfire in the ETO, about 67 percent were repairable. *Panzerfausts* caused similar levels of tank fires: 47 percent of the tanks penetrated in the ETO burned; 69 percent were repairable.

The growing number of Shermans with wet stowage reduced the vulnerability of U.S. tanks according to later after-action reports. A report in 1945 noted that

> Recent experiences reinforce earlier data [that] from 60 to 90% of M4-75mm go by burning and almost all when hit by panzer-faust. The greater proportion of fires originate in the ammunition, a few in the oil of the power-trains or in stowage; the remainder in the engine compartment. Experience of Ninth Army has clearly demonstrated the value of water-protected stowage. It has been their experience that on from 5 to 10% of M4-76mm [wet] burn whereas the usual rates of 60 to 90% fires [would] have occurred otherwise. Records of First Army do not, however, demonstrate any differences insofar as the end result of burning are con-

cerned. Opinion is held by many that wet stowage delays rates of fire initially and more hits are required to start the fire. The practice of loading extra ammunition in the turret and the unprotected ready rack makes evaluation of any benefits from wet stowage difficult.

The number of casualties when a Sherman was knocked out averaged one crewman killed and one injured. One U.S. report concluded that

> When tanks have been penetrated by anti-tank fire, members of the crew who have not been killed or wounded or knocked unconscious usually manage to escape even if the tank is set on fire. Where complete crews are lost, unit commanders attribute casualties to flash ammunition fires which spring up so rapidly that wounded or shocked members cannot evacuate themselves or be evacuated before being overcome by flames. Also it is believed that in a number of cases, exits may have been blocked by wounded members of the crew and thus prevented escape of other members.

The problem of blocked exits was most prevalent in the Shermans built in 1942–43, which had only a single turret hatch over the commander. In the event that the commander was wounded, the gunner and loader had to move his body before they could exit. In October 1943, an additional hatch was added over the loader's station, as the loader was the most vulnerable to being trapped. Statistical studies of tank crew casualties did not find a great disparity between the five crew positions. A U.S. First Army study found that among the crew, the loader was the least likely to be killed (21.4 percent) while the bow gunner and turret gunner were the most likely (27 percent). Of tank crew casualties, about a quarter were killed and three-quarters wounded.

Mines were the next largest source of tank losses, coming in at 20 percent of casualties. In the ETO, the U.S. Army suffered somewhat lower rates of mine loss compared to other theaters—16.5 percent in 1944 and 18.2 percent in 1945. Mines typically

Tank and infantry cooperation was essential in the autumn 1944, by which time tank phones had become commonplace and were generally mounted in a .30-caliber ammo box, as seen above the heads of these two GIs taking shelter under the rear of an M4 near Gleich, Germany, on December 11, 1944.

caused fewer total losses since they less often led to ammunition fires; only 13 percent of American tanks knocked out by mines in the ETO burned, and 76 percent were repairable. Mines by themselves caused few casualties among the crews, as a U.S. Army report noted:

> Commanders have stated that the effect of AT [antitank] mines on personnel riding in the tanks has been very small. It is only in exceptional cases that any member of a tank is injured by the mine. There is considerable shock effect caused by the explosion of a single AT mine, but it is not disabling to the crew. . . . Where tanks have encountered AT mines protected by enemy fire, casualties have occurred in crews due to sniper or machine

gun fire when the vehicle had to be evacuated. Whenever possible, the enemy brings fire on stalled tanks and attempts to destroy them by burning. Even when tanks are disabled out of range of flat trajectory weapons, the enemy will try to bring artillery fire on vehicles to burn them up, cause casualties among the crew, or render recovery difficult during the daylight hours.

Non-enemy causes was the next most prevalent source of tank casualties, at 13 percent. This category mainly consisted of mechanical breakdowns or bogging down, which led to the abandonment of tanks. Antitank rockets were next at 7.5 percent, though this figure is somewhat deceptive since it includes combat in North Africa and Italy in 1942–43, where

An M4A3E2 assault tank probably from the 746th Tank Battalion passes under a destroyed railroad viaduct on December 7, 1944, following the fighting for Langerwehe, the industrial town that was the gateway from the Hürtgen Forest to the Roer plain.

such weapons were not yet fielded. In the ETO, *panzerfausts* and *panzerschrecks* accounted for about 11 percent of tank casualties. The typical engagement range for these weapons was sixty to ninety yards, and the direction of attack was different from that of gunfire, with 31 percent hitting the front of the tank, 51 percent the side, 9.5 percent the rear, and 8.5 percent the roof. Although *panzerfausts* did not necessarily knock out many tanks, they were a frequent source of tank crew casualties since they were so widely used by the German infantry. A report by the 736th Tank Battalion during the fighting in Germany in the spring of 1945 noted that

> Resistance encountered was mainly at defended roadblocks and in towns. Bazookas and panzerfausts caused most of the trouble. Most of the casualties suffered by the 736th occurred outside the tanks. The Germans would disable the tank by panzerfaust or bazooka fire, forcing the crews to abandon the tank. When the crews attempted to abandon the tanks, they would be shot with

machine pistols or machine guns. If crews are well drilled in abandoning tanks, losses inside the tank will be very low. [There's a] need for pistols and shoulder holsters for the whole crew.

Finally, mortars and other miscellaneous weapons, such as artillery, accounted for the remaining 6 percent of tank casualties. Artillery more often than not knocked out tanks by hits on the suspension. A report by a Sherman commander from the 760th Tank Battalion provides a typical viewpoint: "Enemy artillery fire has not done us any harm even at times when we got direct hits on our tanks. The concussion is heavy on near hits, and sometimes knocks men out, but very seldom causes any injuries." Artillery could sometimes penetrate tank armor under freak circumstances. A veteran of the 8th Tank Battalion, 4th Armored Division, recalled an occasion during the fighting in France when his Sherman platoon came under German artillery fire. A round hit a neighboring Sherman on the turret but the fuse failed to detonate, and the projectile had just enough kinetic energy to penetrate the thin roof armor of the tank. The sizzling hot projectile dropped into the lap of the loader, who quickly ran out of the tank in the midst of the barrage and hid under the tank. After the barrage was over, the rest of the crew had a difficult time getting the shocked loader from under the Sherman, and he had to be evacuated to a hospital.

By way of comparison, U.S. studies estimated that German tank losses resulted from a somewhat different mix of causes: 40 percent to gunfire, 20 percent self-destroyed, 20 percent abandoned, 10 percent knocked out by aircraft, and 10 percent knocked out by bazookas and other infantry anti-tank weapons. The high German loss rate to self-destroyed and abandoned vehicles occurred during battles such as the Falaise Gap, Roncey pocket, Seine pocket, Mons pocket, and the Ardennes, where German units were outflanked by Allied maneuver. However, mechanical breakdown was a growing problem for the Wehrmacht in the final year of the war. Gen. Paul Hausser, who commanded the German 7th Army in Normandy, commented that "during long movements to the battle area, 20 percent to 30 percent of all tanks fall out due to mechanical failures. Regarding the remaining tanks, 15 percent are lost through mechanical failures; 20 percent to air attacks; 50 percent to antitank defenses, and 15 percent to artillery. Tanks and tank destroyers are feared most by German tank crews." A German tanker with eight years of combat experience was asked which Allied weapons bothered him the most: "M36 tank destroyers and bazookas." He also noted that more Panthers were disabled moving into the battle area than in combat.

The source of the mechanical breakdowns was not simply production flaws, as noted by a British examination of knocked-out German tanks:

> In the last year of the war there was a very high percentage of failures, due partly to flaws in production, partly to bad driving—itself the result of inadequate training, and partly to the breakdown of railways which compelled tanks to travel on their own tracks. My own impression is that 'availability' so far as the Germans were concerned was affected more by mechanical unserviceability than by battle losses. The Germans tended to handle their armour with a rather brutal stupidity.

CHAPTER 8

Armored Superiority in the Ardennes

THE BATTLE OF THE BULGE SAW THE MOST intense tank fighting of the U.S. Army in World War II. The initial German attack in the Ardennes on December 16, 1944, involved more than 1,750 panzers and AFVs. The U.S. Army had over 4,000 Shermans in the ETO, but in the Ardennes sector, there were only three separate tank battalions with about 170 Shermans—a ratio of about ten-to-one in the Wehrmacht's favor. This imbalance was only transitory; within hours of the start of the attack, the U.S. Army began rushing armored divisions, separate tank battalions, and tank destroyer battalions to the Ardennes. The German equipment advantages were fleeting and success depended on a rapid victory—which was never really within grasp, except in the mind of someone as deranged as Hitler. According to the historian of the German High Command, the Battle of the Bulge proved not only American air superiority, but also armored superiority over the Wehrmacht. It is ironic that in its moment of greatest glory, the Sherman tank came under its most intense criticism. A scandal broke out in the U.S. press about the inadequacies of American weapons in the Ardennes, especially the Sherman.

In the autumn of 1944, Germany was on the brink of defeat. The Wehrmacht had been decisively crushed on both fronts. The Red Army had paused on the central front in Poland so that Stalin could take advantage of political opportunities in the Balkans, an offensive that would strip Germany of its Romanian oil supply. It was only a matter of time before Germany's war economy collapsed and its panzers ground to a halt and the Red Army reactivated its main offensive and crushed the Wehrmacht on the road to Berlin. The timing of this final

Panzer graveyard. These Panthers of the 12th SS Panzer Division were knocked out inside Krinkelt-Rocherath, and the tank in the foreground (tactical number 318) has lost its gun barrel. Although the 12th SS would eventually push the 99th out of the twin villages, it lost so much time that it failed in its mission to reach the Meuse River.

Some of the most savage fighting of the opening phase of the Ardennes campaign took place near the twin villages of Krinkelt-Rocherath when the 12th SS Panzer Division attempted to secure the northern shoulder of the salient by overwhelming the U.S. 99th Infantry Division. Although inexperienced, the 99th put up a legendary fight, and this Panther Ausf. G (tactical number 126) was one of its first victims, knocked out by an M10 tank destroyer along the Wirtzfeld-Krinkelt road on December 17, 1944, after having received multiple antitank and bazooka hits inside the town.

assault was up to Stalin, and there was little Hitler could do to affect Soviet plans.

Hitler's one hope for a miracle was in the west, and even this was largely an illusion because of Hitler's dismissive condescension toward the U.S.

Army. In September 1944, while Hitler was recovering from the concussion of the failed July bomb plot, a chance remark by one of his subordinates reminded him of his most glorious and undisputed military victory of the war, the defeat of the French

After finally pushing through Krinkelt-Rocherath, the 12th SS Panzer Division got tangled up in fierce fighting with the U.S. 1st Infantry Division in the town of Dom Butgenbach on December 19. This PzKpfw IV was knocked out inside the town, possibly by this M36 90mm gun motor carriage of the 634th Tank Destroyer Battalion, which was supporting the infantry. This would be the farthest advance of the 12th SS, far short of its goal.

The fight at Dom Butgenbach hinged on the courage of the infantry's 57mm anti-tank gun crews to stymie the German panzer attacks. This crew of the 1st Battalion, 26th Infantry Regiment, man-handles their gun from its prime mover near Butgenbach on December 17, 1944.

army in 1940 by a clever outflanking maneuver through the Ardennes. Four years later, Hitler desperately needed a similarly stunning victory to reverse the onrushing defeat, and the Ardennes seemed to be his good luck charm.

Hitler's fixation on the Ardennes coincided with American tactical dispositions in the autumn of 1944. As a result of the unexpected shift of the Allied effort northward for Operation Market Garden, Bradley's 12th Army Group found itself spread

A grim reminder of the human cost of bad doctrine and poor equipment. A knocked-out 3-inch gun in Honsfeld is overrun by Kampfgruppe Peiper in the predawn hours of December 17, 1944, during the start of the Ardennes offensive. Two companies from the 612th and 801st Tank Destroyer Battalions were stationed in the town but were quickly overwhelmed.

The threat posed by Kampfgruppe Peiper led to desperate measures. Although the U.S. Army seldom used its 90mm antiaircraft guns for antitank defense as the Germans did with their 88mm guns, the Battle of the Bulge was an exception. Here a 90mm antiaircraft gun of the 143rd Anti-Aircraft Battalion has been set up near a destroyed Panther tank on the outskirts of Malmedy on December 22, supporting the 30th Infantry Division. In the background is the M4 high-speed tractor used to tow the gun. A second battalion, the 110th Anti-Aircraft, also provided antitank defense at Malmedy.

thin from the Netherlands to Alsace. To economize his forces, Bradley held the Ardennes thinly after determining it was the least likely venue for a German counterattack, especially in the foul autumn and winter weather. This split the 12th Army Group, with the heaviest concentration of the U.S. First and Ninth Armies north of the Ardennes facing the Siegfried Line and Patton's Third Army south of the

Ardennes facing the Saar. Bradley was well aware of the German use of the Ardennes in the 1940 campaign, but in 1944, he felt that the autumn weather made any mechanized advance through the area foolish. Bradley was not as desperate as Hitler and fell victim to the classic intelligence failure of "mirror imaging"—expecting an enemy army to do what your own army would do.

During the fighting in Bullingen on December 17, the spearhead of Kampfgruppe Peiper, a company of PzKpfw IV tanks led by SS-Obersturmführer Werner Sternebeck, became disoriented and headed out of town north instead of west toward Wirtzfeld. About a mile out of town, the two lead panzers were knocked out by some M10 3-inch gun motor carriages of the 644th Tank Destroyer Battalion.

The Ardennes was dubbed "the ghost front" with little combat occurring through most of the autumn, except for routine patrolling and the occasional raid. The Ardennes became the "kindergarten and old age home" of the U.S. Army, the sector where Bradley sent newly arrived divisions for a little seasoning and those battered by combat in the neighboring Hürtgen Forest for rebuilding and recuperation. At the time of the German offensive, the Ardennes was held by two divisions that had been crippled in the Hürtgen Forest fighting, the 4th and 28th Infantry Divisions, plus two newly arrived divisions, the 99th and the 106th. Three of the four divisions had separate tank battalions, two of them D-Day veterans, the 70th and the 741st Tank Battalions. The other was the recently arrived 707th Tank Battalion that had been used for training replacement crews in Britain until the shortage of

tank units forced its transfer into combat in October 1944. The hapless 106th Division had no tank support. Unfortunately, tank destroyer support of the infantry divisions consisted only of towed antitank gun battalions that were unwanted elsewhere because of their limited combat effectiveness.

Hitler was attracted to the Ardennes because it seemed to offer a method to split Montgomery's 21st Army Group off from the U.S. Army by a lightening sweep to Antwerp. With the great port in German hands, the British would be obliged to stage another Dunkirk, at least according to Hitler's fevered perspective. That the Wehrmacht in December 1944 did not have the resources to accomplish this mission did not disturb the German leader.

The panzer force in the west had been crippled by the enormous summer losses and was barely on the verge of even partial recovery. Most panzer divisions had lost a third to a half of their panzer crews and suffered even heavier losses in their hard-pressed panzergrenadier ranks. Virtually all their heavy equipment had been lost in France and Belgium, and they didn't receive new panzers until October and November. The ranks were filled by new recruits and personnel from the Luftwaffe and navy, idled by the lack of fuel for their aircraft and warships. The divisional commanders complained that these men had never driven in a tank or fired a tank gun when they arrived for duty, in contrast to the old days when they would have gone through specialist training. If that wasn't bad enough, training was nearly impossible because of the lack of fuel.

The panzer divisions were reequipped with freshly manufactured Panthers, PzKpfw IVs, and even King Tigers, but there were not enough to go around as a result of the Allied bombing campaign against the panzer factories in the early autumn. As impressive as they were on paper, the fresh paint on the panzers concealed the rotting infrastructure of the Third Reich. Steel alloys were becoming scarce, leading to brittle armor and brittle gear teeth in the transmissions. Slave laborers in the panzer factories relished the opportunity to stick debris in the fuel lines. Panzer production was maintained by cutting back on spare parts like engines, final drives, and transmissions, precisely at the time when poor quality control led to premature breakdowns in the field. In the hands of skilled drivers, these problems might be overcome; in the hands of novices, transmission gears became stripped, final drives locked, and the panzers broke down at an alarming rate. Fuel supplies were low, and the new and heavier tanks like the Panther and King Tiger were gas hogs, especially in hilly terrain. None of this was evident to American troops when the panzers came crashing out of the mist and fog in the early morning of December 16, 1944, but it was foremost in the minds of the panzer commanders.

The German plan depended on rapidly breaking through the American lines using second-rate *Volksgrenadier* divisions, at which point panzer divisions would race to the Meuse (Maas) River and then to Antwerp. Hitler had grown distrustful of the regular army since the July 1944 bomb plot, and so put his faith in the loyal Waffen SS. Three armies would take part in the attack, the main thrust coming from the 6th Panzer Army in the north, which had the shortest route to Antwerp, supported on its left by the 5th Panzer Army and the relatively weak 7th Army in the south providing flank security in the Luxembourg hill country against the rest of the U.S. Army.

Hitler misplaced his faith in the Waffen SS, which had grown enormously in the last two years of the war at a time when Germany had lost the strategic initiative and was on the defensive. The Waffen SS panzer commanders did not have the experience in offensive operations like their colleagues in the army. The 6th Panzer Army commander, Sepp Dietrich, was a street brawler and political crony of Hitler's with little formal military education. When Hitler ordered brute-force tactics to break through the American lines, Dietrich willingly obeyed. The neighboring 5th Panzer Army was led by a more traditional German officer, Hasso von Manteuffel, a diminutive and aggressive Prussian officer who had spent most of the past six months fighting the Allies—for example, leading the Lorraine panzer offensive against Patton in September 1944. Manteuffel knew that Hitler's orders to start the offensive with an artillery barrage were futile and dangerous. German artillery lacked the firepower to wreck the American defenses as the shells would simply explode in the pine trees above the U.S. infantry, which would in any event be hunkered down in log bunkers. The barrage would simply alert the Americans, not rout them. Manteuffel realistically appreciated the weaknesses of the beleaguered German infantry of late 1944, and so he favored the textbook German solution to this tactical problem. Instead of relying on ineffective artillery barrages, he would follow the tactics painfully proven since the trench war of 1917: infiltrate the enemy lines with assault groups before the artillery barrage. Stealth and cunning were better than brute force in these circumstances.

As the German assault unfolded on the first two days of the Ardennes offensive, Manteuffel's approach proved the more prudent. He was able to move *Volksgrenadier* divisions to either side of the badly positioned and inexperienced U.S. 106th Infantry Division, eventually forcing one of the largest mass-

As Kampfgruppe Peiper advanced toward La Gleize, it was cut off when the U.S. 30th Infantry Division retook Stavelot. This King Tiger of SS Heavy Tank Battalion 501 stalled while climbing the hill on Rue Haut-Rivage and then rolled back down the hill into this house, where it became stuck.

Another example of a 90mm antiaircraft gun being used in an antitank role to help support the 30th Infantry Division's cordon around Malmedy on December 22. In this case, it has been positioned behind a makeshift defensive work of sandbags and small timber. The 90mm guns were used on several occasions, including the fighting for Stoumont on December 19, where they were credited with three Panthers from Kampfgruppe Peiper.

surrenders by the U.S. Army in World War II. The battered 28th Division was not so easily over-whelmed, and it fought a gallant withdrawal action toward Bastogne. Its supporting 707th Tank Battalion suffered the heaviest casualties of any American tank unit fighting in the Ardennes and was nearly wiped out. Manteuffel's success led to the first German breakthrough, which penetrated toward the road junction at Bastogne. The delay imposed by the 28th Division's heroic fight enabled Bradley to reinforce Bastogne with the 101st Airborne Division and combat commands from the 9th and 10th Armored

This Panther Ausf. G from Kampfgruppe Peiper was lost near the Baugnez crossroads, where the infamous Malmedy massacre occurred.

Divisions, leading to the epic defensive battles around Christmas.

In the north, Dietrich's reliance on Hitler's clumsy artillery tactics led to stalemate along the front as his infantry divisions struggled to penetrate U.S. infantry lines. There were some successes, notably against a weak cavalry screen in the Losheim Gap. But the main thrust by the 1st SS Panzer Division "Leibstandarte Adolf Hitler" and the 12th SS Panzer Division "Hitlerjugend" was held back for more than a day because of the German infantry failures and the stout resistance of American infantry units backed by Sherman tanks.

The inclement autumn weather was both a blessing and a curse for panzer operations. For the first week of the campaign, the skies were overcast with occasional rain showers during the day and sleet and snow at night; this kept away the dreaded American *jabos,* fighter-bombers. On the other hand, the panzers faced the same problem with mud as the U.S. Army had endured through November, which limited the panzers to operations on the road. As a result, each little Belgian stone village straddling a road became a major defense post for U.S. forces and the site of the most critical battles.

In frustration over the initial delays, the Germans prematurely committed the 12th SS Panzer Division in the north before a breakthrough had been made through U.S. infantry defenses. The 12th made a frontal attack against the "twin villages" of Krinkelt-Rocherath, held by elements of the green U.S. 99th Infantry Division and a battalion from the experienced 2nd Infantry Division, supported by Sherman tanks of the 741st Tank Battalion. This was the tank battalion that had taken such heavy losses on Omaha Beach, but it had been rebuilt over and over again during the bloody summer and autumn fighting. The battle for Krinkelt-Rocherath was a case study in failed German tactics with the 12th's Panther battalion sent into the hotly contested villages with insufficient infantry support. In such close quarters, the mighty Panthers had few advantages and were vulnerable to American bazookas, obsolete 57mm antitank guns, and the short 75mm guns of the Sherman.

The commander of the antitank company of the U.S. 9th Infantry Regiment, which held the Lausdell crossroads at the entrance to the village, described their efforts to stop the Panthers with the 57mm gun and bazookas:

The oddest German AFVs to appear in the Ardennes were five of these Panther tanks, reconstructed using sheet metal and painted with American markings to resemble M10 tank destroyers. They were used by Skorzeny's Panzer Brigade 150 in an attack on the town of Malmedy. This one ran over a mine and was abandoned in front of the positions of Company B, 99th "Norwegian" Separate Infantry Battalion, near the Malmedy railroad viaduct.

I saw my guns engage a Panther at 150 yards, firing from the flank at the upper half of the tank. Their first round of AP [armor piercing] glanced off without effect. The second round of sabot penetrated and knocked out the tank. In another case, a Panther approached at 300 yards and a 57mm gun fired a round of AP at the flank of the tank, and the round glanced off. A round of sabot was placed in the gun but misfired. This gun was overrun by the tank. I saw two Panthers knocked out by flanking fire from bazookas. One was 200 yards away when hit, one was 150 yards.

Krinkelt–Rocherath became a panzer graveyard. By the afternoon of December 19, when U.S. forces finally withdrew, the two companies of the 741st Tank Battalion had claimed twenty-seven panzers and six other AFVs at a cost of eight tanks. The M10 tank destroyers of the 644th Tank Destroyer Battalion claimed sixteen, regimental 57mm guns claimed nineteen, and bazooka teams claimed thirty-seven. These were exaggerations, but they give some idea of the intensity of the fighting. Even though the 12th SS Panzer Division managed to wrest control of the twin villages, the cost had been too high in time, men, and equipment. When the advance continued, the Germans were halted a few miles beyond by another tenacious infantry defense of the Dom Butgenbach manor farm by the 26th Infantry of the 1st Infantry Division (the famed Big Red One), supported by a company of Sherman tanks from the 745th Tank Battalion and some M10 tank destroyers. The Americans decisively halted the German attack, and in five days of fighting, the 12th SS Panzer Division lost 60 percent of its initial armored strength and had been unable to penetrate the U.S. defenses.

The neighboring 1st SS Panzer Division achieved no more success. After its advance on the first day was held up by the failure of a poorly led Luftwaffe infantry division, Kampfgruppe (Battle Group) Peiper, with the bulk of the division's panzer strength, charged forward even though the breakthrough had not been secured. The gap in the U.S. defenses was only temporary. Almost as soon as Peiper's panzers passed through Stavelot, newly arriving troops of the 30th Infantry Division retook the town. Kampfgruppe Peiper earned infamy for the Malmedy massacre, but with its rear lines in peril, its penetration to Stoumont was pointless. The Panthers and King Tigers were finally bottled up in La Gleize by the 82nd Airborne Division and its supporting 740th Tank Battalion, which was undoubtedly the oddest American tank unit in the Ardennes. It was a former secret Cassock CDL battalion in the process of converting to a mine-exploder battalion for Patton's Third Army and didn't have any tanks. In the desperate first hours of the Battle of the Bulge, its commander was ordered to scrape together whatever tanks he could find and rush to the aid of the 82nd Airborne. The battalion managed to find about a dozen British Shermans in depot, along with a hodgepodge of other vehicles, including M36 tank destroyers. A single M24 Chaffee light tank was stolen from a convoy earmarked for the Ninth Army, and so this new type would see its combat debut ahead of schedule. The battalion commander liberated an M12 155mm GMC, which would prove instrumental in ending Peiper's stay in La Gleize, bombarding the trapped German battle group at point-blank range with 155mm gunfire.

In a vain attempt to save the doomed 106th Division, Bradley dispatched a pair of armored division combat commands, one from the 7th and one from the 9th Armored Divisions, which eventually set up a defensive perimeter near St. Vith along with the one infantry regiment of the 106th that had managed to avoid encirclement. The St. Vith defense, led by Gen. Bruce Clarke of Arracourt fame, was a "thumb down the German throat" blocking the junction of Manteuffel's 5th Panzer Army with Dietrich's 6th Panzer Army. For nearly a week, the Wehrmacht tried to reduce the salient, and St. Vith came close to becoming surrounded. On the night of December 22, the St. Vith defenders were authorized to withdraw, but there was little confidence that they could do so because of the sodden farmland that threatened to engulf their surviving tanks in mud. But on the night of December 22–23, the weather changed with the advent of a "Russian high," a cold front coming in from the east that froze the ground solid and cleared the skies.

CLEAR SKIES AND HARD GROUND

The weather change on December 23 reinvigorated the German attack since the ground was now solid enough for panzer traffic. No longer confined to the roads or stymied by defenses in each little village, the panzer divisions suddenly regained their mobility. The most dramatic change occurred in the center near St. Vith. The second echelon of the 6th Panzer Army was the II SS Panzer Corps, consisting of the 2nd SS Panzer Division "Das Reich" and the 9th SS Panzer Division, which had been stuck behind the stalled 1st and 12th SS Panzer Divisions. The II SS Panzer Corps was now directed to exploit the withdrawal of the St. Vith garrison. Their objective was

to reach the wooded high ground of the Tailles plateau before the U.S. could establish firm defenses in the villages in the foothills. The 5th Panzer Army sent its 116th Panzer Division along their left flank with much the same objective. At the same time, the 5th Panzer Army freed its panzer divisions from futile assaults on encircled Bastogne and sent the 2nd Panzer and Panzer Lehr Divisions on a race to the Meuse River west of Bastogne.

The change of weather opened the second phase of the Battle of the Bulge and set the stage for the largest tank battles of the campaign. While the 5th and 6th Panzer Armies were taking advantage of the

A 3-inch gun defends a roadblock near Vielsalm, Belgium, on December 23, 1944, during the 7th Armored Division's attempt to withdraw out of the St. Vith salient. The gun has been hastily emplaced as the wheel segments, used to steady the carriage, have not been locked down.

The separate tank battalions supporting the U.S. infantry divisions along the Belgian border were equipped mainly with the 75mm Sherman. The 707th Tank Battalion was attached to the embattled 28th Infantry Division, and one of its M4A3 tanks can be seen knocked out behind a StuG III assault gun in the village of Clervaux after the fighting. The 707th suffered the heaviest casualties of any of the tank battalions serving in the Ardennes.

A Panther Ausf. G of the 2nd SS Panzer Division knocked out in a fork in the road between Manhay and Grandmenil during the fighting on December 23 with the U.S. 3rd Armored Division.

weather, the U.S. Army was preparing the first of a series of counterattacks. To this end, Bradley created a force north of the Ardennes under "Lightning Joe" Collins's VII Corps, based around the 2nd and 3rd Armored Divisions, along with infantry divisions. The VII Corps was sent along the Tailles plateau, with the 3rd Armored assigned to debouch from the plateau and take control of the villages that acted as bottlenecks through the forested hills at the base of the plateau. The 2nd Armored was to continue

farther west and then smash into the flank of the panzer divisions that had bypassed Bastogne.

A second counterattack, involving Patton's Third Army, was also being prepared from the south as well. In the days preceding the German attack, Patton had been on the verge of initiating an early-winter offensive code-named Operation Tink, which was directed toward Frankfurt. His forces were heavily supplied and ready for action. Patton's intelligence chief had been suspicious of the German buildup in

When the II SS Panzer Corps was shifted to the center of the bulge to support Hasso von Manteuffel's attack, much of the subsequent fighting centered around the town of Manhay, astride one of the more valuable road junctions. This M4A1 medium tank of the 3rd Armored Division was positioned on the N494 road going west from Manhay on December 23 in an attempt to halt the advance of the 2nd SS Panzer Division *Das Reich*. It is covered with straw for improvised camouflage.

early December, and after the Third Army's attempts to warn Bradley were dismissed, Patton told his staff to prepare an optional plan to deal with a threat from the Ardennes region if the Germans decided to try to spoil Operation Tink. In the event, the German attack led to the cancellation of Tink, and Patton's staff quickly reconfigured the optional plan as a relief mission to save the "Battlin' Bastards of Bastogne."

The American counterattacks during the second phase of the Battle of the Bulge were predicated on the reliability and mobility offered by the Sherman tank. Patton's Third Army had to rapidly move more than 100 miles under winter conditions and be ready to immediately go into combat, even though in many cases their tanks had not undergone serious maintenance for weeks. For example, Patton's 4th Armored Division, which would spearhead the drive north, was badly understrength after a hard month of fighting, yet it did not have the time to recuperate or reequip. This is a clear example of how

McNair's insistence on "battleworthiness" showed its value. The Sherman proved to be a useful weapon because it was dependable. As would be clear in the next week of fighting, the same could not be said for many of its German opponents.

Over the course of December 22–23, the 3rd Armored Division spilled off the Tailles plateau and headed for road junctions at Baraque de Fraiture, Grandmenil, and Manhay, facing the II SS Panzer Corps, and into the Ourthe River Valley at Hotton and Soy, facing the 116th Panzer Division and a number of *Volksgrenadier* regiments. The 3rd Armored Division, in concert with infantry from the 75th and 84th Infantry Divisions, managed to halt the German advance by Christmas. This ended any German hopes for a penetration along the center axis.

The last remaining German hope was along the southern axis toward Dinant on the Meuse River west of Bastogne. British Shermans of the 29th

An M4 (105mm) assault gun of a headquarters company of the 7th Armored Division waits in hull-down position near Manhay during the fighting there on December 27 with the 2nd SS Panzer Division "Das Reich." The tank is positioned in an entrenchment created by divisional engineers.

An M4A1 (76mm) of the 3rd Armored Division passes by an abandoned Panther Ausf. G of the 2nd SS Panzer Division lost during the fighting near Grandmenil at the end of December 1944.

Armoured Brigade stopped the reconnaissance vanguard of the 2nd Panzer Division on the morning of December 24 within miles of the Meuse River. By the time the leading kampfgruppe reached Celles, it was running desperately short of fuel, and there were ominous warnings from scouts that a major American mechanized force was descending on it from the north. In the ensuing battles on Christmas and the following days, the 2nd Armored Division trapped and destroyed one kampfgruppe in the Celles forest, routed the rest of the division, and brushed back repeated attacks by other units, includ-

A pair of tanks of the 3rd Armored Division in the woods near Houfallize. The Sherman to the left is one of the original M4A1 (76mm) in use with the division since Operation Cobra, while to the right is one of the much-prized M4A3E2 assault tanks.

By early January, the snow had set in throughout Belgium, making mobile operations all the more difficult. The 3rd Armored Division continued its efforts to reduce the northern edge of the bulge around Manhay toward Houfallize. These two M4 medium tanks of the 33rd Armored Regiment, 3rd Armored Division, train their guns on the woods while a tank up ahead is recovered.

ing the 9th Panzer and Panzer Lehr Divisions, which attempted to rescue the trapped 2nd Panzer Division.

With the defeat of the 5th Panzer Army's vanguard west of Bastogne, the German offensive had run out of steam. By December 26, Patton's Third Army had broken through to Bastogne, led by the Sherman tanks of the 37th Tank Battalion, 4th Armored Division, that had fought at Arracourt. Hitler shifted his forces in a vain attempt to overrun Bastogne, but by this time, the mission was hopeless. The U.S. Army was pouring resources into the

This PzKpfw IV (named *Lustmolch*, or "Happy Salamander") of Kampfgruppe Maucke, part of the 15th Panzergrenadier Division, was knocked out during an attack toward Champs on the approaches to Bastogne in an encounter with the American 502nd Parachute Regiment, 101st Airborne Division, on December 26.

Ardennes, and the balance of forces clearly favored the U.S. Army. By early January 1945, even Hitler recognized that the Ardennes attack had been a dismal failure, and he pulled out the 6th Panzer Army for an equally futile and unrealistic offensive against the Red Army in Hungary.

During the fighting in the Ardennes, the Wehrmacht lost about 730 panzers and other AFVs—about 45 percent of its original strength. Equally telling, only a fraction of the surviving panzers were operational. In the case of the Panther tanks, about 180 of the starting force of 415 Panthers were lost (43 percent); another 130 were still in German hands but broken down from battle damage or mechanical problems; and about 105 were operational, only a quarter of the original force. Precise figures on the causes of the losses are lacking, but captured German panzer crewmen complained about the poor mechanical reliability of the new German AFVs and claimed that half were abandoned by their crews or lost to breakdown.

U.S. tank and tank destroyer losses in the Ardennes were about 730 vehicles. In the case of the U.S. First Army, which bore the brunt of the Ardennes fighting, by the end of December it had lost about 320 Sherman tanks, equivalent to a quarter of its average daily strength that month. Because of continual reinforcements, First Army had about 1,085 Shermans on hand at the end of December 1944, with about 980 operational; only 9 percent were dead-lined with mechanical problems or battle damage.

The Wehrmacht launched Operation Nordwind in Alsace in January 1945 against the U.S. 6th Army Group, a much smaller offensive than in the Ardennes and no more successful. When this petered out in early February 1945, it marked the end of major panzer operations in the west. There would be daily encounters with panzer and *panzerjägers* through the end of the war, but large-scale tank-versus-tank encounters no longer took place.

A 3-inch antitank gun lies wrecked at a crossroads outside Humain after it was put out of action by a German tank a few days after Christmas. This particular gun was credited with knocking out fifteen German tanks during the intense fighting around Humain against the 9th Panzer Division.

This trio of Panther Ausf. Gs was abandoned in a field outside Humain, Belgium, on December 28. The 9th Panzer Division attempted to defend the town against an attack by the U.S. 2nd Armored Division but was ejected after a fierce ten-hour battle on the twenty-seventh.

This Panther Ausf. G of the 116th Panzer Division was knocked out during the fighting with the 3rd Armored Division for Hotton on December 26. Note the PzKpfw IV in the background.

The threat posed by the lead elements of Manteuffel's 5th Panzer Army led Montgomery to deploy the British 29th Armoured Brigade along the Meuse River. This Sherman Firefly with its long 17-pounder gun was positioned near the Meuse bridges in Namur on Christmas Day, 1944.

While the British 29th Armoured Brigade blocked to road to the Meuse, the U.S. 2nd Armored Division attacked the exposed flank of the 2nd Panzer Division with full force. Here a group of M4A1 (76mm) carries infantry into an assault near Frandeux on December 27. The 2nd's attacks around Celles shattered Manteuffel's spearhead near the Meuse.

The spearhead for Patton's attempt to relieve Bastogne was the 4th Armored Division's CCA. The first tank to enter Bastogne was *Cobra King*, an M4A3E2 assault tank of Company C, 37th Tank Battalion, command by Lt. Charles P. Boggess. It is seen here after its arrival on December 26. PATTON MUSEUM

With its CCR trapped in Bastogne, the 9th Armored Division's CCA was attached to the 4th Armored Division to take part in operations to relieve the town. An M4A3 (76) of Company C, 19th Tank Battalion, Task Force Collins, moves forward on December 27 as part of the effort to open the road from Neufchateau to Bastogne. This company seized the town of Sibret from the 5th Fallschirmjäger Division that day, capturing about forty prisoners.

German prisoners walk past an M3A1 half-track of the 4th Armored Division on December 27 during the attempts by Patton's Third Army to relieve Bastogne. There was intense fighting along the route for the next several days as the Germans tried to sever the link between Bastogne and the Third Army.

An M4 (105mm) assault gun of the headquarters company, 68th Tank Battalion, 6th Armored Division, moves forward to Bastogne through Habay-la-Neuve on December 29. The 6th Armored Division was sent into Bastogne to take part in efforts to break the encirclement on the eastern side of the town in mid-January.

An M4A3 of the 4th Armored Division passes by the foxhole of armored infantry from the division during operations in the outskirts of Bastogne on January 3, 1945.

The Battle of the Bulge was the debut for the new M4A3 with HVSS suspension, which tankers at the time called the M4A3 (76mm) with 23-inch track and later the M4A3E8. The first batch arrived in the Ardennes and was issued to the badly depleted 4th Armored Division, seen here near Bastogne on January 8, 1945.

This is *Blockbuster*, the M4A3E8 (76mm) tank of Capt. James Leach, the commander of Company B, 37th Tank Battalion, 4th Armored Division.
JAMES LEACH

This M4 medium tank of the 68th Tank Battalion, 6th Armored Division, carries infantry forward during the fighting in mid-January 1945.

An M36 90mm gun motor carriage of the 703rd Tank Destroyer Battalion, 3rd Armored Division, passes by a derelict PzKpfw IV of Panzer Battalion 115, 15th Panzergrenadier Division, south of Langlir on January 13.

This M4A3 (76mm) of the 750th Tank Battalion moves into Salmchateau in support of the 75th Division on January 16. The tank has been thoroughly whitewashed, and on the back deck is a long fluorescent orange air identity panel to prevent strafing by Allied aircraft.

An M4A3 (76mm) of Company C, 774th Tank Battalion, passes by a disabled Panther in the forest near Bovigny on January 17 while supporting the 83rd Infantry Division during the drive to seal the bulge.

A white-washed M4A3E2 assault tank of the 737th Tank Battalion supporting the 5th Infantry Division in operations near Gralingen, Luxembourg, on January 22 on the southern flank of the Ardennes fighting.

The Battle of the Bulge saw the combat debut of the new M24 light tank with the 740th Tank Battalion. The badly mauled 14th Cavalry Group was rebuilt in Belgium following the Ardennes fighting with its M5A1 light tanks replaced by the M24 light tank, seen here with the 18th Cavalry Squadron at Petit Tier, Belgium, on February 3.

RECRIMINATIONS

On January 5, 1945, while the Battle of the Bulge was still raging, the *New York Times* ran the third part of a series on the Ardennes by their military correspondent, Hanson Baldwin, under the headline "New German Tanks Prove Superior to Ours—Inquiry by Congress Urged." The American public was used to hearing that its weapons were the best in the world, and so the charge that its tanks were inferior to German tanks came as a shock. Baldwin's charges were quite blunt:

> Why, at this late stage in the war, are American tank inferior to the enemy's? That they are inferior the fighting in Normandy showed and the recent battles in the Ardennes have again emphatically demonstrated. This has been denied, explained away and hushed up, but the men who are fighting our tanks against much heavier, better armored and more powerfully gunned German monsters know the truth. It is high time that Congress got at the bottom of a situation that does no credit to the War Department.

Baldwin was widely admired and read in Washington, and his column percolated through the Pentagon bureaucracy and eventually to Eisenhower.

On March 18, 1945, Eisenhower sent a personal letter to Brig. Gen. Isaac White, acting commander of the 2nd Armored Division, and a similar letter to Gen. Maurice Rose of the 3rd Armored Division. Eisenhower's letter noted the negative publicity about American tanks in the press in the wake of the Baldwin article and acknowledged that

> Our men, in general, realize the Sherman is not capable of standing up in a ding-dong, head-on fight with a Panther. Neither in gun power nor in armor is the present Sherman justified in undertaking such a contest. On the other hand, most of them realize that we have a job of shipping tanks overseas and therefore do not want unwieldy monsters; that our tank has great reliability, good mobility, and that the gun has been vastly improved. Most of them feel that we have developed tactics that allow them to employ their superior numbers to defeat the Panther tank as long as they are not surprised and can discover the Panther before it has gotten in three or four good shots.

Eisenhower then went on to ask for the commanders' personal opinions on the American tank and the ability of the new T26 Pershing to deal with

Following the fighting at La Gleize, American ordnance troops recovered one of Kampfgruppe Peiper's King Tiger tanks and delivered it to U.S. First Army headquarters at Spa, Belgium, where it was displayed to senior American commanders alongside an M4A3 (76mm). As can be seen, the Sherman was as tall as the King Tiger, though the King Tiger was substantially wider.

the Panther on equal terms and for a digest of the opinions of their units' tankers about tanks and other equipment. White was quick to respond with a personal letter outlining his views on tank development, appending a secret report compiled by the 2nd Armored Division and entitled "United States vs. German Armor"; the report was not declassified until 1958. The seventy-five-page report was a compilation of comments by tank commanders and tankers about their experiences with German tanks and offered grim detail of the numerous occasions when U.S. tanks faced Panthers and King Tigers since Normandy. The battalion commanders were blunt in their assessments. Brig. Gen. J. H. Collier, commanding Combat Command A, wrote that "the consensus of opinion of all personnel in the 66th Armored Regiment is that the German tank and anti-tank weapons are far superior to the American. . . . It is my opinion that press reports of statements by high ranking officers to the effect that we have the best equipment in the world do much to discourage the soldier who is using equipment he knows to be inferior to that of the enemy." This viewpoint was echoed by most of the other officers.

The officers repeatedly questioned the tactical doctrine that tank-versus-tank fighting was not a core mission of the armored divisions. Col. S. R. Hinds, commanding Combat Command B, wrote: "In spite of the often quoted tactical rule that one should not fight tank-versus-tank battles, I have found it necessary, almost invariably, in order to accomplish the mission." Lt. Col. Wilson Hawkins, commanding 3/67th Armored Regiment, hammered this point home: "It has been stated that our tanks are supposed to attack infantry and not be used tank vs. tank. It has been my experience that we have never found this ideal situation, for in all our attacks we must of necessity fight German tanks."

The report contained dozens of short reports on encounters between American and German tanks, focusing on encounters with Panthers and King Tigers. This account from Sgt. Francis Baker was typical:

On the morning of Nov. 20, 1944, I was tank commander of a Sherman medium tank mounting a 76mm gun. The Germans staged a counter-attack with infantry supported by at least three Mark V [Panther] tanks. Ordering my gunner to fire at the closest tank, which was approximately 800 yards away, he placed one right in the side which was completely visible to me. To my amazement and disgust I watched the shell bounce off the side. My gunner fired at least six more rounds at the vehicle hitting it from turret to the track. This German tank, knowing that I possibly would be supported by a tank destroyer, started to pull away. I was completely surprised to see it moving after receiving seven hits from my gun. At this time a tank destroyer mounting a 90mm gun (M36) pulled up on my right flank; motioning to the commander, he acknowledged that he saw the tank. With one well placed shot he put it in flames. Traversing to the left he also put another in flames.

Col. S. R. Hinds summed up the feelings of many fellow officers when he commented that "the reason our armor has engaged the German tank as successfully as it has is not due by any means to a superior tank but to our superior numbers of tanks on the battlefield and the willingness of our tankers to take their losses while maneuvering to a position from which a penetrating shot can be put through a weak spot of the enemy tank."

In the report, several of the officers complained that they had spoken to observers from Washington earlier in the war about the problems with the Sherman but had been ignored. In fact, the White report was the first comprehensive study to document the numerous shortcomings of the Sherman in combat and the first to be widely distributed to senior commanders such as Eisenhower. Earlier observer reports by Ordnance, AGF, Armored Command, and other army organizations prior to D-Day had not found such harsh condemnation of the Sherman or such ardent appeals to provide a better tank. If anything, the general opinion of combat commanders through May 1944 was that a more heavily armored tank like the T26 Pershing with a 90mm gun was not needed. The Sherman had performed very well in Normandy, and although it was occasionally overmatched in sporadic encounters with the Panther, such encounters seldom affected the overall balance of the battle. It was not until the Ardennes, where

The crew of the M4A3 (76) command tank of Capt. John Megglesin of the 42nd Tank Battalion, 11th Armored Division, cross their fingers for luck. This new tank was the third they had been issued in two weeks of fighting in the Ardennes. The two previous tanks had been knocked out, fortunately without the loss of a single crewman. On average, one crewman was killed every time a Sherman was knocked out.

The 3-inch antitank gun was extremely difficult for its crew to maneuver without the assistance of a prime mover, as is evident from this view of a crew of the 801st Tank Destroyer Battalion near Hofen, Germany, on February 2. This battalion converted to M18 76mm gun motor carriage tank destroyers a few weeks later.

the more heavily armored Panther and King Tiger represented more than half of the panzer force, that the outcry began.

This was the fatal flaw of McNair's "battle need" requirement. The commanders in the field were preoccupied with their primary role of leading their troops and consumed by their daily responsibilities. They did not have the luxury to study and ponder the technical intelligence reports on German weapons to anticipate their future needs. By the time battle need was obvious, such as after the Ardennes experience, it was too late for a quick response from Washington. The tepid support for the T26 earlier in

1944 delayed Washington's actions, and so it would be up to GI tankers to improvise their own solutions for dealing with the Panther and King Tiger in the final months of the war.

Another source of bitterness over Sherman performance in 1945 stemmed from the tendency of senior army commanders toward "boosterism" through much of the war. U.S. Army weapons were described as "the best in the world," whether true or not. Some of this was motivated by misinformed but sincere conviction, but often it was a transparent ploy to boost morale. In the end, it led to cynicism among the tank crews who had to fight with inferior equipment.

ARDENNES LESSONS

The main lessons from the Ardennes fighting for the tank battalions and armored divisions were more technical than tactical. Both types of formations had performed well in the Battle of the Bulge in spite of the shortcomings in American armored vehicles. The tankers wanted more armor and firepower.

The German panzer attack had put the tank destroyers to their sternest test, and they had failed in terms of tactical performance and equipment. The four infantry divisions that bore the brunt of the initial German attack had been supported by towed 3-inch tank destroyer battalions. Losses in the 3-inch towed battalions were brutally high, totaling 35 percent in December alone. The hapless 820th Tank Destroyer Battalion was assigned to the 14th Cavalry Group, thinly stretched across the Losheim Gap and at the center of the 6th Panzer Army assault. This battalion was overrun in the first few days of fighting, losing thirty-one of its thirty-six guns. This was the only antitank force available to the thin cavalry screen at the time, and it had utterly failed to have any impact on the fighting. The guns were simply too immobile under actual battlefield circumstances, and even when manned by determined crews, they were easily outmaneuvered and routed from their static positions. The neighboring 801st Tank Destroyer Battalion, assigned to the 99th Division, lost fifteen of its thirty-six guns. In an interview after the tank fighting in Krinkelt-Rocherath, a 2nd Infantry Division officer emphatically stated that "I want the self-propelled guns rather than the towed 3-inch guns because the towed guns are too heavy and sluggish. You can't get them up to the front. My orders have been in almost every case to get the guns up to the front-line troops. I just couldn't do it in the daytime with the 3-inch towed gun. I can get the 57's up pretty well, but you can always get self-propelled guns up better than towed ones."

The lighter 57mm guns had been used with success by the infantry division's own antitank units because they were embedded with the infantry defense and not as easily outmaneuvered by the panzers. They had played a critical role at Krinkelt-Rocherath and the Dom Butgenbach defenses, killed many German tanks in savage close-range duels, and lost many guns and gun crews in the process. The 57mm gun by this stage of the war was obsolete and more a weapon of desperation than a weapon of choice. The bazooka infantry antitank rocket was likewise obsolete, with too small a warhead for current German tanks and lingering problems with the reliability of its warhead. Like the 57mm antitank gun, it had often proved crucial in the early Ardennes fighting even if its dependability and effectiveness were often suspect. U.S. infantry was poorly served in antitank weapons compared to the Germans, and this resulted in no small measure from the infantry's own reluctance to adopt heavier antitank weapons in 1943–44 because of the tactical burden they represented. Many infantry officers regretted these decisions in December 1944.

The Ardennes doomed the towed tank destroyer battalions. The capabilities of the towed battalions had already been found wanting in the summer and autumn of 1944, and the lessons of the Ardennes campaign simply confirmed this. One study concluded that towed tank destroyer battalions fighting independently according to doctrine—and not embedded in an infantry division—suffered a loss ratio of about 3:1 in favor of the attacking panzers. When integrated against doctrine into an infantry defensive position, the towed antitank guns were barely adequate, with an exchange ratio of 1:1.3 in favor of the guns. In contrast, the self-propelled M10 3-inch tank destroyers had a favorable exchange ratio of 1:1.9 when operating independently without infantry support and an excellent ratio of 1:6 when integrated into an infantry defense as a supporting arm. The study noted that the towed 3-inch guns were successful in only two out of nine defensive actions while the M10 tank destroyer battalions were successful in fourteen of sixteen defensive actions against German tanks. The U.S. First Army's tank destroyer losses in the Ardennes totaled 119 weapons, of which 86 were towed guns, a remarkable disproportion that glaringly revealed the vulnerability of the towed guns.

CHAPTER 9

On to the Rhine!

IN THE AFTERMATH OF THE ARDENNES fighting, the tank units in the ETO had become exasperated by Washington's failure to address the German panzer threat in terms of doctrine or equipment. As a result, the beginning of 1945 saw a concerted local effort to adapt to current battlefield realties. This included organizational changes such as the abandonment of the failed towed tank destroyer battalions, as well as technical improvisations such as the addition of appliqué armor on the Sherman and rearming the 75mm tanks with surplus 76mm guns. The theater commanders became much more insistent on equipment improvements, which led to immediate changes in the plans for tank production in 1945.

The performance of the Sherman tank had been found wanting in the Ardennes both in terms of armor and firepower. With the much better Panther now constituting the majority of German tanks, the Sherman was increasingly at a disadvantage in tank-versus-tank battles. The switch to the 76mm version had been slow and uneven. By December 1944, about 30 percent of the Shermans in Bradley's 12th Army Group and Dever's 6th Army Group were 76mm tanks, but some newly arrived units were totally equipped with the new tanks while other long-serving units had few. So for example, of the 3rd Armored Division's 212 Shermans, only 46 were the M4A1 76mm, while the newly arrived 9th Armored Division had all 76mm M4A3 and no 75mm Shermans at all. The separate tank battalions, especially those in the First Army, had fewer 76mm Shermans than average—only about a quarter of their strength—and those battalions in the Ardennes

Tank-infantry cooperation became a well-honed tactic by early 1945. GIs of the 9th Infantry Division prepare to move forward near Bath on February 27 while being supported by a pair of M4A3E2 assault tanks from the 746th Tank Battalion. That day, the division finally captured one of the Roer dams at Schwammenauel—little compensation for the heavy casualties the division had suffered in the bloody Hürtgen Forest.

Various types of assault guns and *panzerjägers* became the most common German AFVs facing the U.S. Army in early 1945. The most impressive was the massive Jagdtiger, a version of the King Tiger fitted with a 128mm antitank gun. Although imposing on paper, these vehicles had poor reliability, and this is one of a pair of Jagdtigers of Heavy Anti-Tank Battalion 653 that broke down near Morsbronn-les-Bains on March 17 and were abandoned by their crews after demolition charges were detonated to sabotage the vehicles.

sector were especially weak in this regard. The four of the five separate battalions that saw the bulk of the early fighting in the first week of the offensive (the 707th with the 28th Division; 741st with the 2nd Division; 745th with the 1st Division; and 740th with the 82nd Division) had none, while the 70th Tank Battalion with the 4th Infantry Division on the southern shoulder had eighteen newly arrived M4A3 (76mm) to make up for their heavy losses in the Hürtgen Forest a month before.

A GI of the 94th Infantry Division walks through a gap in a roadblock in Lampaden past an M4A3 (76mm) of the 778th Tank Battalion that has been knocked out by two gun penetrations through the transmission cover during the fighting for the Saarbrücken bridgehead on March 9.

Victor and vanquished. A Jagdpanther of Heavy Anti-Tank Battalion 654 of Kampfgruppe Paffrath lies by the roadside as a M36 90mm tank destroyer advances past near Kaimig-Ginsterhain on March 13. This was one of three Jagdpanthers knocked out that day. The Jagdpanther combined the hull of the Panther tank with a fixed superstructure mounting an 88mm antitank gun.

FIREPOWER IMPROVEMENTS

If the U.S. Army in the ETO had been reluctant to adopt the 76mm Sherman in June 1944, this attitude had completely changed by January 1945. The outcry about the tank imbalance in the Ardennes was so strong that Eisenhower cabled back to Washington insisting that no more 75mm Shermans be shipped to the theater and that only 76mm Shermans were wanted. There was also pressure to expedite the delivery of more of the 90mm M36 tank destroyers, the long-promised T26 heavy tank, and better ammunition such as the 76mm and 90mm HVAP tungsten carbide projectiles. Ironically, the demand for 76mm tanks led to continued production for Sherman tanks to meet the demand instead of a complete switch to the new T26 Pershing.

As an expedient solution, the 12th Army Group studied the possibility of reequipping the existing 75mm tanks with 76mm guns. This had already been proven as being possible as early as 1942, but there were questions as to whether it could be done in the field by Ordnance units. There was a limited availability of about 100 76mm tubes in theater, which were used to replace gun tubes that had worn out. A small number of trial vehicles were built in February 1945, but by the time the conversions had been completed, the flow of new M4A3 (76mm) from the United States had begun, alleviating the shortage. From its post-Ardennes nadir in January 1945, when 76mm tanks represented 26 percent of Shermans in Bradley's 12th Army Group, the proportion steadily climbed to 30 percent in February, 41 percent in April, and finally 52 percent when the war ended in May 1945. As a result, the 100 gun tubes accumulated for the program were instead installed in the popular M4A3E2 assault tanks.

The dormant American 17-pounder Firefly program was revived in the wake of the Battle of the Bulge. The program began in February 1945, and

Patton's Third Army rearmed its 75mm M4 tanks with the 76mm gun, and a single M4A3 pilot was completed by Ordnance in February 1945. The conversion required the addition of a large slab of steel on the rear of the turret to act as a counterweight. Although feasible, the arrival of the 76mm-equipped M4A3 made the conversions unnecessary. The accumulated 76mm guns were used to rearm about 100 M4A3E2 assault tanks.

About 100 M4 and M4A3 were rearmed with 17-pounder guns by British arsenals in the spring of 1945. They had a number of differences from the British Fireflies—for example, the vision cupola and radio box on the rear of the turret. The smaller tanks in the foreground are M22 Locust airborne tanks. GEORGE BRADFORD

the American M4 (17-pounder) differed from its British counterparts in a number of small details, such as radio fittings. Two U.S. M4A3 (17-pounder) pilots were completed on March 15, 1945, and the first shipment of M4 medium tanks from France back to England for conversion arrived in Southampton on March 9, 1945. The initial order was for 160 conversions, to be completed by April 30. The M4A3 with wet ammunition stowage was preferred for the conversion, but the M4 was also used. A total of eleven conversions were completed by the end of March, and the first batch of five converted M4 (17-pounder) tanks departed Southampton for the continent on March 31.

On April 7, the U.S. Army decided against proceeding with the planned conversion program beyond the first batch of eighty tanks. It was realized that with the war nearing its end, the tanks would

probably never see action and that the process of adding a new caliber of ammunition into the logistics network was not warranted. By the time this change of plan was received by the British arsenals, a total of 100 tanks were already completed or in the process of conversion by May 7. As a result, the excess twenty vehicles were transferred to Britain as part of Lend-Lease. The last three conversions departed Southampton on May 10, after the war had ended. None of the M4A3 (17-pounder) were actually deployed with U.S. Army tank units since by the time they arrived on the continent and were prepared for deployment, the war was almost over. The M4 (17-pounder) tanks were supposed to be issued to tank units of the First and Ninth Armies on an equal basis of forty apiece. In mid-May 1945, Eisenhower's headquarters asked the 6th Army Group if it wanted the M4 and M4A3 (17-pounder) for units

Although the Third Army's 76mm gun program was short-lived, the stock of 76mm guns built up were used to rearm the popular M4A3E2 assault tanks like this example from the 3rd Armored Division during the fighting in Cologne on March 6, 1945.

slated to be deployed to Japan. The 6th recommended against deploying them to the Pacific and instead suggested they be retained in Europe for occupation duty. The fate of these tanks is unclear, and there are no known records of their disposal after the war.

The demand for more powerful guns subsided after the collapse of German tank strength after the failure of the Ardennes offensive and the smaller Operation Nordwind offensive in Alsace in January 1945. The 6th Panzer Army and a number of other panzer divisions were shifted to the Russian front in a forlorn attempt to stem the catastrophe there. By the beginning of February 1945, the Wehrmacht had only 390 tanks on the entire Western Front, and of these, only 190 were operational, a reminder of the pernicious effect of Allied bombing

on the supply of German spare parts. Most of German AFV strength was in the form of StuG III assault guns supporting infantry divisions, as well as *panzerjägers*. German tank strength was so low in the west that panzer battalions were obliged to substitute "Guderian's Duck"—the turretless Panzer IV/70—for regular tanks. These assault guns and *panzerjägers* totaled about 1,020 in February 1945, but only about 610 were operational because of lingering maintenance problems and battle damage. In comparison, American AFV strength in early February included 3,100 Shermans and 1,960 tank destroyers; Montgomery's 21st Army Group had 2,600 tanks and 320 tank destroyers. In terms of actual operational strength, the Allies had a ten-to-one advantage in AFVs following the Ardennes campaign.

MORE ARMOR

If the rapid decline in German AFV strength diminished the pressure to field more powerful tank guns, it did nothing to diminish interest in better armor protection. Although there were fewer German AFVs on the battlefield in early 1945, there was no shortage of antitank weapons. Aside from the ubiquitous 75mm PaK 40 found in all German infantry divisions, U.S. tanks were increasingly threatened by heavy-caliber flak guns as they reached Germany's industrial belt. One of the German responses to the Allied bombing campaign had been the creation of a substantial antiaircraft force to protect the industrial cities, and this had consumed as much as a third of German wartime artillery production. Most of the antibomber weapons were heavy-caliber types in the 88mm to 128mm range, and these all had sec-ondary antitank capabilities. Gunfire remained the main killer of American tanks in 1945, climbing from 47.6 percent in 1944 to 50.9 percent in 1945, even if the balance between the AFVs and towed artillery shifted somewhat. Mines remained a constant threat, accounting for 16.4 percent of U.S. tank losses in 1944 and 18.2 percent in 1945. German antitank rockets, such as *panzerfausts* remained fairly steady at 11.7 percent in 1944 and 11.4 percent in 1945, even though this was not the perception of U.S. tankers. Most American records suggest that these widely used weapons increased considerably in use in the final months of the fighting, but it is also possible that the increased use was not accompanied by increased tank damage because of the declining

In February 1944, Chrysler developed an appliqué armor kit that could be attached in the field to bolster the Sherman's protection. For reasons that remain unclear, the program was cancelled late in February and progressed only as far as this wooden mock-up.

Although the Wehrmacht had lost much of its armor in the Ardennes, the fight was not yet over. Task Force Van Houton from CCB, 2nd Armored Division, was given a rough reception in Rheinberg on the west bank of the Rhine on March 9. German antitank guns and *panzerfausts* knocked out thirty-nine of the fifty-four tanks used in the attack. This M4A3 took five hits, one of them completely shearing off the left drive sprocket.

Ordnance developed kits to deal with the *panzerfaust*, but too late for the war in Europe. The package used low-density HCR2, a mixture of quartz gravel and an asphalt and sawdust mastic. The ten-inch-thick HCR2 was contained within a box with one-inch aluminum plate. Tests in the autumn of 1945 found that the armor substantially improved protection against both the *panzerschreck* and *panzerfaust*, though some penetrations of the sponsons did occur depending on the attack angle.

quality of German troops and the increasing use of untrained forces such as the *Volkssturm* militia.

Regardless of the cause of tank losses, U.S. tankers wanted more armor on their tanks. When Ordnance failed to offer a solution, the tank units themselves came up with improvised solutions. The most popular and widespread improvisation was the use of sandbags, which had been seen in growing profusion since Normandy. Many tanks and tank destroyers had layers of sandbags on their front glacis

Dissatisfaction with the poor armor protection of the M4 tank led many American units to add improvised armor—most often sandbags—to the front of their tanks. The U.S. Seventh Army in Alsace had the most elaborate innovations, like this example from the 14th Armored Division, whose workshops prepared a kit with shelves and frames to hold the sandbags in place.

Some of the first tanks of the 14th Armored Division with the added sandbag armor in February 1945 also were camouflaged with bands of whitewash over the usual olive-drab finish, like this M4A3E8 (76mm).

plate. There were few illusions that these would stop a high-velocity antitank projectile, but many tank crews felt that they did offer a measure of protection against the dreaded *panzerfaust*. Official reaction to the sandbags by senior commanders was mixed but generally supportive. There was considerable contro-versy among Ordnance officers regarding the effec-tiveness of this practice, with most arguing that sandbags offered minimal protection. Tankers dis-agreed, citing numerous examples when sandbagged tanks were not penetrated by *panzerfaust* or *panzer-schreck* hits.

One of the most effective up-armoring programs was undertaken by the Ninth Army, including the 2nd Armored Division as seen here. The tanks had a layer of tracks welded to the glacis plate, covered by sandbags, and then wrapped in camouflage net. The layered armor bears a primitive resemblance to modern laminate armors.

The Ordnance officers of the 12th Armored Division were not entirely convinced of the value of sandbag armor and developed a local expedient in February–March 1945, using concrete applied over the glacis plate and hull sides with steel rebar for internal reinforcement.

Three M10 tank destroyers advance through München-Gladbach on March 1, 1945, when the 29th Infantry Division captured the town during Operation Grenade, the assault over the Roer River. They are fitted with the usual Ninth Army appliqué armor on the glacis plate.

There were few systematic attempts to determine how effective the sandbags were in actual combat. On March 9, 1945, officers from the 1st Armored Group decided to test the standard *Panzerfaust 60* against sandbags. Three rockets fired directly against the side sponsons blew away the sandbags and penetrated the side armor. In order to better simulate a typical German infantry attack in an urban area, subsequent rockets were fired from an angle against the front plate, and these blew away some of the sandbags but failed to penetrate the armor. An observer reported back to the War Department that "these tests are far from conclusive, and the psychological value of the sandbags is the greatest value actually derived." Another observer visiting other units in Germany in March 1945 agreed, reporting that "I gathered that if the bags did nothing more, they were certainly a morale factor as

the crews were thoroughly impressed with them." Most officers recognized that sandbags were a psychological boost for the crew, even if not technically effective, and so condoned the practice even if the ton of sandbags on the Sherman tanks degraded their automotive performance and led to premature transmission failures from the excessive weight concentrated at the front of the tank.

The use of sandbag armor evolved from very simple applications by individual crews to more systematic programs carried out by the ordnance and maintenance battalions. The most systematic program was started by Devers's 6th Army Group in Alsace in January 1945, where the corps ordnance battalions designed a steel basket that allowed sandbag coverage to be extended from the front glacis plate to the hull and turret sides as well, totaling three tons of sandbags per Sherman. The 12th

Armored Division was not entirely convinced of the effectiveness of the sandbag armor and began developing its own solution in the form of concrete armor. The division maintenance unit welded six-inch-long bolts to the glacis plate and sponson sides and then, for reinforcement, two layers of wire mesh at two-inch intervals and a final layer of steel reinforcing rods near the surface. Wooden forms were temporarily attached, and then concrete was poured, creating a rigid protective belt. The use of concrete armor began in February 1945, but only on a small portion of the division's tanks. Little evidence of how effective this proved to be has survived.

Ordnance officers of the Ninth Army on the north wing of Bradley's 12th Army Group felt that they were most valuable on the front glacis plate. They came up with a layered design that may actually have been a crude precursor of modern laminate armors as used in today's main battle tanks. The Ninth Army configuration was a layer of spare steel track blocks welded to the glacis plate, then a layer of sandbags secured by a tightly attached cover of artillery camouflage net. This was used on the tanks of several units, including the 2nd Armored Division after the Ardennes fighting.

The exception to the sandbag armor practice was Patton's Third Army, which devised by far the best armor-protection package for its tanks. In the summer of 1944, the Third Army's ordnance officers convinced Patton that sandbags were worthless and detrimental to the tank's suspension and powertrain, so Patton expressly forbade the use of sandbags in his units. Even Patton could not resist the growing clamor for better protection in the wake of the Battle of the Bulge, so he demanded that his ordnance officers come up with a better solution. The method was obvious—weld on more armor plate. The source was equally obvious—the numerous German and American tanks littering the Ardennes battlefield. In February 1945, Patton ordered that all M4A3 (76mm) in his units be fitted with additional front hull armor as well as turret armor if possible.

With the Third Army's ordnance battalions already overworked, much of the work was handed over to three Belgian factories near Bastogne. The tanks of three armored divisions (the 4th, 6th, and 11th) were modified in this fashion, an average of 36 tanks per division out of their 168 Shermans. The program was both technically successful and very popular with the tank crews blessed with the appliqué armor. A 6th Armored Division tanker recalled how shortly after his M4A3E8 had been fitted with the armor in February 1945, his tank was hit by a 75mm round from a German armored vehicle, which knocked a piece of the appliqué armor from the hull but did not penetrate. This program was continued in March 1945 after Patton acquired a group of salvaged M4 tanks from the neighboring Seventh Army to cannibalize for armor plate.

The Third Army's modernization effort included other improvements as well. The tankers wanted a more powerful coaxial gun than the usual .30-cal machine gun, so some .50-caliber aircraft machine guns were "liberated" and fitted to many tanks. The newly arrived M4A3 (76mm) tanks had a new oval loader's hatch, but in the process, the .50-caliber machine gun was moved to a pintle mount awkwardly positioned behind the tank commander's left shoulder. The tank commander or loader had to fire the machine gun by getting out of the turret and standing on the rear engine deck behind the turret, which was obviously neither safe in combat nor particularly convenient. Some units simply remounted the pintle forward. Other units also added an additional .30-caliber machine gun in front of the commander for added firepower to deal with *panzerfaust*-wielding German infantry.

The Third Army's Sherman program was so successful that Bradley's 12th Army Group borrowed one to write a report back to Washington on how the Sherman should be configured for the ETO. This was never acted upon by any agency in the United States, but it helped establish a model for other units in the ETO.

An M4A1 (76mm) of the 2nd Armored Division passes through München-Gladbach on March 1 as the Roer offensive finally succeeds. Probably one of the M4A1s first used in Cobra the previous July, this tank has been retrofitted with the usual Ninth Army appliqué consisting of steel tank tracks, a layer of sandbags, and a covering of artillery camouflage netting over the glacis plate for added protection against *panzerfausts*.

Patton's Third Army preferred to use armor plate rather than sandbags. This 11th Armored Division M4A3E8 (76mm) shows the added appliqué steel armor. The glacis armor was often from the glacis plate of a knocked-out M4, complete with the associated headlight guards and other features.

The armor for the Third Army's Sherman upgrades was cannibalized from knocked-out German and American tanks. This is an example of a knocked-out M4 105mm assault tank that has been stripped for its hull armor.

Woe to the tank crews that displeased Patton! The general storms back to his staff car after having chewed out the crew of an M4A3E8 (76mm) of 14th Armored Division for their use of sandbag armor. Patton personally disapproved of the practice, creating problems when the 14th Armored Division was transferred from Patch's Seventh Army to Patton's Third on April 22–23, 1945.

The Third Army's Sherman upgrade package impressed Bradley's 12th Army Group headquarters so much that it became the preferred solution to the Sherman's armor problems. This M4A3E8 was used as a model for upgrades in the ETO. Besides the armor improvement, it also included the added .30-caliber machine gun more conveniently located for the commander and a coaxial .50-caliber heavy machine gun in place of the .30-caliber light machine gun.

The ETO upgrade package included numerous changes to the Sherman's machine-gun armament, including better armament and the movement of the pintle mount for the exterior .50-caliber machine gun in front of the loader's hatch.

ZEBRA MISSION

The failure of Ordnance to develop an adequate response to the Panther threat was acutely embarrassing to General Barnes. In an effort to make amends, he accelerated deployment of the T26E2 Pershing heavy tanks and led a special team to the ETO in February 1945, called the Zebra Mission. This included the demonstration of a number of new weapons to senior officers, including a new towed 90mm antitank gun and a new self-propelled 155mm gun. By the end of 1944, forty Pershing tanks had been completed, but they still had mechanical teething problems. The Zebra Mission included a number of specialists to make sure that problems were quickly identified and addressed.

A first batch of twenty T26E3 arrived at the port of Antwerp in January 1945. All were sent to First Army, which had borne the brunt of the Ardennes fighting, split into two groups between the 3rd and 9th Armored Divisions. Training on the new tanks for the crews and maintenance personnel was completed in late February 1945.

The T26E3 were first committed to combat on February 25, 1945, with Task Force Lovelady of the

3rd Armored Division during the fighting for the Roer River. The first tank was knocked out on February 26, when it was ambushed at night by a Tiger I near Elsdorf. Two crewmen were killed, but the tank was repaired and put back into action a few days later. The next day, a Pershing of Company E, 33rd Armored Regiment, knocked out a Tiger I and two PzKpfw IV tanks near Elsdorf. The Tiger was knocked out at 900 yards with the new 90mm T30E16 HVAP, followed by a round of standard T33 armor-piercing ammunition, which penetrated the turret and set off an internal explosion. The two PzKpfw IVs were knocked out at the impressive range of 1,200 yards—beyond the normal engagement ranges for U.S. tanks in World War II, which were closer to 800 yards.

The neighboring 9th Armored Division first committed its Pershings to action during the Roer fighting in the final days of February 1945. One tank was disabled on the night of March 1, when hit twice by a 150mm field gun, but it was later repaired. This left the new heavy tank platoon of the 14th Tank Battalion with only four Pershing tanks

Much to the relief of some tank crews, the first shipment of twenty T26E3 tanks arrived at the port of Antwerp in early February with the Zebra Mission. Since the Pershing was too wide for many railroads, it had to be moved using tank transporters, here being loaded onto an M25 tank transporter in Antwerp harbor on February 9, 1945, using one of the less often seen M26A1 unarmored tractors.

This T26E3 (serial number 36) from Company D, 32nd Armored Regiment, 3rd Armored Division, was one of the first to see combat. Here it is seen on the streets of Cologne on March 6, 1945. This particular tank knocked out two Tigers.

Although two T26E3 were knocked out in the fighting on the approaches to Cologne, only one was a complete loss—this tank (serial number 25) from Company H, 33rd Armored Regiment, 3rd Armored Division. It was hit at 200 yards by an 88mm round from a Nashorn self-propelled tank destroyer, which penetrated the lower bow armor under the transmission, setting off the ammunition in the floor. The round passed between the driver's legs, but surprisingly, the entire crew survived. PATTON MUSEUM

when it took part in one of the most famous actions of World War II. On March 7, 1945, infantry half-tracks of Combat Command B, 9th Armored Division, crested a hill overlooking the town of Remagen on the Rhine River. To their surprise, the Ludendorf railroad bridge was still standing after almost every other bridge over the Rhine had been destroyed by the Wehrmacht to prevent the Allies from crossing the river. The local German com-

mander had hesitated to drop the bridge while trying the extract a large number of his troops still on the western bank of the Rhine. Armored infantry supported by Lt. John Grimball's Pershing platoon fought their way through the town and reached the approaches to the bridge around 2 P.M. A demolition charge on the approaches to the bridge created a crater that prevented tank access, so the T26E3 tanks provided covering fire as the infantry moved

During the battle for Cologne, a Panther Ausf. A tank of the 2nd Battalion, Panzer Regiment 33, 9th Panzer Division, took up a position in front of the cathedral. It knocked out two approaching M4 tanks, but a T26E3 commanded by Sgt. Bob Early from Company E, 32nd Armored Regiment, charged the Panther from the side. The Panther was still slowly turning its turret toward its opponents when the first of three rounds slammed into the tank, causing an internal fire that burned it out, as seen here a few days later.

This is the Pershing platoon of Lt. John Grimball, Company A, 14th Tank Battalion, 9th Armored Division, near Vettweiss, Germany. It would take part in the capture of the bridge at Remagen a week later on March 7, 1945.

across the bridge. A German troop train was spotted moving on the east bank of the river, unaware of the fighting, and the locomotive was destroyed by 90mm high-explosive fire from the tanks.

Another Pershing engagement occurred on March 6, 1945, and was recorded by an army camera crew. A Panther tank from the 9th Panzer Division was stationed in the courtyard in front of the Cologne cathedral, where it ambushed an M4A3 medium tank as it approached. The Pershing tank of Sgt. Bob Early, from Company E, 32nd Armored Regiment, 3rd Armored Division, was sent to deal with it, and the Pershing charged the Panther from the side. The Panther was still slowly turning its turret toward its opponents when the first of three rounds slammed into it, causing an internal fire that destroyed it. The same day, other T26E3 tanks from the 3rd Armored Division knocked out a Tiger I and a PzKpfw IV near the city.

In mid-March, an unusual T26 arrived in Germany, sometimes called the "Super Pershing." This was the original T26E1 pilot tank that had been rearmed with a new long-barreled T15E1 90mm gun to offer performance comparable to the German 88mm KwK 43 gun on the King Tiger. Firing trials in the United States showed it could penetrate 220 millimeters of armor at 1,000 yards at 30 degrees using the new T30E16 tungsten carbide HVAP round—enough to penetrate the thickest German tank armor. This unique tank was deployed with the 3rd Armored Division, and its ordnance battalion decided to further enhance the Super Pershing with appliqué armor plate to bring it closer to the armor on the King Tiger. The five tons of armor were from a 40mm boiler plate on the hull and a plate of 80mm armor taken from a German Panther on the gun mantlet.

The Super Pershing first fired its gun in anger on April 4, 1945, when it engaged and destroyed a German tank, possibly a Tiger or Panther, at a range of 1,500 yards during the fighting along the Weser River. It was credited with another panzer on April 12 shortly after the liberation of the concentration camp at Nordhausen. On April 21, the Super Pershing became involved in a short-range duel with a panzer identified by the crew as a Tiger. (This could have been any type of German tank, since U.S. tank crews regularly called nearly any German tank a Tiger.) As the Super Pershing rounded a corner, the panzer fired the first shot, missing when the round passed over the tank. The Super Pershing fired point-blank, but the shot glanced off the panzer's turret side. The German tank hit the Super Pershing on the turret but failed to penetrate. The panzer began moving forward over some debris in the street, and the American gunner put a round into the panzer's belly, setting off the ammunition. On April 22, after chasing around two panzers in a small town, the Super Pershing accepted the surrender of one of the German tanks after it had run out of ammunition. This was the last tank-versus-tank fighting by the Super Pershing during the war, and its final tally stood at three panzers knocked out and one captured.

A second batch of forty T26E3 Pershing tanks arrived in Antwerp late in March. They were delivered to the Ninth Army, being divided between the 2nd and 5th Armored Divisions. A subsequent batch of thirty tanks was allotted to Patton's Third Army in April, all going to the 11th Armored Division, which was the last unit equipped with the T26E3 in combat. In the final weeks of the war, the T26E3 tanks saw less combat because of the collapse of the German armed forces. By the end of the war, 310 T26E3 had been delivered to Europe, of which 200 had been issued to tank units. However, only the tanks supplied in February 1945 with the Zebra Mission saw extensive combat. The Pershing experience can best be summed up as "too little, too late." A postwar report by First Army assessed the combat trials of the Zebra mission: "Unfortunately for this test, the German armor had been so crippled as to present a very poor opponent and the cessation of hostilities so soon after forming these companies precluded the gaining of any real experience."

The T26E3 tank was received with enthusiasm by American tankers as it offered substantially better armor and firepower than the M4 medium tank. However, it was rushed into service and had a predictable number of problems, the two principal of which related to mobility. It was powered by the same Ford GAA engine as the M4A3 Sherman but weighed about ten tons more, so its automotive performance was unremarkable. It did not have the range of the Sherman, and the large size of the 90mm ammunition reduced the number of rounds it could carry into combat. (In Korea, the M26 was the preferred tank in the 1950 summer campaign when the North Korean Army fielded a significant number of tanks, but in the subsequent fighting in 1951–53, with no enemy tanks present, U.S. tank battalions preferred the more durable and dependable M4A3E8 Sherman.)

Another secret weapon to finally see its combat debut around the time of the Remagen operation was the orphaned Leaflet night-fighting tank. In February 1945, with operations along the Rhine likely, sixty-five Leaflet tanks were taken out of depots and issued to three tank battalions: the 738th Tank Battalion with Hodge's First Army, the 739th Tank Battalion with Simpson's Ninth Army, and the

A T26E3 of Grimball's platoon on the road between Thum and Ginnick, Germany, on March 1 shortly before Remagen. In the background is a T5E1 armored recovery vehicle pushing a set of T1E1 mine exploders.

Since the Ludendorff Bridge was damaged by German demolition charges, the Pershing heavy tanks were not allowed to cross it. Here an M4A3 tank of 14th Tank Battalion passes beyond the two eastern towers that had housed machine-gun positions for the defense of the bridge shortly after the capture of the east bank.

On March 7, 1945, Task Force Engeman of the 9th Armored Division surprised the German defenders of the Ludendorff Bridge at Remagen and seized the Rhine crossing after the demolition charges failed. The attack was led by Lt. John Grimball's platoon of four T26E3 tanks of the 14th Tank Battalion, including this one, photographed a few days later in the town.

Hitler was incensed at the first crossing of the Rhine at Remagen and ordered extensive Luftwaffe attacks against the bridge, including jet bombers. As a result, the U.S. Army moved a considerable amount of antiaircraft artillery into the area, including these M16 quad .50-caliber machine-gun half-tracks.

Among the other new weapons delivered by the Zebra Mission to the ETO was the first of the M26 90mm gun on an M18 carriage. This new weapon had little impact since by this stage of the war, the tank destroyer battalions were fed up with towed guns and wanted all self-propelled weapons.

748th Tank Battalion with Patton's Third Army. These were not intended for use in their original role supporting a major attack, but rather were intended to perform night guard duty when bridges were captured along the Rhine. The Leaflet tanks were seldom used in company strength; usually a platoon of them deployed with each of the three tank companies in each battalion so that two or three bridge sites could be protected.

The first to be deployed was a platoon from Company C, 738th Tank Battalion, which was used to defend the Ludendorff Bridge at Remagen. The Leaflet tanks were used to provide night illumination upstream from the bridge to prevent the Germans from sending boats or frogmen against the bridge. The other units were in action later in March and were also used to provide night illumination to allow the engineers to work around the clock to erect temporary bridges over the Rhine. Several Leaflet tanks were damaged by German mortar and artillery fire during these operations, and a Leaflet tank of Company A, 739th Tank Battalion, sank a German barge on the night of March 25 with four rounds from its 75mm gun, the first known combat engagement of this type. They were also used to provide fire support for a number of infantry operations during the fighting along the Rhine. The Leaflet tanks remained in operation through the middle of April 1945 but were gradually withdrawn as U.S. forces pushed beyond the Rhine into Germany and the searchlights failed because of their prolonged use. The British 35th Armoured Brigade also used its CDL tanks in a similar fashion along the Rhine in March 1945.

The other new tank to appear in 1945, the M24 Chaffee light tank, saw its unintended combat debut in December 1944 with the 740th Tank Battalion during the fighting against Kampfgruppe Peiper near Malmedy. This was a completely new design intended to replace the M5A1 Stuart light tank. The M24 was quickly dubbed the "Panther Pup" because its radically modern design did not have the typical American appearance and so might be mistaken as a panzer. It was one of the best U.S. tank designs of the war, and indeed it would remain in service around the world for nearly half a century. Although it was not much faster or better armored than the Stuart, it was armed with a 75mm gun, giving it firepower comparable to the basic Sherman, and its automotive design, fire controls, and other features were a generation more advanced than the Stuart. It was not available in sufficient numbers to completely replace the M5A1, so it was originally earmarked to go to mechanized cavalry squadrons which desperately needed better equipment to replace their obsolete M5A1 light tanks and sluggish M8 light armored cars.

In the wake of the Ardennes fighting, the towed tank destroyer battalions were scorned by the army in Europe. The army bureaucracy in Washington had failed to act in spite of repeated complaints about the towed battalions since the fighting in Normandy, so in January 1945, Bradley's 12th Army Group took matters into its own hands and began to convert all towed 3-inch battalions to self-propelled battalions. The same policy was later adopted by Devers's 6th Army Group in Alsace after it learned similar lessons during the German Nordwind offensive in January 1945. Commanders preferred to reequip the battalions with the M36 90mm GMC since this was the only tank destroyer that had a reasonably good chance of success against the German Panther tank. Because of shortages of M36s and a surplus of unused M18 tank destroyers, the M18 was used to reequip some of the towed battalions. Lingering shortages of new tank destroyers prevented complete reorganization, and when the war in Europe ended in May 1945, four battalions still had the towed 3-inch guns compared to forty-one with self-propelled tank destroyers. Of these self-propelled battalions, thirteen were equipped with the M18, and the rest were equipped with the M36 or a mixture of M10 and M36 tanks destroyers.

The final production batches of the Sherman for the U.S. Army were the M4A3E8 (76mm) equipped with the new HVSS suspension and twenty-three-inch-wide track. Aside from minor components, such as headlights and periscopes, these tanks did not have a single part in common with the first M4A1 tanks of 1942 and had a different hull, different turret, different gun, different suspension, and different powertrain. The M4A3E8 tank of 1945 was a significantly better tank than the M4A1 of 1942. But the M4A1 could certainly be considered one of the world's best tanks in 1942 and even in 1943; the same could not be said of the M4A3E8 in 1945.

The weight of the new Pershings caused difficulties in crossing rivers. Usually, the Pershings were ferried across using improvised tank ferries made from bridging pontoons, as is the case with this 3rd Armored Division Pershing being ferried across the Rhine in March 1945.

The 3rd Armored Division received the most powerful American tank deployed in World War II, a pilot for the T26E4 armed with the T15 90mm gun. By this stage, the division's ordnance team had already installed appliqué armor on the glacis plate and gun mantlet, though additional armor was later added to cover the turret front.

A column of new Pershing tanks for the 2nd Armored Division approaches the Rhine near Wesel on March 30, 1945.

An M4A3 of Company C, 35th Tank Battalion, 4th Armored Division, moves through the outskirts of Frankfurt on March 28, 1945. This older M4A3 has direct vision slots and has been rebuilt with appliqué armor and other features.

An M4A3 with a squad of infantry on the back moves through Weitzlar on March 28. This is a late-production, wet-stowage M4A3 with the 75mm gun—a fairly common type during the 1945 campaign in Germany, though the stowage box on the hull side is unusual.

A familiar sight in Germany in April 1945: urban warfare. A squad of armored doughs of the 44th Armored Infantry Battalion advances cautiously behind an M4A3E8 medium tank during the fighting by Task Force 44, 6th Armored Division, in Oberdorla, Germany, on April 4. After pushing through the town, the task force participated in the encirclement and capture of Mühlhausen later in the day.

Street fighting was common in the battle for Germany. Here a GI huddles behind a sandbagged M4A3 (76mm) of the 14th Armored Division that was knocked out in the fighting for Lohr on April 3.

After using M4A1 Duplex Drive amphibious tanks in Normandy, the U.S. Army still had about 100 of them, which were refurbished for the Rhine crossing in late March 1945. This is a training exercise by the 781st Tank Battalion near Binau on the Neckar River on April 30. This unit was attached to the Seventh Army in southern Germany and did not participate in the Rhine crossing. It retained its DD tanks for potential future river operations in Germany.

A column from the 15th Tank Battalion, 6th Armored Division, passes a long column of German prisoners of war walking back along the median strip of the autobahn near Giesen, Germany, on March 29 following the surrender of more than 300,000 troops of Army Group B in the Ruhr Pocket. The tank to the right is a new M4A3E8, which, like many of the tanks in Patton's Third Army, has had additional armor plates welded to the turret and hull front.

An M4A3E8 (76mm) of the 6th Armored Division guards an intersection in Offenbach on March 28. This particular tank was one of those fitted with appliqué armor on the glacis plate, though not on the turret. It is painted with the large tactical numbers—in this case, 28—typical of the 6th Armored Division.

This King Tiger was captured by Combat Command R, 7th Armored Division, near Mahmecke on April 11 during the final stages of the battle for the Ruhr Pocket. This may have been one of the King Tigers from the training school at Sennelager that was supporting SS Replacement Brigade Westfalen in the fighting near Paderborn. There was extensive contact with King Tigers in the push across the Ruhr near Cologne since the Henschel production plant was in nearby Kassel.

The crew of an M36 90mm tank destroyer throws food to some liberated Allied prisoners of war on the outskirts of Munich on April 29 shortly before German resistance in the city finally collapsed.

The tanks of the 736th Tank Battalion hold a review in the town square of Piene on May 27. The tanks have been cleaned up and given a new set of markings. The tank in the lower left is one of the late-production M4A1 (76mm) delivered to Europe in the spring of 1945; the tank to the right leading the review is an M4A3E8 (76mm).

The ultimate version of the Sherman tank in U.S. Army service during the war was the M4A3E8, which began appearing in combat in late December 1944. It introduced a new suspension system with wider track, giving the tank better mobility in muddy conditions. This example is with the 21st Tank Battalion, serving with CCA, 10th Armored Division, during the fighting in Rosswalden, Germany, on April 20.

CHAPTER 10

From Bloody Tarawa to the Sands of Iwo Jima

"THE ENEMY'S POWER LIES in their tanks. It has become obvious that our overall battle against the American forces is a battle against their M3 and M4 tanks." So said Gen. Mitsuru Ushijima, the commander of the Japanese 32nd Army on Okinawa, while preparing his troops for the final battle in the spring of 1945. His statement may come as a surprise as tank warfare is seldom associated with the war in the Pacific. Yet tanks played a vital role in nearly all the major campaigns of the Pacific war from 1941 to 1945—and indeed played a decisive tactical role in many battles. A third of all U.S. Army separate tank battalions and all six U.S. Marine Corps tank battalions were deployed in the Pacific theater. There were few epic tank-versus-tank battles in the Pacific, and the Sherman was primarily used to provide fire support for infantry and marines. Unlike the situation in Europe, the Sherman was never seriously challenged by enemy tanks, which were of poor quality. But as in Europe, the threat from determined Japanese infantry attack required constant innovations in the Sherman's protection and its battlefield tactics.

The Pacific theater saw the first combat use of tanks by the U.S. Army in World War II when a number of National Guard tank companies were put under federal control, grandly relabeled the 192nd and 194th Tank Battalions, and trundled off to the Philippines in November 1941. They were soon joined on Luzon by more than 100 freshly assembled M3 light tanks, but the tankers had little time to train before the war started there on December 8, 1941.

Formed into the Provisional Tank Group, the M3 light tanks were used to counterattack the Japanese forces when they landed at Lingayen Gulf later in the month. The first tank-versus-tank engagement took

The fate of many of the U.S. Marine tanks on Tarawa was to drown in shell holes after their engines or electrical systems failed because they did not have deep-wading trunks or sealing. This led to the development of deep-wading gear like that developed in the Mediterranean theater. It was only in 1944 that a standardized deep-wading kit was developed for both the Pacific and European theaters.

The Sherman saw its combat debut in the Pacific theater at Tarawa, landing with Company C, I Marine Amphibious Corps Tank Battalion. This M4A2 (named *Condor*) was one of the few Shermans to make it ashore safely. It was quickly put out of action; official accounts suggest it was accidentally knocked out by a navy dive-bomber, but veterans doubt that story.

place on December 22, 1941, when Type 95 Ha-go light tanks of the Japanese 4th Tank Regiment ambushed a patrol of M3 light tanks from the 192nd Tank Battalion near Damortis. These two opposing tank units continued to skirmish as U.S. forces retreated toward Bataan. Many American tanks were lost during ill-conceived withdrawals—in no small measure because of the inexperience of higher commands with tanks. The surviving M3

light tanks were among the last of the U.S. rearguard to withdraw into the Bataan Peninsula. The last tank-versus-tank action took place on April 7, 1942, when two Japanese tanks were destroyed by the M3 light tanks on Bataan.

Both the U.S. Army and U.S. Marine Corps relied on the M3 light tank for most of the fighting in 1942, including the battle for Guadalcanal that started in August 1942 and was followed by opera-

While the U.S. Marines were attacking Japanese positions on Roi and Namur, U.S. Army units were landing at Enubuj in the Kwajalein atoll on February 2, 1944. The 767th Tank Battalion, equipped with M4A1 medium tanks, supported the U.S. Army 7th Infantry Division during the fighting. A pair of M4A1 medium tanks are seen here landing with their deep-wading trunks.

Operation Backhander on New Britain was the only time that the U.S. Marines used the M4A1 in combat. Company A, Marine 1st Tank Battalion, was supplied with army M4A1 tanks for the Cape Gloucester landings in December 1943, one of which is seen here coming ashore from an LST.

tions on New Georgia. The jungle-covered islands of the South Pacific were not easily accessible by tank, especially the Sherman. When the marines' 1st Tank Battalion landed on Cape Gloucester in the Solomons in December 1943, the enemy strongpoints were so inaccessible that M4A2 medium tanks were loaded onto LCMs (landing craft, medium) and used as miniature battleships to blast Japanese bunkers close to shore.

The most extensive use of Sherman tanks in 1943–44 occurred in the Central Pacific. The Sherman's combat debut was at Tarawa, a coral atoll in the Gilbert Islands that was assaulted by the marines on November 20, 1943. Tank support came from Company C of I Marine Amphibious Corps (IMAC) Tank Battalion, the first marine unit to receive the Sherman. Six M4A2 tanks were landed by LCM at Beach Red 1 from 1,200 yards offshore.

An M4A2 medium tank of the Marine 2nd Separate Tank Company waits along the beach on Perry Island in the Marshalls during the landings there in February 1944. At this stage of the war, the deep-wading trunks were often built by local ordnance teams, and so their shape and configuration differed considerably from the later standardized types.

The marines experimented with specialized tanks as well. Based on magazine articles about British flail tanks, this antimine flail tank was built by the 4th Tank Battalion on Maui in the spring of 1944 after the Marshall Islands campaign.

As they approached the beach, the tank drivers saw a thick carpet of dead and wounded marines in front of them. To avoid running over them, the tanks tried to move to the flanks of the landing area, only to fall victim to Japanese artillery or drown in huge shell holes created by the pre-invasion bombardment. Only two Shermans made it to Beach Red 1. Of these, one had its gun disabled in a duel with a Japanese Type 95 light tank, which was subsequently knocked out by the other Sherman. Company C's eight other M4A2 medium tanks were dropped off at neighboring Beach Red 3, but most of the tanks were lost in the water in shell holes or hit by Japanese shore guns. By the end of the day, only two Shermans were operational, but a third was repaired and put into action the following day. The Sherman tanks proved to be a valuable fire-support weapon, but Tarawa revealed the need for improvements. The 75mm gun was not entirely adequate to deal with the Japanese coconut-log bunkers, and so work was accelerated to field flame-thrower tanks. Also, the loss of many tanks in shell holes clearly indicated the need for waterproofing, and the marines developed their own equivalent of the deep-wading gear used by the U.S. Army in the Mediterranean theater.

The U.S. Army landed on neighboring Makin Island at the same time as the marine landing on Tarawa, a swift and relatively cheap operation by Central Pacific standards. The army operation was supported by a platoon of M3A5 medium tanks of the 193rd Tank Battalion in the only American use of M3 medium tanks in combat in the Pacific. The next objective for U.S. amphibious forces were the Marshall Islands, which included Kwajalein, the largest atoll in the world. Although there was some fear that Kwajalein would turn into another bloody battle like Tarawa, the Japanese garrison was more scattered and not as well equipped. The 4th Marine Division landed on the Roi-Namur Islands of the atoll on February 1, 1944, with tank support that included ten M4A2 medium tanks of the 4th Marine Tank Battalion. The tanks were instrumental in stopping a night counterattack. While the marines stormed Roi-Namur, the army's 7th Division attacked Kwajalein itself, supported by the 767th Tank Battalion. With this atoll subdued, Eniwetok was next. The fighting on Parry Island on February 22 included a short skirmish between marine M4A2 tanks and three Japanese Type 95 light tanks.

By 1944, Japanese weapons were increasingly ineffective against American tanks, especially the Sherman. The Imperial Japanese Army had made extensive use of tanks in China in the 1930s and during the initial victories in the Philippines, Malaysia, and the Dutch East Indies in 1941–42. But Japan's limited industrial resources led to sharp cutbacks in tank and gun production after 1942, with priority given to warship and aircraft production. The most commonly used Japanese tank in 1941–44 was the Type 95 Ha-go, a 1935 design that was thinly armored and armed only with a 37mm gun. It might knock out a Sherman with a lucky hit, but it was a very uneven match. Likewise, the principal infantry antitank gun was the old 37mm, and Japanese infantry lacked an equivalent of the bazooka or *panzerfaust*. As a result, Japanese tactics in 1944 increasingly shifted to desperate close-range attacks using improvised antitank weapons. Lacking antitank rockets, Japanese infantry were given lunge mines, which used a shaped-charge warhead like that on a *panzerfaust* but were mounted on the end of a long pole. The Japanese infantryman had to run toward the tank and strike the mine against it to detonate, usually killing himself in the process. Another widely used Japanese antitank weapon was the magnetic mine, which was hand-planted against the tank before the fuse was ignited.

The Marianas were the first large islands in Japan's inner defense belt to be attacked by the U.S. and the first battle since the Philippines in 1942 to see extensive use of tanks by both sides. The Japanese 9th Tank Regiment was split between Saipan and Guam but had been reinforced with some of the new Type 97-kai Shinhoto Chi-ha tanks with a new 47mm gun that had limited capabilities to defeat a Sherman's frontal armor at close range. Likewise, the Japanese infantry in the Marianas had begun to receive the new Type 1 47mm antitank gun, a towed relative of the weapon that armed the Shinhoto Chi-ha tank. By the summer of 1944, the marine tank battalions had been completely reequipped, each having forty-six M4A2 medium tanks instead of the original fifty-four light tanks; they were supplemented by fourteen to twenty-four M3A1 light tanks armed with Satan flamethrowers. The marines landed their 2nd and 4th Tank Battalions on Saipan on the afternoon of June 15 to support their troops. On June 16, the army's 27th Division landed, supported by a company of M4 medium tanks of the 762nd Tank Battalion, as well as two companies of M5A1 light tanks.

The largest single Japanese tank attack of the Pacific war started in the predawn hours of June 17 when the tank companies of the 9th Tank Regiment

Namur, Marshall Islands, March 1944: *Killer*, the M4A2 of Sgt. Joe Bruno from Company C, Marine 4th Battalion, illustrates the disparity in tanks during much of the war in the Pacific, with a Japanese Type 94 tankette on its engine deck. The photo also shows one of the earliest uses of standoff armor on marine Shermans, an innovation to counter Japanese Type 99 magnetic antitank mines. The wooden planks were spaced four inches from the hull and the void filled with concrete. Also worth noting is the more refined deep-wading trunk on this tank, the first standardized application of these kits in the Pacific.

In stereotypical tank fighting in the Pacific, a tank moves through a dark, fetid jungle followed at close quarters by infantry. Here *Lucky Legs II*, an M4 medium tank of the 754th Tank Battalion, moves forward in support of infantry from Company F, 129th Infantry Regiment, 37th Infantry Division, on Bougainville during the Solomons campaign, March 16, 1944.

attempted a major counterattack against the marines. The Japanese charged across open ground but were soon exposed by naval star shells. Volleys of gunfire, bazookas, and tank fire crushed the attack. Saipan was a complete change from previous Pacific campaigns, since the open terrain permitted freer use of tanks. Sherman losses were quite high because of ambushes by field artillery and hand-emplaced magnetic mines. Japanese infantry mine teams soon learned that their weapons were especially effective if carefully placed on vulnerable points of the M4A2 medium tank, such as the rear fuel tanks. As in the bocage fighting in France in the same time period, the marines learned that there had to be close cooperation between the tanks and infantry to defeat these tactics. By now, the marines had found that telephones mounted on the rear of the tanks were absolutely essential to coordinate their actions with

M4 medium tanks of the 754th Tank Battalion along the Bougainville coast in the Solomons in March 1944. This unit has painted out the large white stars on their tanks, since they made it easier for enemy antitank weapons to target them.

The U.S. Army's 603rd Tank Company saw extensive combat in the Southwest Pacific using M4A1 tanks. *Shangri-La* is seen here during the landings in support of the 41st Infantry Division at Humboldt Bay on Hollandia, New Guinea, on April 22, 1944. Most of their tanks were spring 1943 production with the improved M34A1 gun mount.

the accompanying infantry—again a direct parallel to the situation in France, though it developed independently in both theaters. Saipan was declared secure on July 9, 1944, and was followed by assaults against neighboring Tinian and Guam.

The Saipan campaign made it quite clear that tanks were invaluable in the Central Pacific. Both the marines and the army concluded that further work was needed to improve tank-infantry cooperation, and the marines began a program to reinforce their tanks against the threat of close-in Japanese

suicide antitank tactics by layering wooden planks on the side of their tanks to prevent the attachment of magnetic mines. Shermans of the 1st Marine Tank Battalion were used during the bloody fighting on Peleliu in the Palau Islands starting on September 15, 1944. The Japanese had a divisional light tank company on the island equipped with the obsolete Type 95 light tank, and this unit was wiped out when it made a desperate charge across the island's main airfield, straight into marine antitank defenses.

The campaign in the Philippines, which started with landings on Leyte in October 1944, involved the largest tank operations by either side in the Pacific war. It marked the first time that the Japanese Army committed one of its few armored divisions, the 2nd Tank Division on Luzon, against U.S. forces, while the U.S. Army eventually deployed seven tank battalions, three tank destroyer battalions, and a separate tank company, totaling more than 500 tanks and tank destroyers. The Shermans were used in their standard role for infantry support.

On Luzon, Gen. Tomoyuki Yamashita was not comfortable with the idea of massed use of tanks against the Americans since Saipan showed that Japanese tanks could not compete against the much larger and better armored Shermans. Instead, Yamashita ordered the 2nd Tank Division to disperse and form the nucleus of a series of village strongpoints, intended to slow the American advance while his other units withdrew north. The 2nd's tanks were dug into adobe revetments under heavy camouflage, with some detachments having less than a dozen tanks and two villages having about fifty each. In spite of the large number of Japanese tanks on Luzon, there were very few large-scale tank-versus-tank encounters after the U.S. Army landed on December 15, 1944. The first significant tank battle took place on January 24, 1945, at San Manuel, defended by the Shigemi detachment with about fifty tanks. The U.S. 161st Infantry Regiment attacked the town with the support of a battery of M7 105mm howitzer motor carriages (HMC) and a company of M4 medium tanks from the 716th Tank Battalion. The Japanese defenses were gradually reduced by infantry attacks, and in the early hours of January 28, surviving Japanese troops, backed by the thirty remaining tanks, launched a three-wave charge that was crushed by the heavier firepower available to U.S. forces. The other large Japanese tank concentration, the Ida Detachment at Munoz, was encircled and routed during the first week of February. The surviving Japanese tanks attempted a breakout but were stopped by artillery and the 716th Tank Battalion.

By the beginning of March, the Japanese 2nd Armored Division had been destroyed, already having lost 203 Chi-ha and 19 Ha-go tanks and 2 150mm Ho-ro self-propelled howitzers. Their sacrifice did not substantially affect the campaign, as the poor quality of their tanks did not pose a serious threat to U.S. Army tanks. One of the most curious incidents of the campaign occurred in April 1945 when American forces approached Yamashita's headquarters in Baguio, which was defended by the division's five surviving tanks. Yamashita ordered a *kamikaze* attack by fitting large explosive charges to the front of two tanks, which were then camouflaged with brush along the road. When U.S. M4 medium tanks appeared around a bend in Route 9 on the morning of April 17, the two Japanese tanks raced forward and rammed the Americans, blowing up two Shermans in the process. This was the only known case of *kamikaze* tanks in the Pacific.

Like Tarawa, Iwo Jima would go down in U.S. Marine Corps legend as one of the most bitter battles of the Pacific war. The marines expected the Japanese to make extensive use of bunkers, so large tank deployments totaling three marine tank battalions—the 3rd, 4th, and 5th—were prepared. By the time of the landings on February 19, 1945, the marine tank battalions had again been reinforced with sixty-seven M4A2 or M4A3 tanks each. Nine Shermans in each battalion were armed with E4-5 flamethrowers, replacing the smaller and more vulnerable M3A1 Satan light flamethrower tanks. By 1945, the marines had developed combined-arms tactics to attack the well-fortified Japanese bunkers, dubbed "corkscrew and blowtorch" tactics. The bunkers were suppressed with tank fire or satchel charges and then burned out with backpack or tank-mounted flamethrowers. The main threats to marine Shermans on Iwo Jima were mines, including massive improvised mines made from buried aircraft bombs. Close cooperation between tanks and infantry and the lack of foliage prevented the Japanese infantry from using their normal close-attack tactics against tanks. The only Japanese tanks on the island were from the understrength 26th Tank Regiment, and these were mostly buried up to their turrets as improvised pillboxes. Marine Sherman losses in the fighting were very high, with most battalions barely able to maintain half-strength for much of the campaign.

In the wake of the Iwo Jima campaign, the largest combined amphibious operation of the war

Japanese antitank defenses in the Marianas were improved over previous campaigns with the advent of the new 47mm antitank gun. This M4A2 of the Marine 2nd Separate Tank Company on Guam has suffered two hits against its hull side, which penetrated through the plank stand-off armor.

A platoon of composite-hull M4 medium tanks of Company C, 706th Tank Battalion, during operations near Agana on Guam on August 2, 1944. The composite-hull M4 was similar to the basic M4 medium tank, but the front of the hull was a single casting rather than constructed from the usual welded plates.

The Marianas offered relatively good tank country, with open rolling hills as seen here with *Caesar*, an M4A2 tank of Company C, Marine 2nd Tank Battalion, in July 1944. The late-production M4A2 had the improved forty-seven-degree hull seen on the second-generation Shermans but lacked wet stowage and retained the side appliqué armor panels.

Bushmaster, a late-production composite-hull M4 medium tank of the 763rd Tank Battalion, is thoroughly bogged down in the mud while supporting the 96th Infantry Division during operations on Leyte on November 23, 1944.

M4A2 medium tanks of the Marine 1st Tank Battalion control Peleliu airfield during the Palau campaign of September 1944. During the fighting on Peleliu, the tank company of the Japanese 14th Infantry Division made a charge across this airfield, only to run into intense fire from M4A2 tanks, M3 75mm SPMs, and other antitank weapons.

The fighting on Leyte was followed by American landings on Luzon. Here an M4A1 of the 754th Tank Battalion passes in front of the capitol in Manila on January 9, 1945, during the bitter fighting for the city. Tanks were instrumental in the battle, providing heavy firepower for the infantry during the bloody urban skirmishes.

A composite-hull M4 (named *Battle Baby*) of Company B, 775th Tank Battalion, is led up a sharp curve by the company commander, Lt. Jack Belts, on the Villa Verde Trail on Luzon. These composite-hull M4s used the new wet ammunition stowage and large driver's hatches typical of second-generation M4s.

A composite-hull M4 medium tank moves up a hill overlooking the center of the city of Baguio during fighting on April 27, 1945.

took place at Okinawa in April 1945. After the fruitless experience of its 2nd Tank Division in the Philippines, the Japanese Army decided to hold its best armor for the final defense of the home islands and deploy only a few companies of tanks. The success of American tanks in the Marianas, on the Philippines, and on Iwo Jima led to the decision to commit the heaviest U.S. armor force ever, totaling eight army and two marine tank battalions, as well as

two marine independent tank companies—more than 800 tanks. Gen. Lemuel Shepherd of the 6th Marine Division later commented that "if any one supporting arm can be singled out as having contributed more than any other during the progress of the campaign, the tank would certainly have to be selected."

One of the most curious uses of armor on Okinawa was by the 77th Infantry Division. The

During the later phases of the Burma campaign, Sherman V tanks became available in that theater, like this group from B Squadron of the Indian 5th King Edward VII's Own Lancers (Probyn's Horse) being used to provide fire support for British and Indian units during operations on December 31, 1944.

Supporting the 1st Cavalry Division, a composite-hull M4 opens fire at a concealed Japanese antitank gun that had knocked out another M4 moments before. This unusual overhead photo clearly shows the very large white identification star carried on American tanks in the Philippines to prevent accidental air attacks.

commander of the division was none other than Maj. Gen. A. D. Bruce, former commander of the Tank Destroyer Center. The M18 had been Bruce's pet project, and he was determined to find new missions for it even if it had not proven to be the miracle tank-killer he had sought. Bruce had managed to secure eight M18 tank destroyers to reequip one of his division's three antitank companies, the 306th Anti-Tank Company, to help examine whether these would be a more suitable weapon than towed 37mm or 57mm antitank guns. The M18s saw very little use during the debut with the division on Leyte in the Philippines earlier in 1945, but they were used with some success during the Ie Shima operation during the Okinawa campaign later in the spring of 1945. Bruce was enthusiastic in experimenting with the M18 for infantry antitank support and recommended substituting tank destroyers for towed antitank guns in all infantry divisions in anticipation of forthcoming operations against Japan. In addition, he laid out extensive plans for the Tenth Army to use the M39 armored utility vehicle as a

A composite-hull M4 fitted with an M1 dozer blade from the 775th Tank Battalion moves forward in support of infantry from the 37th Infantry Division during the fighting for Lantap on Luzon on June 12, 1945. The soldier in the foreground is armed with a Browning automatic rifle.

The army came up with its own solutions to the threat of Japanese infantry antitank weapons. The 754th Tank Battalion covered the engine decks of its Shermans with sandbags to reduce the effects of Japanese satchel charges. In addition, it experimented with "crackle paint," a combination of asphalt, sand, pebbles, and normal olive-drab paint that was applied over most of the tank to prevent the adhesion of magnetic antitank mines. This is one of the tanks modified in a depot on Bougainville in September 1944.

scout and resupply vehicle, a turretless derivative of the M18 intended for towing the failed 3-inch anti-tank gun. The war ended before these recommendations could take place.

American plans for the final invasion of the Japanese home islands placed considerable emphasis on tanks as a result of their demonstrated value on Okinawa. One of the few demands from the army's commanders in the Pacific was for a better flamethrowing tank, preferably with a longer-range flame-gun and better armor. Ordnance obliged by redesigning the M4A3E2 assault tanks with a flame-gun, and there were plans to rebuild the surviving assault tanks in Europe in this configuration. The final battle never took place. Curiously enough, the Sherman would form the backbone of the tank force of the rejuvenated Japanese Self-Defense Force in the 1950s. As a result of the war in nearby Korea, four Japanese tank battalions were formed starting in November 1952, based on the M4A3E8.

Chinese tank units raised and trained in Burma were jointly manned by Chinese crews with American advisors. This M4A4 Sherman of the Chinese 1st Provisional Tank Group is seen near Lashio on the Burma Road early in 1945.

An M4 crew from Company C, 754th Tank Battalion, poses in front of its tank (named *Dragon Lady*, after the cartoon character in the popular Milton Cannif cartoon strip, *Steve Canyon*). This is an intermediate-production M4 with the M34A1 gun mantlet, but before the introduction of the improved hull.

The Sherman tank battalions of the Chinese 1st Provisional Tank Group marked their M4A4 tanks with colorful tiger markings, evident on this tank passing through Hsenwi, Burma, on March 24, 1945.

The crew of *Davy Jones*, an M4A3 medium tank of the 5th Marine Tank Battalion, loads 75mm ammunition into the vehicle. This gives a good close-up of the attachment of the extra planking on the hull side, as well as the positioning of the penny nails to prevent Japanese infantry from placing satchel charges directly against the hatches.

A pair of Shermans from Company B, Marine 4th Tank Battalion, along Blue Beach #2 at Iwo Jima in support of the 24th Regiment. The huge invasion fleet is evident in the background. Both tanks are well protected by sandbags and plank armor intended to frustrate Japanese infantry antitank tactics.

This close-up view of the rear end of Lt. Hank Bellmon's *Calcutta*, an M4A3 of Company C, Marine 4th Tank Battalion, shows many interesting features added to ensure better coordination between the tank crew and accompanying marines. As in the ETO, these tanks have been fitted with a field telephone to permit accompanying infantry to communicate with the crew. The "target clock" painted on the wading trunk was intended to remind infantry to call out targets using the clock method when identifying directions. The fuel container on the deck has been rigged for carrying water, with a spigot mounted near the tank phone.

An M4A3 (named *Nitemare II*), a replacement tank sent to the 5th Tank Battalion on March 23, 1945, shortly before the end of the Iwo Jima fighting. On this tank, the protection over the hull hatches is different from the usual 5th Tank Battalion penny-nail style.

Coed, an M4A3 flame tank of the Marine 4th Tank Battalion at the edge of Motoyama airfield. Shortly after this photo was taken, Japanese infantry launched a massed charge against American positions, and this tank played a key role in the carnage that followed, firing deadly canister rounds with considerable effect against the infantry.

One of the more unusual Sherman variants used in small numbers during the initial landings was the M19 device. This was a set of pontoons attached to the Sherman to enable it to swim ashore. A total of 500 M19 kits were built as an alternative to the duplex drive amphibious tank, but only a handful were used on Okinawa.

Composite-hull M4 "blow-torch" medium tanks and M4 105mm howitzer tanks of the 713th (Flamethrower) Tank Battalion take up positions along a ridge line during the landings on Okinawa in April 1945. The tanks in the foreground are flamethrower tanks. The 105mm howitzer tanks are new-production vehicles with HVSS suspension. These vehicles were used by the headquarters company in tank battalions to provide fire support.

An M4 "blow-torch" of the 713th Flamethrower Tank Battalion in action along Coral Ridge on May 17, 1945. The usual tactics of the 713th Tank Battalion were called "corkscrew and blowtorch." Gun tanks would attack enemy bunkers or caves with the normal 75mm tank guns to weaken defenses and prevent the Japanese infantry from returning fire, and then the flamethrowers would move up and attack. The later flamethrower designs like the POW-CWS-H1 were mounted in the gun tube and could not be easily distinguished from other tanks.

A platoon of Shermans of the Marine 1st Tank Battalion during the fighting near Naha on Okinawa in May 1945. The extensive use of track blocks was intended to protect against antitank guns and various types of hand-placed antitank mines. The suspensions of the tanks were often covered with timber or wood planking to prevent Japanese infantry from striking the thin hull armor with lunge mines or other explosive devices.

A composite-hull M4 "blow-torch" of the 713th Flamethrower Tank Battalion attacks Japanese infantry hidden in caves on the southern shores of the island. The battle for Okinawa, the first fought on Japanese soil, was particularly bitter, and the local civilians often joined the soldiers in the caves.

A composite-hull M4 from the 713th Tank Battalion uses its own gun to detonate mines while supporting the 382nd Infantry on Okinawa on June 4, 1945. Notice the telephone box added on the far left side of the hull rear, a vital new addition to help in tank-infantry coordination.

The crew of a M4A3 (W) (named *Angel*) from Company A, 711th Tank Battalion, hurriedly repairs a thrown track while under Japanese sniper fire near Nakaza, Okinawa, on June 16, 1945. Note that the track is fitted with extenders to lower ground pressure.

By the end of the Okinawa campaign, the U.S. Army's tank battalions were showing more interest in the marine practice of adding appliqué armor to protect against close-range Japanese infantry attack. This is an example of a composite-hull M4 of the 713th Tank Battalion fitted out in an army ordnance yard on Okinawa toward the end of the campaign.

The Marine 1st Tank Battalion was dispatched to China for occupation duty with the 1st Marine Division in Tientsin. This is an M4A2 of Company A on parade in the city on May 30, 1946. The 1st Tank Battalion was the last U.S. Marine Corps tank battalion to retain the popular diesel-powered M4A2 after the remaining battalions had shifted to the M4A3 in 1945. The battalion was later reequipped with M4A3s in China.

The ultimate tank for the final assault of Japan was the T33 flamethrower tank. This was based on the M4A3E2 assault tank, but it had a new turret armed with the E12R4 flamethrower along with a 75mm gun. The end of the war in the Pacific led to the cancellation of the program after only three M4A3E2s had been converted.

CHAPTER 11

Cold War Sherman

It is a testament to the Sherman's basic soundness that it remained in widespread use around the globe well into the 1970s. The U.S. Army last used the Sherman in combat in Korea, but thousands of Sherman tanks were distributed to allied forces in the North Atlantic Treaty Organization (NATO) as well as to allies in the Asia-Pacific area. The Sherman would enjoy a final moment of glory in the hands of Israeli tankers in the 1956, 1967, and 1973 wars in the Middle East.

After World War II, the U.S. Army underwent rapid demobilization. Most of its tank force was scrapped, and many Shermans were shipped to allies overseas. At the end of World War II in 1945, the U.S. Army had more than 10,000 Sherman tanks on hand; by 1950, there were only 3,202 M4 tanks still in the American inventory, of which 1,376 were unserviceable. The North Korean People's Army invaded South Korea in the summer of 1950, and the attacks were spearheaded by Soviet-supplied T-34-85 tanks. The ill-equipped South Korean and U.S. units had virtually no tanks, and a crash program was started to rush tank units to Korea. Because of its heavy commitments in Europe, the U.S. Army had only three tank battalions adequately prepared for transfer to Korea. They were equipped with the M26 and M46 Pershing tanks, but the Fort Knox tank training school scraped up two companies of M4A3E8 tanks from Rock Island Arsenal to equip its training unit, the 70th Tank Battalion. The main occupation force in Japan, the U.S. Eighth Army, was able to locate fifty-four M4A3E8 tanks and formed them into the 8072nd (later the 89th) Medium Tank Battalion. The first company from this unit arrived in Korea in late July and went into combat on August 2, 1950. By the end of 1950, American tank units in Korea had received 1,326 tanks, including 679 M4A3E8 Shermans.

The Sherman could accommodate a more powerful gun, and France's Bourges arsenal developed a kit to rearm it with a derivative of the 75mm gun used in the German Panther tank. The Israeli army began upgrading its Shermans with this kit in 1956–57, renaming it the M50 tank. This type saw combat in the 1956 and 1967 Middle East wars. ISRAELI GPO

The heaviest tank-versus-tank fighting of the Korean War took place from August to October 1950 and pitted the M4A3E8 Sherman and M26 Pershing against North Korean T-34-85 tanks. Some 119 tank-versus-tank skirmishes were recorded during the war, and the M4A3E8 saw more combat than any other U.S. tank type. From a technical standpoint, the North Korean T-34-85 and the American M4A3E8 were on fairly equal terms. The 76mm gun of the M4A3E8 was a smaller caliber than the 85mm on the T-34-85, but by the time of Korea, there was an ample supply of HVAP ammunition, enabling the Sherman to defeat the T-34-85's armor. The T-34-85 had no particular problem penetrating the armor of the M4A3E8 at normal combat ranges, so it was an even match in firepower. The critical difference on the battlefield was the quality of the crew training, and the U.S. Army had a clear edge, which resulted in the lop-sided results in favor of American tank battalions during these summer battles. With most of the North Korean tanks destroyed by November 1950, the M4A3E8 tanks switched to their traditional role of providing fire support for infantry units.

In view of the controversies over the Pershing versus Sherman in 1944–45, the Korean War lessons shed some interesting light on this subject. U.S. tank battalions preferred the more heavily armored and armed M26 and M46 Pershing tanks in 1950 when tank-versus-tank fighting was most common. One American report later concluded that the M26 was three times more effective than the Sherman in tank fighting. However, when the mission switched from tank fighting to infantry support in 1951, opinions changed. The M26 was often described as being "lousy," and some tankers thought it was "a complete flop." It was powered by the same engine as the M4A3E8 but was ten tons heavier, and its advanced torquematic transmission was not as reliable as the Sherman's. Those tankers with experience in the M4A3E8 preferred it over the M26 since it was very reliable, easy to maintain, and far more nimble to drive in the hilly Korean countryside.

The use of the Sherman by the Israeli Defense Force (IDF) also provides curious insights into some of the World War II controversies. Israel used a handful of ex-British Shermans in its 1948 war, after which the IDF decided to standardize the Sherman as the most modern tank available on the international arms market. Because of an international arms limitation agreement between the U.S., France, and Britain regarding the Middle East, Israel reinforced its inven-

The most powerful Sherman was no doubt Israel's M51, another effort developed with French cooperation. It was armed with the D1504 105mm gun, a shortened low-pressure version of the weapon developed for France's AMX-30 main battle tank. First converted in 1962, these tanks were gradually rebuilt over the years with new features, especially new Cummins diesel engines, and remained in Israeli service into the 1990s. They saw combat in 1967 and 1973.
ISRAELI GPO

tory by buying Shermans from scrapyards around Europe. The Soviet decision to support the Arab states in the 1950s led to a major arms sales between Egypt and Czechoslovakia involving the purchase of several hundred T-34-85 tanks. Since most Israeli Shermans were armed with the 75mm gun, an antidote was needed to deal with the T-34-85. France began a clandestine program to assist Israel, and one of the stranger results was a joint French-Israeli program to rearm the Sherman. After World War II, France had kept one regiment of captured Panther tanks in service alongside its many Shermans and had come to appreciate its powerful gun. When the French Army began design of the new AMX-13 light tank, the Panther's 75mm gun was reproduced as a French copy. One of the French workshops managed to fit this gun into a Sherman turret, and Israel selected this option to modernize its Sherman force. The resulting tank was called the M50, which would serve in combat in its 1956 and 1967 wars. Oddly enough, the Egyptians ended up with similar capabilities by buying AMX-13 turrets from the French and mounting them on Sherman hulls. A small number of these saw combat in the 1956 war, though there are no accounts of confrontations between the rearmed Israeli and Egyptian Shermans.

After the 1956 war, France began selling surplus 76mm Shermans to Israel, but these quickly became obsolete when the Soviet Union agreed to sell the much more modern T-54A and T-55 to the neighboring Arab states. Aside from buying newer tanks such as the American M48 and the British Centurion, the IDF decided to modernize their Shermans once again, this time using a new French 105mm low-pressure, smooth-bore tank gun. This weapon was the most powerful gun fitted to the Sherman and showed how far the tank could be modernized if the demand was great enough. This version was called the M51 and saw combat in the 1967 and 1973 wars.

During the final half of the 20th century, the Sherman continued to serve in dwindling numbers around the globe and saw combat in numerous wars. Aside from Korea and the Middle East, the most extensive use of the Sherman was by India and Pakistan in their 1967 war. The combat map of Sherman battles spanned the globe, including its use by Castro's rebels in Cuba in the early 1960s, during the Nicaraguan civil war in the 1980s, in the Indochina war of 1948–54, in the Chinese civil war of 1945–49, in the Balkans in the 1990s, and in many small skirmishes too numerous and obscure to mention. Some still remain in the inventories of a number of armies today, though their viability on the modern battlefield has long since passed.

CHAPTER 12

Report Card on the Sherman

The introduction of this book asked the question of whether the Sherman tank was a war-winner or a death trap. As this book has suggested, neither of these two answers does the subject justice, and the real answer must be more nuanced.

The characterization of the Sherman as a death trap and the task of its crews as suicide missions is the most easily dismissed. No tank in combat, even the vaunted Tiger, was invulnerable. Much of the condemnation of the Sherman stems from the shoddy sensationalism of television documentaries over the past decade and similar exaggerations in books and magazines.

From a purely technical standpoint, few tank experts would characterize the Sherman as "the best tank of World War II," though an argument can certainly be made that it was the best tank or one of the best tanks in 1942 and early 1943. The greatest accomplishment of the American tank industry was its remarkable performance in 1941–42 when it progressed from being a third-rate industrial backwater to the world's largest tank production center, turning out tens of thousands of very good armored vehicles. This was not preordained despite America's substantial industrial resources. Britain failed to develop a comparable tank during the war and was obliged to rely on the Sherman.

Unfortunately, the Sherman saw its most extensive combat use by the U.S. Army in 1944 and 1945, by which time it had slipped in quality compared to its opponents. The stagnation in American tank development in 1943 and early 1944 stemmed from a wide range of interlocking institutional problems in the army in World War II. U.S. Army Ground Forces rushed into a unique organizational solution in 1940–41 when shocked into action by the defeat of France. The formation of armored divisions to provide offensive punch and the tank destroyers to create defensive capability was a reasonable response to the lessons of 1940. The problem was that German tactical doctrine evolved beyond the 1940 pattern, and the AGF did not fully understand this evolution nor modify its own forces in 1943 to better cope with the changes. McNair's parochialism, especially his obsession with towed antitank guns as a solution to the panzer threat, unfavorably distorted U.S. Army doctrine and armored vehicle development.

The idea that "tank-versus-tank fighting was not a significant mission for tanks" permeated American doctrine well into 1944, even though the AGF's point of view on this issue was widely viewed as mistaken throughout most of the army. A First Army report written in 1945 concluded that

> Armor must be prepared to meet armor and to destroy it in battle. Armored combat cannot be limited to those missions which can be performed by one type of tank. Tanks for close support of infantry must be capable of destroying hostile armor and have sufficient armor protection to permit them to stay on the battlefield without having to resort to extensive maneuver. Tanks for armored divisions must have gun power to destroy hostile armor and mobility to permit swift, decisive action through maneuver.

Nevertheless, McNair's excessive enthusiasm for the flawed tank destroyer concept would not have mattered as much had Barnes and Ordnance done a better job of integrating technical intelligence on the panzer threat with developments in tank guns and tank armor. The U.S. Army had extensive technical details of new German tank and antitank weapons in the summer of 1943. But unlike the British Army and the Red Army, the U.S. Army failed to appreciate the tactical implications of this technical data, which would have served as the basis for a requirement for better firepower and protection on the Sherman in 1944. There was no technical reason that the U.S. Army should have been the only major army in 1943–44 to fail to develop a new high-velocity tank gun capable of dealing with the panzer threat. The 76mm gun was a mediocre, half-hearted attempt that was inferior to its contemporaries such as the German 75mm KwK 43 on the Panther, the 17-pounder on the British Sherman Firefly, or the Soviet 85mm gun on the T-34-85. In 1944, Ordnance again improvised using the 90mm antiaircraft gun, but this barely matched the capabilities of the smaller and lighter British 76mm gun (17-pounder) or German 75mm gun, and it did not approach the performance of the German 88mm tank gun. British tank officers serving in the United States during the war were mystified why Ordnance didn't exploit the talents of American industry to develop a better tank gun, given the poor performance of government teams in this regard.

Ordnance also failed to address the growing threat of German antitank weapons and had no significant program in place to significantly improve Sherman protection in late 1943 or early 1944. As was shown by Patton's Third Army in February 1945, a field expedient armor appliqué kit could significantly reduce the Sherman's vulnerability without excessive ill effects to its automotive performance.

Ordnance wasted an enormous amount of effort in 1942 and 1943 on programs such as the M7 medium tank and the experimental T20, T22, and T23, which did not offer a significant step forward in tank firepower or protection. For most of 1943, the M4X replacement program was an aimless technological exercise, lacking a firm rationale beyond tinkering with intriguing new technologies. What remains perplexing was Ordnance's complete lack of interest in developing a high-performance tank gun compared to its perpetual enthusiasm for novel transmissions. The failure in gun design remained an institutional problem with American tank design for decades. Over the past fifty years, the U.S. Army has been forced to rely on foreign tank gun designs, first the British 105mm in the 1960s and then the German Rheinmetall 120mm gun in the 1980s.

The technical shortcomings of the Sherman festered during much of 1943 largely because of the army's lack of enough firsthand combat experience in tank fighting. The U.S. Army did not have more than a single armored division in combat until the summer of 1944. Tunisia and Sicily involved only one armored division and small numbers of tank battalions, while the tank fighting in Italy from Salerno to Anzio saw the commitment of parts of one armored division and a few tank battalions. When army leaders in Washington sent observers to the field in Tunisia in 1943, Sicily in 1943, and Italy in 1944, most came back reporting that the troops thought that the Sherman was acceptable or that perhaps it needed some modest improvements of the type that were already underway, such as the 76mm gun version. There was no unanimity over whether more armor was necessary or desirable. Many commanders resisted the adoption of improved Shermans with the 76mm gun as late as May 1944. Both the AGF and Ordnance dismissed British efforts on the powerful 17-pounder as unnecessary.

The power of the newer German tank and anti-tank weapons in Normandy in 1944 came as a sudden shock, but they should not have been such a surprise. The PaK 40 75mm antitank gun was encountered more than a year earlier in Tunisia in February 1943; the Panther had appeared in the summer of 1943. The shock was caused not by the mere appearance of these weapons, but the fact that they had gone from being relatively rare in 1943 to becoming standard and widespread by 1944 at a time when U.S. tank units were not involved in extensive combat with the Wehrmacht. The U.S. Army failed to anticipate this development even though the evidence was at hand. Santayana's maxim that "those who forget history are doomed to repeat it" can be a trap for soldiers. McNair's "battle need" philosophy was just such a trap. Sometimes lessons of past battles are grasped so ardently that soldiers forget that the enemy is learning too and will probably improve before the next battle.

For all of the Sherman's technical shortcomings in 1944, American tank units performed well in the summer battles. Weapons do not operate in isolation, and the quality of troops, their training, their leadership, and their tactical doctrine are usually more important than mere technical issues. U.S. tank units adapted to the circumstances in 1944 and prevailed in spite of the problems with the Sherman.

The disparity between the Sherman and the best German tanks such as the Panther should not be exaggerated. Many of the memoirs from 1944 continually refer to encounters with Tigers and 88s

while accounts from the German side that have become available in recent years make it clear that these were more often StuG III and 75mm guns. Moreover, there has been a tendency in many recent histories to judge the Sherman on the basis of purely paper comparisons with the Panther and the Tiger. Part of this results from the nature of books and television shows about World War II weapons, which are heavily slanted to the enthusiasms of military buffs. This book is no exception; its readers are far more likely to be wargamers, military buffs, and hobbyists than historians or defense analysts. Tank-versus-tank duels are far more intriguing for wargamers, especially with the new generation of highly visual computer games, than the more mundane but common battlefield missions of infantry support. This distorts assessments of tank performance in World War II by focusing on only one of many missions performed by tanks. In reality, the U.S. Army did not face the Panther very often in the summer of 1944, and when it did, such as at Le Desert in July, at Mortain in August, and at Arracourt in September, the Panther did not prove to be a wonder weapon and was defeated by American combined-arms tactics. The Panther and other German AFVs did occasionally extract disproportionate casualties against U.S. tank units in small-scale engagements, but these did not occur often enough to affect the course of any major battle in the ETO.

Such technical comparisons frequently simplify the arms race between the U.S. Army and the Wehrmacht, pitting the best German tanks against the Sherman and ignoring the more common types. Until the Battle of the Bulge, the PzKpfw IV was by far the most common German tank and was no better than the Sherman in most respects and inferior in others. Even after the Panther became the most common tank type by the end of 1944, it did not constitute a majority of the German AFV inventory, which was a complex stew of tanks, assault guns, and tank destroyers, most enjoying less armor protection or firepower than the Panther. For example, at the beginning of the Battle of the Bulge—the highwater mark of the Panther in the west—Panthers constituted only 28 percent of the German AFV force taking part in the offensive.

The technical imbalance between the Sherman and the Panther or Tiger can obscure some of the more substantial advantages that the Sherman enjoyed. McNair's insistence on battleworthiness was his single most important contribution to U.S. tank development during the war. Ordnance frequently tried to foist new and unproven weapons on the U.S. Army, and McNair and AGF adamantly refused to clear them from production until they were adequately tested. Like the Energizer Bunny, the Sherman just kept running, and running, and running. This was not luck, but the result of deliberate AGF policy that placed a premium on durability. The Wehrmacht did not place the same value on durability, and its panzer units suffered from high breakdown rates, especially in the last year of the war. A Panther on the prowl was a fearsome menace; a broken-down Panther was a maintenance burden. There were more Shermans on the battlefield in 1944 because there were fewer dead-lined in need of repair. In December 1944, there were barely 500 Panthers available to the Wehrmacht in the west; there were more than 5,000 Shermans operational in Allied units at the same time.

Warfare in the industrial age requires a careful balance of mass and quality. A single perfect tank cannot offer the same combat power as ten adequate but imperfect tanks. Most American tankers would have preferred to be sitting in a more powerful tank like the Panther, but no commander would have been content to substitute his many Shermans for a much smaller number of Panthers. The Chrysler Corporation history of their tank building effort in World War II concluded that "our tanks were better because the Germans never learned to think in terms of reliability as we use the word, that is, maximum performance with minimum care and replacement. . . . A weakness for technical prowess at the expense of dependability, simplicity and cost is shared by many American engineers, but in this practical nation the engineer is disciplined by the production man and the salesman."

The Sherman was ultimately a better weapon than heavier German tanks like the Panther since it could be fielded in adequate numbers to carry out its many and varied missions and was technically adequate to do its job. The Sherman was built in such large numbers that it could also be used to fill out the separate tank battalions attached to the infantry divisions; German infantry divisions were lucky to get a company of StuG III assault guns. On top of this, the Sherman was the backbone of the British, Canadian, French, and Polish armored divisions in 1943–45 and provided a useful supplement to the Red Army in 1944–45. The combat power of American infantry divisions was substantially enhanced by routine tank support from Sherman battalions, boosting the combat power of the U.S. Army on the battlefield.

The Sherman was not the best tank of World War II, but it was good enough.

Technical and Production Data

1. Sherman Technical Data
2. Sherman Manufacture and Distribution, 1942–45
3. Sherman Production by Plant
4. Sherman Production by Type
5. Armor Penetration of U.S. Tank Guns

1. SHERMAN TECHNICAL DATA			
Type	M4A1	M4A1 (76mm)	M4A3E8 (76mm)
Length (feet)	19.2	24.5	24.7
Width (feet)	8.6	8.6	9.8
Height (feet)	9.0	9.7	9.7
Combat weight (tons)	33.4	35.3	37.7
Main gun	75mm M3	76mm M1A1	76mm M1A2
Elevation	-12 to +25	-10 to +25	-10 +25
Firing rate (rpm)	20	20	20
Co-axial machine gun	.30 cal	.30 cal	.30 cal
Main gun ammo (rounds)	90	71	71
.50-cal HMG ammo	300	600	600
.30-cal LMG ammo	4,750	6,250	6,250
Engine	R-975 C1	R-975 C4	Ford GAA
Horsepower	400	460	500
Fuel stowage (gal)	175	175	168
Range (road, miles)	120	100	100
Max. speed (mph)	24	24	26

1. SHERMAN TECHNICAL DATA *continued*			
Type	**M4A1**	**M4A1 (76mm)**	**M4A3E8 (76mm)**
Armor thickness (mm)			
Hull front	51	64	64
Hull side	38	38	38
Hull rear	38	38	38
Hull top	19	19	19
Hull bottom	25	25	25
Gun shield	76	90	90
Turret front	76	76	76
Turret side	51	63	63
Turret rear	51	63	63
Turret roof	25	25	25

2. SHERMAN MANUFACTURE AND DISTRIBUTION, 1942–45							
Type	**Manufactured**	**Issued to U.S. Army Overseas**	**Issued to U.S. Army Stateside**	**Issued to USMC/USN**	**In Depots 1945**	**Tests/ Other**	**Lend- Lease**
M4 (75mm)	6,748	3,573	372	0	240	414	2,149
M4A1 (75mm)	6,281	2,932	374	0	249	1,780	946
M4A2 (75mm)	8,053	48	1	493	62	36	7,413
M4A3 (75mm)	4,761	2,765	580	330	579	500	7
M4A3E2	254	250	0	0	1	3	0
M4A4	7,499	0	6	1	37	11	7,443
M4A6	75	0	62	0	13	0	0
M4A1/A3 (76mm)	7,968	5,174	545	1	837	81	1,330
M4A2 (76mm)	2,915	0	0	0	704	133	2,078
M4/-A3 (105mm)	4,680	2,009	556	289	1,119	114	593
Total	**49,234**	**16,751**	**2,496**	**1,114**	**3,841**	**3,072**	**21,959**

TANK, MEDIUM, M3
10 September 1942 revision

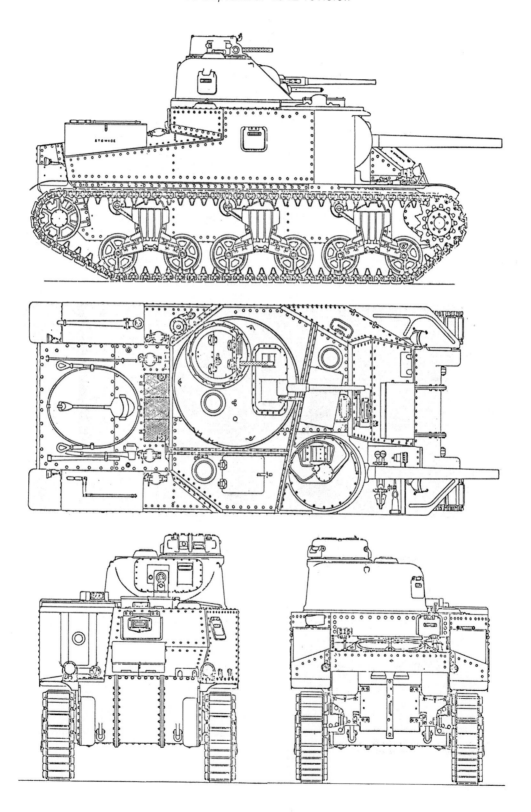

TANK, MEDIUM, M4A1

27 August 1942 revision

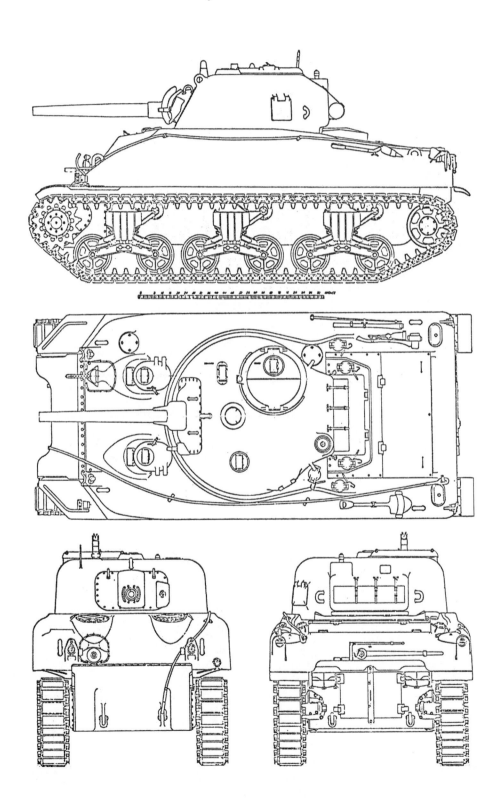

3. SHERMAN PRODUCTION BY PLANT

Plant	Type	1942	1943	1944	1945	Total
American Locomotive Works	M4	0	2,150	0	0	2,150
	M4A2	126	24	0	0	150
Baldwin Locomotive Works	M4	0	1,190	43	0	1,233
	M4A2	12	0	0	0	12
Detroit Tank Arsenal	M4	0	1,528	148	0	1,676
	M4 (105mm)	0	0	1,241	400	1,641
	M4A3 (76mm)	0	0	2,845	1,172	4,017
	M4A3 (105mm)	0	0	1,045	1,994	3,039
	M4A4	2,432	5,067	0	0	7,499
	M4A6	0	16	59	0	75
Federal Machine	M4A2	21	519	0	0	540
Fisher Tank	M4A2	1,540	2,240	834	0	4,614
	M4A2 (76mm)	0	0	1,594	1,300	2,894
	M4A3	0	0	2,420	651	3,071
	M4A3 (76mm)	0	0	525	0	525
	M4A3E2	0	0	254	0	254
Ford Motor	M4A3	514	1,176	0	0	1,690
Lima Locomotive	M4A1	820	835	0	0	1,655
Pacific Car & Foundry	M4A1	266	660	0	0	926
Pressed Steel Car	M4	475	525	0	0	1,000
	M4A1	699	3,001	0	0	3,700
	M4A1 (76mm)	0	0	2,171	1,255	3,426
	M4A2 (76mm)	0	0	0	21	21
Pullman Standard	M4	0	689	0	0	689
	M4A2	1,112	1,625	0	0	2,737
	Total	**8,017**	**21,245**	**13,179**	**6,793**	**49,234**

4. SHERMAN PRODUCTION BY TYPE

Type	1942	1943	1944	1945	Total
M4	475	6,082	191	0	6,748
M4A1	1,785	4,496	0	0	6,281
M4A2	2,811	4,408	834	0	8,053
M4A3	514	1,176	2,420	651	4,761
M4A3E2	0	0	254	0	254
M4A4	2,432	5,067	0	0	7,499
M4A6	0	16	59	0	75
M4A1 (76mm)	0	0	2,171	1,255	3,426
M4A2 (76mm)	0	0	1,594	1,321	2,915
M4A3 (76mm)	0	0	3,370	1,172	4,542
M4 (105mm)	0	0	1,241	400	1,641
M4A3 (105mm)	0	0	1,045	1,994	3,039
Total	8,017	21,245	13,179	6,793	49,234

5. ARMOR PENETRATION OF U.S. TANK GUNS*

Gun	Round	Type	Penetration (in mm)
75mm M3	M61	APC	66
75mm M3	M72	AP	76
76mm M1	M62	APC	93
76mm M1	M79	AP	109
76mm M1	M93	HVAP	157
90mm M3	M82	APC	120
90mm M3	T33	AP	119
90mm M3	T30E16	HVAP	221
90mm T15E2	T43	AP	132
90mm T15E2	T44	HVAP	244

* At 500 yards range, homogenous armor plate at 30 degrees

TANK, MEDIUM, M4A3E8 (76MM)

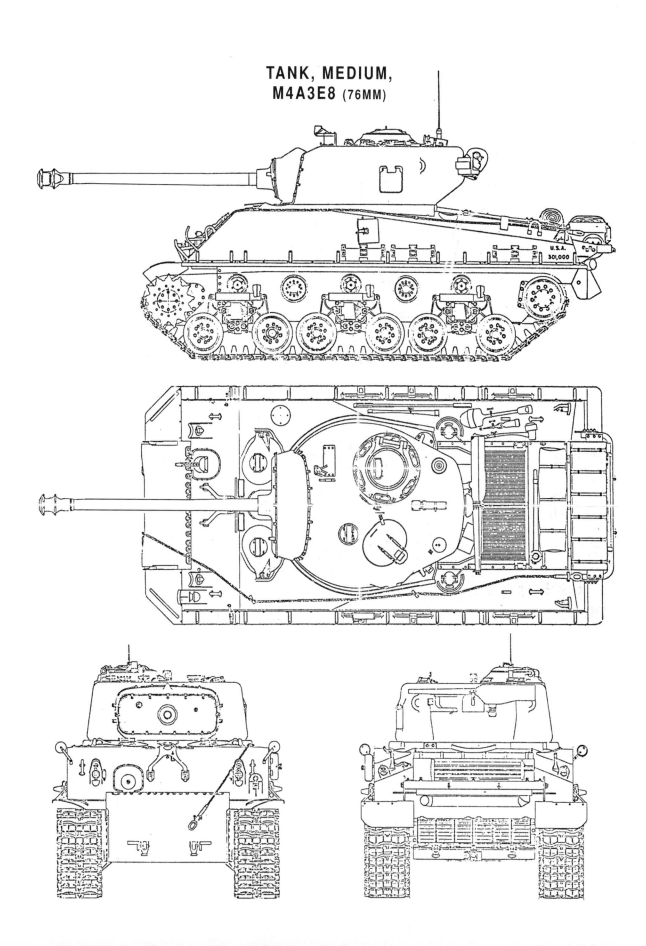

Strength and Loss Statistics

1. U.S. 1st Armored Division Medium Tank Strength in Tunisia, 1943
2. U.S. Fifth Army Sherman Losses in the Italian Campaign, 1943–45
3. U.S. First Army Sherman Strength and Losses in Normandy, June–August 1944
4. U.S. Armored Division Sherman Strength (75mm vs. 76mm) in the ETO, 1944–45
5. U.S. 12th Army Group Separate Tank Battalion Sherman Strength (75mm vs. 76 mm)
6. U.S. 12th Army Group Sherman Strength (75 mm vs. 76 mm), 1944–45
7. U.S. 12th Army Group Sherman (76mm) Losses by Army, 1944–45
8. U.S. 6th Army Group Sherman Strength (75mm vs. 76mm)
9. U.S. Army Sherman Losses in the ETO, 1944–45
10. U.S. Army Sherman Losses in the ETO by Unit
11. Delivery of M4A3E8 (76mm) to Armies of the 12th Army Group in the ETO, 1944–45
12. U.S. Army Self-Propelled Tank Destroyer Strength and Losses in the ETO, 1944–45
13. T26E3 (M26) Pershing Deployed Strength in the ETO, 1945

1. U.S. 1ST ARMORED DIVISION MEDIUM TANK STRENGTH IN TUNISIA, 1943							
	13 Feb 43*	3 March 43	9 Mar 43*	12 Mar 43	22 Mar 43	26 Mar 43	May 43
M3 medium tank	20	93	71	77	86	86	51
M4 medium tank	182	100	80	97	125	120	178
Total	**202**	**193**	**151**	**174**	**179**	**206**	**229**

* Type breakdowns are estimates on these dates

2. U.S. FIFTH ARMY SHERMAN LOSSES IN THE ITALIAN CAMPAIGN, 1943–45

	9-30 Sep 43	30 Sep-11 Nov 43	11 Nov-20 Jan 44	20 Jan-29 Mar 44	30 Mar-8 Jun 44	9 Jun-12 Aug 44	20 Aug-26 Nov 44	26 Nov 30 Mar 45	31 Mar-11 MayTotal 45	Total
M4, M4A1	24	9	26	125	265	151	148	226	98	**1,072**
M4A3(76)							9	30	39	**78**
M4 (105mm)							5	4	12	**21**
Total	**24**	**9**	**26**	**125**	**265**	**151**	**162**	**260**	**149**	**1,171**

3. U.S. FIRST ARMY SHERMAN STRENGTH AND LOSSES IN NORMANDY, JUNE–AUGUST 1944

	Strength*			Losses		
	June	July	August	June	July	August
70th Tank Bn	40	44	50	33	18	13
709th Tank Bn		54			10	
712th Tank Bn		51	47		19	0
735th Tank Bn			53			0
737th Tank Bn		49	51		4	15
741st Tank Bn	36	55	46	53	6	2
743rd Tank Bn	39	48	46	16	26	11
745th Tank Bn	52	54	50	6	1	3
746th Tank Bn	34	39	50	43	45	7
747th Tank Bn	44	50	49	37	8	18
749th Tank Bn		48	54		12	0
2nd Armored Div	206	221	224	21	45	40
3rd Armored Div	195	249	226	0	40	74
5th Armored Div			160			21
2nd (French) AD			176			19
Total	**646**	**962**	**1,282**	**209**	**234**	**223**

* Strength is average operative Sherman strength through the month

4. U.S. ARMORED DIVISION SHERMAN STRENGTH (75MM VS. 76MM) IN THE ETO, 1944–45

Division	Jun	Jul	Aug	1944 Sep	Oct	Nov	Dec	Jan	Feb	1945 Mar	Apr	May
2	219/0	210/0	171/45	153/68	156/65	128/60	125/60	117/21	143/66	143/65	143/87	95/95
3	204/0	201/0	184/50	159/65	115/60	138/60	165/48	138/40	155/44	143/51	119/40	86/90
4			160/0	137/18	108/13	132/18	128/17	68/16	112/42	91/49	48/68	54/105
5			166/0	136/19	125/15	127/16	119/21	127/10	123/35	114/35	106/66	77/62
6			156/0	153/0	153/0	157/2	122/11	139/11	66/44	87/56	45/74	30/128
7				94/12	62/49	78/32	77/49	61/36	94/41	118/50	77/61	72/80
8									107/47	116/47	80/70	77/70
9						167/0	0/168	13/95	51/116	50/116	55/97	52/96
10						114/51	116/49	85/34	84/49	86/43	84/84	66/100
11								98/44	81/58	91/61	88/61	68/74
12								109/52	93/44	78/90	84/84	86/83
13												91/70
14											83/88	65/68
16											117/51	115/49
20											117/51	0/165
% 76mm	0	0	10.2	17.9	21.9	18.6	33.1	27.3	34.5	37.2	44.0	56.3

5. U.S. 12TH ARMY GROUP SEPARATE TANK BATTALION SHERMAN STRENGTH (75MM VS. 76MM)

	Jun	Jul	Aug	1944 Sep	Oct	Nov	Dec	Jan	Feb	1945 Mar	Apr	May
75mm	245	370	650	527	508	647	525	695	733	781	669	567
76mm	0	0	0	95	37	166	177	259	216	305	438	607
Total	**245**	**370**	**650**	**622**	**545**	**813**	**702**	**954**	**949**	**1086**	**1107**	**1174**
76mm %	0	0	0	15.2	6.7	20.4	25.2	27.1	22.7	28.1	39.5	51.7

Data at beginning of each month

6. U.S. 12TH ARMY GROUP SHERMAN STRENGTH (75MM VS. 76MM), 1944–45

	Jun	Jul	Aug	1944 Sep	Oct	Nov	Dec	Jan	Feb	1945 Mar	Apr	May
75mm tanks	646	781	1317	1367	1267	1521	1377	1695	1749	1937	1664	1449
76mm (arm'd div.)			95	117	202	406	418	350	542	624	726	987
76mm (tank bn.)				95	37	166	177	259	216	305	438	607
Subtotal 76mm			95	212	239	572	595	609	758	929	1164	1594
Total	646	781	1,412	1,579	1,506	2,093	1,972	2,304	2,507	2,866	2,828	3,043
% 76mm tanks	0	0	6.7	13.4	15.8	27.3	30.1	26.4	30.2	32.4	41.1	52.3

7. U.S. 12TH ARMY GROUP SHERMAN (76MM) LOSSES BY ARMY, 1944–45

	Jun	Jul	Aug	1944 Sep	Oct	Nov	Dec	Jan	Feb	1945 Mar	Apr	Total
First Army	0	12	38	33	0	14	100	29	7	48	26	307
Third Army	0	0	0	61	0	7	72	127	25	82	38	412
Ninth Army	0	0	0	0	3	16	5	2	18	39	28	111
Total	0	12	38	94	3	37	177	158	50	169	92	830

8. U.S. 6TH ARMY GROUP SHERMAN STRENGTH (75MM VS. 76MM)

	Jan	Feb	Mar	Apr	May
U.S. Seventh Army					
75mm tank	422	381	332	434	523
76mm tanks	185	208	366	478	557
% 76mm tanks	30.4	35.3	52.4	52.4	51.5
Seventh Army Subtotal	**607**	**589**	**698**	**912**	**1,080**
French First Army					
75mm tanks		420	513	537	546
76mm tanks		53	52	51	50
French First Army Subtotal		**473**	**565**	**588**	**596**
% 76mm tanks		11.2	9.3	8.6	8.3
6th Army Group Total		**1,062**	**1,263**	**1,500**	**1,676**

9. U.S. ARMY SHERMAN LOSSES IN THE ETO, 1944–45

	Jun	Jul	Aug	1944 Sep	Oct	Nov	Dec	Jan	Feb	1945 Mar	Apr	Total
Losses	167	121	557	436	237	257	495	585	319	462	554	207
Unit Strength	2,202	2,093	2,557	2,423	2,464	2,832	4,076	4,561	5,297	6,229	5,555	6,107
% of strength	15.0	5.8	21.8	18.0	9.8	9.1	11.7	12.8	6.0	7.4	9.7	6.6

Data as of twentieth of each month. U.S. Seventh Army (6th Army Group) figures are included starting in November.

10. U.S. ARMY SHERMAN LOSSES IN THE ETO BY UNIT

Separate Tank Battalions

70 TB	90
191 TB	140
701 TB	15
702 TB	56
707 TB	93
709 TB	60
712 TB	68
717 TB	2
735 TB	51
736 TB	15
737 TB	66
738 TB	4
739 TB	8
741 TB	86
740 TB	55
743 TB	96
744 TB	1
745 TB	50
746 TB	124
747 TB	70
748 TB	6
749 TB	52
750 TB	
753 TB	62
756 TB	77
761 TB	71
759 TB	42
771 TB	34
772 TB	8
774 TB	56
777 TB	16

10. U.S. ARMY SHERMAN LOSSES IN THE ETO BY UNIT *continued*

Separate Tank Battalions

778 TB	16
781 TB	16
782 TB	1
784 TB	18
786 TB	11
787 TB	0

Armored Divisions

2AD	276
3AD	632
4AD	316
5AD	116
6AD	202
7AD	360
8AD	58
9AD	162
10AD	181
11AD	82
12AD	129
13AD	27
14AD	101
16AD	0
20AD	17
Separate Tank Battalion Losses	1,636
Armored Division Losses	2,659
Total Losses	**4,295**

11. DELIVERY OF M4A3E8 (76MM) TO ARMIES OF 12TH ARMY GROUP IN THE ETO, 1944–45

Army	Dec 1944	Jan 1945	Feb 1945	Mar 1945	Apr 1945	Total
First		29	19	57	153	258
Third	21	28	62	13	132	256
Ninth		33	72	45	64	214
Fifteenth		24				24
Total	**21**	**114**	**153**	**115**	**349**	**752**

12. U.S. ARMY SELF-PROPELLED TANK DESTROYER STRENGTH AND LOSSES IN THE ETO, 1944–45*

	M10 Strength	M36 Strength	M18 Strength	Total Strength	M10 Losses	M36 Losses	M18 Losses	Total Losses
June 1944	691	—	146	**837**	1	—	—	**1**
July 1944	743	—	141	**884**	17	—	—	**17**
August 1944	758	—	176	**934**	28	—	6	**34**
Sep 1944	763	—	170	**933**	40	—	6	**46**
Oct 1944	486	170	189	**845**	71	2	14	**87**
Nov 1944	573	183	252	**1,008**	45	5	7	**57**
Dec 1944	790	236	306	**1,332**	62	21	44	**127**
January 1945	760	365	312	**1,437**	69	26	27	**122**
Feb 1945	686	826	448	**1,960**	106	18	16	**140**
March 1945	684	884	540	**2,108**	27	21	21	**69**
April 1945	427	1,054	427	**1,908**	37	34	55	**126**
May 1945	427	1,029	427	**1,908**	37	25	21	**83**

* Data as of twentieth of each month. U.S. Seventh Army (6th Army Group) figures are included starting in November.

13. T26E3 (M26) PERSHING DEPLOYED STRENGTH IN THE ETO, 1945

Division	Mar	Apr	May
2nd Armored	19	21	
3rd Armored	10	10	18
5th Armored	17		
9th Armored	10	10	17
11th Armored	32		
Total	**20**	**39**	**105**

Allied Data

1. British–Canadian 21st Army Group Strength in the Northwest Europe Campaign
2. British Sherman Designations
3. Sherman Lend-Lease Shipments, 1942–45

1. BRITISH-CANADIAN 12TH ARMY GROUP SHERMAN STRENGTH IN THE NORTHWEST EUROPE CAMPAIGN										
Type	M4	M4A1	M4A2	M4A4	M4A1 (76)	M4 (105)	M4 17 17-pdr	M4A4 17-pdr	DD	Crab	Total
Unit strength	223	192	340	794	0	0	2	316	251	180	2,298
Parks, reserve	52	50	150	178	0	0	0	24	251	45	750
Total, June 1944	**275**	**242**	**490**	**972**	**0**	**0**	**2**	**340**	**502**	**225**	**3,048**
Unit strength	106	164	193	595	135	0	408	228	54	105	1,988
Parks, reserve	75	71	193	370	51	0	357	180	94	93	1,484
Total, 27 Jan 1945	**181**	**235**	**386**	**965**	**186**	**0**	**765**	**408**	**148**	**198**	**3,472**
Unit strength	63	106	220	708	142	64	485	224	48	101	2,161
Parks, reserve	99	57	333	329	149	30	295	231	58	89	1,670
Total, 5 May 1945	**162**	**163**	**553**	**1037**	**291**	**94**	**780**	**455**	**106**	**190**	**3,831**

2. BRITISH SHERMAN DESIGNATIONS

British	US Army
Sherman I	M4
Sherman Hybrid I	M4 (with composite cast/welded hull)
Sherman IB	M4 (105mm)
Sherman IC	M4 with 17-pdr, usually on composite hull
Sherman II	M4A1
Sherman IIA	M4A1 (76mm)
Sherman IIC	M4A1 with 17-pdr
Sherman III	M4A2
Sherman IIIA	M4A2 (76mm)
Sherman IV	M4A3
Sherman IVB	M4A3 (105mm)
Sherman V	M4A4
Sherman Vc	M4A4 with 17-pdr

3. SHERMAN LEND-LEASE SHIPMENTS, 1942–45

Shipping Period	1942	1943	1944	1945	Total
UK					
M4/M4A1	268	752	2018	90	3,128
M4A1 (76)	0	0	1,330	0	1,330
M4A2	456	4,083	501	8	5,048
M4A2 (76)	0	0	0	20	20
M4A4	147	5,385	1,631	5	7,168
M4 (105)	0	0	488	105	593
Subtotal	871	10,220	5,698	228	17,287
USSR					
M4A2	227	1,086	727	0	2,040
M4A2 (76)	0	0	1,482	613	2,095
M4A4	2	0	0	0	2
Subtotal	229	1,086	5,968	228	17,287
France					
M4A2	0	363	20	0	383
M4A4	0	274	0	0	274
Subtotal	0	637	20	0	657
Other	0	4	53	0	57
Total	**1,100**	**11,947**	**8,250**	**841**	**22,138**

Bibliographic Essay

THE U.S. ARMY HAS NOT been especially interested in the history of its weapons technology in World War II—or in the Cold War years either. The army's excellent Green Book series of histories of World War II are focused on the army's campaigns. Three volumes are devoted to Ordnance, but these are from an institutional perspective and do not offer a balanced look at the controversies of wartime tank development. This inattention is not confined to the history of tank programs; there is a similar gap in published histories of U.S. Army field artillery development, radar development, radio/communication development, and most other fields of technology. This is especially noticeable when comparing the army's indifference to technological history to the air force and navy.

An even more glaring shortcoming can be seen in the preservation of historical artifacts, with the army's collection of World War II tank and AFV designs rusting away at Aberdeen Proving Ground while the U.S. Air Force carefully preserves and displays its aircraft at Wright-Patterson Air Force Base. U.S. Army museums in the United States do not contain a single Sherman that was an actual combat veteran of World War II. "Cobra King," the M4A3E2 assault tank that led Patton's relief of Bastogne, is sitting as a gate guard in Vilseck, Germany, its true identity largely unknown outside a small circle of Sherman buffs. A combat veteran M4 tank knocked out in the Netherlands in the autumn of 1944 and formerly at the Overloon museum was recently sold off to serve as a memorial to the Canadian troops who fought at Ortona, Italy. Most of the Sherman tanks that served in the ETO were given away to NATO allies or expended as range targets during the Cold War.

Technical histories of the various armored vehicle programs of World War II were written by Ordnance after the war but never published. These are from its perspective, although AGF also published a rather modest history of its own involvement in armored vehicle development as well. The Ordnance histories are still available at the U.S. National Archives and Records Administration (NARA) at College Park, Maryland. For those readers not willing or able to travel to NARA for these documents, the next best thing is the superb series of books by Richard Hunnicutt, including his volume on the Sherman, which are heavily based on Ordnance records.

In view of the large number of photos used in this book, a few words about World War II photographic archives are necessary. Unless otherwise noted, all the photos in this book are official U.S. Army photos, primarily taken by the U.S. Signal Corps but also by the Ordnance Department, Armored Board, and other official organizations. The main Signal Corps collection was maintained at the Pentagon through the 1970s, then transferred to the Defense Audio-Visual Agency in Anacostia in the 1980s, and finally to NARA, where they currently reside as Record Group 111-SC. There are two main finding aids for this collection, a card collection, and a collection of bound photos Record Group 111-SCA, which formerly served as the primary finding aid when the collection was held at the Pentagon. The Signal Corps collection at NARA is not the only collection of army World War II photos though it is the most comprehensive; there are other collections at the U.S. Army Military History Institute at Carlisle Barracks, Pennsylvania, and at the U.S. Army Center for Military History at Fort McNair outside Washington, DC. All wartime army photos did not end up in the Signal Corps collection. So for example, some photos taken in the ETO can be found in the Office of War Information photo collection at NARA. Ordnance photos can be found primarily in the Ordnance records rather than photo collections at NARA, primarily in RG 165. NARA also has U.S. Navy and U.S. Marine Corps photo collections which contain a significant amount of photographic material on tanks in World War II. The U.S. Marine Corps Museum at Quantico also has a significant photographic record of U.S. Marine units in the Pacific in World War II.

The Patton Museum at Fort Knox has one of the richest collections of photographs dealing with U.S. tank development in World War II. Following World War II, various Ordnance offices at Aberdeen Proving Grounds dumped many of their records in the trash. Col. Robert Icks could not bear to see these unique photo records destroyed, and he collected what he could before they were destroyed. His collection is now preserved at the Patton Museum. Likewise, Richard Hunnicutt donated his very extensive collection of photos and documents to the Patton Museum, making it an especially fruitful location for research on U.S. tank history. The Military History Institute at Carlisle Barracks has a number of personal photo collections that were donated over the years that contain a good many unique World War II tank photos. The U.S. Military Academy at West Point also has some private collections, including the Bradley Collection, with photos not found elsewhere.

UNPUBLISHED DOCUMENTS AT NARA

National Archives and Records Administration II (NARA II) in College Park, Maryland, is the primary repository of U.S. government documents. The files are organized under record groups (RG), and fortunately, most of the major World War II U.S. Army record groups have finding aids located in the NARA II researcher's room. The list below covers the principal record groups that I examined over the years while researching American AFVs.

Ordnance Department records are located in RG 156 and consist of several distinct subcollections. Entry 646A contains a large number of histories and studies compiled by Ordnance during and after the war, and provides a particularly handy survey of tank and weapons development. They are

scattered throughout about 100 boxes (A709–809); the principal ones dealing with the Sherman tank and related subjects are listed below in more detail than the other record groups. Many of these can also be located in the Hunnicutt Collection at the Patton Museum at Fort Knox.

Entry 62 contains a large number of technical reports from various Ordnance facilities on testing and evaluation of AFVs during World War II, mainly at Aberdeen Proving Ground. A related series is in Entry 894, which consists of the corresponding tests by the Armored Forces Board at Fort Knox, and RG 337 Entry 87 on the Tank Destroyer Board at Fort Hood.

Entry 886 is the Ordnance Department Technical Information File, also known as the OKD File. This file contains the foreign technical intelligence collected by the Ordnance Department since 1918. Unfortunately, there is no finding aid at NARA, and since the collection is more than 500 archive boxes, this is a significant problem. RG 165 contains the files of the Military Intelligence Division, and I found the files dealing with 1930–39 to be particularly illuminating about the extent of U.S. knowledge of foreign developments in AFVs, armored tactics, and armored unit organization.

RG 377 and RG 338 contain records of the higher commands and their associated headquarters. The records of the AFV&W sections, also known as armored sections, are particularly useful. Some of these are also available in a condensed form in the published higher headquarters histories, such as those by the 12th Army Group, First Army, and Third Army.

For readers interested in combat records of tank units, RG 407 contains the main collection of unit after-action reports (AARs) for armored divisions, armored (tank) groups, and separate tank battalions. These vary considerably in size and quality, and a useful finding aid is available at NARA II. These provide detailed day-by-day chronicles of the units deployed to the ETO and the Pacific. Tank buffs will probably be surprised at how little detail is in these records regarding the tanks in the unit. For example, I went through most of the records of the 1st Armored Division from the time of the Kasserine battles, trying to track the introduction of the M4

Sherman and the replacement of the older M3 medium tanks. It may be a mild exaggeration, but I don't think I ever saw the term M4 or M3 crop up in a single document, only the generic term "medium tank."

Technical issues are far better covered in ordnance reports or in higher headquarters reports. For example, there is far more detail in the AFV&W section reports on issues such as sandbag armor for tanks than in the individual unit files. Likewise in the case of separate tank battalions, the records of the armored (tank) group headquarters are often better on these issues than the individual battalion records since these commands were often coordinating such programs amongst their attached tank battalions and so sometimes have summary reports on the programs. It's also worth noting that these unit histories seldom contain any photos of the unit, with some very rare exceptions.

RG 156 (Entry 649A) Office of Chief of Ordnance, Technical Division

37mm Gun Motor Carriages (1962)

37mm Tank Guns

3-Inch Gun Motor Carriages

57mm Gun Motor Carriages (1958)

75mm Gun Motor Carriages (1945)

75mm Howitzer Motor Carriages (1945)

76mm Gun Motor Carriage T70, 90mm Gun Motor Carriage T71

90mm Ammunition Design, Development (Special report No. 103, 1945)

Armor Plate, Development and Production 1940–1945

Combat Vehicles, Series V, Study No. 2; The Armistice Period 1919–1940; The Tank From WWI to 1939

Development History of 76mm Gun Motor Carriages

Development of the US Medium Tanks M3 & M4 (1943)

Documentation Project report No. 45 on Medium and Heavy Tanks, Vol. 1: Medium Tanks

Documentation Project report No. 45 on Medium and Heavy Tanks, Vol. 2: Heavy Tanks

ETO Report, Fires in Tanks: Gas vs. Diesel Engines (1943)

Evolution of American and German Medium Tanks (January 1943)

Heavy Anti-Tank Carriages (1944)

Heavy Tanks and Assault Tanks

History of Tank development by Ordnance Department in World War II

History of Tank Guns (October 1944)

History of the Heavy Tanks M6

History of the Medium Tank M4 (76mm)

History of the Medium Tank T20 Series

Hypervelocity Development, Guns and Ammunition

Light Tank T7 Series

Mine Exploder Mission to ETO 4 April 1944–19 October 1944.

New Tanks and Gun Motor Carriages (January 1946)

New Tanks for 1944 (July 1943)

Record of Army Ordnance Research and Development, Tank Development 1940–45

Record of Development of Gun Motor Carriages from 1 July 1944 to 20 March 1945 (1945)

Record of Developmental and Experimental Ordnance, Vol. 1, Tanks

Record of the Development of Combat Vehicles from 1 Sept 42 to 30 Jun 44 (1944)

Self-propelled Artillery and Anti-Tank Guns (1958)

Special Mission New Weapons & Demonstration Board in ETO & NATO (1944)

Statistical Summary of Accomplishments, Tank Automotive Material (1945)

Summary Report of Acceptances, Tank-Automotive Material 1940–1945

RG 156 (Entry 894) Records of Armored Force Board, Ft. Knox

RG 160 Records of the Headquarters, Army Service Forces

RG 165 US Army Military Intelligence Division

RG 331 6th Army Group, G-3 Records

RG 331 Records of Headquarters, Supreme Headquarters Allied Expeditionary Force

RG 331 Headquarters, 12th Army Group Special Staff, Ordnance Section

RG 331 Headquarters, 12th Army Group
Special Staff, Armored (AFV&W) Section

RG 337 Headquarters, Army Ground Forces

RG 337 Headquarters, Army Ground Forces,
Requirements Division

RG 337 Records of Tank Destroyer Board,
Ft. Hood

RG 337 Records of Armored School

RG 337 Records of Cavalry School

RG 338 Records of US Third Army 1945–47

RG 338 Records of US 12th Army Group
1945–47

RG 338 Headquarters, ETO US Army,
Armored Vehicles Section Ordnance Section

RG 338 AFV&W Section, Headquarters,
European Theatre of Operations US Army

RG 338 Headquarters, G-3, First US Army
Group

RG 338 Headquarters, 12th Army Group

RG 338 Headquarters, Armored Force

RG 407, Headquarters, 12th Army Group,
Armored Section

RG 407, US Army ETO, US Armored Division,
Armored Group, Tank Battalion, Tank
Destroyer Battalion after-action reports

PERSONAL COLLECTIONS

Besides the formal organizational histories, a number of generals have donated their personal collections of documents to various archives. Gen. Lesley McNair was killed in action at the start of Operation Cobra on July 25, 1944, so researchers are obliged to scour through Army Ground Force headquarters documents for his correspondence. Jacob Devers left his papers to the archives of the York County Heritage Trust in York, Pennsylvania; these include the reports he made following his visit to Tunisia in 1943. A great deal of material from Gen. Gladeon Barnes of ordnance can be found in the RG 165 Ordnance files at NARA. Gen. Andrew Bruce left his papers to the U.S. Army Military History Institute, and they contain a significant amount of material on the various controversies swirling around the tank destroyer force.

MHI also has numerous personal collections of armored officers, which have some bearing on Sherman history. For example, Gen. Bruce Clarke's collec-

tion has a good deal of fresh material on tank tactics in World War II. MHI has also been conducting a veterans survey, which includes both an attempt to retrieve any photos taken by veterans during the war and any documentary material still in their possession. In addition, MHI has been asking veterans to fill out a survey form to collect details of their service career. Cameras were not officially permitted in front-line U.S. combat units in World War II, but some sneaked through (though certainly not on the scale seen in the Wehrmacht). MHI has one of the larger collections of such photos, but tank buffs will probably be disappointed by the thin pickings in these collections. I actually found more photos of German AFVs in the survey collection than American AFVs. The Patton Museum has a number of unique collections of personal material by tankers. George S. Patton's personal photos reside at the Library of Congress.

ARMY REPORTS AND STUDIES

This category straddles the archival records listed above and the books listed further below. I have included official U.S. histories available to the public through the Government Printing Office with more conventional books below. These army studies were published for internal circulation in limited print runs and were not intended for wide public distribution. Some are large, formally published books such as the *Report of Operations* compiled by the major field commands, though they were usually classified for a period of time and so are not widely available outside army libraries or archives. Some of the smaller printed documents are far less formal, often mimeographed reports. I have primarily used the collection of these documents at the U.S. Army's Military History Institute, part of the Army Heritage and Education Center at Carlisle Barracks, Pennsylvania. Many of these reports are also available at NARA but are much harder or more time-consuming to locate.

MHI also has several other major collections worth mentioning, though I have not listed them here. The library has a full set of the wartime TO&E (table of organization and equipment) documents that detail the authorized configuration of all army units. MHI also has excellent collections of army technical publications, including the TM (technical manuals), which are operator manuals for tanks and other weapons; the TB (technical bulletins), which are small publications usually consisting of instructions about modification of equipment in the field; the SNL (standard nomenclature lists), which are parts catalogs for major weapons such as tanks and AFVs; and the FM (field manuals), which are the army's tactical handbooks.

Another collection worth mentioning is the Foreign Military Studies collection, which was undertaken by the U.S. Army's Office of the Chief of Military History in the late 1940s and early 1950s. These are studies compiled by German officers dealing with their experiences in World War II. They are primarily campaign oriented, with a heavy emphasis on campaigns fought against the U.S. Army, but with considerable Russian front coverage as well. There are several hundred of these reports, ranging from a few pages to hundreds of pages per report and varying enormously in content and detail. MHI has both German and English language editions, and they provide a unique resource for readers interested in the German perspective on many of the battles fought in the ETO. I have not listed them here, but they are in the bibliographies of the Osprey campaign books I have written on many of the major campaigns of the U.S. Army in the ETO.

The Ordnance Committee Meeting (OCM) reports are worth special mention since they form the chronological skeleton of any study of AFV development by the U.S. Army in World War II. I have generally used the excellent bound collection at MHI, but it lacks the secret reports. A full set, including the classified reports (now declassified), is at NARA II.

The armored school reports are part of a series done by officers at Fort Knox in the years immediately after the war, and I found copies both at the Patton Museum and at MHI. The British technical documents come primarily from the library of The Tank Museum and Bovington Camp in Dorset, Great Britain, and my thanks go to the indefatigable David Fletcher for help in obtaining these.

British Army

Preliminary Report on Armour Quality and Vulnerability of Pz.Kw. Mk V Panther (Department of Tank Design, Chobham Report M6815A/3)

Investigations in Germany by Tank Armament Research, Ministry of Supply (British Intelligence Objectives Sub-Committee, 1946)

Maj. G. H. Gee, *Tank Battle Analysis* (Department of the Scientific Advisor to the Army Council, Military Research Report #3, November 1946)

Maj. G. H. Gee, *The Comparative Performance of German Anti-Tank Weapons During World War II* (Department of the Scientific Advisor to the Army Council, Military Research Report #16, May 1950)

Maj. G. H. Gee, *A Survey of Tank Warfare in Europe from D-Day to 12th August 1944* (Army Operational Research Group, Memorandum C.6, May 1952)

U.S. Army Studies

First United States Army, Report of Operations 1943–45 (1946)

First Army, Combat Operations Data, First Army Europe 1944–45 (1945)

Third Army, Report of Operations, August 1944–May 1945 (1946)

Seventh Army, Report of Operations: France and Germany 1944–45 (1946)

12th Army Group, Report of Operations: Final After Action Report (1946)

Armored Force Replacement Center, *Tankers in Tunisia* (July 1943)

Armored School, Fort Knox, *American Armor at Anzio* (May 1949)

Armored School, Fort Knox, *American Armor at Faid-Kasserine* (September 1949)

Armored School, Fort Knox, *Armor at Bastogne* (May 1949)

Armored School, Fort Knox, *Armor under Adverse Conditions: 2nd and 3rd Armored Divisions in the Ardennes Campaign* (1949)

Armored School, Fort Knox, *Armor in the Attack of Fortified Positions* (May 1950)

Armored School, Fort Knox, *Armor in Night Attack* (June 1950)

Armored School, Fort Knox, *Armor in Winter Warfare* (June 1950)

Armored School, Fort Knox, *Armored Action in WWII: Use of Armor in Defense* (May 1950)

Armored School, Fort Knox, *A Critical Analysis of the History of Armor in World War II* (April 1953)

Armored School, Fort Knox, *Employment of Armor in Korea: The First Year* (1952)

Armored School, Fort Knox, *2nd Armored Division in the Ardennes* (1948)

Armored School, Fort Knox, *The Separate Tank Battalion in Support of Infantry in River Crossing Operations in the ETO* (May 1950)

Army Concepts Analysis Agency, *Ardennes Campaign Data Base* (1995)

Army Ground Forces, Historical Section, *Tank Destroyer History* (Study No. 29, 1946)

Army Ground Forces, Historical Section, *The Role of Army Ground Forces in the Development of Equipment* (Study No. 24, 1946)

Army Ground Forces, *Historical Section, History of the Armored Force, Command, and Center* (Study No. 27, 1946)

Army Ground Forces, Observer Board, ETO, *Reports of Observers-ETO: 1944–45* (Volume I-VI, 1945)

Army Service Forces, The Design, Development and Production of Tanks in World War II (1944)

Army Service Forces, Report of the New Weapons Board (27 April 1944)

Army Service Forces, Summary report of Acceptances: Tank-Automotive Materiel, 1940–45 (December 1945)

Ballistics Research Laboratories, *Data on WWII Tank Engagements involving the U.S. Third and Fourth Armored Divisions* (Memo report No. 798, 1954)

General Board, U.S. Forces, European Theater, *Organization, Equipment and Tactical Employment of Tank Destroyer Units* (Study No. 60, 1946)

General Board, U.S. Forces, European Theater, *Tank Gunnery* (Study No. 53, 1946)

General Board, U.S. Forces, European Theater, *Mechanized Cavalry Units* (Study No. 49, 1946)

General Board, U.S. Forces, European Theater, *The Armored Group* (Study No. 51, 1946)

General Board, U.S. Forces, European Theater, *Organization, Equipment and Tactical Employment of Separate Tank Battalions* (Study No. 50, 1946)

General Board, US Forces, European Theater, *Armored Special Equipment* (Study No. 52, 1946)

Infantry School, *Employment of Tanks in the Spanish Civil War* (1938)

Ordnance Department, Ordnance Technical Committee Meeting Minutes (1939–1945)

Office of the Chief of Military History, *Tank Fight of Rocherath-Krinkelt (Belgium) 17–19 December 1944* (1952)

Office of the Chief of Military History, *Ardennes Campaign Statistics, 16 December 1944–19 January 1945* (1952)

Office of the Chief of Military History, The US Army in World War II, Statistics, Procurement (1952)

Operational Research Office, *Survey of Allied Tank Casualties in World War II* (ORO-T-117 March 1951)

Operational Research Office, *Tank-vs.-Tank Combat in Korea* (ORO-T-278 September 1954)

Tank Destroyer School, *TD Combat in Tunisia* (January 1944)

US Strategic Bombing Survey, *(German) Tank Industry Report* (1947)

US Strategic Bombing Survey, *Maschinenfabrik Augsberg-Nurnberg, Nurnberg, Germany* (1947)

US Strategic Bombing Survey, *Maybach Motor Works, Friedrichshafen, Germany* (1947)

War Department, *Lessons from the Tunisian Campaign* (October 15, 1943)

War Department, *Medium Tank M4 (105mm Howitzer) and Medium Tank M4A1 (76mm Gun)* (TM9-731AA, June 1944)

War Department, Field Manual 17-5, *Organization and Tactics of Tank Destroyer Units* (June 16, 1942)

War Department, Field Manual 17-10, *Tactics and Techniques* (March 7, 1942)

War Department, Field Manual 17-32, *Tank Company* (August 2, 1942, revised March 15, 1944)

War Department, Field Manual 17-33, *Armored Battalion, Light and Medium* (September 18, 1942)

War Department, Field Manual 17-33, *Tank Battalion* (November 1944)

War Department, Field Manual 17-36, *Employment of Tanks with Infantry* (March 13, 1944)

War Department, Field Manual 17-42, *Armored Infantry Battalion* (November 1944)

War Department, Field Manual 17-100 *Armored Division* (January 15, 1944)

War Department, Field Manual 18-5, *Organization and Tactics of Tank Destroyer Units* (July 18, 1944)

War Department, Field Manual 18-21, *Tank Destroyer Towed Gun Platoon* (April 1, 1944)

War Production Board, Official Munitions Production of the United States July 1, 1940–August 31, 1945 (May 1947)

BOOKS

Numerous books have been published about the Sherman tank over the years. The best single book on Sherman development is Richard Hunnicutt's massive study, part of his multivolume history of American AFV development that is an essential cornerstone for anyone interested in U.S. tank history. Charles Baily's book *Faint Praise* was the first study to examine the interplay between Ordnance and the Army Ground Forces in U.S. Army AFV development during World War II, and it remains a very useful guide to these controversies, even if a bit hard to find. Many of the histories of the Sherman tank are badly dated, like the classic book by Peter Chamberlain and Chris Ellis, and I have not listed all of them here for that reason. There are also many histories of the Sherman mainly aimed at hobbyists, and I have not listed all of them here. I have listed many of my Osprey New Vanguard books here as they provide a quick way to locate concise and inexpensive histories of most major American AFVs of World War II. Coverage of German tank development and combat operations in World War II is generally more comprehensive than American tanks, though there is a heavier focus on cult classics such as the Tiger than on the more mundane types like the PzKpfw IV. I have stayed away from listing the many military campaign histories of World War II, as they seldom treat AFV issues in any detail; I have listed only a few of these books here as there are hundreds. I have included a few campaign histories which involve major tank actions or deal with issues central to the Sherman story, such as infantry-tank cooperation.

I have also included a list of U.S. unit histories, primarily the armored divisions and separate tank battalions. Many of the rare divisional histories have been republished by Battery Press. This list is far from comprehensive so far as tank battalion histories are concerned since there are many obscure self-published histories. The U.S. Army Military History Institute has a very good selection. Readers with a more casual interest would be better off with Harry Yeide's book on the separate tank battalions, which contains a good deal of material culled from the archival after-action reports; the same is true of his volume on tank destroyer battalions.

Baily, Charles. *Faint Praise: American Tanks and Tank Destroyers during World War II.* Hamden, CT: Archon, 1983.

Beale, Peter. *Death by Design: British Tank Development in the Second World War.* Stroud, England: Sutton, 1998.

Bellis, Malcom. *U.S. Tank Destroyers of World War Two.* Self-published.

Bird, Lorrin, and Robert Livingstone. *World War II Ballistics: Armor and Gunnery.* Albany, NY: Overmatch, 2001.

Blackburn, Mark. *The U.S. Army and the Motor Truck: A Case Study in Standardization.* Westport, CT: Greenwood, 1996.

Buckley, John. *British Armour in the Normandy Campaign, 1944.* London: Frank Cass, 2004.

Cavanagh, William. *The Battle East of Elsenborn and the Twin Villages.* Barnsley, England: Pen and Sword, 2004.

Chamberlain, Peter, and Hilary Doyle. *Encyclopedia of German Tanks of World War Two.* London: Arms and Armour Press, 1978.

Chamberlain, Peter, and Stevenson Pugh. *T3 Christie Tank.* Leatherhead, England: Profile Publications, 1968.

Cooper, Belton. *Death Traps: The Survival of an American Armored Division in World War II.* Navato, CA: Presidio, 1998.

de Vries, G, and B. J. Martens. *German Anti-Tank Weapons: Panzerbüsche, Panzerfaust and Panzerschreck.* N.p.: Special Interest Publications, 2005.

Doubler, Michael. *Closing with the Enemy: How GIs Fought the War in Europe, 1941–45.* Lawrence, Kan.: University of Kansas: 1994.

Dugdale, J. *Panzer Divisions, Panzer Grenadier Divisions, Panzer Brigades of the Army and Waffen SS in the West: Ardennes and Nordwind, Their Detailed and Precise Strengths and Organizations* Vol. 1. Milton Keynes, England: Military Press: 2000–05.

Estes, Kenneth. *Marines under Armor: The Marines Corps and the Armored Fighting Vehicle, 1916–2000.* Annapolis, Md.: Naval Institute Press, 2000.

Fleischer, Wolfgang. *Panzerfaust and Other German Infantry Anti-Tank Weapons.* Atglen, PA: Schiffer, 1994.

Fleischer, Wolfgang, and Richard Eiermann. *German Anti-Tank (Panzerjäger) Troops in World War II.* Atglen, PA: Schiffer, 2004.

Fletcher, David. *Sherman Vc M4A4 Firefly.* Darlington, MD: n.p., 1997.

Fletcher, David. *The Great Tank Scandal: British Armour in the Second World War, Part 1.* London: HMSO, 1989.

Fletcher, David. *The Universal Tank: British Armour in the Second World War, Part 2.* London: HMSO, 1993.

Frieser, Karl-Heinz. *The Blitzkrieg Legend: The 1940 Campaign in the West.* Annapolis, Md.: Naval Institute Press, 2005.

Gabel, Christopher. *Seek, Strike, and Destroy: U.S. Army Tank Destroyer Doctrine in World War II.* Fort Leavenworth, Kan.: U.S. Army CGSC, 1985.

Gabel, Christopher. *The U.S. Army GHQ Maneuvers of 1941.* Washington, DC: GPO: 1991.

Gilbert, Oscar. *Marine Tank Battles in the Pacific.* Conshohocken, PA: Combined Publishing, 2001.

Gill, Lonnie. *Tank Destroyer Forces: WWII.* Paducah, Ky.: Turner, 1992.

Gott, Kendall. *Breaking the Mold: Tanks in the Cities.* Fort Leavenworth, Kan.: Combat Studies Institute, 2006.

Green, Constance, et. al. *The U.S. Army in World War II: The Technical Services, Ordnance Department: Planning Munitions for War.* Washington, DC: GPO, 1955.

Gillie, Mildred H. *Forging the Thunderbolt: A History of the Development of the Armored Force.* Harrisburg, PA: Military Service Publishing, 1947.

Hahn, Fritz. *Waffen und Geheimwaffen des deutschen Heeres, 1933–45.* Vol. 2, *Panzer und Sonderfahrzeuge, Wunderwaffen, Verbrauch und Verluste.* Koblenz, Germany: Berard and Graefe, 1987.

Hays, J. J. *United States Army Ground Forces Tables of Organization and Equipment in World War II: The Armored Division, 1940–45.* Vol. 2. Milton Keynes, England: Military Press: 2003.

Hayward, Mark. *Sherman Firefly.* Tiptree, England: Barbarossa, 2001.

Hofmann, George. *Through Mobility We Conquer: The Mechanization of the U.S. Cavalry.* Lexington, Ky.: University Press of Kentucky, 2007.

Hofmann, George, and Donn Starry, eds. *Camp Colt to Desert Storm: The History of the U.S. Armored Forces.* Lexington, Ky.: University Press of Kentucky, 1999.

Hunnicutt, Richard. *Firepower: A History of the American Heavy Tank.* Navato, CA: Presidio, 1998.

Hunnicutt, Richard. *Pershing: A History of the Medium Tank T20 Series.* Bellingham, WA: Feist, 1971.

Hunnicutt, Richard. *Sherman: A History of the American Medium Tank.* Belmont, CA: Taurus, 1978.

Hunnicutt, Richard. *Stuart: A History of the American Light Tank.* Navato, CA: Presidio, 1992.

Icks, Robert. *The M6 Heavy and M26 Pershing.* London: Profile Publications, 1971.

Irzyk, Albin. *He Rode Up Front for Patton.* Raleigh, NC: Pentland Press, 1996.

Jarymowycz, Roman. *Tank Tactics from Normandy to Lorraine.* Boulder, CO: Lynne Rienner, 2001.

Jentz, Thomas. *Germany's Panther Tank: The Quest for Combat Supremacy.* Atglen, PA: Schiffer: 1995.

Jentz, Thomas. *Panzer Truppen: The Complete Guide to the Creation and Combat Employment of Germany's Tank Force 1943–1945.* Vol. 2. Atglen, PA: Schiffer, 1996.

Johnson, David E. *Fast Tanks and Heavy Bombers: Innovation in the U.S. Army, 1917–1945.* Ithaca, NY: Cornell University Press, 1998.

Liddell Hart, B. H. *The Tanks: The History of the Royal Tank Regiment.* London: Cassell, 1959.

Mayo, Lida. *The U.S. Army in World War II, The Technical Services, Ordnance Department: On Beachhead and Battlefront.* Washington, DC: GPO, 1991.

McGhee, Addison. *He's in the Armored Force Now.* New York: McBride, 1942.

Ross, G. MacLeod. *The Business of Tanks.* Ilfracombe, England: Arthur Stockwell, 1976.

Mansoor, Peter. *The GI Offensive in Europe: The Triumph of American Infantry Divisions, 1941–1945.* Lawrence, Kan.: University Press of Kansas, 1999.

Nafziger, George. *The American Army in World War II.* Vol. 3, *Independent Armored, Mechanized Cavalry, Artillery, Anti-Aircraft, and Engineer Battalions.* N.p.: Nafziger, 2000.

Nafziger, George. *The American Army in World War II.* Vol. 4, *Armored Divisions.* N.p.: Nafziger, 2000.

Odom, William. *After the Trenches: The Transformation of U.S. Army Doctrine, 1918–1939.* College Station, TX: Texas A&M, 1998.

Perrett, Bryan. *The Lee/Grant Tanks in British Service.* London: Osprey, 1978.

Reardon, Mark. *Victory at Mortain: Stopping Hitler's Panzer Counteroffensive.* Lawrence, Kan.: University Press of Kansas, 2002.

Robinett, Paul. *Armor Command.* Washington, DC: McGregor and Werner, 1958.

Sorley, Lewis. *Thunderbolt: Gen. Creighton Abrams and the Army of His Times.* New York: Simon & Schuster, 1992.

Spielberger, Walter. *Panther and Its Variants.* Atglen, PA: Schiffer, 1993.

Stout, Wesley. *Tanks Are Mighty Fine Things.* Detroit, Mich.: Chrysler, 1946.

Thomson, Harry, and Lida Mayo. *The U.S. Army in World War II, The Technical Services, Ordnance Department: Procurement and Supply.* Washington, DC: GPO, 1991.

Triplet, William. *A Colonel in the Armored Divisions.* Columbia, MO: University of Missouri, 2001.

Vannoy, Allyn, and Jay Karamales. *Against the Panzers: U.S. Infantry vs. German Tanks, 1944–45.* Jefferson, NC: McFarland, 1996.

Wilson, John. *Maneuver and Firepower: The Evolution of Divisions and Separate Brigades.* Washington, DC: U.S. Army Center of Military History, 1998.

Yeide, Harry. *Steel Victory: The Heroic Story of America's Independent Tank Battalions at War in Europe.* New York: Random House, 2003.

Yeide, Harry. *The Tank Killers: A History of America's World War II Tank Destroyer Force.* Havertown, PA: Casemate, 2004.

Zaloga, Steven. *Amtracs: American Amphibious Assault Vehicles.* London: Osprey, 1987.

———. *Anzio: The Beleaguered Beachhead.* London: Osprey, 2005.

———. *Armor at War: The Battle of the Bulge.* Hong Kong: Concord Publications, 2001.

———. *Armour of the Pacific War, 1937–45.* London: Osprey, 1983.

———. *Battle of the Ardennes (1): St. Vith and Northern Shoulder, 1944.* London: Osprey, 2002.

———. *Battle of the Ardennes (2): Bastogne.* London: Osprey, 2004.

———. *Battle of the Bulge.* London: Arms and Armour Press, 1983.

———. *D-Day: Omaha Beach, June 1944.* London: Osprey, 2003.

———. *D-Day: Utah Beach and the Airborne Operations.* London: Osprey, 2003.

———. *Kasserine: Rommel's Last Victory?* London: Osprey, 2005.

———. *Lorraine 1944: Patton vs. Manteuffel.* London: Osprey, 2000.

———. *M10/M36 Tank Destroyer.* London: Osprey, 2002.

———. *M18 Hellcat Tank Destroyer.* London: Osprey, 2004.

———. *M24 Chaffee Light Tank, 1944–1964.* London: Osprey, 2003.

———. *M26/M46 Pershing Tank.* London: Osprey, 2000.

———. *M3 Lee/Grant Medium Tank.* London: Osprey, 2005.

———. *M3/M5 Stuart Light Tank.* London: Osprey, 1999.

———. *M4(76mm) Tank, 1943–1953.* London: Osprey, 2003.

———. *Operation Cobra: The Normandy Breakout, 1944.* London: Osprey, 2001.

———. *Paris 1944: Patton's Race for the Seine.* London: Osprey, 2008.

———. *Patton's Tanks.* London: Arms and Armour Press, 1984.

———. *Poland 1939: The Birth of Blitzkrieg.* London: Osprey, 2002.

———. *Remagen 1945: Endgame against the Third Reich.* London: Osprey, 2006.

———. *Siegfried Line, 1944–45: Battles on the German Frontier.* London: Osprey, 2007.

————. *Sherman Tank at War: The European Theatre, 1942–45 (1)*. Hong Kong: Concord Publications, 1994.

————. *Sherman Tank at War: The European Theatre, 1942–45 (2)*. Hong Kong: Concord Publications, 2000.

————. *Sherman Tank in U.S. and Allied Service*. London: Osprey, 1981.

————. *Stalin Heavy Tanks*. London: Osprey, 1993.

————. *T-34-85 Tank, 1944–1994*. London: Osprey, 1996.

————. *Tank Battles of the Mid East Wars, 1948–73*. Hong Kong: Concord Publications, 1996.

————. *Tank Battles of the Pacific War, 1941–45*. Hong Kong: Concord Publications, 1995.

————. *U.S. Anti-Tank Artillery, 1941–45*. London: Osprey, 2005.

————. *U.S. Armored Artillery of World War 2*. Hong Kong: Concord Publications, 2002.

————. *U.S. Armored Divisions in the ETO, 1944–45*. London: Osprey, 2003.

————. *U.S. Armored Units in the North African and Italian Campaigns, 1942–45*. London: Osprey, 2004.

————. *U.S. Army Tank Crewman, 1941–45*. London: Osprey, 1984.

————. *U.S. Armour Camouflage and Markings, 1917–45*. London: Osprey, 1984.

————. *U.S. Field Artillery, 1941–45*. London: Osprey, 2005.

————. *U.S. Light Tanks, 1944–84*. London: Osprey, 1984.

————. *U.S. Light Tanks in Combat, 1941–45*. Hong Kong: Concord Publications, 2001.

————. *U.S. Tank and Tank Destroyer Battalions in the ETO, 1944–45*. London: Osprey, 2004.

————. *U.S. Tank Battles in France, 1944–45*. Hong Kong: Concord Publications, 2003.

————. *U.S. Tank Battles in Germany, 1944–45*. Hong Kong: Concord Publications, 2003.

————. *U.S. Tank Battles in North Africa and Italy*. Hong Kong: Concord Publications, 2004.

————. *U.S. Tank Destroyers at War, 1941–1945*. Hong Kong: Concord Publications, 1996.

————. *U.S. Tank Destroyers of WW2*. London: Arms and Armour Press, 1985.

Zaloga, Steven, and George Balin. *D-Day Tank Warfare*. Hong Kong: Concord Publications, 1994.

————. *Tank Warfare in Korea, 1950–53*. Hong Kong: Concord Publications, 1994.

Zaloga, Steven, and James Grandsen. *Soviet Tanks and Combat Vehicles of World War II*. London: Arms and Armour Press: 1984.

Zaloga, Steven, and Leland Ness. *Handbook of the Red Army, 1941–45*. London: Sutton Publishing, 1999.

U.S. Army World War II Armored Division Histories (in numerical order by division)

Houston, Donald. *Hell on Wheels: The 2nd Armored Division*. Navato, CA: Presidio Press, 1977.

Blaker, Gordon. *Iron Knights: The U.S. 66th Armored Regiment* (2nd Armored Division). Shippensburg, PA: White Mane, 1999; Mechanicsburg, PA: Stackpole Books, 2008.

Smith, J. A. *Spearhead in the West: The 3rd Armored Division in World War II*. Frankfurt, Germany: F. J. Henrich, 1945; Nashville, Tenn.: Battery Press, 1980, 1998.

Koyen, Kenneth. *The 4th Armored Division: From the Beaches to Bavaria*. Self-published, 1946; Nashville, Tenn.: Battery Press, 1980.

Fox, Don. *Patton's Vanguard: The U.S. Army 4th Armored Division*. Jefferson, NC: McFarland, 2003.

Frankel, Ned. *Patton's Best: An Informal History of the 4th Armored Division*. New York: Hawthorn Books, 1978.

Hillery, V., and E. F. Hurley. *Paths of Armor: The 5th Armored Division in World War II*. Atlanta: A. Love Enterprises, 1950; Nashville, Tenn.: Battery Press, 1985.

Hofmann, George. *The Super Sixth: History of the 6th Armored Division in World War II*. Louisville, Ky.: Sixth Armored Division Association, 1975; Nashville, Tenn.: Battery Press, 1998.

Chapin, Neil. et. al. *The Lucky Seventh: The 7th Armored Division and Association*. Farmington Hills, Mich.: Taylor Publishing, 1982.

Leach, Charles. *In Tornado's Wake: A History of the 8th Armored Division*. Chicago: Eighth Armored Division Association, 1956; Nashville, Tenn.: Battery Press, 1992.

Reichelt, Walter. *Phantom Nine: The 9th Armored Division, 1942–45.* Austin, TX: Presidial Press, 1987.

Nichols, L. M. *Impact: The Battle Story of the 10th Armored Division in World War II.* New York: Gateway, 1954; Nashville, Tenn.: Battery Press, 1985.

Steward, H. D. *Thunderbolt: The History of the 11th Armored Division.* Washington, DC: 11th Armored Division Association, 1948, Nashville, Tenn.: Battery Press, 1981.

N.a., *Hellcats: The 12th Armored Division in World War II.* N.p., 1946, Nashville, Tenn.: Battery Press, 1978.

Ferguson, John. *Hellcats: The 12th Armored Division in World War II.* Abilene, TX: State House Press, 2004.

N.a. *The 13th Armored Division: A History of the Black Cats.* N.p., 1947.

Carter, Joseph. *The History of the 14th Armored Division.* Atlanta: Albert Love Enterprises, 1946.

N.a., *Armor in the ETO: The 20th Armored Division.* Atlanta: Albert Love Enterprises, 1946.

U.S. Army World War II Separate Tank and Tank Destroyer Battalion Histories (in numerical order by battalion)

N.a. *History of the 70th Tank Battalion, 5 June 1940–22 May 1946.* Self-published, 1946.

Jensen, Marvin. *Strike Swiftly: The 70th Tank Battalion from North Africa to Normandy to Germany.* Navato, CA: Presidio, 1997.

DeBevoise, Charles. *Voodoo: History of the 81st Tank Battalion.* Self-published, 1947.

Evans, Thomas. *Reluctant Valor: the 704th Tank Destroyer Battalion.* Latrobe, PA: St. Vincent College, 1995.

Gill, Lonnie. *Code Name: Harpoon, The Combat History of the 704th Tank Destroyer Battalion.* N.p.: Baron Publishing, 1982.

Elson, Aaron. *Tanks for the Memories: An Oral History of the 712th Tank Battalion from WWII.* Hackensack, NJ: Chi Chi Press, 1992.

Baty, Roger, and Eddie Maddox. *Where Heroes Trained: 736th Medium Tank Battalion (Special).* Tucson, Ariz.: Fenestra, 2004.

Rubel, George. *Daredevil Tankers: The Story of the 740th Tank Battalion.* Self-published, 1945.

Heintzleman, Al. *The 741st Tank Battalion, D-Day to VE Day.* Self-published, 1982.

N.a., *Move Out and Verify: The Combat Story of the 743rd Tank Battalion.* Self-published, 1946.

Folkestad, William. *The View from the Turret: The 743rd Tank Battalion during World War II.* Shippensburg, PA: White Mane, 1996.

Robinson, Wayne. *Barbara* (743rd Tank Battalion). New York: Doubleday, 1962.

N.a. *History of the 745th Tank Battalion.* Self-published, 1945.

Blanchard, W. J. *Our Liberators: The Combat History of the 746th Tank Battalion during WWII.* Tucson, Ariz.: Fenestra Books, 2003.

Fazendin, Roger. *The 756th Tank Battalion in the Battle of Cassino, 1944.* Bloomington, IN: iUniverse: 1991.

Krebs, John. *To Rome and Beyond: B Company, 760th Tank Battalion, Italy, 1943–1945.* Self-published, 1981.

Wilson, Joe. *The 761st Black Panther Tank Battalion in World War II.* Jefferson, NC: McFarland, 1999.

Montgomery, Jim. *B Company, 776 Tank Destroyer Battalion, in Combat.* Baltimore, Md.: Gateway, 1983.

Wilson, Joe. *The 784th Tank Battalion in World War II.* Jefferson, NC: McFarland, 2007.

Chase, Patrick. *Seek, Strike, Destroy: The History of the 894th Tank Destroyer Battalion in World War II.* Baltimore, Md.: Gateway, 1995.

Index

Page numbers in italics indicate illustrations or tables